Taxation and Public Finances in the Spanish Empire

The emergence and consolidation of the so-called modern state was one of the most remarkable features of the early modern period and went hand in hand with the development of fiscal and financial systems.

This book explores the case of the Spanish Habsburgs who ruled over a vast collection of states and principalities in the burgeoning Spanish empire. In this edited volume, a cast of expert economic historians each explores the fiscal and financial systems created in the different territories of the Spanish Monarchy, including Castile, Aragón, Navarre, Spanish America, Portugal, the Italian States and the Southern Low Countries. While each of the components of this 'composite monarchy' laboriously created its own fiscal and financial apparatus, there are interesting similarities behind the at-first-sight impenetrable jungle of different fiscal and financial institutions which indicates more commonality than is sometimes assumed. Also, the medieval heritage of these fiscal systems did not preclude change and evolution, as the massive expansion of public credit in Portugal and Castile demonstrates. However, the chapters also provide convincing evidence to question the adequacy of the almighty fiscal state paradigm which dominates similar work on the Dutch and British empires and shows that a unified imperial fiscal and financial bureaucracy never existed. The book demonstrates that the imperial center consistently observed local privileges and rights while negotiating its mounting fiscal requests with the Empire's different cities, territories and corporations separately.

This book will find ready readers among all those interested in European and American economic history, early modern history and the history of public finance.

José Ignacio Andrés Ucendo is an Associate Professor of Economic History at the University of the Basque Country (EHU/UPV).

Xabier Lamikiz is an Associate Professor of Economic History at the University of the Basque Country.

Ramón Lanza García is a Full Professor of Economic History at Universidad Autónoma de Madrid.

Perspectives in Economic and Social History
Series Editors: Andrew August and Jari Eloranta

Queer Trades, Sex and Society
Male Prostitution and the War on Homosexuality in Interwar Scotland
Jeffrey Meek

History of Finance Capital in America
The Great Depression and Interwar Years
Go Tian Kang

History of Economic Management in North Korea
From Planned Economy to Socialist Enterprise System
Phillip H. Park

National Wealth, Income and the History of Economic Growth
Finland from the Late 19th Century until the Second World War
Heikki Mikkonen

Economic, Politics and Prosperity in Restoration England
An Intellectual History of the Works of Sir William Temple
Juha Haavisto

History of Regional Trade in Southeast Asia
Singapore as an Entrepôt
Atsushi Kobayashi

Taxation and Public Finances in the Spanish Empire
1550–1750
Edited by José Ignacio Andrés Ucendo, Xabier Lamikiz and Ramón Lanza García

For more information about this series, please visit: www.routledge.com/Perspectives-in-Economic-and-Social-History/book-series/PESH

Taxation and Public Finances in the Spanish Empire

1550–1750

Edited by José Ignacio Andrés Ucendo, Xabier Lamikiz and Ramón Lanza García

Routledge
Taylor & Francis Group
LONDON AND NEW YORK

First published 2026

by Routledge
4 Park Square, Milton Park, Abingdon, Oxon OX14 4RN

and by Routledge
605 Third Avenue, New York, NY 10158

Routledge is an imprint of the Taylor & Francis Group, an informa business

British Library Cataloguing-in-Publication Data
A catalogue record for this book is available from the British Library

ISBN: 978-1-041-10082-9 (hbk)
ISBN: 978-1-041-10083-6 (pbk)
ISBN: 978-1-003-65330-1 (ebk)

DOI: 10.4324/9781003653301

Typeset in Times New Roman
by Newgen Publishing UK

Contents

Figures

About the editors

José Ignacio Andrés Ucendo is an Associate Professor of Economic History at the University of the Basque Country (EHU/UPV). Together with M. Limberger, he edited *Taxation and Debt in the Early Modern City*, London: Pickering and Chatto, 2012. He is also the co-author (together with Ramón Lanza García) of "Prices and Real Wages in Seventeenth-Century Madrid", *Economic History Review*, vol. 67, no. 3, pp. 607–626 and "Prices and Wages in Segovia, 1571-1807", *Revista de Historia Económica/Journal of Iberian and Latin American Economic History*, vol. 38, no. 2, pp. 221–248.

Xabier Lamikiz (PhD, Royal Holloway, 2006) is an Associate Professor of Economic History at the University of the Basque Country. He is the author of *Trade and Trust in the Eighteenth-Century Atlantic World* (Woodbridge: Boydell & Brewer, 2010). His research on merchant networks, economic institutions, taxation and trade in the Spanish Atlantic has appeared in *Revista de Historia Económica*, *Hispanic American Historical Review*, *Colonial Latin American Review* and in various edited collections. He has been a member of several research projects on Spain's early modern economy.

Ramón Lanza García is a Full Professor of Economic History at Universidad Autónoma de Madrid. His research includes several works on taxation, prices and wages, economic inequality and urban history in Modern Spain. He has recently coordinated the publication of collective works such as *Las instituciones económicas, las finanzas públicas y el declive de España en la Edad Moderna*, Madrid: Universidad Autónoma de Madrid, 2017; *Finanzas y crisis financieras en la Monarquía Hispánica, siglos XVI–XVII*, Madrid: Marcial Pons, 2023 and *Los dineros de la Corona. Hacienda y cambio fiscal en la Monarquía hispánica, siglos XVI–XVII*, Granada: Editorial Comares, 2023.

Contributors

Leonor Freire Costa is a Professor of Economic History at ISEG/Universidade de Lisboa/Social Science Department – History.

Mario García-Zúñiga is a Senior Lecturer of Economic History at the University of the Basque Country (UPV-EHU).

Michael Limberger is a Professor of Early Modern History at Ghent University.

Roberto López Vela is a Professor of Early Modern History at the Universidad de Cantabria.

María del Pilar Martínez López-Cano is a Senior Researcher at the Institute of Historical Research – UNAM.

Luciano Pezzolo is a Professor of Early Modern History at the Dipartamento de Studi Umanistici della Universitá Ca' Foscari di Venezia.

Íñigo Ena Sanjuán is a Marie Skłodowska-Curie Postdoctoral Fellow at the Instituto Pirenaico de Ecología, Consejo Superior de Investigaciones Científicas (Spain).

Sergio Sardone is an Associate Professor of Economic History at the Università di Napoli Federico II.

Acknowledgement

We would like to thank the Ministerio de Ciencia e Investigación del Gobierno de España, whose support through the Research Project "Crisis fiscal y declive económico en la Monarquía Hispánica, 1550-1740", PID2020-118287GB-I00 has funded the research for the chapters of this book. Preliminary drafts of these chapters were debated in a Research Seminar held on 25 October 2024 at the Arts Faculty of the Universidad del País Vasco/Euskal Herriko Unibertsitatea (Vitoria–Gasteiz).

Introduction

Fiscal and financial policies in the Spanish Empire, 1550–1750: An overview

José Ignacio, Andrés Ucendo, Xabier Lamikiz and Ramón Lanza García

Spanning from the Philippine Islands and Spanish America to the Southern Low Countries and Sicily, the Spanish Empire was the European hegemon during the sixteenth century and the first half of the seventeenth century. At its peak between 1580 and 1640, the Spanish Habsburgs ruled over a collection of territories, including Portugal and its sprawling Overseas Empire.[1] The Spanish kings controlled the richest silver mines on earth and patrolled the vital trade routes of the Atlantic, which was virtually a Spanish lake during most of the sixteenth century. They also ruled over some of Europe's most important concentrations of wealth and economic activity, such as the Low Countries, the Duchy of Milan, Naples and Sicily. This aroused the hostility of other European states and forced the Spanish kings to continually raise human, fiscal and financial resources for the defence of their vast Empire. The purpose of the essays included in this book is to shed light on the fiscal and financial systems created in the territories of the Spanish Empire between 1500 and 1750.

Felt everywhere in Europe in the sixteenth and seventeenth centuries, the need to mobilise resources for the increasingly expensive wars of the period led to the emergence and expansion of a new historical actor: the fiscal-military state. An influential school sees in the fiscal-military state an all-powerful Leviathan, whose rise rested on the advance of centralisation and the consolidation of complex bureaucratic organisations.[2] Under the influence of the seminal works of North and Weingast (1989) and Brewer (1989), eighteenth-century England/Britain has been considered the textbook example of a successful Fiscal State, especially when compared with the absolutist monarchies of France and Spain. This view emphasises two points: firstly, the consolidation of representative government, followed by the strict commitment of the post-1688 English/British Parliament to the enforcement of property rights; and secondly, the subsequent expansion of British public debt, funded by revenues obtained from a tax system in the hands of a competent, professional and bureaucratic fiscal administration. This enabled the British Imperial State to provide a set of public goods, namely the conquest and defence of the expanding colonial markets, which played a pivotal role in the expansion of the eighteenth-century British economy and paved the way for the arrival of the British high-wage economy and the Industrial Revolution.[3]

DOI: 10.4324/9781003653301-1

Compared to Britain, early modern France and Spain have often been depicted in rather bleak terms, as absolutist states ruled by predatory governments with a feeble commitment to property rights.[4] French public finances are famous for the collapse of John Law's system in the 1720s, the subsequent bankruptcies in 1726, 1759, 1763 and 1772, and the financial crisis of 1788, which led to the French Revolution.[5] As for Spain, the Castilian bankruptcies of 1557, 1575, 1596, 1607, 1627, 1647, 1652 and 1662 have led some scholars to conclude that the Spanish Habsburgs were serial defaulters.[6] French and Castilian defaults are seen as attacks on the property rights of public debt holders, and similar consideration is given to the frequent retentions of interest payments ordered by the Castilian Crown during the seventeenth century. According to this interpretation, the development of reliable public credit systems in France and Castile/Spain became impossible, thereby hampering their prospects for economic growth.

Although this view persists in some circles,[7] a re-evaluation is now necessary, especially regarding the Spanish Empire. Critical to North and Weingast's theory is that limited and representative government was the most effective antidote for the predatory propensities of the absolutist French and Spanish monarchies in the early modern period. Today, this argument no longer seems tenable, if only because medieval and early modern Europe abounded in cases of small urban republics that ruthlessly exploited their rural hinterlands.[8] Another strand of North and Weingast's argument emphasises that, by virtue of its strict enforcement of property rights from 1688, the English/British Parliament created a favourable environment that lowered the interest rate on its public debt, granting Britain considerable financial superiority over its rivals. This view implies that the interest rates of the annuities issued by European republics and parliamentary states during the early modern period were significantly lower than those of absolutist states. Such possibility was tested by Epstein (2000: 19–22), who found that public debt interest rates fell everywhere in early-modern Europe, and that there were only minor differences between representative polities and absolutist states from the middle of the sixteenth century onward. England was one of the main exceptions to this trend in the sixteenth and seventeenth centuries. Interest rates in the London financial market began to converge with the European trend in the central decades of the seventeenth century. Still, the interest rates paid by the English Treasury remained high by European standards until the second third of the eighteenth century. They then entered a rapid decline brought about by the introduction of the "consols".[9]

Another problem with North and Weingast's view is that it has often led to property-rights determinism, which tends to overlook the specific content of such rights and their impact on economic growth. Hoffman (1996) reminds us that the mere enforcement of property rights per se is not necessarily conducive to growth and prosperity, as the State may enforce the wrong set of rights, with deleterious effects on economic growth. This point was effectively illustrated by his analysis of French agriculture during the early modern period, where he found that the commitment of the French monarchy to some forms of property proved hugely detrimental to economic growth, as it made it virtually impossible to expropriate privately owned plots of land for public purposes, such as the building of roads and irrigation systems.[10] Another illustration of this point, crucial for our book, comes from the research carried out in recent decades, which convincingly proves that the Spanish Habsburgs' commitment to property rights was reasonably strong, in line with their traditional respect for local privileges, liberties and franchises and the prevailing political doctrines of the time.[11] By the standards of its era, Habsburg Spain was a reasonably well-ruled set of kingdoms with little room for arbitrariness. Staffed by professional bureaucrats trained in Roman Law, the courts of law and the central government's ministries were habitually inclined to safeguard the property rights of owners of economic assets, and expropriations were admitted only for public purposes after due process of law (which included the payment of indemnities to those affected).[12] If anything, Spain seems to have suffered from the negative impact of certain well-entrenched and highly protected forms of property, such as entailed estates (*mayorazgos*) and mortmain, on its long-term economic performance.

The reassessment of the commitment of French and Spanish monarchies to the enforcement of property rights during the early modern period undermines the view held by North and Weingast (1989) that both cases were exemplary instances of the negative economic consequences of predatory governments. It proves that their theory does not entirely fit the historical record. North and Weingast held that the strict enforcement of property rights became one of the main concerns of the English government and Parliament after the Glorious Revolution, which put an end to the wave of expropriations and arbitrariness that had characterised the Stuart period. However, building on the research of other scholars on various aspects of eighteenth-century British political and institutional history, Hoppit (2011) concludes that property rights became less secure after 1688, not more so. As he explains, the key contribution of the Glorious Revolution was not an increase in the security of property, but the fact that it granted Parliament the power not only to expropriate but even extinguish some forms of property. The British Parliament made wide use of this faculty, leading to a wave of expropriations as older forms of property (such as hereditary offices and enslaved Africans) were abolished. Property rights were reformulated in a way that was more conducive to economic growth, granting the British economy the flexibility needed to seize new economic opportunities.

The rise of an administrative organisation staffed by a growing number of professional public servants was the other element stressed by those who saw England/Britain as the most successful Fiscal State of the day.[13] However, there are compelling reasons to reassess this view. There is no denying that vast amounts of professionalism, rationality and efficiency characterised the British fiscal and financial administration, but this does not mean it was exceptional. Many territories of the Spanish Empire also saw the consolidation of an administrative apparatus staffed by competent royal ministers, with a remarkable command of the most advanced fiscal and financial techniques of the time and high levels of professional competence.[14] This resulted from the competitive pressures that drove the development of improved administrative methods and institutions in European polities seeking to navigate the intense mercantilist competition of the time, regardless of their political constitution. This also accounts for the long coexistence, within every European State, of refined bureaucratic institutions in some branches of government, with more conservative and traditional methods in others. Plainly visible in France and Spain, such coexistence can also be found in the eighteenth-century British Imperial state,[15] whose centralised and professional fiscal and financial administration functioned alongside a much more traditional institutional framework and even with instances of venality and cronyism in some branches of government.[16]

The above considerations set the stage for a reappraisal of the fiscal and financial systems developed in the different territories of the Spanish Empire. As indicated below, this revision is already underway, at least as far as Castile and some Italian territories (such as Milan) are concerned, shedding new light on traditional topics that have long drawn the interest of scholars and researchers.

A long tradition, which dates back to the seventeenth century, held Habsburg rule largely responsible for the economic decline of Lombardy, the ruin of the Italian Mezzogiorno and the Castilian decadence. The consolidation of supposedly predatory and extractive fiscal and financial systems during the Habsburg period was seen as one of the main causes of the economic difficulties of these territories.[17] As the readers of Manzoni's "The Betrothed" (*"I Promessi Sposi"*, 1827) know well, the Spanish kings and their Milanese Governor Generals and Neapolitan viceroys were depicted as rapacious and extractive rulers that trampled on local rights, franchises and parliamentary assemblies to raise the resources required for their ruinous imperial wars. The growth of the fiscal burden in these territories led to the introduction of new taxes, especially in the mid-seventeenth century. The proliferation of indirect taxes was significant in Naples, Lombardy and Castile.[18] Many contemporary essayists saw such proliferation as one of the main causes behind the rise of production costs and the fall in real wages and consumption levels, which supposedly played a pivotal role in the collapse of the Lombard and Castilian urban industries during the seventeenth century.[19]

The above view, shared by eighteenth-century Italian and Spanish enlightened writers and their nineteenth-century liberal successors, was generally accepted until the first decades of the twentieth century. However, today it is far less convincing.[20] Nowadays, most historians agree that Habsburg fiscal and financial policy played a smaller role in the Mezzogiorno's backwardness or Lombardy's industrial decline than previously thought.[21] Sella (1997) points out that the traditional high-quality wool industries of the Italian states outside the Habsburg domain, such as those of Venice and Florence, also declined during the seventeenth century. Complaints about the adverse effects of indirect taxation on the competitiveness of urban economies were also heard in seventeenth-century Castile.[22] What is the truth behind these complaints? To the best of our knowledge, the plausible idea that the proliferation of indirect taxes had led to the decline of Lombard industries remains largely untested. As far as Habsburg Italy is concerned, the scarce evidence at our disposal suggests that the impact of taxation on production costs might have been smaller than what Lombard essayists assumed. Taxes accounted for perhaps two percent of the price of Milanese woollen cloth; something similar happened in other Italian states, with the remarkable exception of Venice.[23] In the case of Castile, the main fiscal burden fell on meat and wine, and the taxes directly levied on textiles were light. Taxation increased Madrid's price levels by 16–20 percent during the last third of the century, reducing real wages to the same extent.[24] These are significant figures that indicate a higher impact of taxes on production costs in Castile than in Lombardy, but still lower than what could be expected if one were to believe the eloquent complaints of the Castilian economic thinkers of the time. The previous data suggest that the fiscal burden on the Castilian economy could well have been less than previously thought, at least for most of the seventeenth century, an idea which resurfaces when adopting a comparative approach. While, as we have just seen, the impact of taxes on production costs was higher in Castile than in Lombardy, the fiscal burden in terms of daily wages was lighter in Castile than in the seventeenth-century United Provinces and in eighteenth-century England.[25]

At the same time, a more nuanced view of Castilian public finances during the Habsburg period has emerged in recent decades.[26] The new perspective emphasises the sustainability of Castilian public debt, at least until the beginning of the seventeenth century, if not beyond. It also stresses that the famous financial defaults of the Spanish kings were not evidence of the perpetual financial disarray that they supposedly experienced, but served as a means to free up revenue for further borrowing by converting floating debt into long-term, low-interest debt. Debt conversions were also relatively frequent in other European States of the time. In light of this, the retentions in the interest rates that accrued to holders of Castilian and Neapolitan annuities during the seventeenth century seem little different from the taxes levied on the interest earned by buyers of similar assets in Holland.[27]

The fact that there never was a central treasury setting a uniform set of fiscal and financial policies, rules and methods for the whole of the Empire means that each of its territories developed its existing fiscal and financial systems. How can we characterise the variegated fiscal and financial systems developed in the different components of the Spanish Empire? While the fiscal-military State paradigm might provide a guide for this purpose, our reservations outlined above have led us to seek an alternative approach. After all, if the enforcement of property rights and strides in the development of a bureaucratic fiscal and financial administration are the main attributes of the fiscal-military State, then the term encompasses substantially different kinds of polities, ranging from parliamentarian England/Britain and the Dutch Republic to the Spanish Empire and absolutist Sweden.[28] This is why we have turned to another paradigm, that of composite monarchy, which appears more fruitful for accounting for the specificities in the fiscal and financial history of the lands once ruled by the Spanish Habsburgs.[29]

An aggregate of diverse territories, from some of the old traditional European kingdoms such as Aragon, Castile and Naples to a group of smaller polities and fiefdoms scattered across Northern and Central Europe, the Spanish Empire was the result of military expansion and dynastic marriages.[30] To ease the incorporation of new territories, each with its own political, legal and administrative framework, and to enlist the cooperation of local elites, the Spanish Habsburgs were always ready to respect regional laws, privileges and institutions. That was one of the keys to the monarchy's survival. Still, it came at a price, as it precluded constitutional change in the imperial territories, blocked any political and administrative unification project, and prevented the implementation of a uniform mercantilist trade policy. The closest thing to a global Imperial plan was the 1626 *Unión de Armas*, an ambitious project for a more balanced apportionment of the costs of imperial defence, whose final failure eloquently proved the opposition of local elites in imperial territories to this kind of design.[31] The lack of a unified framework meant that every part of the Empire clung to its own traditional fiscal and financial institutions.[32] From this perspective, the lack of a common institutional framework was the essence of the Spanish Empire's fiscal and financial history. While there is some truth in the previous assertion, it should not hide the existence of some common traits that provide, in our view, some unity to what could initially seem little more than a juxtaposition of disparate cases.

Firstly, Habsburg rulers knew that the relative differences in wealth and economic development of the diverse territories of their Empire impinged on their capacity to raise fiscal and financial resources. This is why they focused on maximising the fiscal and financial resources coming from the Indies (mainly silver) and Castile, followed, at some distance, by those from Naples, Sicily and Milan. These territories constituted the fiscal and financial core of the Empire.[33] The contributions of the other territories were always smaller, and the Spanish Habsburgs seem to have been comfortable with this imbalance. That was likely due to their realisation that the political costs involved in any project to raise the revenues drawn from the smaller and more peripheral components of the Empire outweighed any potential fiscal and financial gains. Consequently, the Spanish kings decided to carefully conserve their political capital by refusing to enter into potentially explosive conflicts with the local elites of the Empire's peripheral territories, where there was no realistic prospect of sound fiscal returns.

This leads us to the second recurring factor. It is frequently stated that the transit from the Domain State (where the bulk of revenues came from the Crown's patrimonial domains and rights) to the Tax State (where revenues came from regular taxes and services) was a crucial step in the emergence of the Fiscal State.[34] This ran simultaneously to the consolidation of parliamentary assemblies, such as the Castilian, Aragonese, Valencian, Catalan and Navarrese *Cortes*, the Sicilian Parliament, the Estates of Flanders and Brabant and other representative bodies.[35] Given the prevailing scholastic political culture of the time, the introduction of new taxes and monetary aids required the consent of these institutions, leading to prolonged negotiations between them and the Crown. The willingness of the Spanish kings to negotiate with local parliaments and intermediate bodies reflected their adherence to the basic tenets of political scholasticism, but also their pragmatic desire to secure the cooperation of institutions whose intermediation was necessary to increase the Crown's revenues at an acceptable political cost. The same desire, coupled with the intention of saving administrative costs, explains the devolution of substantial fiscal competences to parliaments, intermediate bodies, cities, corporations and even private individuals, who were often responsible for assessing the tax base, the collection of taxes and even the payment of interest to public debt holders.[36]

With the invaluable help of a favourable economic situation, negotiation and fiscal devolution, the Spanish Habsburgs increased revenues from the core imperial areas until the mid-seventeenth century. However, both methods had their fair share of problems, which lead us to the third factor that resurfaces time and again throughout this book. In the case of Castile, fiscal devolution drove the development of a relatively decentralised fiscal system, similar in some respects to the Dutch one.[37] However, fiscal devolution could also result in the consolidation of well-entrenched local interests capable of blocking any fiscal reform, significantly contributing to the fiscal stagnation experienced by many European polities by the mid-seventeenth century.[38] As for negotiation, its purpose was to enable an increase in the State's fiscal revenues at an acceptable price (in political terms) for both the ruler and the ruled. But what if one side deemed the price unacceptably high or low? This was a familiar problem for many of the monarchies of the period. Kings and emperors requested increased taxes and services from parliaments and intermediate bodies, which were usually reluctant to grant such requests without strict conditions to ensure the proper use of funds granted to the monarch. Frequently, this was unacceptable for the ruler, who could decide to dispense with parliamentary cooperation and turn instead to other measures and expedients.[39]

To summarise, the fiscal and financial systems developed in the territories of the Spanish Empire conformed to the rules and norms of the composite states of the time rather than the pattern of predatory absolutism.[40] Conscious of the relative differences in wealth and economic development across the territories under their domain, Spanish kings modulated their fiscal and financial demands accordingly, creating a visible imbalance between a core group of heavily taxed territories and a more peripheral group of lightly taxed ones. Spanish kings relied on negotiation and fiscal devolution to increase their fiscal revenues. This enabled them to increase fiscal revenues until sometime in the mid-seventeenth century, when fiscal exhaustion set in and the limitations of the whole system became apparent.

The first part of our argument (the difference between core and peripheral fiscal areas) is addressed by the chapters by García-Zúñiga and Pezzolo, which show that the heaviest fiscal burden fell on Castile. Castile was followed by some distance by other (mainly Italian) territories. According to Pezzolo's estimates, the fiscal revenues raised by the Crown from Castile in 1650 amounted to 412 tons of pure silver, and those from Naples, Milan and Sicily to 41, 35.2 and 16 tons respectively. The fiscal burden that fell on other territories, such as Navarre, was lighter, but as García-Zúñiga points out, this was due to strategic concerns. As a frontier territory, imperial policymakers saw Navarre as the first line of defence against a potential French invasion. They sought to enlist the Navarrese in defending the frontier by granting them broad fiscal exemptions.

The second part of our argument (the prevalence of negotiation and fiscal devolution) is discussed in most chapters of the book. Negotiations took place at different levels. As Pezzolo shows, the incorporation of new territories into the

Empire was usually followed by negotiations to establish the fiscal regime under which the newly incorporated polities would operate. Given their traditional adherence to the political thinking of the time and their willingness to respect all kinds of privileges and franchises, the Spanish Habsburgs were usually ready to embrace the traditional institutions and norms of their new dominions, as in post-1513 Navarre (García-Zúñiga). There was strong continuity between the Navarrese fiscal system before and after its incorporation into the Empire, which accounts for the local *Cortes*' centrality during the early modern period. The emphasis on continuity is also evident in other imperial territories, though the Habsburgs' arrival could prompt profound fiscal changes, as in sixteenth-century Lombardy.[41]

At another level, the fiscal history of many imperial territories during the Habsburg period was presided by continuous negotiations between the Crown and their parliamentary assemblies, such as the *Cortes* of Castile, Navarre and those of the Aragonese territories (Catalonia, Aragón and Valencia) or the provincial Estates of Flanders and Brabant (Andrés Ucendo and Lanza García; Sardone; García-Zúñiga; Ena; Limberger). This was the continuation of a long-term process that dated back to the Middle Ages. It was initially admitted that kings and rulers had to draw their revenues from their patrimonial domains and rights. If those revenues were insufficient, the rulers turned to regional parliaments and asked for extraordinary contributions (Castilian and Aragonese *servicios*, Navarrese aids, Brabantine subsidies). Schumpeter (1954 [1918]) emphasises that the consolidation of parliamentary assemblies due to the fiscal shortcomings of the Dominion State was a key step in the emergence of the Fiscal State. The process was already well underway in the late Middle Ages, if not before, in the Iberian kingdoms, due to the need of the Castilian and Aragonese kings to raise revenues for their military campaigns against Muslims. It was also visible in other territories that, over time, would become part of the Spanish Empire. The close involvement of local parliaments, such as the *Cortes* of Castile and those of the Aragonese territories, in the Crown's fiscal policy remained constant, at least until the 1660s. As a result, the Spanish kings grew accustomed to lengthy negotiations with the parliamentary assemblies of the territories they ruled over. This enhanced the political profile of some of these assemblies, such as the Castilian *Cortes*.[42]

Nevertheless, there were some exceptions. Perhaps the most important was the Portuguese. Until the mid-fifteenth century, Portugal seemed intent on pursuing the same fiscal course as other Iberian and European states, and the Domain State appeared on the verge of extinction. Since 1336, the country's municipalities had collected a sales tax (*sisa*) whenever the king asked for extraordinary subsidies. Initially, it was a temporary, voluntary tax conceded by the towns to the Crown, but it became permanent in 1387 when the *Cortes* granted the *sisa* to João I to fund the war effort against Castile. At the end of his reign, the *sisa* provided 74 percent of the Crown's revenue.[43] This seemed to be the prelude to the birth of the Portuguese branch of the Fiscal State, but the process ended with the arrival of the Imperial Age. As Costa remarks in her chapter, the expansion of the overseas empire and trade drove the rise of the Portuguese kings' revenues from sources within the Crown's domain, such as royal monopolies and customs, granting them remarkable independence from the local *Cortes* in fiscal and financial matters. This reinvigorated the main features of the Domain State until the 1620s, when the rising fiscal and military demands of the Spanish Habsburgs ultimately created a favourable context for Portuguese independence in 1640, followed by substantial changes in the country's fiscal and financial structure.[44]

The key fiscal role of parliamentary assemblies in the Spanish Empire is evident in the fact that, between 1600 and 1660, a substantial portion of the revenues raised by the Castilian Crown came from contributions granted by the *Cortes*. However, this should not obscure the importance of the negotiations between the Crown and other institutions, such as the Church and the Seville merchant court (*Consulado*). This aspect is analysed by López Vela and Lamikiz in their chapters. López Vela focuses on the negotiations over the religious subsidies of 1707–1709 between Philip V, the Spanish Church and the Papacy. The Spanish and Italian churches ranked among the wealthiest in Latin Christendom, something which did not escape the Spanish Habsburgs. Our estimates suggest that between 1600 and 1640, the religious contributions (*subsidio*, *excusado* and *cruzada*) granted by the Church provided between 10 and 15 percent of the Royal Treasury's yearly revenue. This led to complex negotiations between the Crown, the Papacy and the Castilian Church. A special committee represented the latter, the *Congregación del Clero de las Iglesias de Castilla*, charged with apportioning the contributions granted by the local (and then Spanish) church among the archbishoprics, bishoprics, religious orders and ecclesiastical institutions of Castile and Spain. In his chapter, López Vela examines the circumstances surrounding the Spanish Church's grants of the subsidies of 1707 and 1709 to Philip V, as well as the involvement of the *Congregación* and the Papacy in the process. Lamikiz's chapter on the taxation of the *Carrera de Indias* (the Spanish system of transatlantic trade and navigation) examines the ongoing tension between the Crown and transatlantic merchants to determine an appropriate level of coercion that would secure both ordinary and extraordinary tax revenues for the king without damaging transatlantic trade during the seventeenth century. Ultimately, the chapter delves into the reasons that compelled merchants to pay what the king demanded. State coercion often turned predatory before the 1650s. Silver requisitions brought the Spanish colonial trade system to the cusp of collapse. This forced a major reform in 1660, giving the Seville *Consulado* more control over the collection of certain taxes and the extraordinary subsidies demanded by the Crown. However, the Crown managed to maintain a strong level of coercion, greatly facilitated by the one-port policy and the periodic fleets system, while at the same time granting important privileges to the merchants involved in the American trade and the *Consulado*.

Negotiation went hand in hand with fiscal devolution. The latter enabled the Crown to transfer the political costs of taxation to other fiscal agents, such as cities and corporations, which usually welcomed this possibility, since it reduced the risk of unwelcome Crown interference in their economic activities and daily affairs. This issue is addressed in the chapters by Andrés Ucendo and Lanza García, Sardone, García-Zúñiga, Lamikiz, Limberger, Ena and Martínez López-Cano.

During the reign of Charles I, following the precedent set by the preceding *Trastámara* dynasty at the end of the medieval period, the Castilian *Cortes* granted and collected extraordinary contributions for the Crown (Sardone). To this, it should be added that some of the central taxes levied in Castile (*millones* and *alcabalas*) were collected by the cities under the surveillance of parliamentary committees (Andrés Ucendo and Lanza García). Simultaneously, the Navarrese and Aragonese *Cortes* and the Brabantine States were responsible for collecting the aids and subsidies they granted to the king (García-Zúñiga, Ena and Limberger). More examples of this trend can be found in the chapters by López Vela and Lamikiz, which deal with the involvement of the *Congregación del Clero de las Iglesias de Castilla* in the collection of the 1707–1709 subsidy and the Seville *Consulado* in the collection of the new *avería* tax and the extraordinary contributions (*indultos*, *servicios* and *donativos*). The Castilian, Navarrese and Aragonese *Cortes*, the Brabantine Estates, the *Congregación del Clero*, and even the Seville *Consulado* were institutions that, in a broad sense, represented the specific interests of relevant social groups. Fiscal devolution granted these institutions some say in shaping the Crown's fiscal policy, which was the price the latter gladly paid to avoid the costs of recruiting and building the administrative apparatus required to collect royal taxes. Another way to address the same problem was to outsource some key fiscal functions to private individuals. Martínez López-Cano addresses this issue in her chapter on the merchants of Mexico City hired by the Crown to collect the revenues obtained from the crusade bull (*bula de cruzada*) in New Spain between 1590 and 1659. As the conquered American territories were legally deemed Castilian provinces rather than mere colonial dependencies, numerous Castilian fiscal and financial institutions were transplanted to Spanish America after 1492. In 1574, the *alcabala*, the most critical Castilian tax until the 1630s, and the crusade bull began to be levied in New Spain (Martínez López-Cano).[45] The latter was collected through the involvement of the Mexico City merchants, who acted as commission agents, selling the bulls to the inhabitants of the Viceroyalty. They could fulfil this task because, as Martínez López-Cano convincingly proves, they were wealthy and influential individuals with many years of experience and a vast network of contacts all over New Spain (which included, at least as far as the collection of the *cruzada* is concerned, the Philippine Islands), ensuring quality of service.

With a favourable economic climate that lasted until the beginning of the seventeenth century, the emphasis on negotiation and fiscal devolution helped secure the political consensus required to raise royal revenues. The figures presented by Pezzolo show that royal revenue in Castile rose from 107 silver tons in 1551 to 430 in 1600, then fell to 412 by mid-century. In the same period, the revenues drawn from the Italian dominions (Milan, Naples and Sicily) followed a similar pattern, rising from 70.7 tons in 1550 to a maximum of 143.1 tons in 1600, before falling to 92.2 tons in 1650. Andrés Ucendo and Lanza García's data indicate that, both in current and silver terms, the Castilian Crown's revenues peaked around 1635–45, while those of García-Zúñiga prove that the fiscal ceiling was reached in Navarre in 1630–39. This indicates that the Spanish Habsburgs' fiscal revenue reached its peak sometime during the first half of the seventeenth century. Then stagnation set in for the rest of the century. By 1700, the revenue from Castile had declined to 219 silver tons, down to the pre-1600 level, and that from Milan, Naples and Sicily to little more than 76 tons. Remarkably, the royal revenue in Navarre during the same period showed a similar trend.

Such pattern may be explained by the seventeenth-century economic crisis, which profoundly affected the fiscal systems of the Habsburg Empire's territories. In many cases, these systems rested on indirect taxes on consumption and trade, the burden of which fell mainly on Castilian and Italian cities. While the growth of the Castilian and Italian economies during the sixteenth century had created favourable conditions for the fiscal expansion of the time, the opposite happened during the seventeenth. The impact of the crisis was devastating across the Mediterranean.[46] The shocks of the demographic slump and the economic recession in Castilian and Italian cities negatively affected fiscal systems. In this context, the possibilities for introducing fiscal reform and adaptations were narrowed by the emergence of serious agency problems and the distortions created by the expedients the government used to sidestep the constraints imposed by parliamentary assemblies. This is the third point of our argument, which is addressed in the chapters by Andrés Ucendo and Lanza García, Ena, Costa, Lamikiz and Limberger.

Implicit in fiscal devolution was the potential emergence of agency problems brought about by the consolidation of well-entrenched institutions and constituencies, as their distinct interests might differ from the Crown's. The expansion of municipal debt in the Aragonese, Flandrian and Brabantine cities provides a case in point, as shown in the chapters by Ena and Limberger. To raise the subsidies granted to the Crown, the cities of these territories issued annuities funded through the taxes collected by the municipalities themselves. This led to the consolidation of rentier groups, primarily urban. These rentiers had a stake in perpetuating regressive urban taxation systems that supplied the revenues needed to cover interest payments. As Ena and Limberger indicate, at the beginning of the eighteenth century, the belief that the municipal debt was disastrous and had to be defaulted on was widespread among government circles and many essayists. However, they faced strong opposition from annuity holders. Urban indebtedness was a general problem in the territories of the old Spanish Habsburg Empire at the beginning of the eighteenth century. This was merely the tip of a serious structural problem, which led the Bourbon dynasty, upon its arrival in Spain in the 1700s, to conclude that the country's tax systems served only the urban rentiers and other powerful constituencies. This explains the Bourbons' interest in promoting the Treasury's direct involvement in collecting the most critical taxes, while simultaneously subjecting the local treasuries of Castilian and Spanish cities to close control.[47]

In territories such as Castile, the rise of municipal debt was more than paralleled by the unremitting growth of the Crown's indebtedness, which has long drawn the interest of historians.[48] The chapters by Andrés Ucendo and Lanza García, and Costa, address some aspects of this process. The growth of public debt in Castile meant that a substantial part of the Crown's revenues was earmarked for servicing its long- and short-term debt (Andrés Ucendo and Lanza García, and Costa).

A discount (*media anata*) on the interest payments of the long-term debt bonds (*juros*) was introduced in 1635, and soon became an important source of revenue for the beleaguered Castilian Treasury. Although the *media anata* was admitted by the *Cortes* and the Crown compensated the *juros* holders (*juristas*) with new bonds until around 1675, its levying was strongly resented as an arbitrary attack on the property rights of the *juristas*, many of whom were members of the powerful Castilian Church. As described by Ena, this was essentially the same reasoning invoked at the beginning of the eighteenth century by the Aragonese judges of the Royal Court, who were opposed to any default of the municipal debt.

Compared to Castile, Portuguese public debt as examined by Costa offers a remarkable contrast.[49] The two countries shared some similarities, including extensive overseas empires that provided substantial fiscal and financial resources. However, the most significant difference between them is that, after regaining its independence in 1640, Portugal was able to develop sound public credit. This is shown by the fact that the supposedly absolutist kings of the Braganza dynasty issued public debt bonds (*xuros*) at interest rates that ranked among the lowest in seventeenth-century Europe, thereby challenging theories that see the consolidation of representative government as a fundamental step in the development of sound public debt.

Aside from the *media anata*, in the seventeenth century, the Castilian Crown also resorted to other expedients, such as extraordinary contributions and devaluations of the bullion currency. Both expedients, analysed in the chapters by Andrés Ucendo and Lanza García and Lamikiz, were simple ways to raise royal revenue, but at the cost of causing severe long-term economic distortions in the fabric of the Castilian economy.

As explained by Lamikiz, there was a shift in the taxes levied on the Castilian transatlantic trade during the seventeenth century, from a system based on customs duties to one dependent on extraordinary contributions (*indultos*, *donativos* and *servicios*) imposed on transatlantic merchants. These contributions required a measured level of coercion to be effective. However, the line separating an appropriate level of State coercion from outright predation was often blurred, as evidenced by the Crown's requisitions of American precious metal imports. Unsurprisingly, these requisitions caused distortions and uncertainties that hampered transatlantic trade – a vital branch of the Castilian economy.

The manipulations of the bullion coinage in seventeenth-century Castile were also highly disruptive of domestic economic activity. Both contemporary authors and modern historians agree that such manipulations had disastrous economic consequences.[50] Andrés Ucendo and Lanza García's chapter shows that monetary manipulations were also responsible for the final fiscal and financial crisis of the Castilian Treasury in the first half of the 1680s. Drelichman and Voth (2014) have proved that the fiscal and financial system of Habsburg Castile was more resilient than traditionally thought, but that resilience vanished in the mid-seventeenth century. The economic crisis of the period fell mainly on the Castilian cities, ending the Crown's capacity to raise the fiscal revenue required for servicing its short- and long-term public debt.[51] In the short run, *vellón* manipulations played a key role in the crisis. Copper currency devaluations generated substantial income for the Treasury. Still, it was at the cost of undermining the foundations of the Castilian economy and, therefore, the basis of its fiscal and financial organisation, as discussed in the chapter by Andrés Ucendo and Lanza García.

The *media anata*, the confiscations of American bullion and the manipulations of the Castilian petty copper currency could be seen as an unremitting offensive of the Castilian Crown against property rights. Under the strain of funding the imperial policy, the Spanish rulers ultimately adopted measures that diverged from their traditional adherence to the principles of a composite Empire. As a result, their commitment to the property rights of holders of financial assets such as the *juros*, those who owned American silver brought by treasury fleets, and the public, who held *vellón* currency in their pockets, was progressively weakened. This strengthens the long-held image of the Spanish monarchy as a relentless predatory force determined to disregard the local institutions and privileges of its various territories in a quest for fiscal and financial resources, presumably leaving behind a set of rules and norms that hindered economic development. However, when we broaden our perspective to include the evidence presented in this book's chapters, it becomes clear that the Spanish Habsburgs governed in accordance with the fundamental tenets of a composite state and upheld their subjects' property rights. That is why the Spanish Habsburgs and their representatives in the imperial territories continuously resorted to prolonged negotiations with local parliaments and intermediate bodies to raise their revenues, rather than to a unilateral, arbitrary introduction of new taxes. It is also why substantial fiscal competencies were devolved to parliaments, intermediate bodies, cities, corporations and even individuals. The chapters of this book therefore offer a new and, we believe, more nuanced view of the fiscal and financial systems created in some territories of the Spanish Empire during the Habsburg period. If they also help to dispel some old theories which are still rather influential, then the book will have served its purpose.

Notes

1 Artola, 1999; Elliott, 1963.
2 Ertman, 1997; Glete, 2001; Storrs, 2009; Tilly, 1975 and 1990.
3 O'Brien, 2011 and 2018.
4 North and Thomas 1973; Davis 1973. See also Levi, 1988.
5 Norberg, 1994; Collins, 1995.
6 As it is said by Reinhart and Rogoff, 2009 and Stasavage, 2016. See also more recent studies by Fortea Pérez, 2023 and 2025, and Gelabert, 2017 and 2023.
7 Cameron, 1989; Landes, 1998.
8 Epstein, 2000.
9 Sussman, 2022; Sussman and Yafeh, 2006.
10 Hoffman, 1996.
11 Thompson, 1994b and 1996; Artola 1999; Elliott, 1963; Fortea Pérez 2025; Kagan 1991.
12 Gallego Anabitarte, 2009 [1971]; García Martín, 2010 and San Emeterio, 2005.
13 Brewer, 1989: 69–85; Bowen, 1998: 30–31.

14 Muto, 1995: 234–235 and 240; Ruiz Martín, 1990: 179.
15 Langford, 1989: 692–700, and 1991: 390–410; Innes, 1994: 118.
16 Langford, 1989: 710–719.
17 Andrés Ucendo and Lanza García, 2013: 162–166; Andrés Ucendo, 2023: 84; Galasso, 1975: 20; Malanima, 2002: 308 and Sella, 1979: VII, 63–74 and 1997: 32.
18 Calabria, 1991: 43 and 53–67; Sella, 1997: 37–38; Domínguez Ortiz, 1960: 20–100.
19 García Sanz, 1991; Andrés Ucendo and Lanza García, 2013: 162–166; Lanza García, 2020; Sella, 1979: 63–74.
20 Andrés Ucendo, 2023a: 85–90; Galasso, 2000: 187 and 214; Koenigsberger, 1989: 163.
21 For an exception to this agreement, see Calabria, 1991: 4.
22 Andrés Ucendo and Lanza García, 2013: 162–166.
23 Sella, 1997: 36–37.
24 Andrés Ucendo and Lanza García, 2013: 182–186.
25 Thompson, 1994a; Hoffman and Norberg, 1994; van Zanden and Prak, 2006; Lanza García, 2019.
26 Fortea Pérez, 2008 and 2023; Drelichman and Voth, 2014; Álvarez Nogal and Chamley, 2014.
27 Toboso, 1986; Gelabert, 2017; Calabria, 1991: 73 and 128–129; Fritschy, 2017; Fortea Pérez, 2023; Lanza García, 2026.
28 Glete, 2001.
29 For the concept of composite monarchy, see Elliott, 1992 and Koenigsberger, 1989.
30 Elliott, 1963; Artola, 1999.
31 Elliott, 1986.
32 Muto, 1995: 233.
33 Andrés Ucendo and Lanza García, 2008; Domínguez Ortiz, 1960: 151–161; Elliott, 1986; Yun-Casalilla, 2012; Biblioteca Nacional de España (BNE), Ms 9372, fols. 43–52.
34 Schumpeter, 1954 [1918].
35 Fernández Albaladejo, 1992; Fortea Pérez, 2008; González Antón, 1989; Koenigsberger, 1989; Sella, 1979: 31 and 141–143.
36 Yun-Casalilla, 2012: 14–15; Calabria, 1991: 44; Muto, 1995: 239; O'Brien, 2011: 421–25 and 434; Sella, 1979: 33.
37 Fritschy, 2017: 64–80.
38 O'Brien, 2011: 435 and 2018: 108.
39 Dincecco, 2009: 55.
40 Fernández Albaladejo, 1992; Fortea Pérez 2025; Thompson, 1994a, 1994b and 1996.
41 Sella, 1997; Vigo, 1979.
42 Fortea Pérez, 1990 and 2008; Fernández Albaladejo, 1992; Fernández de Pinedo, 1993; Thompson, 1994a and 1994b.
43 Disney 2013; Costa, Lains and Miranda, 2018: 41; Mata, 2012: 215.
44 Mata, 2012: 215.
45 On the Novo-Hispania taxation see Martínez López-Cano, Sánchez Santiró and Souto Mantecón, 2015.
46 Alfani, 2013; De Vries, 2009; Fortea Pérez, 1995; Gelabert, 1994 and 2012; Lanza García, 2025.
47 Fernández Albaladejo, 1992; García García, 1996.
48 Calabria, 1991; Toboso, 1986.
49 Costa and Miranda, 2023.
50 Hamilton, 1934 and 1947; and the international comparison in Braudel and Spooner, 1967.
51 Andrés Ucendo, 2023b; Lanza García, 2025.

Bibliography

Alfani, Guido (2013), "Plague in Seventeenth-Century Europe and the Decline of Italy: An Epidemiological Hypothesis", *European Review of Economic History*, 17, 4, pp. 408–430.

Álvarez-Nogal, Carlos and Chamley, Christophe (2014), "Debt Policy under Constraints: Philip II, the Cortes and the Genoese Bankers", *Economic History Review*, 67, 1, pp. 192–213.

Andrés Ucendo, José Ignacio (2023a), "Sobre el sistema financiero de la Castilla de los Austrias", in Ramón Lanza García and Roberto López Vela, coords., *Ciudades y Corona. Fiscalidad, representación y gobierno en la Monarquía Hispánica en la Edad Moderna*, Santander: Universidad de Cantabria, pp. 83–101.

Andrés Ucendo, José Ignacio (2023b), "Hacienda y Crédito Público en Castilla en el siglo XVII", in Ramón Lanza García, coord., *Finanzas y crisis financieras en la Monarquía Hispánica, siglos XVI-XVII*, Madrid: Marcial Pons, pp. 251–283.

Andrés Ucendo, José Ignacio and Lanza García, Ramón (2013), "Impuestos municipales, precios y salarios reales en la Castilla del siglo XVII: el caso de Madrid", *Hispania*, 73, pp. 162–191.

Andrés Ucendo, José Ignacio and Lanza García, Ramón (2008), "Estructura y evolución de los ingresos de la Real Hacienda de Castilla en el siglo XVII", *Studia Historica. Historia Moderna*, 30, pp. 111–155.

Artola, Miguel (1999), *La Monarquía de España*, Madrid: Alianza.

Bowen, Henry V. (1998), *War and British Society, 1688–1815*, Cambridge: Cambridge University Press.

Braudel, Fernand, and Spooner, F. C. (1967), "Prices in Europe from 1450 to 1750", in E.E. Rich and C.H. Wilson, eds., *The Cambridge Economic History of Europe*. IV. *The Economy of Expanding Europe in the Sixteenth and Seventeenth Centuries*, Cambridge: Cambridge University Press, pp. 374–486.

Brewer, John (1989), *The Sinews of Power: War, Money and the English State, 1688–1783*, Cambridge, MA: Harvard University Press.

Calabria, Antonio (1991), *The Cost of Empire: The Finances of the Kingdom of Naples in the Time of Spanish Rule*, Cambridge: Cambridge University Press.

Cameron, Rondo (1989), *A Concise Economic History of the World: From Palaeolithic Times to the Present*, Oxford: Oxford University Press.

Collins, James B. (1995), *The State in Early Modern France*, Cambridge: Cambridge University Press.

Costa, Leonor Freire and Miranda, Susana Münch (2023), "Reputational Recovery under Political Instability: Public Debt, Portugal, 1461–1683", *Economic History Review*, 76, 3, pp. 871–891.

Costa, Leonor Freire, Lains, Pedro and Miranda, Susana Münch (2018), *An Economic History of Portugal, 1143–2010*, Cambridge: Cambridge University Press.

Davis, Ralph (1973), *The Rise of the Atlantic Economies*, London: Weidenfeld and Nicolson.

De Vries, Jan (2009), "The Economic Crisis of the Seventeenth Century after Fifty Years", *Journal of Interdisciplinary History*, 40, 2, pp. 151–194.

Dincecco, Mark (2009), "Fiscal Centralization, Limited Government, and Public Revenues in Europe, 1650–1913", *Journal of Economic History*, 69, 1, pp. 48–103.

Disney, Antony R. (2013), *A History of Portugal and the Portuguese Empire*, vol. I, Cambridge: Cambridge University Press.

Domínguez Ortiz, Antonio (1960), *Política y Hacienda de Felipe IV*, Madrid: Pegaso.

Drelichman, Mauricio and Voth, Hans-Joachim (2014), *Lending to the Borrower from Hell: Debt, Taxes and Defaults in the Age of Philip II*, Princeton, NJ: Princeton University Press.

Elliott, John H. (1963), *Imperial Spain, 1469–1716*, London: Edward Arnold.

Elliott, John H. (1986), *The Count Duke of Olivares: The Statesman in an Age of Decline*, New Haven, CT: Yale University Press.

Elliott, John H. (1992), "A Europe of Composite Monarchies", *Past and Present*, 137, pp. 48–71.

Epstein, Stephen (2000), *Freedom and Growth: The Rise of States and Markets in Europe, 1300–1750*, London: Routledge.

Ertman, Thomas (1997), *Birth of the Leviathan: Building States and Regimes in Medieval and Early Modern Europe*, Cambridge: Cambridge University Press.

Fernández Albaladejo, Pablo (1992), *Fragmentos de Monarquía*, Madrid: Alianza.

Fernández de Pinedo, Emiliano (1993), "Fiscalidad y absolutismo en Castilla en la primera mitad del siglo XVII", in José Ignacio Fortea and María del Carmen Cremades, eds., *Política y Hacienda en el Antiguo Régimen*, Murcia: Universidad de Murcia, vol. I, pp. 33–51.

Fortea Pérez, José Ignacio (1990), *Monarquía y Cortes en la Corona de Castilla. Las ciudades ante la política fiscal de Felipe II*, Cortes de Castilla y León (the Regional Parliament), Valladolid: Cortes de Castilla y León.

Fortea Pérez, José Ignacio (1995), "Las ciudades de la Corona de Castilla en el Antiguo Régimen: una revisión historiográfica", *Revista de Demografía Histórica*, 13, 3, pp. 19–60.

Fortea Pérez, José Ignacio (2008), *Las Cortes de Castilla y León bajo los Austrias*, Junta de Castilla y León (the Regional Government), Valladolid: Junta de Castilla y León.

Fortea Pérez, José Ignacio (2025), "Las ciudades, la deuda pública y la *revolución financiera* (1500-1700): una reflexión desde el sur de Europa", in *As Cidades na História: Economia. Atas III Congreso Histórico Internacional 25 a 27 de outubro de 2023*. Guimarães: Câmara Municipal de Guimarães (Forthcoming).

Fortea Pérez, José Ignacio (2023), "Fiscalidad y deuda pública bajo los Austrias: las últimas bancarrotas de Felipe IV (1647, 1652, 1662)", in Ángel GALÁN Sánchez, José Ramón Díaz de Durana Y ORTIZ DE Urbina, and José Manuel Triano, eds., *Oficio de príncipes. Conflicto militar, economía y circuitos financieros en la Península Ibérica (siglos XIII-XVII)*, Granada: Comares, pp. 229–286.

Fritschy, Wantje (2017), *Public Finance of the Dutch Republic in a Comparative Perspective: The Viability of an Early Modern Federal State* (1570s–1795), Leiden: Brill.

Galasso, Giuseppe (1975), *Mezzogiorno medievale e moderno*, Torino: Einaudi.

Galasso, Giuseppe (2000), *En la periferia del Imperio. La monarquía hispánica y el reino de Nápoles*, Madrid: Península.

Gallego Anabitarte, Alfredo (2009 [1971]), *Poder y Derecho. Del Antiguo Régimen al Estado Constitucional en España. Siglos XVIII a XIX*, Madrid: Marcial Pons.

García García, Carmen (1996): *La crisis de las Haciendas Locales: de la reforma administrativa a la reforma fiscal*, Valladolid: Junta de Castilla y León.

García Martín, Javier (2010), "*Auferre rem privation* o título versus *potestas*. La expropiación en los juristas castellanos del *ius comune*", in Salustiano de Dios, Javier Infante, Ricardo Robledo, Eugenia Torrijano, coords., *Historia de la Propiedad. La expropiación*, Salamanca: Ediciones de la Universidad de Salamanca/Servicio de Estudios del Colegio de Registradores, pp. 99–193.

García Sanz, Ángel (1991), "Repercusiones de la fiscalidad sobre la economía castellana en los siglos XVI y XVII", *Hacienda Pública Española. Homenaje a Felipe Ruiz Martín*, I, pp. 15–23.

Gelabert, Juan Eloy (1994), "Urbanization and Deurbanization in Castile, 1500–1800", in I.A.A. Thompson and Bartolomé Yun-Casalilla, eds., *The Castilian Crisis of the Seventeenth Century*, Cambridge: Cambridge University Press, pp. 182–206.

Gelabert, Juan Eloy (2012), "La fortuna de las ciudades, 1500–1700", *Studia Historica. Historia Moderna*, 34, pp. 25–59.

Gelabert, Juan Eloy (2017), "La 'banqueroute deguisée' de *Messieur* Sully (1598–1610)", in Julio Pardos, Julen Viejo, José María Iñurritegui, José María Portillo and Fernando Andrés, eds., *Historia en fragmentos. Estudios en Homenaje a Pablo Fernández Albaladejo*, Madrid: Universidad Autónoma de Madrid, pp. 257–274.

Gelabert, Juan Eloy (2023), "El dedo y la luna. Política, hacienda y crédito en la Monarquía hispana, 1573–1597", in Ramón Lanza García, coord., *Finanzas y crisis financieras en la Monarquía Hispánica en los siglos XVI y XVII*, Marcial Pons: Madrid, pp. 129–186.

Glete, Jan (2001), *War and the State in Early Modern Europe*, London: Routledge.

González Antón, Luis (1989), *Las Cortes en la España del Antiguo Régimen*, Madrid: Siglo XXI.

Hamilton, Earl J. (1934), *American Treasure and the Price Revolution in Spain, 1500–1650*, Cambridge, MA: Harvard University Press.

Hamilton, Earl J. (1947), *War and Prices in Spain, 1651–1800*, Cambridge, MA: Harvard University Press.

Hoffman, Philip (1996), *Growth in a Traditional Society: The French Countryside, 1450–1815*, Princeton, NJ: Princeton University Press.

Hoffman, Philip and Norberg, Kathryn (1994), "Conclusion", in Philip Hoffman and Kathryn Norberg, eds., *Fiscal Crises, Liberty, and Representative Government, 1450–1789*, Stanford, CA: Stanford University Press, pp. 299–310.

Hoppit, Julian (2011), "Compulsion, Compensation and Property Rights in Britain, 1688–1833", *Past and Present*, 210, pp. 93–128.

Innes, Joana (1994), "The Domestic Face of the Military-Fiscal State: Government and Society in Eighteenth-Century Britain", in Lawrence Stone, ed., *An Imperial State at War: Britain from 1689–1815*, London: Routledge, pp. 96–127.

Kagan, Richard (1991), *Pleitos y pleiteantes en Castilla, 1500–1700*, Valladolid: Junta de Castilla y León.

Koenigsberger, Helmuth (1989), *La práctica del Imperio*, Madrid: Alianza.

Landes, David (1998), *The Wealth and Poverty of Nations*, London: Little Brown.

Langford, Philip (1989), *A Polite and Commercial People: England 1727–1783*, Oxford: Oxford University Press.

Langford, Philip (1991), *Public Life and the Propertied Englishman, 1689–1798*, Oxford: Oxford University Press.

Lanza García, Ramón (2019), "Carga tributaria, ciudadanía y moral fiscal en la Castilla del siglo XVII", in Roberto López Vela, coord., *Ciudades, gentes e intercambios en la Monarquía Hispánica en la Edad Moderna*, Santander: Universidad de Cantabria, pp. 267–329.

Lanza García, Ramón (2020), "Guerra, hacienda y economía en la Monarquía de España en la crisis del siglo XVII", in José Ignacio Fortea Pérez, Juan Eloy Gelabert, Roberto López Vela and Elena Postigo, coords., *Monarquías en conflicto*, Madrid: Fundación Española de Historia Moderna/Universidad de Cantabria, pp. 197–255.

Lanza García, Ramón (2025), "Las ciudades en la España Moderna: crecimiento económico, crisis y reconstrucción, 1500–1800", *Memoria y Civilización*, 28, I, pp. 39–72.

Lanza García, Ramón (2026), "Juros, media anata de juros y el problema de la deuda pública de los últimos Habsburgo españoles", *Studia Historica. Historia Moderna*, 48, 1, forthcoming.

Levi, Margaret (1988), *Of Rule and Revenue*, Berkeley and Los Angeles: University of California Press.

Malanima, Paolo (2002), *L'economia italiana. Dalla crescita medievale alla crescita contemporanea*, Bologna: Il Mulino.

López-Cano, Martínez, del Pilar, María, Sánchez Santiró, Ernest and Souto Mantecón, Matilde, coords. (2015), *La fiscalidad novo-hispana en el Imperio español. Conceptualizaciones, proyectos y contradicciones* , México: Instituto Mora-Conacyt-UNAM.

Mata, Eugenia (2012), "From pioneer mercantile state to ordinary fiscal state: Portugal, 1498–1914", in Bartolomé Yun-Casalilla; Patrick K. O'Brien, and Francisco COMÍN Comín, eds., *The Rise of Fiscal States: A Global History, 1500–1914*, Cambridge: Cambridge University Press, pp. 215–233.

Muto, Giovanni, (1995), "The Spanish System", in Richard Bonney, ed., *Economic Systems and State Finance*, Oxford: Oxford University Press, pp. 231–260.

Norberg, Kathryn (1994), "The French Fiscal Crisis of 1788 and the Financial Origins of the Revolution of 1789", en Philip T. Hoffman and Kathryn Norberg, eds., *Fiscal Crises, Liberty, and Representative Government, 1450–1789*, Stanford, Cal.: Stanford University Press, pp. 253–298.

North, Douglass C. and Thomas, Robert P. (1973), *The Birth of the Western World: A New Economic History*, Cambridge: Cambridge University Press.

North, Douglass C. and Weingast, Barry R. (1989), "Constitutions and Commitment: The Evolution of Institutions Governing Public Choice in Seventeenth-Century England", *Journal of Economic History*, 49, 4, pp. 803–832.

O'Brien, Patrick K. (2011), "The Nature and Historical Evolution of an Exceptional Fiscal State and Its Possible Significance for the Precocious Commercialization and Industrialization of the British Economy from Cromwell to Nelson", *Economic History Review*, 64, 2, pp. 408–446.

O'Brien, Patrick K. (2018), "The Costs and Benefits of Mercantilist Warfare", *Financial History Review*, 25, 1, pp. 97–113.

Reinhart, Carmen and Rogoff, Kenneth (2009), *This Time Is Different: Eight Centuries of Financial Folly*, Princeton, NJ: Princeton University Press.

Ruiz Martín, Felipe (1990), *Las finanzas de la Monarquía Hispánica en tiempos de Felipe IV*, Madrid: Real Academia de la Historia.

San Emeterio, Nieves (2005), *Sobre la propiedad. El concepto de propiedad en la Edad Moderna*, Madrid: Tecnos.

Schumpeter, Joseph (1954 [1918]), "The Crisis of the Tax State", *International Economic Papers*, 4, pp. 5–38.

Sella, Domenico (1979), *Crisis and Continuity: The Economy of Spanish Lombardy in the Seventeenth Century*, Cambridge, MA: Harvard University Press.

Sella, Domenico (1997), *Italy in the Seventeenth Century*, London: Longman.

Stasavage, D. (2016), "What We Can Learn from the Early History of Sovereign Debt?", *Explorations in Economic History*, 59, pp. 1–16.

Storrs, Christopher, ed. (2009), *The Fiscal-Military State in Eighteenth-Century Europe*, Ashgate: Farnham.

Sussman, Nathan (2022), "Financial Development in London in the Seventeenth Century: The Financial Revolution Revisited", *Journal of Economic History*, 82, 2, pp. 480–515.

Sussman, Nathan and Yafeh, Yishay (2006), "Institutional Reforms, Financial Development and Sovereign Debt: Britain 1690–1790", *Journal of Economic History* 66, 4, pp. 906–35.

Thompson, Irving A.A. (1996), "Absolutism, Legalism, and the Law in Castile: 1500–1700", in Ronald G. Ash and Heinz Duchardt, eds., *Der Absolutismus – ein Mythos?*

Strukturwandel monarchischer Herresachaft in West- und Mitteleuropa (ca. 1550–1700), Köln Weimar Wien: Böhlau Verlag, pp. 185–228.

Thompson, Irving A.A. (1994a), "Castile: Polity, Fiscality, and Fiscal Crises", in Philip T. Hoffman and Kathryn Norberg, eds., *Fiscal Crises, Liberty, and Representative Government, 1450–1789*, Stanford, CA: Stanford University Press, pp. 140–180.

Thompson, Irving A.A. (1994b), "Castile: Absolutism, Constitutionalism, and Liberty", in Philip T. Hoffman and Kathryn Norberg, eds., *Fiscal Crises, Liberty, and Representative Government, 1450–1789*, Stanford, CA: Stanford University Press, pp. 181–225.

Tilly, Charles, ed., (1975), *The Formation of National States in Western Europe*, Princeton, NJ: Princeton University Press.

Tilly, Charles (1990), *Coercion, Capital and European States, AD 990–1990*, Oxford: Blackwell.

Toboso, Pilar (1986), *La deuda pública castellana durante el Antiguo Régimen (juros)*, Madrid: Instituto de Estudios Fiscales.

Van Zanden, Jan Luyten and Prak, Maarten (2006), "State Formation and Citizenship: the Dutch Republic between Medieval Communes and Modern Nation States", *European Review of Economic History*, 10, pp. 111–145.

Vigo, Giovanni (1979), *Fisco e società nella Lombardia del Cinquecento*, Bologna: Il Mulino.

Yun-Casalilla, Bartolomé (2012), "Introduction: The Rise of the Fiscal State in Europe from a Global, Comparative and Transnational Perspective", in Bartolomé Yun-Casalilla, Philip K. O'Brien and Francisco Comín Comín, eds., *The Rise of Fiscal States: A Global History*, Cambridge: Cambridge University Press, pp. 1–34.

1 The Castilian fiscal and financial system in the 16th and 17th centuries (1561–1700)

José Ignacio Andrés Ucendo and Ramón Lanza García

Introduction

The purpose of this chapter is to present an overview of the main lines in the evolution of the Castilian fiscal and financial system from 1561 to 1700. Our view emphasises several key points. First, the way the Castilian fiscal and financial system evolved during this period was shaped by an increasingly expensive imperial policy. This forced the Crown to make continuous requests for monetary aid (*servicios*) from the Castilian parliamentary assembly (*Cortes*) and led to a process that reinvigorated the political role of the assembly, especially from 1575 to 1664. Second, trying to escape from its dependence on streams of revenue granted by the *Cortes*, the Crown also resorted to sources of revenue free from parliamentary involvement from the early 17th century. Prominent among them were the manipulations of its petty copper currency (*vellón*). These manipulations involved an end to its traditional commitment to the stability of the country's monetary system and were one of the main factors responsible for the Castilian economic crisis of the 17th century.[1] The Castilian rulers were aware of these problems, but *vellón* manipulations enabled the Crown to raise substantial revenues without the costs of protracted negotiations with the *Cortes*, and this outweighed any other consideration.

Third and last, if the capacity for raising revenues is the test for the success of any fiscal and financial system, then the Castilian one passed with flying colours until the mid-17th century, despite the famous defaults of 1557–60, 1575, 1596, 1607, 1627, 1647, 1652 and 1662. Sometimes, such defaults were the pretext invoked by the Crown to present to the *Cortes* the necessity of deep fiscal reform, yet these projects came to nothing. In the absence of any real fiscal reform, the Crown surmounted each default by converting its short-term debt into long-term debt.[2] The conversion freed revenues for obtaining more short-term credit from international financiers (*asentistas*). To pay the interest on the long-term bonds (*juros*) issued in each episode, the Treasury usually relied on new services granted by the *Cortes* and taxes.[3] The system worked well until the mid-17th century when the Crown showed a remarkable ability to balance its income with its spending, an ability that vanished for two reasons. The economic crisis of the period, first, reduced the yields of taxes and *servicios*,[4] while the rising inflation levels driven

DOI: 10.4324/9781003653301-2

by *vellón* manipulations, second, drove the sudden increase of one particularly important item of expenditure: the so-called *reducciones*. This set the scene for an episode that can be considered the last chapter in the list of fiscal and financial crises of the Spanish Habsburgs: the Castilian 1680–88 monetary, fiscal and financial stabilisation programme. Triggered by the 1680 deflation, this episode put into stark relief the problems of the Castilian Crown's fiscal and monetary policy. The deflation led to a drop in the Crown's revenues, which fell by 45 percent between 1679 and 1687. This prompted substantial cuts in the interest that accrued to the owners (*juristas*) of the Castilian long-term bonds (*juros*), which fell by the same extent.

This last point deserves some consideration. Early modern Castile was ruled by kings who adhered to the main tenets of the prevailing political culture of the time.[5] Always willing to negotiate their fiscal and financial requests with the *Cortes* and the cities, Castilian kings were also keen on enforcing the property rights and privileges of their subjects. Royal courts strictly enforced Castilian law and did not hesitate to rule where necessary against the Crown. It was argued decades ago that the problem with 17th-century Castile seems to have been an excessive respect for legal procedure and due process of law by its rulers, which created a legalistic mindset shared by a broad section of the country's population.[6] While our chapter shares the view we have just outlined, it is worth adding a nuance: 17th-century Castilian kings found growing space for departing from their traditional enforcement of the law and property rights in the monetary, fiscal and financial arenas. This is the conclusion we may draw from the frequent *vellón* manipulations and the cuts in the interest that accrued to the *juristas*. This shows how in some key areas of the Castilian economy and society during the 17th century the otherwise strong commitment of the Crown to the enforcement of property rights was progressively weakened, with long-lasting consequences for the country's subsequent progression.

Part 1 deals with the sources used in the article. To develop our argument, part 2 presents our series of yearly revenues of the Castilian Crown between 1561 and 1700. In part 3, we analyse the evolution of the Crown's spending between 1561 and 1700. Lastly, in part 4, we deal with the circumstances that led to the Castilian 1680–88 monetary, fiscal and financial stabilisation programme and its implications.

The sources

In a 1998 article, J. Gelabert described the Spanish Monarchy as the largest machine for the raising of fiscal and financial resources in Western Europe until the middle of the 17th century.[7] In the same article, the author went on to point out the difficulties faced by today's historians when trying to compile the Crown's revenues and its spending. While many of the problems found by J. Gelabert remain, there have been some advances in the last decades. Today we have reliable series of the revenues raised by the Crown from some of its main taxes (the *millones*, the *cuatro cientos*), plus estimates of the yields of *donativos* granted to the Crown by the most important Castilian cities, such as Seville and Madrid.[8] Together with the large secondary literature on the issue, plus the sources preserved in the *Archivo General de Simancas* (AGS), this has enabled us to compile the Castilian Treasury's yearly revenues between 1561 and 1700.

While the reconstruction of our revenue series has been possible thanks to the documentary sources filed in the AGS and the large secondary literature at our disposal, our effort to reconstruct the Crown's spending from 1561 to 1700 has proved rather less successful due to obstacles posed by the sources. Because of this, we have resorted, first, to the research carried out by some scholars, which has provided us with the Crown's spending in 1566–74, 1575–84, 1585–96, 1598, 1601, 1608, 1614, 1615, 1617, 1621 and 1703-4.[9] Secondly, we have also consulted a set of contemporary reports about the Crown's spending for 1621–40, 1647, 1648–50, 1648, 1649–54, 1648–60, 1651, 1659–60, 1663, 1666, 1678 and 1680.[10] These reports come from the pens of royal officials. Some of them indicate the expenditures effectively carried out (1621–40, 1649–54 and 1648–60) while others (1647, 1648–50, 1651, 1659–60, 1663, 1666, 1678 and 1680) are mere spending forecasts (*provisiones*) for those years.

Two of these reports stand out: the report (*tanteo*) written by Tomás de Aguilar at the beginning of the 1640s and the speech delivered in 1660 to the *Cortes* of Castile by Juan de Góngora.[11] Both Aguilar and Góngora were well-placed Crown officials, with firsthand knowledge of the Castilian public finances gained during their long years of service. In his *tanteo*, deservedly famous among historians, Aguilar recorded the Castilian Treasury's revenues and expenditures in the first two decades of the reign of Philip IV. Although the reader will not find here yearly series of the Crown's revenues and spending, Aguilar took good care to mention the total value of these two variables between 1621 and 1640, so we can easily arrive at their annual average value. Góngora's speech indicated the total amount of the Crown's ordinary spending between 1648 and 1660, so, again, it is possible to estimate its yearly average value. Góngora also informed the *Cortes* of the financial costs involved in the short-term loans granted to the Crown by its *asentistas*. Unlike Aguilar, however, he did not mention the amounts earmarked by the Treasury for the service of its long-term public debt (*situado*).

As for the *provisiones*, we have unearthed those of 1647, 1651, 1659–60, 1663, 1666, 1678 and 1680. The *provisiones* were an estimate produced by royal officers at the end of the year of the Crown's spending for the following year. Servicing the public debt was not included in them. When estimating the *provisiones*, royal officials had to ponder how they were going to raise the revenues needed to fund the planned expenditures and how such funds would then be transferred to all those charged with the task of making the payments, either royal officials or private contractors inside Castile or abroad. This was far from straightforward, and it frequently derailed, so at least a part of the *provisiones* never turned into real spending. Taking this into consideration, and the fact that the *provisiones* did not include the service of public debt, we decided not to display them in Figure 1.2, which shows the revenue and spending of the Castilian Crown in some years and periods from 1566 to 1660 and 1703–4. This does not imply that the analysis of the *provisiones* is useless. Together with the service of the public debt, the *provisiones* give us an accurate idea of the spending level deemed necessary by the Crown to implement its political agenda. Moreover, the need to raise revenues to fund the payments outlined in the *provisiones* was paramount to the concerns of the royal officials and informed the Crown's major decisions in the areas of fiscal and monetary policy. Our sources provide us with particularly accurate information about the *provisiones* of 1659, 1660, 1678 and 1680,[12] and this gives us an insight into the causes behind the deep changes in the Castilian fiscal and monetary policies of the 1680s (part 4).

The Crown's revenues

A pioneer, together with Tudor England and Valois France, in the expansion of the so-called Modern State, Habsburg Castile was also a pioneer in the development of one of the first modern fiscal and financial systems. The roots of the Castilian fiscal system date back to the medieval period. As was usual in the Europe of the time, it was supposed that the king had to fund his expenditures with the revenues obtained from the royal patrimony. As this was not sufficient, Castilian kings were forced to ask for monetary aid (*servicios*) from the *Cortes* and the cities. This led to continuous negotiations between both sides within the framework provided by the political thought of the time, which required a just cause for the introduction of new taxes and proportionality between the sums demanded by the Crown and the purpose for which those sums were asked.[13]

The process was already visible in 1342, when the Cortes granted the *alcabala*: a 10 percent sales tax for funding the siege of Algeciras. A temporary (3 years) expedient for the payment of a *servicio* at first, the *alcabala* soon became a permanent tax, collected from 1536 through the *encabezamiento general del reino*. The *encabezamiento* was a periodically renewed agreement between the king and the *Cortes* in which the king relinquished his right to collect the tax in return for a lump sum.[14] The agreement enabled the Castilian cities to collect the *alcabala* under the surveillance of a parliamentary committee, the *Diputación del Reino*, at a rate of 3–4 percent, well below the legal 10 percent.[15] The *alcabala* set a precedent followed by some of the most important taxes of the Royal Treasury, such as the *servicio ordinario y extraordinario* and, especially, the *servicio de millones*, introduced for the first time in 1590 and then, permanently, in 1601. In both cases what started as a temporary aid granted by the *Cortes* began to be periodically renewed after negotiations between the Crown and the assembly and finally turned into a permanent tax. As in the case of the *alcabala*, the cities collected the *millones* under the surveillance of another parliamentary committee, the *Comisión de Millones*. To raise the sums granted to the Crown, the *Cortes* resorted to a wine, vinegar and olive oil excise, plus a group of monetary charges on these staples and cow, pork and mutton from 1603.[16] Parliamentary involvement was also visible in another important tax: the four *unos por ciento*, introduced in 1639, 1642, 1656 and 1662 after negotiations between the Crown and the *Cortes*. Each *ciento* consisted of a 1-percent sales tax, so the four *cientos* amounted to a 4 percent tax. The first three *cientos* were created to complete the yields of the *millones*, while the fourth and last was introduced for the service of the *juros.*[17] Lastly, to enlist the cooperation of the Church in the funding of its ambitious imperial policy the Crown was also driven into continuous negotiations with the wealthy Castilian Church. Such negotiations had an extra-layer of complexity as they frequently not only involved the high circles of the local church, but also the Pope, who was usually rather reluctant to admit the fiscal requests of the Castilian kings.[18]

The *alcabala, servicio ordinario y extraordinario, millones, cientos* and Church contributions provided the Treasury with around 55–60 percent of its total yearly revenues, a figure that in some moments rose to 60–65 percent. Aware of the importance of their cooperation for the Royal Treasury, the *Cortes* and the cities imposed stringent conditions in return for the granting and renewal of these taxes, which led to a substantial strengthening of the role played by the assembly especially between 1575 and 1664. Unsurprisingly, the Crown consistently tried to curb the growing influence of the *Cortes* and the cities in the fiscal field, reducing the control of the assembly over the *millones* and promoting centralising measures which led to a delicate political balance between both sides during the first two-thirds of the 17th century.[19] This also accounts for the government's interest in those sources of revenue, which the Treasury could dispose of free from any parliamentary involvement, such as customs, many monopolies, the *media annata* (a tax on the interest that accrued to the owners of *juros*) and the *quinto real* (a 20-percent tax on the remittances of American silver). Lastly, the Crown also relied on a group of extraordinary sources of revenue, considered as such by its accountants on the basis of the discontinuities in their collection, such as sales of taxes, royal and municipal offices, nobility titles and vassals; donatives granted by cities and corporations and, especially, the manipulations of the Castilian low-value copper currency.[20]

The Castilian monetary system of the 16th and 17th centuries rested on the coexistence between the copper *maravedí* and the silver *real*. It had been decided in 1497 that the copper *maravedí* had to include a small silver content (3 percent).[21] Given that monetary policy was one of the most treasured regalian rights of Castilian kings, the *Cortes* had no say in this area. In turn, the possibility of increasing the nominal value of the copper *maravedí* while keeping its silver content (*resello*) or issuing pure copper pieces with no silver at all was highly appealing for the Crown, which resorted to them in 1603–6, 1617–26, 1636–38, 1641–42, 1651–52, 1658 and 1660–65.[22]

Since the revenues raised by the Crown were insufficient, Castilian kings had to borrow funds by way of short-term debt contracts, mainly from German, first, and then Italian – Genovese and Florentine – and Portuguese financiers.[23] The excessive accumulation of short-term debt was responsible for the famous financial defaults of the period. Those defaults basically were debt conversions in which the Crown reached an agreement with its lenders (*Medio General*). Typically, the short-term debt was converted into long-term debt with a lesser interest rate. To compensate its *asentistas* for their losses, the Crown typically issued massive amounts of long-term bonds in each *bancarrota*, the interest of which was frequently serviced through new services granted by the *Cortes* and taxes.[24] Although there could be other reasons behind the issue of this kind of financial asset, the defaults of the period were the main factor responsible for most of the new issues of *juros* between 1561 and 1664.[25] The expansion of the Castilian long-term public debt ended at the end of Philip IV's reign, but as the Crown had virtually renounced amortising the *juros* long ago its service remained as one of the most pressing problems of Castilian public finances between 1561 and 1700 for the simple fact that it drew a substantial part of the government's revenues.

Figure 1.1 displays the evolution of the fiscal revenues raised by the Castilian Treasury between 1561 and 1700. Figure 1.1 also includes the amounts coming from extraordinary revenues, but not those raised from the long and short-term debt. Our data are presented both in copper and silver *reales* (1 Castilian *real* = 34 copper *maravedís*). Most of the Castilian Crown's revenues were raised in low-value copper currency (*maravedí*). As a substantial part of its spending was abroad, where the Castilian *maravedí* could not be used, the Treasury had to exchange the sums collected inside Castile in copper *maravedís* into gold (in the 16th century) and silver (in the 17th).[26] At the beginning of the 17th century, the Crown raised enough silver for its payments abroad. After the *vellón* manipulations, however, this became increasingly difficult and in the last decades of the century, the Castilian authorities had to almost exclusively use the devalued copper pieces for their payments. This is why Figure 1.1 also charts the evolution of the Crown's total revenues in silver *reales*.

Measured in current terms, the Crown's yearly revenues went through a remarkable growth after 1575, driven by the increase of the *alcabala* when they rose from 59.5 million *reales* in 1574 to 95 in 1596.[27] Then, the arrival of the *servicios de millones* in 1590 and its definitive introduction in 1600 drove another rise from 90 million *reales* to 117 in 1621.[28] The increase gained pace in the first two decades of Philip IV's reign, between 1621 and 1642, when revenues rose from 117 million *reales* to 234. After a small fall, revenues stabilised around 200–220 million *reales* until 1683, when they decreased to 175 million. The decline lasted until the end of the century and in 1700 revenues had fallen to 150 million *reales* annually.[29]

The continuous rise of its long-term debt affected the evolution of the Castilian fiscal system between 1561 and 1700. The *juros* were issued on the pledge of some of the most important Crown taxes, such as the *alcabala, servicio ordinario and extraordinario, customs* and monopolies.[30] Already in 1573, the *situado* amounted to more than 80 percent of the total value of these taxes,[31] which accounts for the 1575 default and the rise of the *encabezamiento de alcabalas* in 1575. At the end of the century the situation was even worse, as 90 percent of the yields of *alcabala, servicio ordinario, customs* and *monopolies* were earmarked for the payment of the interest which accrued to the owners of *juros*. This left very little for other expenditures, which was one of the reasons behind the definitive introduction of the *millones* in 1601 and the strategic retrenchment of the reign of Philip III. Such a stance ended with the arrival of Philip IV and his famous *valido*, the Count Duke of Olivares.[32] Both Philip IV and Olivares supported a much more forward policy, funded through the resort to sources of revenue unencumbered by the *juros*, such

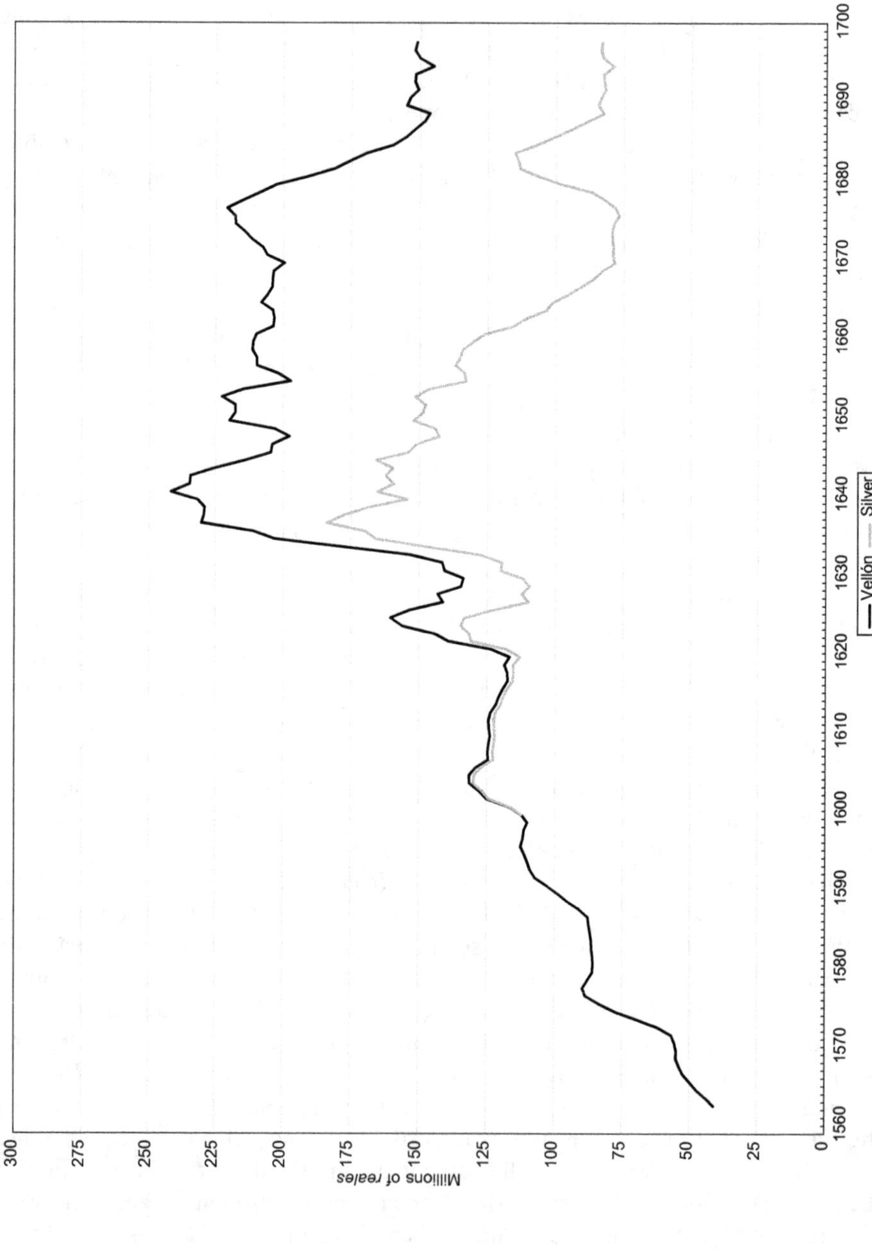
Millions of reales
0
25
50
75
100
125
150
175
200
225
250
275
300
1560
1570
1580
1590
1600
1610
1620
1630
1640
1650
1660
1670
1680
1690
1700
Vellón
Silver

Figure 1.1 Total revenues of the Castilian Treasury, 1561–1700.

Sources: For the total revenues of the Crown during the reign of Philip II, Bilbao (1990). In our compilation of the revenues of the Crown during the 17th century we have grouped the taxes and sources of revenue of the Royal Treasury under the same headings as Bilbao. For the yearly value of the *alcabalas*, *cientos* and *millones*: Andrés Ucendo, 1999, 2006, 2008 and 2023. The data on *rentas arrendables*: Artola, 1982; Alloza Aparicio, 2019 and AGS, Contadurías Generales, leg. 1093–1259. The subsidies granted by the Church and *excusado*: AGS, Comisaría de Cruzada, leg. 26–76 and 145–171. The American silver remittances: Hamilton, 1934; García Fuentes, 1980: 383–404; Álvarez-Nogal, 1998: 453–89. The seigniorage: Motomura, 1994: 104–27; García Guerra, 2014: 83–108; Hamilton, 1947 and Domínguez Ortiz, 1960. The proceeds from the alienations of royal taxes (*ventas de rentas reales*): Marcos Martín, 2006: 206 and 2007: 13–35. The Crusade (*Cruzada*): Lanza García, 2020a. The donatives (*donativos*) and other incomes: Bernal, 1992; Domínguez Ortiz, 1960, 1964, 1970, 1984, 1992 and 2003; Gutiérrez Alonso, 1989; Martínez Ruiz 1992; Mosácula, 2001; Quintana Toret, 1988; Rodríguez Vicente, 1977; Sánchez Belén, 1996; and the authors′ database. The revenues in a sample of years from 1577 to 1688 can also be consulted at Andrés Ucendo and Lanza García, 2008. Nominal values have been deflated by the price index of Andrés Ucendo and Lanza García, 2014 and 2020.

Note: Data in millions of *reales de vellón* and *reales de plata*. 5-Year moving averages.

as the *millones* and a long list of new taxes, plus all kinds of expedients introduced between 1621 and 1641.[33] In these two decades, the average yearly Crown revenues amounted to 182 million *reales*, 55 million higher than in 1598–1621. The *millones* were responsible for slightly over 50 percent of this rise, and although they began to be employed as collateral for new issues of *juros* from the middle of 1626, in 1641 less than 20 percent of their yields were allocated to that end. Although the *millones* were important, they were not alone, and in this period many other taxes were introduced (the first *uno por ciento*; new monopolies on tobacco, soap, stamp paper, chocolate and fish and the *media annata*), together with surcharges on taxes already in place, such as the salt tax.[34] Lastly, the Treasury also resorted to extraordinary sources of revenue, such as the donatives granted by the kingdom in 1625, 1629, 1631 and 1635 and the currency manipulations of 1617–26, 1636–38 and 1641–42.

The rise of 1621–41 was difficult to maintain in the adverse economic and political climate of the beginning of the 1640s. The key problem was that most of the Crown's revenues came from taxes levied upon internal trade and consumption, so their burden fell on the Castilian cities, at a period when the country's previously flourishing urban network was going through a phase of crisis and decadence.[35] The real wages earned by building labourers in Madrid and nearby Segovia fell by 33 and 26 percent respectively between 1621 and 1641.[36] In the same period, the Crown's revenues increased by nearly 130 percent. The imbalance between a growing tax burden and the progressive impoverishment of the Castilian taxpayers was untenable and contributed to the dismissal of Olivares at the beginning of 1643.[37] The departure of Olivares defused what had threatened to become an explosive political situation, and not by chance from 1643 the yearly value of the Crown revenues stabilised around 200–220 million *reales*. This lasted until 1686, when the fiscal relief programme promoted by the government reduced its yearly revenues to 140–150 million.

The 1683–86 fiscal relief programme was prompted by the 1680 deflation, which ended the *maravedí* manipulations, the main cause of the rise of inflation during the mid-century. As can be seen in Figure 1.1, the impact of inflation on the Crown's revenues in silver terms became visible from the beginning of the 1630s. Measured in silver *reales*, the remarkable rise of this decade was rather less noticeable. Even more importantly, Treasury revenues began to fall from the beginning of the 1640s, which was particularly visible during the mid-century, during the peak of *vellón* inflation. From 1660, the Crown's revenues dropped to the levels of the first third of the century.

The Crown's spending

Figure 1.2 displays the Castilian Crown's total spending in current terms, in a sample of years and periods from 1566 to 1660 and in 1703–4.

Government spending rose from 77.8 million *reales* annually in 1566–74 to 151.2 in 1598. This figure fell to 131.5 million in 1601. Not surprisingly, given the strategic retrenchment of Philip III's reign,[38] spending levels fell in 1601, 1608

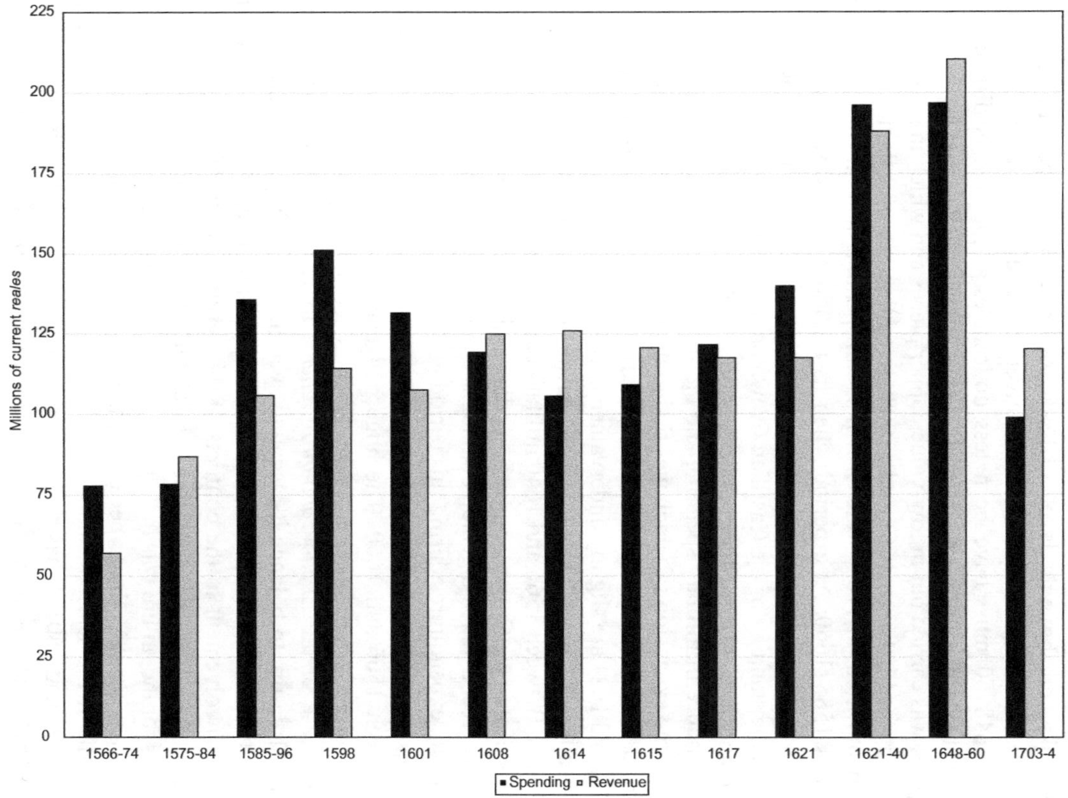

Figure 1.2 Spending and revenue of the Castilian Crown, 1566–1660 and 1703–4.

Notes: Data in current millions of Castilian *reales;* 1566–74, 1575–84, 1585–96, 1621–40, 1648–60 and 1703–4: data in yearly averages.

Source: Drelichman and Voth, 2014; Andrés Ucendo and Lanza García, 2024 and Figure 1.1.

and, especially, 1614 and 1615, but began to rise in 1617. The arrival of Philip IV embodied the resurgence of a more assertive Castilian foreign policy[39] and in the first year of his reign, 1621, spending rose to 140 million *reales*. The reign of Philip IV was the decisive phase in the Castilian bid for European hegemony, which fuelled a substantial increase in government spending. Measured in yearly averages, total spending was 195.8 million *reales* in 1621–40 and 209.7 in 1648–60, at its peak, well above the levels of 1598, 1601 and 1608. In part, this growth was due to *vellón* inflation. Measured in silver terms, the rise of 1621–40 and, especially, 1648–60 must have been less noticeable, although it is difficult to know to what extent as our sources simply do not tell us which part of government expenditures was carried out in low-value copper pieces and which in silver.

What happened between 1661 and 1700? Given the lack of reliable data, it is difficult to know, but in 1703–4 the Crown's total spending had fallen well below the levels of 1585–1660. At a period when its traditional rivals, such as France or England, were able to increase their spending levels, this remarkable fall undermined the standing of the Castilian Crown on the European scene.

The composition of Castilian public spending (Table 1.1) was presided over by the importance of military spending and the service of the long and short-term public debt, the expansion of which was tied to the need to fund the ongoing wars of the period. It should be noted that the financial expenditures of 1601, 1608, 1614, 1615, 1617 and 1621 are slightly undervalued as our sources do not inform us about the money allocated by the Treasury for the payment of the interest on the *asientos* in these years. Between 1566 and 1640 military expenditures hovered around 29.2 and 56.4 percent of the Crown's annual spending and financial expenditures around 35.5 and 56 percent. Taken together, both items amounted to around 85–90 percent of government expenditures during this period.

Going back to Figure 1.2, it shows the budgetary situation of the Castilian Crown between 1566 and 1660. The huge budgetary deficit of 1566–75, when expenditures were 36 percent higher than revenues, led to the famous 1575 default and the increase of the *Encabezamiento General* in 1575–76.[40] Both measures enabled the Treasury to balance its accounts, yet this was only a temporary solution. The years 1585–96 saw the resurgence of substantial budgetary deficits after the Crown's involvement in the conflicts of the period.[41] As in 1575, this led to another default in 1596, but this time the default proved ineffective. One of the main reasons for the failure was that unlike 1575 the Crown was unable to increase its revenues, among other things because of the unwillingness of the Castilian cities to grant Philip II the *servicio de los 500 cuentos*.[42] This failure accounts for the deficits of 1598 and 1601. It has recently been suggested[43] that the financial crisis opened in 1596 was closed by the definitive introduction of the *millones* in 1601. After 2 years (1601 and 1602) in which the annual yields of the *millones* were below the government's expectations, their yields substantially increased in 1603.[44] If we also remember that the strategic retrenchment of the reign of Philip III caused a remarkable drop in expenditures, the capacity of the Crown to balance its books – and even achieve budgetary surpluses – in 1608, 1614, 1615 and 1617 is easy to account for.

Table 1.1 Composition of Castilian government spending, 1566–1640 and 1703–4 (in percentages)

	1566–74	*1575–84*	*1585–96*	*1601*	*1608*	*1614*	*1615*	*1617*	*1621*	*1621–40*	*1703–4*
Long term	*33.2*	*42.2*	*31.7*	*38.8*	*48.5*	*56.4*	*54.6*	*49.8*	*44.1*	*29.7*	*36.6*
Short term	*10.9*	*6.6*	*6.4*							*5.8*	*5.5*
Financial	44.1	48.8	38.1	38.8	48.5	56.4	54.6	49.8	44.1	35.5	42.2
Military	48	42.8	56.4	52.8	39.2	29.2	31.3	34.4	47.2	56.1	23.6
Non-military	7.9	8.4	5.5	8.8	12.6	14.3	14.05	15.6	8.5	8.3	34.0

Notes: Long-term: long-term debt service (situado). Short-term: short-term debt service. Financial: Long and short-term debt service.
Sources: Drelichman and Voth, 2014; Andrés Ucendo and Lanza García, 2024.

Remarkably, the Crown also managed to balance its revenues with its expenditures in 1621–40 and 1648–60. In the light of the vast historical literature, which has traditionally described the Treasury's budgetary and financial position during these decades in bleak terms,[45] this might seem surprising. The Treasury's ability to balance its accounts between 1621 and 1640 could be attributed to the sudden rise of its revenues described in the previous section. More difficult to explain is the budgetary stability of 1648–60. The history of Castilian public finances at this time was presided over by the consequences of the financial defaults of 1647 and 1652.[46] As always, the main purpose of both defaults was, precisely, to improve the Treasury's financial and budgetary position, and the evidence provided by Figure 1.2 could be seen as proof of their success. Some authors, however, have noted that no taxes were introduced in these years, so the usual link between financial default and the widening of the Crown's tax base is missing here.[47] Consequently, both defaults were something of a failure, which poses an intriguing question that deserves further research.

Figure 1.2 shows that at least between 1561 and 1640/60 the Castilian fiscal and financial system was more resilient than traditionally thought and that the Crown was able to balance its accounts. To achieve this objective the government usually resorted to the introduction of new taxes and sources of revenue, frequently – but not always – related to the financial defaults of the period. Nevertheless, any capacity the Castilian Crown might have had to balance its accounts vanished during the 1660s and 1670s, mainly as a result of the stagnation of the Castilian economy[48] and the rise of *vellón* inflation. The latter fuelled the sudden increase of a new item of expenditure, the *reducciones*. The impact of the *reducciones* on the Crown's fiscal and financial woes is best revealed through an analysis of the *provisiones* of 1659, 1660, 1678 and 1680, which we address in the next section.

The 1680–86 stabilisation and its aftermath

Table 1.2 shows the three most important components of the Crown's planned spending for 1659, 1660, 1678 and 1680. Ordinary expenditures and *reducciones*

Table 1.2 Composition of the Crown's planned spending for 1659, 1660, 1678 and 1680 (in millions of Castilian *reales*)

	1659	*1660*	*1678*	*1680*
Financial	59.5	59.1	66.1	61.7
Reducciones	95.9	37.5	103.6	71.6
Ordinary	122.4	105.8	108.1	106.9
Total Spending	277.9	202.4	277.8	240.2
Total Revenues	244.8	206.2	732.7	194.1
	-12%	+1.9%	-16.3%	-19.2%

Notes: Financial: service of the long and short-term public debt. Ordinary: ordinary spending (military and non-military spending).

Sources: Archivo Histórico Nacional, AHN, Estado, leg. 4834; AGS, Consejo y Juntas de Hacienda, CJH, leg. 1913; Canga Argüelles, 1834: II, 95 and 106.

were included by the Crown officers in the *provisiones* for those years. The service of the Castilian public debt, on the contrary, never was, but thanks to the secondary sources at our disposal, it has been possible to estimate the amounts earmarked by the Treasury to such end.[49]

The importance of the *reducciones* in 1659, 1678 and 1680 is one of the most relevant lessons of Table 1.2. The *reducciones* originated in the fact that the Crown raised most of its revenues in copper *maravedís* while it had to pay many of its creditors and suppliers using gold and, from the beginning of the 17th century, silver currency and bars. That had been the norm until the central decades of the century. Then, as a result of the drop in the revenues raised in silver terms the Crown began to pay the sums originally due in silver by resorting to the devaluated copper pieces, plus an additional compensation in *vellón* to cover for the losses experienced by their recipients because of its progressive devaluation. Such a compensation is, precisely, what our sources call "*reducciones de plata a vellón*". To have an idea of its amount, royal accountants began to estimate the expenditures of the Crown in *vellón* terms, after converting those expenditures due in silver currency into *vellón*. They did so in 1678 and 1680, and such is the method we have followed in Table 1.2.[50]

The *reducciones* were of small import in the early 17th century. Remarkably, neither Tomás de Aguilar nor Juan de Góngora deemed it necessary to list them separately and they grouped *reducciones* together with financial expenditures. In 1659–60, however, things had changed, and royal officials recorded the *reducciones* separately. In 1659, the amount of the *reducciones* was far higher than that of financial expenditures, being one of the main causes of the imbalance (-12 percent) between the planned government spending for the year and its revenue. This helps to understand the signing of the Treaty of the Pyrenees (November 1659), which reduced the Crown's silver payments abroad and, in turn, the *reducciones* to 40 percent of its 1659 level. The relief brought by the treaty was short-lived because immediately after, the Crown decided to focus on the war with Portugal. To pay for what proved to be the last – and ultimately failed – effort to recover Portugal, between 1660 and 1664 the government resorted to new issues of petty copper currency, this time with a small silver content but still below that established in 1497.[51] Together with massive arrivals of counterfeit copper currency from abroad, this fuelled a renewed upsurge in inflation rates and, in turn, in *reducciones,* which in 1678 had a very similar value to the Crown's ordinary spending. This was untenable and the awareness of the problem prompted the famous February 1680 deflation.[52]

By reducing the face value of the copper pieces coined between 1660 and 1664 by 75 percent and that of the counterfeited ones by 75–85 percent, Castilian authorities tried to curb the *reducciones* and increase their revenues in silver terms,[53] something plainly admitted by the head of the Crown's financial council (*Consejo de Hacienda*), Don Antonio de Monsalve years later.[54] What was the effect of the reform? Its impact on the *reducciones* is not fully visible in Table 1.2. The *provisiones* for 1680 were settled in 1679, before the February deflation, so in 1680 their total amount still outweighed the service of public debt. Other indicators, however, suggest that the government achieved its basic objective of ending the *reducciones*. While price levels fell by 43 percent between 1679 and 1682, the Crown's total revenues in silver terms rose by 65 percent in the same period.[55] More importantly, after 1680 the need to pay expensive *reducciones* vanished and in 1703–4 they had disappeared from the expenditure items of the government.

The success of the 1680 deflation came at a heavy price. In March of the same year, the government decided to issue a new copper *maravedí* to provide the public with the petty currency necessary to prevent the paralysis of the Castilian economy, but this proved to be a failure. After decades of continuous manipulations, the public had lost its confidence in the government's commitment to monetary stability[56] and by drastically reducing the monetary assets in the pockets of the Castilians, deflation plunged the Castilian economy into a disarray that would last for decades.[57] Already in 1680, the Crown's revenues had fallen by 24 percent and the continuing stagnation of the Castilian economy forced the government to introduce drastic tax cuts in 1683 and in 1686,[58] so in 1687 its total revenues were 46 percent less than in 1679.

With the drop in the Crown's revenues between 1679 and 1686, a familiar problem came to the fore. The 1680 deflation might have solved the difficulties caused by the *reducciones*, but the need to service the Castilian public debt remained and Table 1.3 gives us some figures to understand the extent of the problem:

In 1667 and 1669, the *situado* amounted to 52.2 and 60.8 percent of the Crown's total revenues respectively, a figure which rose to 86.5 in 1687. The situation was even worse for the progressive rise of what the sources call a *cabimiento* problem, a term coined by royal officials to indicate their inability to pay the *situado* for the simple fact that the revenues for that were insufficient. Already in 1667 and 1669 the *situado* was 16 and 18.8 percent higher than the revenues allocated for its service and this figure widened to 50 percent in 1687. In the latter year, the *situado* was 122.4 million *reales*, while the revenues for its service amounted to 81.5 and the rest (41.9 million) were, simply, left unpaid.

That the Crown had *cabimiento* for servicing 84 and 66.5 percent of its *situado* in 1669 and 1687 does not mean it paid it completely. In 1635, the Crown had

Table 1.3 Service of Castilian public debt in 1667, 1669, 1687 and 1688 (in millions of *reales*)

	1667	*1669*	*1687*	*1688*
Total Revenues	223.9	194.1	141.1	144.4
Situado	116.9	118	122.4	122.4
Cabimiento	100.8	99.4	81.5	
Media anata		33.3	25.3	25.3
Paid to *juristas*		66.1	56.1	37.1

Notes: Total Revenues: total revenues of the Crown. *Situado*: total amount of interest of the *juros*. *Cabimiento*: revenues earmarked by the Crown for servicing the *situado*. *Media anata*: tax on the interest that accrued to the *juristas*. Paid to *juristas*: amounts of money effectively paid to the owners of *juros*.

Sources: Archivo Histórico Nacional, AHN, Estado, leg. 4834; AGS, Consejo y Juntas de Hacienda, CJH, leg. 1913; Canga Argüelles, 1834: II, 95 and 106.

introduced a tax (*media annata*) on the interest of the *juros*. The tax was levied on those bonds for which there was *cabimiento*, although some categories were exempt, such as the *juros* owned by religious institutions and widows. In 1669 the *media annata* yielded 33 million *reales*. Once we take into account the lack of *cabimiento* and the impact of media *annata* we find (Table 1.3) that in this year the Treasury hardly paid 56 percent of its *situado*. Given that the *situado*, revenues earmarked for its service, and *media annata* yields remained stable through the 1670s at near-1669 levels, the Castilian Treasury likely paid 56 percent of the interest owed to its bondholders until at least 1680. This figure further fell to 46 percent in 1687 and 30.3 percent in 1688.[59]

The decline in 1688 was the result of the spending cuts implemented by the Crown in the same year, as an unavoidable consequence of the 46-percent drop in its revenues between 1679 and 1686. By 1687, if not before, Treasury officials were thinking of ways to reduce public spending. This led to the Royal Order of 6 February 1688 which implemented the so-called *Decreto de los 4 millones de la Causa Pública.*[60] In essence, the *Decreto* was a rearrangement of the priorities of government spending. Its most important aspect was that ordinary expenditures (plus the service of short-term debt and some other items of lesser importance) were cut to the bare bones: 42 million *reales* annually, soon raised to 47 million.[61] These expenditures would be paid through the yields coming from ordinary revenues. Remarkably, the *Decreto* did not include extraordinary expenditures, which would be funded through the *quinto real*, the remittances of American silver, the *media annata*, church contributions and extraordinary revenues. In 1688, the Treasury's ordinary revenues consisted of the *alcabala*, *cientos*, *millones*, *servicio ordinario* and *extraordinario*, *customs*, monopolies and other taxes of lesser importance. These were, precisely, the same revenues earmarked for servicing the *situado* and their net yield in 1687 was, according to the head of the *Consejo de Hacienda*, the Marquis of Los Vélez, 84 million *reales*,[62] although, for reasons unknown, the Crown finally allocated 81.5 million.[63] Had the government paid in 1688 the same amount as in 1687 to the owners of *juros*, 56 million *reales*, this would have left 28 million *reales* for the funding of ordinary expenditures, well below the objectives of the *Decreto*. Not surprisingly, then, in 1688 the Treasury decided to cut the service of its long-term public debt from 56.1 million *reales* to 37, which freed up the amount required for the 47 million *reales* allocated to ordinary expenditures in 1688. As a result, in that same year the Castilian Crown hardly paid 30 percent of its *situado*. If we consider that the government must have serviced around 56 percent of its long-term debt until 1679, then it is clear that the 1680 monetary stabilisation and the drop in the Crown's revenues were responsible for a 46-percent fall in the interest that accrued to the owners of the *juros* between 1679 and 1688. Needless to say, this contributed to the general disrepute surrounding these assets and the decadence of the Castilian long-term debt.

The 1680 deflation set the scene for the later evolution of the Castilian and Spanish (after the arrival of the new Bourbon dynasty) fiscal and financial system. The economic stagnation of Castilian cities discouraged the introduction of more indirect taxes and was the main obstacle to any increase in the yields of those already existing. Simultaneously, political constraints also discouraged the resort to direct taxation. Given the difficulties in increasing its tax revenues, the government relied on a myriad of administrative changes to tighten its grip on the fiscal system and improve its efficiency. These reforms were a continuation of transformations that had already appeared in the 17th century. One of the most important of these was the unification of the collection of the *alcabalas*, *cientos* and *millones* levied in each fiscal district into large provincial tax-farms (*rentas provinciales*).[64] This created an environment for the consolidation of an emerging group of Spanish tax-farmers who simultaneously advanced credit to the Treasury. The group partially filled the void left by the decadence of the *asientos* in the mid-17th century.[65] To avoid the problems posed by its excessive reliance on a group of tax-farmers and to ensure cheaper access to their credit, the government promoted fierce competition among its members, although this could not prevent the last financial default of early modern Spain in 1739.[66] The fiscal debate sparked by the default prompted the replacement of tax-farming by the direct involvement of the Treasury in the collection of the most important taxes (*administración directa*) in the mid-century, with Spain being the first European state to take on such responsibility.[67] The *administración directa* culminated the trend towards improving the management of Spanish taxes through administrative reforms. Together with the growing tax revenues coming from the expanding colonial silver mining and trade in the second half of the century, these were destined to be the main pillars of Spanish taxation until the end of the 18th century.[68]

Concluding remarks

It is hard to overstate the importance of the deflation of 1680. It was one of the main factors responsible for the deep transformation in the Castilian fiscal and financial system at the turn of the 17th to the 18th century. During the 16th century, Charles I and Philip II had laboriously built a fiscal system that rested on the indirect taxes collected from the cities and the *quinto real* and they also promoted the expansion of public credit through *asientos* and *juros*. Although far from perfect, the system was resilient and the Crown was able to surmount the financial defaults of the period and balance its accounts thanks to its capacity to widen its tax base through new taxes and services, frequently negotiated with the *Cortes*.

By the mid-17th century, however, the system was under strain. The crisis of the Castilian economy, compounded by *vellón* manipulations, dealt a heavy blow to the Crown's ability to raise its revenues through indirect taxes and undermined the foundations of its short-term credit. Thanks to the increase of the *encabezamiento general* in 1575, a key part of the strategy followed by the Treasury in the default of that same year, its total revenues rose by 30.6 percent. Nearly a century later, the fourth *uno por ciento*, introduced to service the *juros* issued after the 1662 default, hardly increased its revenues by 1 percent. In political terms the system was also under strain. The Crown looked with suspicion on its growing dependence on the *Cortes* and the cities, owing to its adherence to a political culture that forced the government to negotiate with intermediate bodies its demand for *servicios*. Trying to escape from this dependence, the Crown resorted to other alternatives such as the *vellón* manipulations. The issues of pure petty copper currency and the *resellos* caused the rise of the *reducciones* and the 1680 deflation which, in turn, prompted substantial tax and spending cuts and finally a 46-percent cut in the interest that accrued to the owners of *juros*. This was the last step in the Castilian public credit crisis.

To conclude with the general overview about the fiscal and financial system of Habsburg Spain carried out in the previous pages, we would like to present a final thought. As the heads of a composite monarchy, Castilian kings were strongly committed to the privileges and franchises of intermediate bodies – as the *Cortes* and the cities of the country – and the enforcement of property rights. But during the 17th century we may discern the slow expansion of a grey area where their willingness to follow traditional principles and attitudes coexisted with the resort to a set of policies which could be perceived as coercive and even predatory. This grey area may be found in the field of fiscal and monetary policy, which at times seemed particularly propitious for the virtually unchecked expansion of royal power. The government needed no permission from the *Cortes* to manipulate its petty copper currency or reduce the interest paid to the owners of *juros*, and that is what it did. Rather naturally, these measures were resented among Castilians. Not by chance, in his famous *Tratado y discurso contra la moneda de vellón*, the Jesuit Juan de Mariana (1609: 75) described the issues of pure petty copper currency as simple theft. There is little doubt that most of his contemporaries wholeheartedly agreed with Mariana, and that most saw in these kind of policies proof of the apparently untrammelled growth of royal power. But the growing assertiveness of the latter in the fiscal and financial arena century should not hide that the principles of the political constitution of the country still retained its influence, shaping the form taken by some measures with a tinge of arbitrariness dangerously close to mere expropriation. Two instances will suffice to illustrate the point. In 1628 the Crown reduced the nominal value of the Castilian copper currency by 50 percent, but not without proposing the cities to look for a way to compensate the public for the massive losses that the operation was going to cause. If, finally, there was no compensation it was because the cities themselves soon admitted the impossibility of raising the amount of money required for that.[69] Another instance of the same tension between the way the Crown faced its need for growing fiscal and financial resources and its readiness to enforce traditional norms and rules might be found in that an important (but still unknown) part of the juros issued during the 17th century was created, precisely, to compensate the *juristas* for the losses they suffered as a result of the levying of the media annata.[70] These examples suggest that it would be wrong to describe the fiscal history of Habsburg Castile either in terms of the progressive consolidation of an absolutist power or, on the contrary, as an example of the consolidation of the *Cortes* and local powers against the Crown. What we find instead is an uneasy balance between both sides with no clear winner, but one thing seems, we believe, quite clear: as a result of the tension between the centre and the periphery, the Crown ended up by promoting a set of measures such as the manipulations of its low value copper currency with damaging consequences for the stability of its fiscal and financial system and the country's economic growth.

Acknowledgement

This work was supported the Spanish Ministry of Economy and Business (MINECO) through the research project "Crisis fiscal y declive económico en la Monarquía Hispánica, 1550-1740", PID 2020-118287 GB-100, and the Regional Basque Government through the Grupo de Investigación Consolidado del Gobierno Vasco (IT 1523–22).

Notes

1 Hamilton, 1934 and 1947.
2 Carande, 2000 [1943, 1949 and 1967]; Ruiz Martín, 2016 [1979] and Ulloa, 1986.
3 Fortea Pérez, 2017: 95–134 and 2023: 229–86. All these operations are debt conversions, not defaults. Reinhart and Rogoff (2009).
4 Andrés Ucendo, 2023.
5 Elliott, 2002; Fernández Albaladejo, 1992; Fortea Pérez, 1990 and 2008.
6 Kagan, 1991.
7 Gelabert, 1998: 265.
8 Andrés Ucendo, 1999, 2006 and 2008, Andrés Ucendo and Lanza García, 2008 and 2013; Martínez Ruiz, 1992.
9 Drelichman and Voth, 2014; Kamen, 1974; Pulido Bueno, 1996, and Thompson, 1992.
10 Andrés Ucendo and Lanza García, 2024: 2–22.
11 Andrés Ucendo and Lanza García, 2024: 6 and 9; Valladares, 2002.
12 Andrés Ucendo and Lanza García, 2024: 10 and 12.
13 Artola, 1982; Fortea Pérez, 1990 and 2008; Fernández Albaladejo, 1992.
14 Carande, 2000 [1943]; Artola, 1982; Fortea Pérez, 1990.
15 Fortea Pérez, 1990; Zabala Aguirre, 2000.
16 Andrés Ucendo, 1999.
17 Artola, 1982: 101; López Juana Pinilla, 1840: IV, 463–65; AGS, Contadurías Generales (CG), leg. 1358.
18 Artola, 1982; Carande, 2000 [1943]; Ulloa, 1986.
19 Andrés Ucendo, 1999; Fernández de Pinedo, 1993.
20 Andrés Ucendo, 2023 and Lanza García, 2020b.
21 Hamilton, 1934.
22 Hamilton, 1934.
23 Álvarez-Nogal and Chamley, 2013 and 2016; Carande, 2000 [1943]; Ulloa, 1986; Ruiz Martín, 1968, 1990b and 2016 [1979].
24 Artola, 1982; Domínguez Ortiz, 1960; Ruiz Martín, 2016 [1979].
25 Ruiz Martín, 2016 [1979] and Toboso, 1986.
26 Ruiz Martín, 1990a and 2016 [1979].
27 Artola, 1982 and Fortea Pérez, 1990.
28 Andrés Ucendo, 1999.
29 See also, Andrés Ucendo and Lanza García, 2008 and Lanza García, 2020b.
30 Toboso, 1986.
31 Álvarez-Nogal and Chamley, 2013: 195.
32 Elliott, 1986; Gelabert, 2001.
33 Domínguez Ortiz, 1960 and Gelabert, 2001.
34 Artola, 1982 and Domínguez Ortiz, 1960.
35 Fortea Pérez, 1995; Gelabert, 2001; Lanza García, 2025.
36 Andrés Ucendo and Lanza García, 2014 and 2020.

37 Domínguez Ortiz, 1960; Elliott, 1986 and Gelabert, 2001.
38 Elliott, 1986.
39 Domínguez Ortiz, 1960; Elliott, 1986 and Gelabert, 2001.
40 Fortea Pérez, 1990 and Gelabert, 2023.
41 Parker, 2014.
42 Fortea Pérez, 1990.
43 Fortea Pérez, 2017: 111–12.
44 Andrés Ucendo, 1999.
45 Domínguez Ortiz, 1960; Ruiz Martín, 1990b and 2016 [1979].
46 Domínguez Ortiz, 1960; Fortea Pérez, 2023; Ruiz Martín, 2016 [1979].
47 Domínguez Ortiz, 1960 and Fortea Pérez, 2023.
48 Andrés Ucendo, 2023.
49 Domínguez Ortiz, 1960 and Toboso, 1986.
50 Andrés Ucendo, 2023; Andrés Ucendo and Lanza García, 2024.
51 Domínguez Ortiz, 1960; Hamilton, 1947.
52 Kamen, 1997 and Lanza García, 2023.
53 Lanza García, 2023.
54 Andrés Ucendo and Lanza García, 2024.
55 Andrés Ucendo and Lanza García, 2014 and 2020.
56 Hamilton, 1947; Lanza García, 2023: 394.
57 Lanza García, 2023.
58 Sánchez Belén, 1986; Andrés Ucendo, 1999 and 2006.
59 Artola, 1982; Domínguez Ortiz, 1960; Toboso, 1986; Lanza García, 2026.
60 Kamen, 1981 and 1997.
61 Kamen, 1974 and 1997.
62 Kamen, 1997: 277.
63 Canga Argüelles, 1834, II: 106.
64 González Enciso, 2020: 166–67; Fortea Pérez, 2008 and Sánchez Belén, 1996.
65 Sanz Ayán, 1989 and 2013.
66 Fernández Albaladejo, 1977.
67 González Enciso, 2020: 127 and 137.
68 Andrés Ucendo and Comín Comín, 2021.
69 AHN, Consejos, leg. 51359-18.
70 Toboso, 1986.

Bibliography

Álvarez-Nogal, Carlos (1998), "Las remesas americanas en las finanzas de la Real Hacienda. La cuantificación del dinero de la Corona, 1621–1675", *Revista de Historia Económica*, 16, pp. 453–89.

Álvarez-Nogal, Carlos and Chamley, Christophe, (2013), "La crisis financiera de Castilla en 1575–1577. Fiscalidad y estrategia", *Revista de la Historia de la Economía y de la Empresa*, 7, pp. 187–211.

Álvarez-Nogal, Carlos and Chamley, Christoph, (2016), "Philip II against the Cortes and the Credit Freeze of 1575-77", *Revista de Historia Económica/Journal of Iberian and Latin American Economic History*, 34, 3, pp. 351–382.

Alloza Aparicio, Ángel (2019), *El Sistema aduanero de la Corona de Castilla (1550–1700)*, Valladolid: Universidad de Valladolid.

Andrés Ucendo, José Ignacio (1999), *La Fiscalidad en Castilla el siglo XVII: los servicios de millones, 1601–1700*, Lejona: Universidad del País Vasco.

Andrés Ucendo, José Ignacio (2006), "Fiscalidad real y fiscalidad municipal en Castilla durante el siglo XVII: el caso de Madrid", *Investigaciones de Historia Económica*, 5, pp. 41–70.

Andrés Ucendo, José Ignacio (2008), "Government Policies and the Development of Financial Markets: The Case of Madrid in the Seventeenth Century", in Fausto Piola Caselli, ed., *Government Debts and Financial Markets in Europe*, London: Pickering, pp. 67–79.

Andrés Ucendo, José Ignacio (2023), "Hacienda y Crédito Público en la Castilla del siglo XVII", in Ramón Lanza García, coord., *Finanzas y crisis financieras en la Monarquía Hispánica, siglos XVI-XVII*, Madrid: Marcial Pons, pp. 251–285.

Andrés Ucendo, José Ignacio and Comín Comín, Francisco (2021), "Evolución y estructura de los ingresos de la Real Hacienda en el largo siglo XVIII, (1680-1807)", *Investigaciones de Historia Económica*, 17, 3, pp. 40–50.

Andrés Ucendo, José Ignacio, and Lanza García, Ramón (2008), "Estructura y evolución de los ingresos de la Real Hacienda de Castilla en el siglo XVII", *Studia Historica. Historia Moderna*, 30, pp. 111–155.

Andrés Ucendo, José Ignacio and Lanza García, Ramón (2013), "Impuestos municipales, precios y salarios reales en la Castilla del siglo XVII: el caso de Madrid", *Hispania: Revista española de Historia*, LXXIII, 243, pp. 161–92.

Andrés Ucendo, José Ignacio and Lanza García, Ramón (2014), "Prices and Real Wages in Seventeenth-Century Madrid", *Economic History Review*, 67, 3, pp. 607–626.

Andrés Ucendo, José Ignacio and Lanza García, Ramón (2020), "Prices and Wages in Segovia, 1571–1807", *Revista de Historia Económica/Journal of Iberian and Latin American Economic History*, 38, 2, pp. 221–48.

Andrés Ucendo, José Ignacio and Lanza García, Ramón (2024), "Estructura y tendencias del gasto de la Hacienda Real de Castilla en el siglo XVII", *Obradoiro de Historia Moderna*, 34, pp. 2–23.

Artola, Miguel (1982), *La Hacienda del Antiguo Régimen*, Madrid: Alianza.

Bernal, Antonio Miguel (1992): *La financiación de la Carrera de Indias. Dinero y Crédito en el comercio colonial español con América, 1500–1824*, Sevilla: Tabapress.

Bilbao Bilbao, Luis María (1990), "Ensayo de reconstrucción histórica de la presión fiscal en Castilla durante el siglo XVI", in Emiliano Fernández de Pinedo, coord., *Haciendas Forales y Hacienda Real: Homenaje a Felipe Ruiz Martín*, Lejona: Universidad del País Vasco, 1990, pp. 37–61.

Canga Argüelles, José (1968 [1833 and 1834]), *Diccionario de Hacienda con aplicación a España*, Madrid: Instituto de Estudios Fiscales.

Carande, Ramón (2000 [1943, 1949 and 1967]), *Carlos V y sus banqueros*, Barcelona: Crítica, 3 vols.

Domínguez Ortiz, Antonio (1960), *Política y Hacienda de Felipe IV*, Madrid: Pegaso.

Domínguez Ortiz, Antonio (1964), "Ventas y exenciones de lugares durante el reinado de Felipe IV", *Anuario de Historia del Derecho Español*, 34, pp. 163–208.

Domínguez Ortiz, Antonio (1970), "La venta de cargos y oficios públicos en Castilla y sus consecuencias económicas y sociales", *Anuario de Historia Económica y Social*, III, pp. 105–137.

Domínguez Ortiz, Antonio (1984 [1961]), "Concesiones de votos en Cortes a ciudades castellanas en el siglo XVII", in Antonio Domínguez Ortiz, *Instituciones y sociedad en la España de los Austrias*, Barcelona: Ariel, pp. 99–111.

Domínguez Ortiz, Antonio (1992 [1964]), *La sociedad española en el siglo XVII. Vol. 1. La nobleza* , Granada: Universidad de Granada.

Domínguez Ortiz, Antonio (2003 [1946]), *Orto y Ocaso de Sevilla. Estudio sobre la prosperidad y decadencia de la ciudad en los siglos XVI y XVII*, Sevilla: Ayuntamiento de Sevilla.

Drelichman, Mauricio and Voth, Hans-Joachim (2104), *Lending to the Borrower of Hell. Debt, Taxes and Default in the Age of Philip II*, Princeton, NJ: Princeton University Press.

Elliott, John H. (1986), *The Count-Duke of Olivares. The Statesman in an Age of Decline*, Yale, CT: Yale University Press.

Elliott, John H. (2002), *Imperial Spain, 1469–1716*, London: Penguin.

Fernández Albaladejo, Pablo (1977), "El decreto de suspensión de pagos de 1739: análisis e implicaciones", *Moneda y Crédito*, 142, pp. 51–86.

Fernández Albaladejo, Pablo (1992), *Fragmentos de Monarquía*, Madrid: Alianza.

Fernández De Pinedo, Emiliano (1993), "Fiscalidad y Absolutismo en Castilla en la primera mitad del siglo XVII", in José Ignacio Fortea Pérez and María del Carmen Cremades Griñán, eds., *Política y Hacienda en el Antiguo Régimen*, vol. 1, Murcia: Universidad de Murcia, pp. 33–51.

Fortea Pérez, José Ignacio (1990), *Monarquía y Cortes en la Corona de Castilla: Las ciudades ante la política fiscal de Felipe II*, Valladolid: Cortes de Castilla y León.

Fortea Pérez, José Ignacio (1995), "Las ciudades de Castilla en el Antiguo Régimen: una revisión historiográfica", *Boletín de la Asociación Española de Demografía Histórica*, 13, 3, pp. 19–59.

Fortea Pérez, José Ignacio (2008), *Las Cortes de Castilla y León bajo los Austrias. Una interpretación*, Valladolid: Junta de Castilla y León.

Fortea Pérez, José Ignacio (2017), "Deuda, desempeño y bancarrota: la economía política de la reforma fiscal bajo los Austrias", in Ramón Lanza García, coord., *Las instituciones económicas, las finanzas públicas y el declive de España en la Edad Moderna*, Madrid: Universidad Autónoma de Madrid, pp. 95–134.

Fortea Pérez, José Ignacio (2023), "Fiscalidad y deuda pública bajo los Austrias: las últimas bancarrotas de Felipe IV (1647, 1652, 1662)", in Ángel Galán Sánchez, José Ramón Díaz de Durana Ortiz de Urbina, and José Manuel Triano Millán, coords., *Oficio de príncipes: conflicto militar, economía y circuitos financieros en la Península Ibérica (siglos XIII al XVII)*, Granada: Comares, pp. 229–286.

García Fuentes, Lutgardo (1980), *El comercio español con América*, Sevilla: CSIC–Escuela de Estudios Hispano-Americanos/Diputación Provincial de Sevilla.

García Guerra, Elena (2014), "The deflation of 1652 Fractional Coin. Bad Business for the Castilian Tax System in Early Modern Castile", *The Journal of European Economic History*, 43, 1, pp. 83–122.

Gelabert, Juan Eloy (1998), "La evolución del gasto de la Monarquía Hispánica entre 1598 y 1650. Los asientos de Felipe III y Felipe IV", *Studia Historica. Historia Moderna*, 18, pp. 265–98.

Gelabert, Juan Eloy (2001), *Castilla convulsa, (1631–1652)*, Madrid: Marcial Pons.

Gelabert, Juan Eloy (2023), "El dedo y la luna. Política y crédito en la Monarquía Hispánica", in Ramón Lanza García, coord., *Finanzas y crisis financieras en la Monarquía Hispánica, siglos XVI y XVII*, Madrid: Marcial Pons, pp. 130–86.

González Enciso, Agustín (2020), *Los sistemas financieros en la Europa del siglo XVIII. Bancos privados, fiscalidad y deuda pública para la guerra* , Madrid: Síntesis.

Gutiérrez Alonso, Adriano (1989), *Estudio sobre la decadencia de Castilla. La ciudad de Valladolid en el siglo XVII*, Valladolid: Universidad de Valladolid.

Hamilton, Earl J. (1934), *American Treasure and the Price Revolution in Spain, 1500*-1650, Cambridge, MA: Harvard University Press.

Hamilton, Earl J. (1947), *War and Prices in Spain, 1651–1800*, Cambridge, MA: Harvard University Press.

Kagan, Richard (1991), *Pleitos y pleiteantes en Castilla, 1500–1700*, Salamanca: Junta de Castilla y León.

Kamen, Henry (1974), *La Guerra de Sucesión en España, 1700–1715*, Barcelona: Grijalbo.

Kamen, Henry (1981), *La España de Carlos II*, Barcelona: Crítica.

Kamen, Henry (1997), "España en la Europa de Luis XIV", in *Historia de España de Menéndez Pidal, vol. XXVIII. Transición del siglo XVII al XVIII. Entre la decadencia y la reconstrucción*, Madrid: Espasa-Calpe, pp. 207–302.

Lanza García, Ramón (2020a), "Plata y vellón para la Cruzada", in Ramón Lanza García, coord., *Fisco y Moneda. El uso del dinero en las economías de los reinos hispanos, siglos XIV-XVIII*. Santander: Universidad de Cantabria, pp. 381–441.

Lanza García, Ramón (2020b), "Guerra, hacienda y economía en la Monarquía de España en la crisis del siglo XVII", in José Ignacio Fortea, Juan Eloy Gelabert, Roberto López Vela and Elena Postigo Castellanos, coords., *Monarquías en conflicto*, Madrid: Fundación Española de Historia Moderna/Universidad de Cantabria, pp. 197–255.

Lanza García, Ramón (2023), "La reforma monetaria de 1680-86 y la depresión económica de Castilla", in Ramón Lanza García, coord., *Finanzas y crisis financieras en la Monarquía Hispánica, siglos XVI-XVII*, Madrid: Marcial Pons, pp. 380–436.

Lanza García, Ramón (2025), "Las ciudades en la España Moderna: crecimiento económico, crisis y reconstrucción, 1500–1800", *Memoria y Civilización*, 28, I, pp. 39–72.

Lanza García, Ramón (2026), "Juros, media anata de juros y el problema de la deuda pública de los últimos Habsburgo españoles", *Studia Historica. Historia Moderna*, 1.

López Juana Pinilla, José (1840), *Biblioteca de Hacienda de España*, vol. IV, Madrid: Eusebio Aguado Impresor.

Marcos Martín, Alberto (2006), "Fue la fiscalidad regia un factor de crisis en la Castilla del siglo XVII", in Geoffrey Parker, coord., *La crisis de la Monarquía de Felipe IV*, Barcelona: Crítica, pp. 173–254.

Marcos Martín, Alberto (2007), "Las ventas de oficios en Castilla en tiempos de suspensión de ventas", *Chronica Nova*, 33, pp. 13–35.

Mariana, Juan, (1609 [2017]), *Tratado y discurso sobre la moneda de vellón*, Barcelona: Ediciones Deusto.

Martínez Ruiz, José Ignacio (1992), *Finanzas municipales y crédito público en la España Moderna. La Hacienda de la ciudad de Sevilla, 1528–1768*, Sevilla: Ayuntamiento de Sevilla.

Mosácula, Francisco Javier (2001), "Los regidores municipales de Segovia durante los reinados de Felipe II, Felipe III y Felipe IV", *Espacio, Tiempo y Forma. Historia Moderna*, 14, pp. 245–314.

Motomura, Akira (1994), "The Best and Worst of Currencies: Seigniorage and Currency Policy in Spain, 1621–1675", *Journal of Economic History*, 54, pp. 104–27.

Parker, Geoffrey (2014), *An Imprudent King. A New Life of Philip II*, New Haven, CT: Yale University Press.

Pulido Bueno, Ildefonso (1996), *La Hacienda de Felipe III*, Huelva.

Quintana Toret, Francisco Javier (1988), "Los "asientos" del concejo malagueño en el siglo XVII. ¿Una alternativa fiscal de la Monarquía Absoluta?", in *Fiscalidad Estatal i Hisenda Local (ss. XVI-XIX),* Palma de Mallorca: Institut d'Estudis Baleàrics, pp. 466–79.

Reinhart, Carmen and Rogoff, Kenneth (2009), *This Time Is Different: Eight Centuries of Financial Folly*, Princeton, NJ: Princeton University Press.

Rodríguez Vicente, María Encarnación (1977), "Los cargadores a Indias y su contribución a los gastos de la Monarquía, 1555–1750", *Anuario de Estudios Americanos*, XXXIV, pp. 211–32.

Ruiz Martín, Felipe (1968), "Las finanzas españolas durante el reinado de Felipe II. Alternativas de participación que se dieron para Francia", *Hispania*, número extra, 2, pp. 109–74.

Ruiz Martín, Felipe (1990a), *Pequeño capitalismo y gran capitalismo. Simón Ruiz y sus negocios en Florencia*, Barcelona: Crítica.

Ruiz Martín, Felipe (1990b), *Las finanzas de la Monarquía Hispánica en tiempos de Felipe IV*, Madrid: Real Academia de la Historia.

Ruiz Martín, Felipe (2016 [1979]), *La Banca en España hasta 1782*, Madrid: Urgoiti.

Sánchez Belén, Juan Antonio (1996), *La política fiscal en Castilla durante el reinado de Carlos II*, Madrid: Siglo XXI.

Sanz Ayán, Carmen (1989), *Los banqueros de Carlos II*, Valladolid: Universidad de Valladolid.

Sanz Ayán, Carmen (2013), *Los banqueros y la crisis de la Monarquía Hispánica de 1640*, Madrid: Marcial Pons.

Thompson, Irving A.A. (1992), "Taxation, Military Spending and the Domestic Economy in Castile in the Later 16th century", in *War and Society in Habsburg Spain*, London: Ashgate, pp. 1–21.

Toboso, Pilar (1986), *La Deuda Pública Castellana en el Antiguo Régimen. Los juros*, Madrid: Instituto de estudios Fiscales.

Ulloa, Modesto (1986), *La Hacienda Real de Castilla en el reinado de Felipe II*, Madrid: Fundación Universitaria Española.

Valladares, Rafael (2002), *Banqueros y vasallos: Felipe IV y el Medio General, 1630–1670*, Cuenca: Universidad de Castilla la Mancha.

Zabala Aguirre, Pilar, (2000), *La alcabala y la Hacienda Real de Castilla: siglo XVI*, Santander: Universidad de Cantabria.

2 Royal revenues and fiscal privileges in Early Modern Navarre

Mario García-Zúñiga

Constraints to the rise of Royal Revenues

Like other European states, the Spanish monarchy faced revenue shortfalls, structural deficits and chronic indebtedness during the early modern period. These problems were exacerbated until the mid-17th century by the substantial costs of warfare abroad. Oversimplifying somewhat, two partially intertwined factors limited the monarchy's ability to increase its tax revenues: the strong fiscal inequalities and the predominantly indirect nature of taxes.[1]

The development of Castilian taxation had been carried out without interfering in the collection of land rent and tithes, the main sources of income for the nobility and the clergy. This accounts for the reliance on indirect taxes.

During periods of economic growth, population rise, increased commercial activity and rising prices allowed for high tax revenues, although inflation tended to reduce the extent of such increases in real terms, which contributed to the well-known bankruptcies of 1557 and 1575. Conversely, at times of recession and/or war, commercial transactions slowed, mortality reduced the number of taxpayers, and the decrease in their purchasing power reduced consumption levels. It then became necessary to implement spending cuts and/or look for new sources of income. These typically included new levies and higher rates on existing taxes, the creation of new monopolies on the sales of a broad range of products and the use of a wide range of extraordinary expedients (currency manipulations, grants, donations and the sale of offices and jurisdictions). Such were the limits of a fiscal system that drew most of its revenues from indirect taxes and that was heavily dependent on the economic cycle.

The weight of Church tithes is one of the key factors that helps to explain the absence of direct taxation in Castile and the stabilisation of the amounts of Crown revenues derived from the services paid by the non-noble Castilian population (*pecheros*) by the mid-16th century. It is often overlooked that the Castilian Church extracted around 10–12 percent of the gross agricultural product, a figure which in net terms must have been higher. Tithes and first fruits constituted a formidable obstacle to the implementation of any land tax, which would also clash with the interests of the landed nobility. As both the Church and the Castilian nobility knew only too well, the imposition of any land tax would limit their ability to increase

DOI: 10.4324/9781003653301-3

land rents beyond a certain level. Such a level could come close to eliminating the surplus of their tenants, even reducing to some extent the self-consumption of their household units, but it could not be exceeded without endangering both their economic viability and demographic reproduction. As E. Fernández de Pinedo (1991, 98) pointed out, for many liberal economists and policy makers, the connections between tithe suppression and land taxes were clear. The 1845 Mon's tax reform proved this; only after tithes were abolished could the State levy a land tax and landowners raise their income simultaneously.

Another constraint was the pronounced personal and geographical inequalities in the distribution of the fiscal burden, a defining characteristic of most tax systems during developed feudalism. Allegedly, the privileged Estates (nobility and the Church) were largely, but not entirely, exempt from taxation. Any attempt to increase their contribution to the fiscal burden of the monarchy by taxing their wealth or levying taxes that might endanger the collection of land rent or tithes was doomed to failure. This happened in 1590 with Philip II's plan to collect the first *servicio de millones* through direct taxes and, two centuries and a half later, not only with the Cadastre, but also with the recurrent, and ultimately failed projects of imposing taxes on flour and salt discussed at the time.[2]

On the other hand, political unity did not imply uniformity or administrative centralisation. In the composite European monarchies of the 16th–18th centuries, a single monarch ruled over different polities, each zealously preserving their own peculiarities, inherited from the Middle Ages. In the fiscal sphere, this was reflected in the coexistence of different fiscal systems[3] and in the limited contribution of non-Castilian territories to the financial burdens of the monarchy, something not too different from what occurred in the rest of Europe. As M. t'Hart (1995, 282) pointed out, "Invariably, the 'core' regions of states became those most heavily taxed [...] Peripheral provinces paid relatively less".

A well-known estimate of the Spanish Monarchy's revenues in 1577 reflects this. The revenues collected from the Basque Country and the kingdoms of Navarre and Aragon amounted to 300,000 ducats, representing only two percent of the overall income (excluding the revenues from religious contributions to the Crown—Crusade Bull, *Subsidio* and *Excusado*—which were recorded on an aggregate basis). But while those coming from Navarre (173,500 inhabitants) amounted to 95,000 ducats, those from Aragon (1 million inhabitants) were slightly more than double and those from the Basque Country were negligible.[4] A similar pattern is reflected in a *Relación de la Real Hacienda* for the year 1616, published by A. Domínguez Ortiz (1983, 152).

The territorial fiscal disparities between the kingdoms of the Crown of Castile and Aragon were mitigated after the War of Succession, when the Bourbon dynasty extended the Castilian fiscal system to the latter, though not to the Basque Country or Navarre.

This chapter aims to analyse the continuities and changes in the revenues obtained by the Royal Treasury from one of the fiscally privileged territories of the Spanish Monarchy: the small northern Kingdom of Navarre. The chapter is organised into three sections. Part 1 describes the main features of the Navarrese fiscal system, largely inherited from the arrangements in place at the time of the kingdom's incorporation into the Spanish Monarchy in 1513. With only minor changes, this system remained largely unchanged until the last two decades of the 17th century. Part 2 focuses on the changes introduced in 1684 in the subsidies (*donativos*) granted by the Navarrese parliamentary assemblies (*Cortes*). Finally, the transformations that took place from 1716 onwards are analysed in part 3. These changes did not entail the introduction of new taxes, but instead involved administrative reforms and the transfer of specific financial obligations which were handled by the central government in other parts of Spain.. As a result, the contribution of the kingdom to the total expenditures of the Spanish Monarchy was increased. Nevertheless, by the end of the 18th century, Navarre continued to enjoy extensive tax exemptions.

The Navarrese fiscal system under Habsburg rule

A medieval legacy

With both French and Castilian influences and created during the late medieval crisis, the Navarrese fiscal system during the Habsburg period essentially relied on customs duties (*tablas*) and especially on parliamentary grants *(donativos)*.

Regular financial aids began in 1355.[5] Over time, several methods were tested to raise the money, but by the turn of the 16th century, the prevailing collection method involved levying a direct tax (*cuartel*) and an indirect one (*alcabala*). At the end of the Middle Ages, their amounts were known in advance, and the *Cortes* voted, according to the financial needs of the monarch, for as many *cuarteles* and years of *alcabala* as deemed necessary. This was the same method used to collect the Castilian *monedaje*[6] or the *aides* granted to the dukes of Burgundy by their counties of Artois and Flanders.[7]

The *cuarteles*—Navarre's version of the widespread medieval direct and proportional taxes on wealth—were in their beginnings as both a fiscal and temporal unit. Fiscally, each *cuartel* represented a lump sum of money, first settled at 10,000 pounds and soon after at 10,000 florins, an amount that was gradually reduced throughout the 15th century. Temporally, the term referred to the period within which this sum had to be collected, originally on a quarterly basis, hence the name *cuartel*. As a quota tax, its assessment seems to have relied on demographic criteria and some kind of estimate of the wealth of taxpayers, something not too different from what would happen with the first *servicio de millones* in late 16th century Castile.[8] Given that the amount of the first *cuartel* granted in 1377–79 (10,000 pounds) corresponded to the theoretical number of taxable hearths (*fuegos*) of the kingdom, it is plausible, as G. Dupont Ferrier (1932, 13) pointed out for the *taille* in France, that the *cuartel* was no more than a new denomination for the previous hearth taxes (*fogajes*).

It is uncertain when or how the first *encabezamiento* (the establishment and distribution of a predetermined total amount owed to the Treasury) was carried out. However, as noted by M. Berthe (1984, 584), the stability of the quotas earmarked for the *Merindad* (an administrative district) of Estella between 1390 and 1427 points to the earlier date. This is consistent with the appointment of inquisitors in response to complaints about tax collectors, as reported by the King in February 1389.[9] The perpetuation of the quotas at a time of population slump increased their burden *per capita*, and gave rise to marked territorial inequalities. In response to the grievances, the kings first granted tax relief measures and, in 1427, ordered a comprehensive survey for a more equitable reassessment of the burden.[10]

Completed in 1428, this survey included—albeit with some discrepancies—the distribution of the "old assessment" among taxpayers, so it does not provide an accurate portrait of the wealth of the kingdom. After being examined by the "Queen, our lady, and the officials of her treasury, in great council [...] a certain ordinance" was issued establishing new tax quotas,[11] but the criteria underlying the new assessment remain unknown. The new rules were already applied to the aid granted in 1429, resulting in an overall reduction of 27 percent in the amounts yielded. Except for occasional reductions granted to certain localities, in 1462, King John II halved the quotas (and cut them by one-third in the *Merindad* of Tudela) because of the war, but the general reassessment mentioned by Queen Leonor in 1474 when she halved the quotas of Carcastillo never took place. The amount of a *cuartel* was definitively fixed, as were its apportionments.[12]

With a slight delay compared to Castile, and at the same time as the French levying of 12 *deniers* per *livre* on all sales established by the ordinance of 5 December 1360,[13] the sales tax (*alcabala)* appeared in 1362. In their session of 11 January, the *Cortes* of Tudela granted, at the request of Charles II, a temporary aid of 5 percent ("one out of every twenty dineros") on all sales and purchases for five years.[14] Having been renewed in the successive assemblies, the levying of the *alcabala* became a virtually yearly tax and the number of taxed products grew.[15] By the late 15th century, the amount due under the *alcabala* had been effectively fixed. Each town and village agreed to contribute a predetermined sum, and the Kingdom became responsible *in solidum* for its collection.[16] Navarrese kings were unsuccessful in securing the right to levy the *alcabala* without the consent of the Cortes. Nor was the tax rate raised. Unlike Castile, where the *alcabala* became a regular tax set at 10 percent, in Navarre it remained a means of raising the sums approved through parliamentary grants. This was what happened with the Catalan *imposicions*[17] and even with the Castilian *alcabalas generales* initially, according to an old theory by J.M. Pérez Prendes (1964: 494).

On the eve of their incorporation into the Crown of Castile, the primary source of Royal Revenue in Navarre was the grants provided by the Three Estates; customs duties accounted for less than 10 percent of the Crown's total income. The political instability and warfare after the death of Queen Blanca in 1441 threw the administration and collection of Royal Revenues into disarray. Therefore, from their accession to the throne in 1494, Catherine of Foix and John of Albret undertook a determined (albeit ultimately unsuccessful) campaign to gather detailed information on the Crown's revenues, reform the taxes levied in the Kingdom and overturn the privileges and exemptions awarded by them and their predecessors that had undermined the Royal Domain.[18] This was basically the same fiscal policy pursued during the same period by the Catholic Kings in Castile. With the support of (or perhaps in agreement with) the ecclesiastical and noble estates (*brazos*), they also tried to introduce changes in the subsidies granted by the *Cortes*, reducing the weight of direct taxation.

On average, according to the records of 1501 and 1503, the *cuarteles* provided 79.5 percent of the net revenue coming from the parliamentary grants, with the *alcabala* accounting for the remaining 20.5.[19] Although collection methods varied, a 1534–35 survey suggests that, to some extent, it rested on the wealth of taxpayers. This is clear from the most common answers given in the survey, which show that the quotas levied on each town and village were apportioned among their inhabitants taking into account their properties and the livestock they owned. Possibly influenced by the Castilian fiscal system, in the *Cortes* of 1505, the representatives of the ecclesiastical and military *brazos* proposed to their counterparts from the towns (*universidades*) to halve the *cuarteles*, doubling the *alcabala*. The reason for this was that the tax burden levied on the local peasantry was too high. The *universidades* rejected the proposal, so the ecclesiastical and noble estates unsuccessfully insisted again three years later. Remarkably, the same request was put forward by the monarchs themselves in 1511.[20]

Attempts to increase Royal Revenues in the 16th century

The taxes levied in Navarre from the late medieval crisis closely resembled those in Castile: Navarrese *alcabalas*, *tablas* and *cuarteles* corresponded to the Castilian *alcabalas*, customs duties and ordinary and extraordinary services (*servicios*) respectively. However, while Castilian taxes had largely become permanent, only customs duties held this status in Navarre.

Setting aside any attempts to reform the fiscal and financial institutions, the new rulers focused on three objectives: first, to compile reliable estimates of revenues in the newly conquered kingdom; second, to reassess the *encabezamientos* of the *cuarteles* and *alcabalas*; and third, to make the *alcabala* a permanent tax.

One of the first decisions taken by Ferdinand the Catholic was to review the tax quotas traditionally earmarked for the administrative and fiscal districts of the Kingdom. In 1513, Charles de Góngora was commissioned to investigate the quotas of *cuarteles* and *alcabalas* paid.[21] New commissioners were appointed in 1528 to oversee the tax rates levied to collect the *alcabalas*. Finally, in 1534 an *ad hoc* royal minister (*visitador*), Antonio Fonseca, was charged with conducting a comprehensive survey of the amounts paid by towns and villages for both *cuarteles* and *alcabalas*, as well as contributions owed to the Royal Domain.[22] It is surely no coincidence that this activity coincided with similar inquiries undertaken by the Castilian Crown between 1525 and 1540. Remarkably, the general instructions issued to the Castilian commissioners[23] do not differ greatly from those of the Navarrese survey of 1534, which in turn reflect the procedures established in the 1513 inquiry.

Thanks to these inquiries, the Royal Treasury regained the *cuarteles* and *alcabalas* paid by certain localities which had disappeared from the tax records.

Excluding the northernmost *Merindad* of Ultrapuertos, the amounts of the *encabezamientos* recorded by the treasurers in 1534–35 for the *cuarteles*, and in 1546–47 for the *alcabalas,* increased by 10 and 3 percent respectively, compared with 1513. Thereafter, between 1546–47 and 1566–67, the quotas remained virtually stable. Table 2.1 shows how the rise in 1534–35 was more pronounced in the *merindades* where the nobility held greater influence (Estella, Olite and Tudela). Nevertheless, since the *cuarteles* and *alcabalas* paid by most of the newly recorded places had previously been alienated in favour of the local nobility, the overall increase in the Crown's revenues was relatively modest.

The new rulers soon tried to circumvent their obligation to summon the *Cortes* to obtain financial aids. As early as 1517, the Crown ordered the collection of the *alcabala* without prior consent. However, this first attempt, along with those of 1529 and 1542, ultimately proved unsuccessful.[24]

The Crown's efforts to increase the *encabezamientos* of *cuarteles* by leveraging local grievances over the unequal distribution of the tax burden had limited success. To this end, a general hearth census was conducted in 1553,[25] but failed to produce the intended results. Protests from the valleys of Santesteban de Lerín, Basaburúa Mayor and Basaburúa Menor, presented to the *Cortes* of 1554, prompted the Three Estates to postpone any decision on the matter.[26] By the final decades of the 16th century, at a time of increasing economic hardship, unrest grew and demands for fiscal reform surfaced once again.[27] With this in mind, in the first quarter of the 17th century, an extensive survey of taxable assets—houses, land and livestock—was undertaken to reassess the *cuarteles*. While the survey remains an invaluable historical source, its practical effects were minimal, likely due to opposition from the Three Estates. In fact, the minutes of the 17th-century *Cortes* hardly refer to this issue, suggesting that the light tax burden on Navarrese taxpayers must have made more bearable an assessment system that was still based on the criteria established in 1428. The tax reform demanded by Catherine I and John III at the end of the 15th century never took place.[28]

The only viable means of increasing Crown revenues was through the introduction of new taxes and the negotiation of larger grants in the Cortes, something in which the monarchy achieved only limited success.

In addition to the revenues raised from customs and parliamentary grants, income from the Royal Domain and receipts from Justice, an additional annual sum of 20,000 silver rs. was secured from 1561 onwards through a contract (*asiento*) known as the *composición de camas*, signed between the viceroy Gabriel de la Cueva and the kingdom's capital, Pamplona. These revenues were further supplemented by the ecclesiastical contributions of subsidy (*subsidio*) and *excusado*, the former collected under a special regime.[29]

On the other hand, the average number of *cuarteles* granted by the *Cortes* increased from 26.5 in 1513–19 to 39–40 in the 1590s, a figure that appears to have represented the upper limit. This yielded a net annual revenue of around 200,000 silver rs. for the Royal Treasury. Nonetheless, the net income derived from the *cuarteles* did not even double over the century. In contrast, revenues from *servicios* in Castile rose from a base index of 100 in 1500 to 284 by 1558, after which they

Table 2.1 Variations in the cuarteles and alcabalas' encabezamientos between 1513 and 1566, according to the treasury records (in Navarrese silver reales)

	Cuarteles					*Alcabalas*				
	1513	*1534–35*	*2/1*	*1566–67*	*3/2*	*1513*	*1546–47*	*2/1*	*1566–67*	*3/2*
	1	*2*		*3*		*1*	*2*		*3*	
M. Estella	[a]931.7	1,378.1	47.9	1,378.1		3,496.7	3,815.0	9.1	3,815.0	
M. Pamplona	1,647.1	1,647.1		1,647.1		12,558.3	12,558.3		12,558.3	
M. Olite	925.0	1,056.7	14.2	1,060.0	0.32	4,987.5	5,525.0	10.8	5,525.0	
M. Sangüesa	1,985.0	1,985.0		1,986.6	0.08	9,078.3	9,078.3		9,085.0	0.07
M. Tudela	649,9	699.1	7.6	699.1		8,500.0	8,876.3	4.4	8,876.3	
Total	6,138.6	6,765.9	10,2	6,770.8	0.07	38,620.8	39,852.9	3.2	39,859.6	0.02
Ultrapuertos	632.6					3,479.9				
Total	6,771.2					42,150.8				

Sources: AGN, RC, 2ª serie, 1, 16, 25 and 35.

M: merindad. Note a: the rise between 1513 and 1534–35 was due to the annulment of the graces previously enjoyed by the Constable and the Marquis of Falces.

stagnated, while income from the *alcabalas* grew from an index of 100 to just over 300 between 1537 and 1578.[30]

The evolution of Royal Revenues in the 16th and 17th centuries

Based on the revenues raised from parliamentary grants and customs duties, the evolution of Royal Revenues in Navarre during the 16th and 17th centuries can be divided into three distinct phases. The first, until 1580–89, was characterised by a noticeable increase in revenue, albeit much lower than in Castile. Royal income more than doubled, rising from 175,000 silver rs. in 1513–19 to 420,000 by the 1580s. Despite this upward trend, revenues remained insufficient to cover all expenses, and, as in other Habsburg territories, the defence of the kingdom continued to rely heavily on financial support from the Castilian Treasury.

As mentioned previously, the monarchy was unable to convert the *alcabala* into a fixed and permanent tax. It also failed to raise the *encabezamientos* of *cuarteles* and *alcabalas*. If the monarchy accepted these failures, it may well have been due to the recent conquest of the kingdom and its still uncertain allegiance, and also because 16th-century Navarre was the Iberian kingdom which contributed most to the Royal Treasury *per capita.*

The reliance on parliamentary grants made Navarre's fiscal system very similar to those of the Basque provinces and the kingdoms of the Crown of Aragon, though with two significant differences. First, until the mid-17th century, subsidies in Navarre were practically annual. Though formally considered as "gracious and voluntary gifts", in practice they became a regular source of income for the King. Between 1513 and 1651, 133 services were granted (nearly one per year), yielding a total net revenue of 24 million silver rs., around 172,000 annually. By comparison, services collected in Catalonia between 1519 and 1650 amounted to 3.6 million Catalan pounds, around 32,000 annually.[31] In *reales de vellón*, the figures were similar but, by 1590, the Catalonian population was double that of Navarre and four times higher by 1768.

Secondly, unlike in the Aragonese kingdoms, where customs duties (*Generalidades*) were administered by the *Diputación* (a standing parliamentary committee), Navarrese customs were a regalian right. Over the course of the 16th century, the annual average value from Navarrese *tablas* rose eightfold, from 34,000 silver rs. in 1513–19 to a peak of 278,000 in 1609–10. To some extent, this increase (surpassed only by that achieved in Castile[32]) was due to the low starting-point of our series, but also to the growth in transit trade through Navarre after 1513. As the revenues collected from the *services* granted by the *Cortes* grew more modestly, from the 1560s more than half of the Royal Revenues came from custom duties, thereby increasing the weight of indirect taxation in Navarre.

The second phase (1580–89 to 1630–39) was characterised by remarkable stability, with ordinary revenues fluctuating at around 400,000 silver rs. The third phase began in the 1640s and was marked by a significant decline in royal income. This fall was driven by both a reduction in customs revenues (brought about by the war with France, population decline and the rise of smuggling) and a decrease in

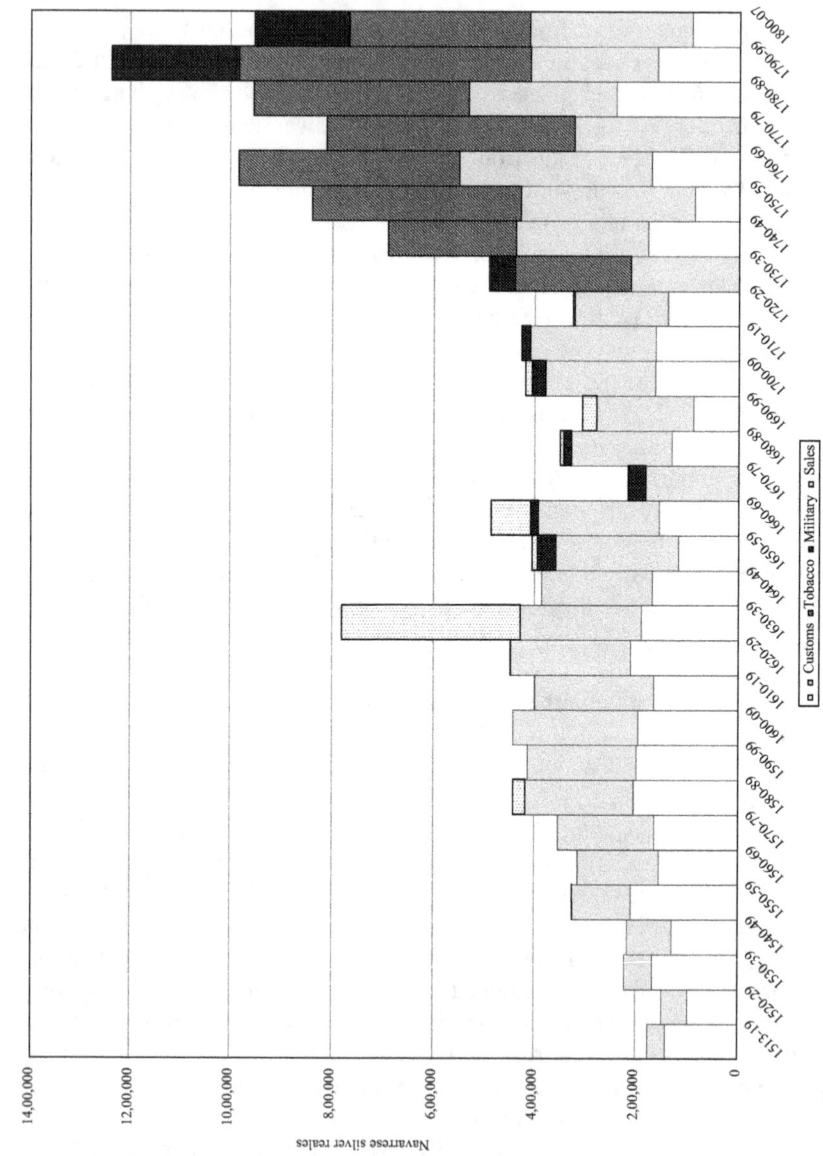

Figure 2.1 Ordinary and extraordinary revenues of the Royal Treasury in Navarre (ten-year averages in Navarrese silver reales).

Sources: See text.

parliamentary grants. The decline gained pace in the 1670s, when Royal Revenues dropped by approximately 50 percent.

In the 17th century, the Crown sought to compensate for the stagnation and decline of its tax revenues. However, unlike in Castile, no new taxes were introduced, as this would have required the approval of the *Cortes*, and existing tax rates remained unchanged. Instead, invoking its regalian rights, the Crown imposed a 50 percent levy on all graces and privileges previously granted to individuals and institutions (*media annata de mercedes*). It also introduced certain monopolies (*estancos*), though the revenues from two of them—tobacco (1642) and chocolate (1678)—were earmarked for repaying the debts of the local treasury (*Hacienda Foral*). Another monopoly, on playing cards (*naipes*), requested by the *Cortes* in 1621 and 1628 for the same purpose, was sold in 1630 to the General Hospital of Pamplona.[33] The Crown's decision to grant these concessions to Navarrese local authorities was likely driven, at least in part, by the aim to curb the widespread smuggling of tobacco, chocolate and *naipes* that was undermining the revenues generated by the Royal Treasury in Castile from its own monopolies on these goods. Ultimately, only the meagre yields from the gunpowder monopoly (*estanco de la pólvora*) accrued directly to the Crown.[34] Additionally, from 1634 onwards, the Crown earned between 1,000 and 1,500 ducats annually from the leasing of liquor canteens serving royal troops stationed in Pamplona.

Extraordinary measures were taken to increase revenues. Although not totally free from manipulation, Navarrese currency was hardly altered, unlike the Castilian petty copper currency (*vellón*), and taxes continued to be paid in silver coin. The Crown primarily relied on the sale of offices, jurisdictions, noble titles and other "graces". It also intensified its demand for military contributions and supplies for the maintenance and repair of fortifications. According to our still provisional estimates, the net proceeds from venality during the 17th century amounted to nearly 5 million silver rs. Most of them took place in 1630–33 (65 percent) and 1664–67 (15 percent).

Military contributions increased significantly from 1635 onwards. After the resumption of hostilities with France, the western Pyrenees became an important base of operations.[35] In accordance with Navarrese local laws (*fueros*), part of the cost of defending the border had to be shouldered by the Kingdom. The failed 1636 military expedition to Labourd, the defence of Fuenterrabía two years later, and the need to protect the borders, prompted the mobilisation of approximately 14,000 men between 1636 and 1640—roughly 9% of the population—at an economic cost that it is difficult to estimate. Military demands continued into the 1640s with the wars in Catalonia and Portugal. Like other Iberian territories, Navarre faced increased pressure from the Crown to provide troops and partially or fully fund their equipment and wages. The *Cortes* were also asked for extraordinary monetary contributions to support the war effort.

Except in the 1630s and 60s, revenues from sales and military contributions did not alter the downward trend in income, which reached its nadir in 1670–79, a deep slump that lasted until well into the 18th century (Figure 2.2). In constant terms, the revenue trajectory reveals greater fluctuation, but from the 1620s

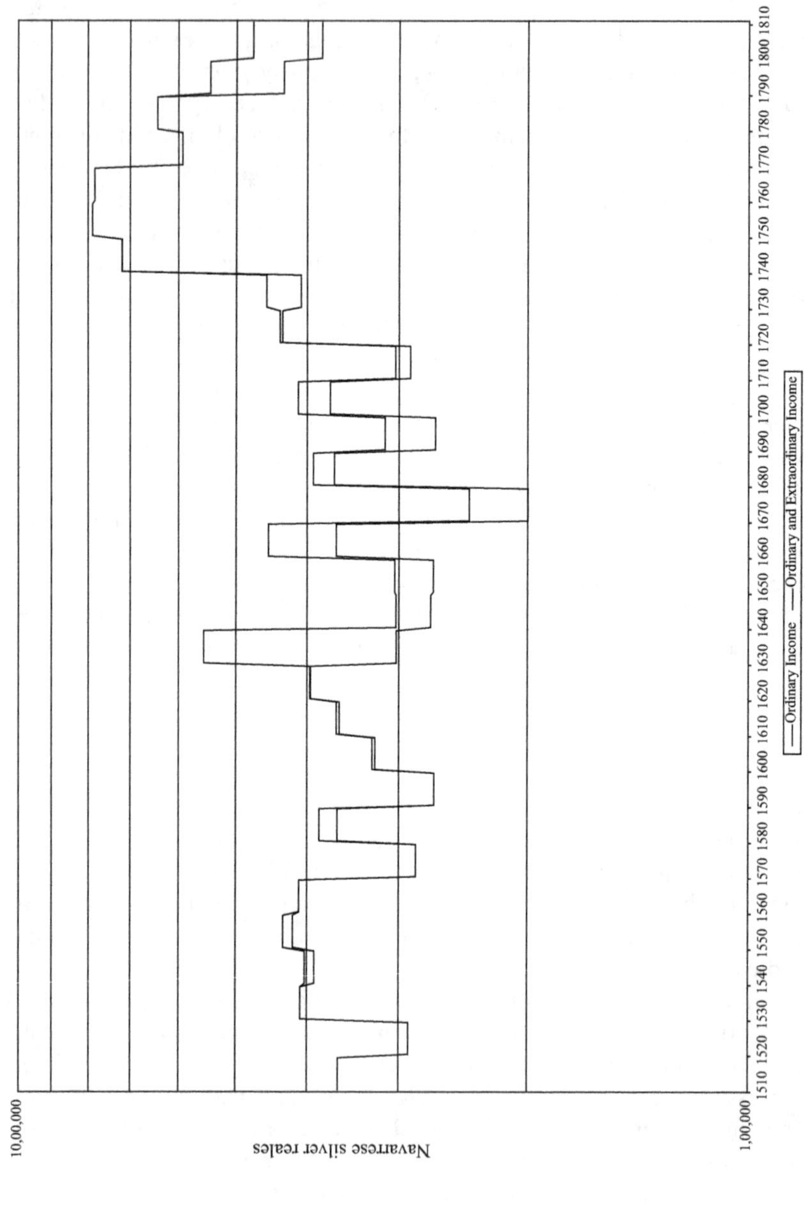

Figure 2.2 Ordinary and extraordinary revenues of the Royal Treasury in Navarre at constant prices of 1720–49 (ten-year averages in Navarrese silver rs).

Sources: See text.

(ordinary revenues) and the 1630s (ordinary and extraordinary) a clear downward trend emerges. In nominal terms, the fiscal contribution of the kingdom during the second half of the 17th century was lower than it had been in the mid-16th century. In real terms, it had fallen to its lowest point.

The evolution of the Crown revenues in the 16th and 17th centuries in Navarre is very different from that of the income raised from the major sources of revenue for the Castilian Treasury, such as *alcabalas*, *cientos* and *millones,*[36] but is similar to that found by Fernández de Pinedo (1990, 1997) for Catalonia and Mugartegui for Guipúzcoa (1990), respectively. The fact that these were border territories may well be a factor in their light taxation.[37]

It seems that, like other European monarchies,[38] the Spanish Crown had decided it was better to have loyal but lightly-taxed subjects, willing to defend its borders, than heavily-taxed and discontented ones. This was the same reason given in 1624 by the Estates of Béarn to justify the survival of their "traditional liberties" after the incorporation of the viscounty and Lower Navarre into France.[39] The evolution of the revenues raised by the French Crown from Lower Navarre, very similar to that of Spanish Navarre, corroborates the above assertion. The 32 *cuarteles* that the former paid as a gift between 1622 and 1632 rose to 34 in 1640 (5,695 pounds), and decreased in 1649 to 31 and 28 in 1664 (4,690 pounds). To this amount a new contribution was added for the maintenance of troops in 1643. This levy was first settled at 5,000 pounds, then reduced to 4,000 and to 2,000 in 1664. Thus, the contribution of Lower Navarre to the French monarchy fell from 10,695 pounds at the beginning of the 1640s to 6,690 at the end of the 1660s (37 percent lower).[40]

A transitional Stage: Fiscal Relations between Navarre and the Crown, 1684–1715

Despite growing tensions in the mid-17th century—caused, as elsewhere, by the Crown's constant demands for men and money and the ever-thorny issue of the transit and billeting of royal troops—there was no fiscal rupture between King and kingdom. Although the *Cortes* were convened less frequently than in earlier periods, Navarre, along with Aragon, remained the few territories where parliamentary assemblies continued to be held during the reign of Charles II.

It is not entirely clear whether the Estates were formally obligated to grant annual subsidies. Nevertheless, with the exception of the tense 1652–54 meeting,[41] until 1662, they continued to approve as many services of *cuarteles* and *alcabalas* as years had elapsed since the previous assembly. Furthermore, from 1642, they also granted many *tercios* for the wars in Catalonia and Portugal, which were funded wholly or partially by the Kingdom.

The rupture took place at the *Cortes* held in Pamplona in 1677–78. The session began with the approval of a new *tercio* of 600 men for the Catalonian campaign, fully clothed, armed and paid for by the Kingdom. Soon after, however, the *Cortes* refused to deliberate on further grants until the grievances were addressed, and to raise another *tercio* in 1678. As a result, tensions between the Estates and the Crown began to mount. Disagreements over the amount of the service finally offered by the *Cortes* (one year of *cuarteles* and *alcabalas* and 26,000 ds. instead of the requested *tercio*, and an additional 8,000 ds. earmarked for repaying the debts of the *Hacienda Foral*), and the conditions required for its allocation (a ban on foreign wine imports) eventually led to a crisis. Rather than give in, the monarchy refused to accept more revenues from Navarre. The viceroy accepted only the annuity of *cuarteles* and *alcabalas*, rejected the remaining offer and proceeded to dissolve the assembly. Although the *Cortes* held him responsible for the breakdown, the attempts made in Madrid to persuade the King to accept the Navarrese proposal for the service were unsuccessful.[42] This caused a significant financial crisis between 1668 and 1684, which forced the transfer of funds from Castile and empowered the viceroys to "grant certain favours" for money, in order to raise the sums needed to pay the troops and undertake the most essential work on the fortifications, which had suffered from a lack of investment in maintenance and improvement.[43]

On 21 March 1684, just six days after the beginning of the *Cortes*' assembly, a brief French incursion across the border exposed the Kingdom's defensive vulnerabilities. In response, the *Cortes* promptly agreed to provide financial support for defence costs. However, rather than granting additional *cuarteles* and *alcabalas*, they reverted to a proposal similar to that of 1677, approving 30,000 ducats—later increased to 40,000—raised through two mechanisms: an undifferentiated hearth tax and one year of *cuarteles* and *alcabalas.*[44] This decision established a precedent that would be followed in subsequent *Cortes* meetings.

The seven assemblies held between 1684 and 1709 granted seven years of *cuarteles* and *alcabalas*, which, in gross terms, amounted to approximately 2.1 million silver rs., plus another 2.7 million earmarked for fortifications. We should also include the three 600-man regiments raised in 1705, the cost of which remains difficult to estimate. Even including the nearly 450,000 silver rs. generated by reducing royal grants and privileges to individuals and corporations (*valimientos*) between 1709 and 1716,[45] the total revenue approved by the *Cortes* for the Crown during this period amounted to just over 5.25 million silver rs. In net terms, this figure drops to approximately 4.5 million, an average of 140,000 reales per year assuming payments were made between 1685 and the start of the next parliamentary session.

The reasons behind the decision to modify the structure of parliamentary aids in 1684 remain unclear. Had the traditional method of *cuarteles* and *alcabalas* continued, Navarrese taxpayers would have paid some 17.6 million silver rs. for the annual services owed since 1659 (58 years at an average of 39 *cuarteles* and the *alcabala* per year). Excluding the sums allocated to the *Hacienda Foral*, around 11 million would have gone to the Crown, roughly 60 percent more than the 4.5 million rs. actually collected. There were other losers besides the Crown, however. Among these are the nobles whose incomes rested on the broad range of gifts and privileges granted by the Crown, such as pensions (*acostamientos*), subsidies and alienated taxes, the value of which declined because of the lesser weight of *cuarteles* and *alcabalas.*[46] A local financier, José de Soraburu, blamed the change on the Third Estate.[47] Yet, given that any agreement required the unanimous consent of all three Estates, his explanation appears unconvincing. Furthermore, after 1684, the share of parliamentary aids paid by the eight towns and cities with more than 400 inhabitants—each represented in the *brazo de las universidades* of the *Cortes*—increased from 11 to 19 percent of the total.

As before, the Crown tried to increase its resources through spending cuts and the implementation of extraordinary expedients. In 1694, all royal "graces" were suspended, with the sole exception of military pensions (*acostamientos*). The savings obtained were invested in the repairs of fortifications.[48] Even this special kind of *acostamientos* ceased to be paid from the parliamentary grants of 1695, 1701 and 1705.

The War of Spanish Succession (1702–1715) marked a critical period for Navarre, which supported Philip V with troops, funds and provisions. In gratitude for this loyalty, the new King respected its *Fueros* and privileges. However, in the aftermath of the conflict, the fiscal relationship between the Crown and Navarre began to shift.

Raising revenues without fiscal reform: The Navarrese tax system under the Bourbon dynasty

The turning point came with the *Cortes* held in 1716–17. In his opening address, the viceroy formally requested, as was customary, a financial service from the assembly and proposed institutionalising the levying of *cuarteles* and *alcabalas* on an annual basis. Additionally, he proposed updating the amounts of money granted in each aid to account for the effects of currency manipulations. Lastly, he requested an additional 1.5 million *pesos* —a little more or less—to cover arrears allegedly owed by Navarre to the Crown. In response, the *Cortes* recalled the efforts made during the war in support of the new Bourbon monarchy, as well as the extensive body of *fueros* and legal traditions that reinforced their position regarding the voluntary and non-annual character of parliamentary aids. It seemed to be the usual bargaining between the King and the Estates, yet it soon became apparent that something more was at stake.

Following surprisingly smooth deliberations (from 13 to 26 August), the *Cortes* voted in a new tax duty on both imports and exports conducted by Navarrese merchants (*nuevo impuesto* or *expediente de mercaderías*).[49] More significantly, they granted a service of 117 *cuarteles* and three years of *alcabalas.* As had been the norm since 1695, the service was to be rendered without any *acostamientos* being deducted from the amounts collected. In return, all *valimientos* would be suspended and, more importantly, the Royal Treasury would formally acknowledge that the alleged arrears of 1.5 million *pesos* had been fully settled.

The viceroy accepted the proposal without hesitation, despite the wide gap between his initial request and the amount ultimately granted by the assembly. However, just two days later, alongside the customary letter of royal gratitude, the Crown announced its decision to take direct control over the tobacco monopoly, the main source of revenue for the *Hacienda Foral*, citing the rise in contraband entering Castile, Aragon and Valencia. The royal decision provoked an intense debate that extended until December, when it was resolved in favour of the Crown.[50] From then on, the *estanco del tabaco* could be regarded, for all practical purposes, as another source of revenue for the Royal Treasury, although formal ownership remained with the *Hacienda Foral*.

Following the Crown's assumption of control over the tobacco monopoly, customs became the next target of reform. The Royal Decree of 31 August 1717 ordered the relocation of the inland customs posts in the Basque Country and Navarre to the coast and the Pyrenean border, respectively. This was a continuation of the measures adopted three years earlier in the kingdoms of the Crown of Aragon. However, the order provoked widespread resistance, with popular protests compelling the Crown to reconsider its position. The Royal Law of 16 December 1722 ordered the return of the customs posts to their former position from 1 January 1723.

This failure did not deter the Crown from pursuing increased revenue extraction from Navarre. The *Cortes* of 1716–17 and the unsuccessful attempt to relocate customs posts signalled the emergence of two major points of conflict between the Crown and the kingdom throughout the 18th century: the fiscal contribution to the monarchy and the contraband; the third was military conscription (*quintas*).[51]

To combat smuggling, two main measures were implemented: a tax on goods imported by Navarrese merchants, who were also required to declare both the merchandise and its destination, along with strengthened surveillance.

Suspended in August 1717 by the relocation of customs posts, the new tax duty was renewed by all the *Cortes* after 1724, first as a means of payment for the service granted and then to fund the building of the road network. This measure ended the long-standing privilege of the Navarrese to import any goods freely, which had facilitated the rise of smuggling.[52] The impact of the tax must have been substantial, as evidenced by the local merchants' attempt to avoid its imposition by offering an annual donation of 240,000 rs. for five years—an amount equivalent to the average income yielded by the *tablas* between 1710 and 1716. When the assembly rejected their proposal, the merchants expressed their willingness to farm out the tax collection, but without success. They would make similar attempts again, also unsuccessfully, in subsequent *Cortes*.[53]

One of the initial measures undertaken by the Crown upon assuming control over the tobacco monopoly was to expand the number of tobacco guards. This deployment was further expanded in 1748, when the Crown assumed direct control over the customs, which had previously been administered by the local Chamber of Accounts, the financial authority of the Kingdom. The growth in consumption, trade and prices during the economic expansion of the 18th century, combined with more effective anti-smuggling efforts, led to a significant increase in revenues from the tobacco monopoly and customs duties. Nevertheless, these gains were offset by the substantial costs incurred in maintaining the surveillance apparatus. The resulting deficit necessitated regular monetary transfers from other Royal Treasuries. This fiscal imbalance was a key factor behind the Crown's persistent efforts to relocate customs posts to the Pyrenean frontier, so as to reduce surveillance costs. Not surprisingly, the issue of customs relocation emerged as a contentious topic during the sessions of the *Cortes* in 1757 and 1780, although, in both cases, the assembly rejected the royal proposals. In response, the Crown implemented the 1782 tariff, followed by successive decrees with the primary objective of impeding Navarrese exports.[54]

Simultaneously, the monarchy increased pressure to secure further substantial aids under more favourable conditions. In 1724, it requested that the *Cortes* approve the automatic extension, from early 1721, of the levy of the *cuarteles* and *alcabalas* service, as well as the new import duties which had been suspended due to the customs relocation. This request was refused by the *Cortes* and, consequently, parliamentary grants continued to depend on negotiation. However, the Three Estates found themselves increasingly compelled to include clauses in the grants that were more detrimental to their own interests. From 1724 (partially at first, and fully from 1765–66 onwards), financial contributions had to be paid upon the promulgation of the law. From 1743 onward, negotiations with the Crown became increasingly difficult, as the King ceased to accept the assembly's initial proposal. This shift stemmed either from the King's aim to increase the immediate payment (1743–44, 1757, 1765–66), or because he deemed the proposed amounts insufficient (1780–81, 1794–97).

Table 2.2 shows that the monarch secured increasing amounts, in part by abolishing the deductions previously applied to the *Hacienda Foral*. If we estimate the average annual revenue from these grants by spreading each *donativo* over the interval between successive sessions of the *Cortes*, a clear upward trend emerges until the mid-1790s. At the same time, there were notable changes in the allocation of the funds raised. Although there were some exceptions, the prevailing norm, until the *Cortes* of 1743–44, was that the sums collected in Navarre were to be spent within the kingdom. From then on, the King was granted the authority to freely dispose of the funds, which were transferred (initially in part and later entirely) out of Navarre, and into the General Treasury in Madrid or the regional treasuries of the Spanish army.

These changes did not result in increased revenues for the Crown, be it in nominal or real terms. The total amount collected from the seven services approved between 1716 and 1794, plus the 340,000 silver rs. advanced by the *Diputación* following the failed *Cortes* of 1801 on account of the service to be granted at a later stage (127,500 in 1801 and 212,500 in 1805),[55] amounted to approximately 10.9 million (around 120,000 annually). This figure was 50 percent lower than the yearly average value of the subsidies raised between the mid-16th and mid-18th centuries, and even lower than those of the services collected between 1684 and 1716. To some extent, this decline can be attributed to the less frequent convening of the *Cortes* during the 18th century. From 1716 to 1805, when the last parliamentary aid was paid, there were 33 gap years in which no revenue was collected from this source. Consequently, the relative weight of services in the monarchy's revenue significantly diminished, while the share of indirect taxes continued to rise. From 1716 onward, tobacco and customs duties accounted, on average, for 80 percent of ordinary revenues, with services contributing a mere 15 percent.

The transformations of the 18th century overturned the foundations of Navarrese taxation. The Crown began to draw most of its resources from a revenue source

Table 2.2 Parliamentary grants (000 silver reales)

Parliamentary assemblies	*Initial proposal*		*Definitive concession*						*Annual average*
	Total 1	*Immediate* 2	*Total* 3	*Immediate* 4	*3/1* %	*4/2* %	*To the king* 5	*5/3* %	
1716–17			[a]823.6				[b]757.2	92	94,649
1724–26	1,119.2	328.0					[c]1,057.0	88	55,632
1743–44	1,600.0	800.0	1,600.0	1,200.0		150	[d]1,600.0	100	114,286
1757	1,200.0	400.0	1,200.0	480.0		120	[c]1,099.4	92	137,419
1765–66	1,440.0	480.0	1,440.0	1,440.0		300	1,440.0	100	160,000
1780–81	2,080.0	2,080.0	2,400.0	2,400.0	115		2,400.0	100	171,429
1794–97	1,440.0	1,440.0	2,000.0	1,600.0	139		2,000.0	100	166,667

Sources: AGN, CA, legs. 4–5, Cuentas de Cuarteles y Alcabalas, legs. 1–5 and RC, 2ª Serie, 81–82, 85 and 88.

Notes: (a) Estimated income from the *nuevo impuesto* at 62,500 rs.; (b) Deducting 6,000 ducats allocated to the *Hacienda Foral*, plus the 1,500 of the annuity granted in 1705 and still pending collection; (c) Deducted the 3,000 ds. and the 4 percent withholding on the hearth tax allocated to the *Hacienda Foral*; (d) No deductions. By order of the Chamber of Castile of 5 May 1745, the 50,000 pesos that were to come from the *cuarteles* and al*cabalas* were paid in full in 1745 and 1748.

it did not formally own and that suffered from a chronic deficit: the *estanco del tabaco*. The brief return of the monopoly to Navarre's local treasury in 1742–44 suggests that the Crown initially doubted the arrangement's financial benefits, but it soon regained control, valuing strategic advantages over monetary concerns.

The Royal Treasury's control over tobacco and customs revenues enabled the redeployment of many guards from the Castilian and Aragonese borders to the inland of the kingdom. This may be seen in the stark contrast between the small surveillance apparatus of the tobacco monopoly (*resguardo del tabaco*) in Soria—comprising just six members, including a notary—and the much larger Navarrese *resguardo*, with 210 to 220 personnel.[56] Since they were now largely funded by revenue collected in Navarre, it is reasonable to conclude that this shift resulted in considerable savings for the Royal Treasury. It is also likely that a presumably more efficient surveillance system reduced revenue losses from smuggling.[57] When contraband increased in the early 1780s, the government's response appears to have been relatively successful. French sources report a drop in the arrival of Spanish silver piastres to Labourd and Lower Navarre since the summer of 1786, which they attributed to the strict surveillance enforced by the Spanish authorities.[58] Thus, the deficits of the tobacco monopoly and customs duties in Navarre were likely offset by higher tax revenues in other Spanish territories and by the reduced costs of maintaining customs enforcement.

Without modifying its fiscal system and making only relatively minor administrative adjustments to existing taxes, Navarre ended up contributing more to the Spanish monarchy during the 18th century than it had over the two previous centuries. Nevertheless, although its fiscal privileges were reduced during this period, the kingdom remained one of the least heavily taxed regions in Spain, surpassed only by the Basque Country.[59]

The view of Navarre as a lightly taxed area which emerges from the analysis of the royal tax records is not entirely accurate, however. Royal records are particularly reliable when reconstructing the evolution of ordinary revenues, but less so when compiling that of extraordinary revenues and total spending. Given that part of the latter was shouldered by institutions other than the Royal Treasury—such as the Provincial Treasuries of the Spanish army and, especially, the *Hacienda Foral* and the municipal treasuries—this point deserves further consideration.

Financing the seven volunteer battalions raised during the War of the Pyrenees (1793–1795) required approximately 2.3 million silver rs. To this conservative estimate, we should add an amount that is impossible to quantify, but probably very similar, paid by the towns that granted enlistment bonuses to attract recruits and pay for the *apellido*,[60] as settled by the *Fueros*. The total cost of the war must have been close to the 9,709,862 rs. vn. (5.5 million silver rs.) that the *Diputación* estimated with remarkable accuracy;[61] its upward estimate was likely offset by the expenditures incurred by the municipalities, which were not included in the calculation. The *Hacienda Foral* covered the war expenditure through borrowing and an extraordinary levy of 200,000 *pesos*,[62] while municipal treasuries were forced to incur debt, likely to a much greater extent.[63]

The indebtedness of the *Hacienda Foral* and municipalities was preceded by similar borrowing efforts that began in 1784 to finance the construction of a road network—an undertaking that, as in the rest of Spain, gained momentum in the mid-18th century. A Royal Decree of 6 May 1751, transferred authority over public works from the Royal Council to the viceroy, Count of Gajes. Initially, he attempted to minimise costs by relying on compulsory labour from local residents, and a special tax levied on the clergy, who immediately opposed it. As Gajes himself stated in a letter to Minister Ensenada on 28 April, this cost-cutting strategy failed, and was met with widespread complaints.[64] Grievances—first from the *Diputación*, and later from the *Cortes* convened in 1757—led to this policy being abandoned, making it necessary to seek alternative sources of funding.[65]

In a Royal Decree dated 8 February 1780, the King called upon the *Cortes* to propose mechanisms for maintaining and expanding the existing road network. The assembly's proposal to assume all costs in exchange for full authority over roadworks being transferred to the *Diputación* initially failed. However, a final agreement was reached in October 1783 with Count Floridablanca. Between 1784 and 1807, total expenditures on road construction and maintenance (excluding interest payments and minor amortisations) amounted to 12.3 million silver reales—almost half a million per year.[66] This figure slightly exceeded the average annual income from the tobacco monopoly. As in the Basque Country during the same period, the Crown successfully modernised the Navarrese road network without directly funding it.

In return, the monarchy ceded full control over road infrastructure to the Basque and Navarrese *diputaciones*, thereby reinforcing their economic and political authority. Lacking sufficient revenue to repay the loans, public debt accumulated. According to a report from 1817, the principal amounted to 8,736,704 silver rs., around 16.5 million *vellon* rs., plus 1.5 million in overdue interest. According to the report, it would take nearly 33 years to settle this debt.[67] This financial burden would later become a key factor in the persistence of Basque and Navarrese fiscal privileges during the liberal reforms of the 19th century.[68]

Acknowledgement

This work has been funded by the Ministry of Economy, Industry and Competitiveness (Agencia Estatal de Investigación)/European Regional Development Fund (ERDF), project HAR 2016-78026-P, and by the Basque Government (Consolidated Research Group IT897-16 UPV-EHU). I thank Emiliano Fernández de Pinedo for the extraordinary generosity of his comments.

Notes

1 On the characteristics of the taxation of developed feudalism, Fernández de Pinedo, 1980: especially 12 and 73.

2 Fernández de Pinedo, 2014: 21 and 78–80.

3 Koenigsberger, 1978: 202 *et seq*; Elliott, 1992; Muto, 1995: 232–234; Comín Comín and Yun Casalilla, 2012: 233–234.
4 Published, among others, by Canga Argüelles, 1968: II, 442–443. The population data in García-Zúñiga, 1996: 176, and Nadal, 1984: 74.
5 Extraordinary taxes started being used in Navarre only after 1328. Mugueta, 2008.
6 Ladero Quesada, 1973: 201–202; Menjot, 1979: 93–96.
7 Derville, 1992: 38–39.
8 Fernández de Pinedo, 2014: 19 and 22.
9 Archivo Real y General de Navarra (hereinafter AGN), Registros de Comptos (hereinafter RC), 1ª serie, 202, ff. 1r–2r.
10 The commission for the reform in AGN, Libro de fuegos de la Merindad de Pamplona, fols. 1r–v.
11 AGN, RC, 1ª serie, 395, ff. 123r–v.
12 AGN, Comptos, caj. 162, nº 48, and Yanguas, 1964: I, 54, who dates the reform in 1472. The correction of the date in Monteano, 1999: 292–293.
13 Prévost, 1885: LIV.
14 With the exception of the sales of horses and weapons, real state transactions, and currency exchanges. AGN, Cuarteles y alcabalas (hereafter CA), leg. 1, c. 1.
15 Carrasco, 2012.
16 AGN, Comptos, caj. 164, nº 30; Papeles Sueltos de Comptos (hereafter PSC), 1ª serie, leg 20, c. 9.
17 Sánchez Martínez, 1992: 369–375.
18 At least in 1496, 1501 and 1502 commissioners were appointed, and instructions were issued for the reform of the Royal Domain, *alcabalas* and *cuarteles*. AGN, Comptos, caj. 165, nº 71, caj. 167, nos. 8, 17 and 19, caj. 168, nº 10, caj. 177, nº 9, caj. 179, nos. 13–15, and caj. 193, nº 43; PSC, 1ª serie, leg. 20, cs. 20 and 23; CA, leg. 1, cs. 15, 16 and 23; Guerra, leg. 1, c. 6.
19 AGN, RC, 1ª serie, 527bis and 531.
20 AGN, Recopilación de Actas de Cortes, years 1503–1531, sessions of 14 March 1505 and 22 December 1508, ff. 25v and 59v; CA, leg. 1, cs. 28 and 31.
21 Beaumont's commission also enabled him to review all kinds of rebates, tax-exemptions and the number of beneficiaries of tax-privileges, exempted palaces and deserted hearths. Huici, 1996: 204–205; Monteano 2000: 410–414.
22 AGN, Comptos, caj. 179, nº 48-X, and RC, 1ª serie, 550.
23 Carretero Zamora, 2008: I, 66–67.
24 AGN, CA, leg. 4, c. 12; *Novissima Recopilacion de las Leyes del Reino de Navarra...* (hereinafter NR), 1.14.10. A similar attempt by the Prince of Viana had already been declared contrafuero in 1448. *Actas de las Cortes de Navarra* (hereinafter ACN), book 6, cortes de Pamplona of 1716–17, session of 6 August 1716: p. 122.
25 Floristán Imízcoz, 1982: 213.
26 ACN, book 1, cortes de Pamplona of 1554, session of 26 February: 248.
27 Cortes de Pamplona of 1596, law 41. NR, 1.14.13.
28 After the hearth census of 1553, no more censuses were conducted until 1646 (the one of 1644–45 was discarded), but the *Cortes* agreed not to publish it to avoid "disputes among themselves [the towns] whether the *repartimientos* carried out by the Kingdom were equitable or not". ACN, book 3, cortes de Pamplona of 1652–54, session of 2 October 1652: 194.
29 Azcona, 1988: 46.

30 Carretero Zamora, 2017: 164–165; Artola, 1982: 464–465.
31 Fernández de Pinedo, 1997: 70–73.
32 For the values of customs revenues, Artola, 1982: 76–77.
33 AGN, Beneficencia, tit. 8, caj. 1, nos 1–2 and 6.
34 The sources date it in 1659. AGN, CA, leg. 2, c. 62.
35 French reports from 1639 encouraged the King of France to invade Navarre, highlighting the vulnerability of its defences. Archives des Affaires Étrangères. Mémoires et Documents. Fonds Divers. Espagne. Correspondance Politique, vol. 19, fols. 491r–493v and 506r–509v; vol. 20, ff. 363r–364r.
36 Fernández de Pinedo, 1997: 82–83; Andrés Ucendo, 2001: 612 and 614.
37 This was always paramount in the minds of Castilian kings and policymakers, who preferred to maintain the border along the Pyrenees. In fact, this was precisely the justification Charles I gave in 1538 in response to the complaints raised by some representatives at the Castilian *Cortes* held in Toledo. They protested over the fact that the Castilian Treasury had to fund, totally or partially, the fortifications of Navarre, Perpignan (in Catalonia) and the Balearic Islands, plus the squadron of Genoese galleys of Andrea Doria. *Actas de las antiguas cortes de León y Castilla*: V, 716.
38 See, among others, O'Brien and Hunt, 1999: 78, for the neighbouring English counties of Wales and Scotland, and Potter, 1993: 236, for French Picardy.
39 Loirette, 1964: 67 and 69.
40 Destrée, 1955: 236–237.
41 This assembly voted to raise of a 500-man infantry unit (*tercio*), 20,000 ducats for its recruitment, and four years of *cuarteles* and *alcabalas*, instead of the theoretical eight.
42 ACN, book 4, Pamplona cortes of 1677–78: pp. 337–341, 344–345, 454–457, 466–468 and 494–498, 521–546; AGN, CA, leg. 2, cs. 69–70.
43 AGN, Fortificationes, leg. 1, c. 39, and leg. 2, cs. 12 and 21. The commissions issued to the viceroys to "grant favours" would continue throughout the 1690s. Presumido Casado, 2023: 394.
44 AGN, Fortificationes, leg. 1, cs. 10 and 12.
45 AGN, PSC, 1ª serie, leg. 142, cs. 7–9, 144, cs. 4–5 and 27, 145, cs. 4–6, 147, c. 6, and 149, cs. 12–14 and 16, and Archivo Secreto de la Cámara, tit. 35, nº 40.
46 García-Zúñiga, 2013: 373–374.
47 Rodríguez Garraza, 1996: 365.
48 Huici, 1996: 246.
49 The Navarrese enjoyed complete freedom to import foreign goods, while foreign merchants were subject to a 3⅓ percent duty on the value of their imports. Exports were taxed at 5 percent, except for wool, wine and iron, which enjoyed tariff advantages.
50 ACN, book 6, Pamplona assemblies of 1716–17: 100–101, 120–125, 145–146, 171–175, 181–183 and 235–241, among others.
51 The decision to extend the system of *quintas*, established by the R.O. of 3 November 1770, to Navarre in 1772, sparked a prolonged debate among the institutions. García Pérez, 2008: 205–232. What the kingdom's institutions did achieve was that substitutes could be put in place (1775), replaced by *levas de vagos* (1786) and volunteers (1793), and, from 1803, the possibility of redeeming them in cash.
52 García-Zúñiga, 1993: 311.
53 Hernández Escayola, 2004: 183–184 and 303.
54 García-Zúñiga, 1994: 85–86.
55 AGN, CA, leg. 8, c. 51; Cuentas del Vínculo, libro nº 5.

56 Archivo General de Simancas (hereinafter AGS), DGR, 1ª Remesa, legs. 2452–53, and 2471–72.
57 The observed decrease in the seizures of smuggled tobacco could be interpreted as evidence of more effective fraud prevention. García-Zúñiga, 2006: 120–121.
58 Dermigny, 1954: 265–266.
59 García-Zúñiga, Mugartegui and De la Torre, 1991.
60 The obligation to defend the territory at their own expense against any enemy incursion and that, at least in theory, affected all Navarrese between the ages of 16 and 60 capable of taking up arms.
61 Archivo Histórico Nacional (hereinafter AHN), Estado, leg. 3952.
62 García-Zúñiga, 1992: 15.
63 The War of the Pyrenees significantly worsened the financial situation of local councils, ultimately leading many to bankruptcy. This mounting municipal debt was later addressed through an early phase of civil disentailment. Fernández de Pinedo, 1974; De la Torre, 1991.
64 AGS, SSH, leg. 920, and AHN, Ministerio de Hacienda, leg. 229, exp. 18.
65 CC, Cortes de Pamplona of 1757, ley 24.
66 García-Zúñiga, 1992: 12.
67 AGN, Vínculo, leg. 8, c. 13.
68 Fernández de Pinedo, 1991: 97; De la Torre and García-Zúñiga, 1995: 82–83.

Bibliography

Actas de las antiguas Cortes de León y Castilla (1903), Madrid: Sucesores de Rivadeneyra, volumen V.

Actas de las Cortes de Navarra (1530–1829) (1991–1996), Pamplona: Parlamento de Navarra.

Andrés Ucendo, José Ignacio (2001), "Castile's Tax System in the Seventeenth Century", *Journal of European Economic History*, 30, 3, pp. 597–617.

Artola, Miguel (1982), *La Hacienda del Antiguo Régimen*, Madrid: Alianza.

Azcona, Tarsicio de (1988), "El pago del subsidio y del excusado a la corona por la iglesia de Navarra en el siglo XVI", *Príncipe de Viana*, anejo 9, pp. 35–46.

Berthe, Maurice (1984), *Famines et épidémies dans les campagnes navarraises à la fin du Moyen Age*, Paris: SFIED.

Canga Argüelles, José (1968 [1833–34]), *Diccionario de hacienda con aplicación a España*, Madrid: Instituto de Estudios Fiscales.

Carrasco, Juan (2012), "Monarquía y fiscalidad indirecta en Navarra. El lento predominio de la 'imposición' (1362–1386)", in Ernesto García Fernández and Imanol Vitores Casado, eds., *Tesoreros, 'arrendadores' y financieros en los reinos hispánicos: la Corona de Castilla y el Reino de Navarra (siglos XIV-XVII)*, Madrid: Instituto de Estudios Fiscales, pp. 9–49,

Carretero Zamora, José Manuel (2008), *La averiguación de la corona de Castilla, 1525–1540, Los pecheros y el dinero del reino en la época de Carlos V*, Salamanca: Junta de Castilla y León.

Carretero Zamora, José Manuel (2017), *Gobernar es gastar. Carlos V, el servicio de las cortes de Castilla y la deuda de la monarquía hispánica, 1516–1556*, Madrid: Sílex.

Comín Comín, Francisco and Yun-Casalilla, Bartolomé (2012), "Spain: From Composite Monarchy to Nation-State, 1492–1914. An Exceptional Case?", in Bartolomé

Yun-Casalilla, Patrick K. O'Brien with Francisco Comín Comín, eds., *The Rise of Fiscal States: A Global History, 1500–1914*, Cambridge: Cambridge University Press, pp. 233–266.

Cuadernos de las Leyes y Agravios reparados por los tres Estados del Reino de Navarra (1964), Pamplona: Aranzadi.

De la Torre, Joseba (1991), *Los campesinos navarros ante la guerra napoleónica, Financiación bélica y desamortización civil*, Madrid: Ministerio de Agricultura, Pesca y Alimentación.

De la Torre, Joseba and García-Zúñiga, Mario (1995), "Revolución burguesa y privilegios fiscales: la hacienda foral de Navarra (1780–1860)", in José María Donézar and Manuel Pérez Ledesma, eds., *Antiguo Régimen y liberalismo, Homenaje a Miguel Artola, 2. Economía y Sociedad*, Madrid: Alianza Editorial/UAM, pp. 81–85,

Dermigny, Louis (1954), "Circuits de l'argent et milieux d'affaires au XVIIIe siècle", *Revue Historique*, 212, 2, pp. 239–278,

Derville, Alain (1992), "La fiscalité d'État dans l'Artois et la Flandre Wallone avant 1569", *Revue du Nord*, 74, 294, pp. 25–52,

Destrée, Alain (1954), *La Basse Navarre et ses institutions. De 1620 à la Révolution*, Zaragoza: Librería General.

Domínguez Ortiz, Antonio (1983), *Política y hacienda de Felipe IV*, Madrid: Pegaso.

Dupont-Ferrier, Gustave (1932), *Études sur les institutions financières de la France à la fin du Moyen Âge, Tome second: Les finances extraordinaires et leur mécanisme*, Paris: Firmin-Didot et Cie.

Elliott, John H. (1992), "A Europe of composite monarchies", *Past and Present*, 137, pp. 48–71.

Fernández de Pinedo, Emiliano (1974), "La entrada de la tierra en el circuito comercial: la desamortización en Vascongadas. Planteamiento y primeros resultados", in Gabriel Tortella Casares and Jordi Nadal, coords., *Agricultura, comercio colonial y crecimiento económico en la España contemporánea* , Barcelona: Ariel, pp. 100–128.

Fernández de Pinedo, Emiliano (1980), "Coyuntura y política económicas", in Manuel Tuñón de Lara, ed., *Centralismo, ilustración y agonía del Antiguo Régimen*, Barcelona: Labor, pp. 9–173,

Fernández de Pinedo, Emiliano (1990), "Ingresos y gastos de la Hacienda catalana en el siglo XVII", in Emiliano Fernández de Pinedo, ed., *Haciendas Forales y Hacienda Real, Homenaje a D. Miguel Artola y D. Felipe Ruiz Martín*, Bilbao: Universidad del País Vasco, pp. 207–224.

Fernández de Pinedo, Emiliano (1991), "Gasto público y reformas fiscales, Las haciendas forales vascas", *Hacienda Pública Española*, monografías 1, pp. 93–100.

Fernández de Pinedo, Emiliano (1997), "La participación fiscal catalana en la monarquía hispánica (1599–1640)", *Manuscrits*, 15, pp. 65–96.

Fernández de Pinedo, Emiliano (2014), *El censo de la sal (1631). Hacienda y consumo*, Bilbao: Universidad del País Vasco.

Floristán Imízcoz, Alfredo (1982), "La población de Navarra en el siglo XVI", *Príncipe de Viana*, 43, 165, pp. 211–261.

García Pérez, Rafael D. (2008), *Antes leyes que reyes, Cultura jurídica y constitución política en la edad moderna (Navarra, 1512–1808)*, Milan: Giuffré.

García-Zúñiga, Mario (1990), "Los ingresos de la hacienda real en Navarra (siglos XVI-XVII)", in Emiliano Fernández de Pinedo, ed., *Haciendas Forales y Hacienda Real, Homenaje a D. Miguel Artola y D. Felipe Ruiz Martín* , Bilbao: Universidad del País Vasco, pp. 195–206.

García-Zúñiga, Mario (1992), "Orígenes, evolución y crisis de una hacienda foral: Navarra, 1642–1820", *Gerónimo de Uztariz*, 6–7, pp. 5–24.

García-Zúñiga, Mario (1993), "Haciendas forales y reformas borbónicas, Navarra, 1700–1808", *Revista de Historia Económica*, 11, 2, pp. 307–334.

García-Zúñiga, Mario (1994), "Comercio y contrabando en Navarra durante el feudalismo desarrollado", *Hacienda Pública Española*, monografías 1, pp. 79–87.

García-Zúñiga, Mario (1996), *Hacienda, población y precios (siglos XVI-XVIII)*, Pamplona: Gobierno de Navarra.

García-Zúñiga, Mario (2006), "El estanco del tabaco en Navarra, 1642–1841.Valores, consumo y contrabando", *Gerónimo de Uztariz*, 22, pp. 107–139.

García-Zúñiga, Mario (2013), "El gasto en un reino periférico. Navarra (siglos XVI-XVII)", in Ángel Galán Sánchez and Juan Manuel Carretero Zamora, eds., *El alimento del Estado y la salud de la* Res Publica: *Orígenes, estructura y desarrollo del gasto público en Europa*, Madrid: Instituto de Estudios Fiscales, pp. 357–379.

García-Zúñiga, Mario, Mugartegui, Isabel and De la Torre, Joseba (1991), "Evolución de la carga tributaria en la España del Setecientos", *Hacienda Pública Española*, monografías 1, pp. 81–91.

Hernández Escayola, Mª Concepción (2004), *Negocio y servicio: Finanzas públicas y hombres de negocios en Navarra en la primera mitad del siglo XVIII*, Pamplona: EUNSA.

Huici, Mª Puy (1996), *La Cámara de Comptos de Navarra en los siglos XVI y XVII*, Pamplona: Gobierno de Navarra.

Koenigsberger, Helmut G. (1978), "Monarchies and Parliaments in Early Modern Europe. Dominium Regale or Dominium Politicum et Regale", *Theory and Society*, 5, 2, pp. 191–217.

Ladero Quesada, Miguel Ángel (1973), *La hacienda real de Castilla en el siglo XV*, La Laguna: Universidad de La Laguna.

Loirette, Francis (1964), "L'administration royale en Béarn de l'Union à l'Intendance (1620–1682), Essai sur le rattachement à la France d'une province frontière au XVIIe siècle", *XVIIe siècle*, 65, pp. 66–108.

Menjot, Denis (1979), "La fiscalité royale directe en Castille sous les premiers Trastamare: remarques sur l'évolution d'une pratique financière dans un cadre urbain (1374-début du XVe siècle)", in *Études sur la fiscalité au Moyen Âge, Actes du 102e Congrès National des Sociétés Savantes*, Paris: Bibliothèque Nationale, vol, I, pp. 91–107.

Monteano, Peio J. (1999), *Los navarros ante el hambre, la peste, la guerra y la fiscalidad, Siglos XV y XVI.* Pamplona: Universidad Pública de Navarra.

Monteano, Peio J. (2000), "La población navarra a comienzos del siglo XVI: el Recuento de casas de 1514", *Príncipe de Viana*, 61, 220, pp. 407–431.

Mugartegui, Isabel (1990), "La exención fiscal de los territorios forales vascos: el caso guipuzcoano en los siglos XVI y XVII", in Fernández de Pinedo, Emiliano Fernández de Pinedo (ed), *Haciendas Forales y Hacienda Real, Homenaje a D. Miguel Artola y D. Felipe Ruiz Martín*, Bilbao: Universidad del País Vasco, pp. 175–194.

Mugueta Moreno, Iñigo (2008), *El dinero de los Evreux: hacienda y fiscalidad en el reino de Navarra (1328–1349)*, Pamplona: Gobierno de Navarra.

Muto, Giovanni (1995), "The Spanish System: Centre and Periphery", in Richard Bonney, ed., *Economic Systems and State Finance*, Oxford: Oxford University Press, pp. 231–259.

Nadal, Jordi (1984), *La población española (siglos XVI a XX)*, Barcelona: Ariel.

Novissima Recopilacion de las Leyes del Reino de Navarra hechas en sus Cortes Generales desde el año de 1512 hasta el de 1716 inclusive (1964 [1735]), Pamplona: Aranzadi.

O'Brien, Patrick K. and Hunt, Philip A. (1999), "England, 1485–1815", in Richard Bonney ed., *The Rise of the Fiscal State in Europe, c, 1200–1815*, Oxford: Oxford University Press, pp. 53–100.

Ordenanças del Consejo Real del Reyno de Navarra (1622), Pamplona: Nicolás de Assiayn.

Pérez Prendes, José Manuel (1964), *Apuntes de historia del derecho español*, Madrid: Gráficas Menor.

Potter, D (1993), *War and Government in the French Provinces: Picardy, 1470–1570*, Cambridge: Cambridge University Press.

Presumido Casado, Pablo (2023), "Servir al rey para servirse a sí mismo: navarros al servicio de Carlos II de Austria", *Revista de Historia Moderna*, 41, pp. 383–418.

Prévost, Gustave-Alphonse (1885), "Introduction", in Eugène Izard, *Le Compte des recettes et dépenses du Roi de Navarre en France et en Normandie de 1367 à 1370*, Paris: Alphonse Picard, pp. I–CXLVI.

Rodríguez Garraza, Rodrigo (1996), "La guerra de Sucesión en Navarra, I, Financiación de la misma y capitalización de los asentistas autóctonos (1705–1711)", *Príncipe de Viana*, 57, 208, pp. 359–388.

Sánchez Martínez, Manuel (1992), "La fiscalidad real en Cataluña (siglo XIV)", *Anuario de Estudios Medievales*, 22, pp. 341–376.

't Hart, Marjolein (1995), "The Emergence and Consolidation of the 'Tax State'. The Seventeenth Century", in Richard Bonney, ed., *Economic Systems and State Finance*, Oxford: Oxford University Press, pp. 281–293.

Yanguas y Miranda, José (1964 [1840]), *Diccionario de Antigüedades del Reino de Navarra*, Pamplona: Institución Príncipe de Viana.

Appendix 2.1 Revenues of the Royal Treasury in Navarre, 1513–1807 (ten-year averages in silver reales)

	Customs	[a] *Parliamentary grants*	*Royal Domain*	*Receipts from Justice*	*Tobacco monopoly*	*Military services*	*Sales*	*Revenues A*	*Revenues B*	*Index prices 1720-49 =100*	*At constant prices*	
											Revenues A	*Revenues B*
1513–19	33,869	141,416	?	?				175,285	175,285	48	362,769	362,769
1520–29	49,811	98,547	?	?				148,357	148,357	51	291,089	291,089
1530–39	54,633	166,990	?	8,403				221,623	221,623	54	408,653	408,653
1540–49	86,734	129,238	?	15,513		6,600		215,971	222,571	55	390,985	402,934
1550–59	116,224	208,920	?	27,594		10,000		325,145	335,145	78	418,586	431,460
1560–69	159,699	154,700	11,184	28,439				314,399	314,399	77	410,161	410,161
1570–79	189,702	163,870	14,557	46,249				353,572	353,572	124	284,375	284,375
1580–89	214,204	203,910	13,465	47,154			24,237	418,114	442,350	115	363,889	384,982
1590–99	214,655	198,368	15,195	46,615				413,023	413,023	154	268,431	268,431
1600–09	246,676	195,202	15,412	42,790			4,400	441,878	446,278	137	323,149	326,367
1610–19	233,741	165,108	12,706	38,772			3,630	398,849	402,479	110	361,599	364,890
1620–29	237,445	210,409	11,725	30,821			484	447,853	448,337	113	395,830	396,258
1630–39	238,886	189,500	12,321	?		1,800	352,386	428,386	782,571	142	302,548	552,692
1640–49	217,641	168,174	12,395	17,779		33,180	10,940	385,814	429,934	142	271,629	302,691
1650–59	242,148	116,975	?	29,919		35,797	10,397	359,122	405,316	133	269,329	303,973
1660–69	238,511	155,038	10,310	32,013		14,717	78,735	393,549	487,001	108	365,307	452,053
1670–79	181,565	0	9,236	30,105		34,614	2,540	181,565	218,719	91	199,621	240,470
1680–89	197,128	130,828	8,996	16,338		15,429	6,942	327,956	350,327	89	367,442	392,506
1690–99	190,244	88,088	8,187	13,750		20,080	27,677	278,332	326,090	104	267,576	313,487
1700–09	216,058	163,118	?	10,152		26,615	13,292	379,175	419,082	102	372,409	411,604
1710–19	[b]247,500	162,088	6,697	14,244		16,747	2,780	409,588	429,115	141	289,628	303,436
1720–29	[b]182,178	139,292	6,143	15,787	[c]93,000		2,995	414,469	417,465	96	433,050	436,180
1730–39	211,375	0	7,520	25,469	228,797	47,595	3,394	440,172	491,161	108	407,780	455,016
1740–49	260,725	177,604	7,667	33,648	253,405		220	691,733	691,953	96	717,960	718,188
1750–59	342,151	86,160	7,580	34,849	411,895			840,205	840,205	107	788,683	788,683

(*Continued*)

Appendix 2.1 (Continued)

	Customs	[a] *Parliamentary grants*	*Royal Domain*	*Receipts from Justice*	*Tobacco monopoly*	*Military services*	*Sales*	*Revenues A*	*Revenues B*	*Index prices 1720-49 =100*	*At constant prices*	
											Revenues A	*Revenues B*
1760–69	380,476	171,076	8,812	34,912	432,446		50	983,997	984,047	126	782,900	782,940
1770–79	322,678	0	11,446	39,952	489,431			812,109	812,109	137	592,144	592,144
1780–89	292,646	240,000	11,358	31,446	423,022			955,668	955,668	149	641,659	641,659
1790–99	[c]250,000	160,000	14,772	45,322	574,585	253,163		984,585	1,237,748	229	430,875	541,665
1800–07	319,693	92,500	?	46,839	356,598	185,672		768,790	954,462	201	382,584	474,982

Sources: García-Zúñiga, 1996: 43–51, 61–74, 82–94, 99–104, 139–140 and 226–230; Sales: data from a work in progress.

Notes: (a) Net income. Deducted the sums allocated to the *Hacienda Foral*; (b) Excluding customs relocation period; (c) Estimate. Revenues A: customs+donation+tobacco, Revenues B: the same plus military services and sales.

3 State, taxation and finance in Italy. Some comparative issues

Luciano Pezzolo

Introduction

This essay proposes a comparison of several fiscal and financial features of the major Italian states between the mid-sixteenth and late seventeenth centuries. It should be premised that some methodological problems weaken the basis of the documentation. First, the quantitative data have large margins of uncertainty, due to the very nature of old regime budgets; moreover, satisfactory series on population, prices, wages, budgets, interest rates and currencies are not available for all the states considered.

The states considered are the Republic of Genoa, the State of Milan, the Republic of Venice, the Grand Duchy of Tuscany, the State of the Church, the Kingdom of Naples and, finally, the Kingdom of Sicily. As can be seen, we have different constitutional systems (republics and monarchies); different political contexts (some independent states and others subject to a foreign crown); different origins (some arose from the territorial expansion of one city Genoa, Milan, Florence and Venice), while others are characterised by a long monarchical tradition (Rome, Naples and Sicily); and different sizes (Genoa and Florence have rather limited areas; the southern kingdoms and Milan are larger in size; Rome is a political centre but is mainly the capital of the Catholic Church; Venice holds territories in the Adriatic and eastern Mediterranean seas). Apart from Genoa and Florence, the other states are more or less frequently engaged in conflicts, either directly (first and foremost Venice in the Mediterranean, and occasionally Milan) or indirectly, by means of supplies of men, goods, services and especially money (the Habsburg territories), or only by providing subsidies to Catholic allies (the Holy See). The picture, therefore, is extremely complex and varied. On the one hand, this stimulates comparison and the identification of similarities and differences between the various polities; on the other, it complicates the possibility of satisfactorily comparing data due to differences in the availability of adequate studies and sources. In recent decades, however, financial history in Italy (as well as in the rest of Europe) has been seeing a fruitful period of scholarship.

Comparing typologies

Taxation and state constitute a pair that has spanned the centuries, maintaining an enviable union. The exploration of these closely interrelated aspects is by no means

DOI: 10.4324/9781003653301-4

new; the warlike origins of the late medieval and early modern state have been the subject of much attention by both historians and sociologists. Norbert Elias has effectively described the process:

> The society of what we call the modern age is characterised, above all in the West, by a certain level of monopolisation. Free use of military weapons is denied to the individual and reserved to a central authority of whatever kind, and likewise the taxation of the property or income of individuals is concentrated in the hands of a central social authority. The financial resources thus flowing into this central authority maintain its monopoly of military force, while this in turn maintains the monopoly of taxation. Neither has in any sense precedence over the other; they are two sides of the same monopoly.[1]

The most well-known reference, among many, can be identified in the ordinances of Charles VII of France of November 1439, which established the collection of taxes reserved exclusively for the Crown and imposed the royal prerogative to recruit soldiers.[2] This typology reflects the evolving idea of the absolute state in France and especially in Prussia, which has an illustrious tradition. At the beginning of the twentieth century, Otto Hintze, one of the most prestigious German historians of the time, emphasised the decisive role that the army had played not only as the armed arm of the absolute state but also as a matrix for the development of the bureaucratic system underlying the so-called 'modern' state.[3] Army, taxation and permanent bureaucracy were essentially the three pillars on which the 'modern' state had been built. Charles Tilly later reconsidered the issue by proposing a dynamic, long-term model. Growing military needs pushed political elites towards centralisation and control of coercive and financial resources; governments developed bureaucratic apparatuses for the purpose of collecting taxes and financing war; as a result, the space managed by civilians to negotiate the extraction of resources from the holders of those resources increased.[4] The fiscal-military model effectively applied by Brewer to eighteenth-century England found further stimulation in the work of Downing and Ertman.[5] The growing fiscal, and thus financial, capacity of the state enabled the mobilisation of enormous military resources in the context of new relations between ruled and rulers in the aftermath of the Glorious Revolution of 1688. The English case was then applied to the rest of Europe.[6] Eighteenth-century parliamentary England thus replaced absolutist France as the archetype of the 'modern' European state.

The general typology has been subjected to numerous verifications in recent years, which have sharply diminished the concept of the absolute state and, in some cases, criticised the genealogical line that starts from the Renaissance monarchic state and leads to the nineteenth- and twentieth-century liberal state. The starting point, in fact, reveals serious limitations for those who wish to discern its characteristics of modernity, and – upon closer examination – even the end point could be seen more as a myth than a centralised bureaucratic system.[7] It could even be argued that the topic no longer holds any interest. Yet new syntheses and further typologies have recently been proposed, highlighting the importance of military organisation and the fiscal-financial system in determining the different paths taken by the major polities in late medieval and early modern Europe. The problem of the state, although in different forms, is always current because it indicates political, social and ideological changes. Thus, what a few years ago could have appeared 'modern' – the centralised, national and bureaucratic state – is now viewed more critically in the light of the political-institutional changes affecting Europe. It is no coincidence that the notion of the composite state – i.e. a polity characterised by particularisms and pluralisms, generally institutionalised – has gained traction precisely when there is a trend, almost everywhere, towards both the creation of supranational bodies and an emphasis on regionalism rather than the nation-state.[8] A state that leaves wide room for action to its citizens is also currently considered a much more 'modern' system than traditional centralised states. The concept of the state is therefore mutable, undergoing significant transformations and variations in relation to the times and experiences that people are living through.

The focus on the pair of state and finance might seem a peculiar exercise in the Italian case. If the tendency for a legal monopoly of violence appears to be a prerogative of great monarchies, the Italian states, or at least most of them, would instead represent the exception to the rule; the (failed) Mediterranean path to Northern absolutism, and therefore to modernity, with all that entails. It is significant that a relatively recent publication on Italian states in the Renaissance offered a wide range of topics (cities, rural communities, fiefs, classes, factions, women, offices, diplomacy, political languages, justice, economy) neglecting military and fiscal-financial aspects.[9] This appears to indicate a widespread bias that sees war and finance as traditional and 'statist' fields of study. However, the aim of this paper is not to draw an evolutionary line towards a fanciful 'modern' state, but to shed light, through a particular perspective, upon some features of Italian polities in the early modern age. The peninsula offers the extraordinary opportunity to set up a comparative analysis of institutions in different contexts, where traditions, historical events, and geographical and political structures influence institutional processes, and vice versa. Institutional changes exert significant influence on power structures, possibilities for economic growth, and the responses that various systems adopt to economic conjunctures. The complex and varied institutional landscape of Renaissance and Baroque Italy thus offers a privileged laboratory to test some dynamics and propose some hypotheses. Republics and principalities do not appear as mere constitutional containers but, especially in some areas, show marked differences, to the point of determining the destinies of some states. The following section considers, albeit briefly, the different cases.

Cases

Let us start with Genoa. Thanks to the work of Giorgio Felloni, it is possible to outline with reasonable approximation the long-term trend of Genoese state finance, at least in terms of basic data.[10] Between the mid-sixteenth and mid-eighteenth centuries, state revenues grew in nominal terms fourfold, due to the increase in direct taxation, both in the capital city and in the subject territory, and to a lesser extent from consumption duties. Considering some parameters, however, it is noticeable that the revenue increase is considerably scaled down. The value (in current currency) of Genoese port trade in the same period grew less than twice; the price of grain increased almost fivefold, while state revenues expressed in silver went from 9.4 tons in 1550, to 19.8 tons a century later. The performance of Genoese public finance, unlike private finance, certainly does not appear noteworthy. Faced with the changing international context and the growing needs of state expenditure, the Republic shows itself incapable of expanding the budget due to the structural limits of its power system – a power system centred on the hegemony of the patriciate and the pre-eminence of the capital over the rest of the territory, according to the classic models of the city-state. The constraints imposed by the communities subject to the central government's action were quite strong and thus prevented effective resource collection. Consequently, it was necessary to find money among the capital's taxpayers, who nonetheless were unable to provide adequately for the needs. Thus, the "pragmatic compromise between the will to power and tenacious individualism" prevented Genoa from playing a significant role on the European stage of the old regime.

After the end of the ducal dynasty following the death of Francesco II Sforza in 1535, the State of Milan had passed to Emperor Charles V and would remain under the Habsburg Eagle until 1706. Although new conquerors usually tend to act with some caution, and although the ambassadors of Milan hastened to ask the new sovereign for the abolition – which was not granted – of all "unusual taxes and increases in duties and other revenues", the arrival of the Spaniards introduced significant changes in the Milanese finance.[11] This is hardly surprising. The new rule fully entered the sphere of Habsburg imperial policy with the consequent honours and, above all, burdens. Certainly, in 1536 the Spanish governor reduced the tax on wheat milling and abolished the tax on millet and rye. But it was a merely symbolic act, as the clouds of war against France were looming. And indeed, in the same year the *mensuale* was decreed, the revenue from which became the pillar of Milan's budget.

Once the government decided how much money had to be collected from the State of Milan, the burden was distributed among the nine provinces and, within each, between the city and its rural district (the *contado*). Usually, the cities paid their share through indirect taxes, and if that was not sufficient, direct taxation was applied on the land income of citizens. In the countryside, on the other hand, direct levies prevailed, affecting both the land and the "heads". It should be emphasised, however, that citizens did not pay taxes on land owned in rural communities, nor were they subject to the obligation to lodge troops. The marked inequality between urban and rural taxpayers is evident, dating back to centuries earlier, when the cities expanded their control over the surrounding countryside.

The imposition of the *mensuale* represented a crucial event in the relations between Lombard tax bodies and the Spanish government. First, its nature as an extraordinary tax quickly disappeared. Certainly, its collection ceased in 1546 at the end of the war against France, but it was resumed a year later and never stopped again. Moreover, the amount to be paid increased from 12,000 scudi per month to

20,000 and then to 25,000. The notary Simone Del Pozzo was right when he wrote that "Extraordinarily: they use this word to console the People". But what gave it importance was its distribution among the taxpayers, which became the model for other taxes. The *mensuale*, as expected, provoked strong resistance and loud complaints among Lombard subjects. But among them there were those who had more reasons to complain. When Charles V decreed the *mensuale* tax in 1536, he certainly did not think that it would provoke a conflict among his new subjects that would last three generations. In fact, the new tax challenged the traditional fiscal arrangements of Lombardy and in some ways became a subversive element in local power relations. Following the introduction of the *mensuale*, in March 1543 the government ordered the formation of a general assessment (*estimo*), which had to include both real estate and commercial activities. The emperor's aim was to balance, as far as possible, the marked disparities among the tax bodies and to expand the taxable wealth base. To the usual opposing actors, the cities and rural communities, merchants were now added, affected for the first time in their business. The strongest opposition came from Milan, which aimed to maintain its prerogatives over the other cities, which in turn supported the new assessment to put the Milanese in difficulty. Moreover, the cities were opposed to the rural communities, which were determined to take advantage of the new apportionment to shift part of their burdens onto urban landowners, and finally the merchants, especially those of Milan, who saw their businesses threatened by the tax inspectors. The obstacles and delays on the part of the protagonists prevented the timely conclusion of the operations; the assessment of land property was completed in the late 1560s, and that of movable wealth dragged on even into the early seventeenth century, although some important results were achieved. The taxable land area doubled compared to that assessed in 1531.[12] Similarly, incomes from commercial and artisan activities were taxed, which until then had barely been touched by the hand of the fiscal authorities.[13] The *mensuale* provided the Treasury with a large sum, which became the main source of financing for the duchy. Progressively, additional taxes were introduced alongside it that paralleled the traditional taxes established during the period of the Visconti and Sforza rule and that, above all, distributed their burden in a less unbalanced way.[14] The burden of lodging troops, which was initially assigned solely to rural communities, was extended also to cities by the end of the sixteenth century.[15] The gap between urban and rural taxpayers did not disappear but undoubtedly decreased, thanks also to the formation of political and administrative institutions that represented rural communities – namely local elites – at both provincial and state levels. Thus, the state of Milan at the beginning of the seventeenth century presented political and institutional balances quite different from the past. Although it may be optimistic to speak of a revenge of the rural population, it is nevertheless undeniable that the fiscal policy implemented by the Spanish decisively contributed to reducing the centuries-old disparities among nobles, city dwellers and rural inhabitants.

Some similarities can be found in the neighbouring Republic of Venice. Between the mid-sixteenth and the early eighteenth centuries, its income doubled from about forty-nine tons of silver to over ninety-six tons.[16] This increase is not at all remarkable, considering that during the same period the French Crown saw a five-fold growth rate, and England as much as seventeen times. Moreover, throughout the seventeenth century, Venice, like the rest of the Italian peninsula, was undergoing an economic and political downsizing compared to the dynamism of the north-western area of Europe. Nevertheless, the financial history of the Serenissima is by no means monotonous or lacking in interest.

In principle all the subjects of the Venetian Republic were called to fiscal duty: lay people and ecclesiastics, female household heads, citizens and peasants, nobles, merchants and landowners. The Doge himself had to pay taxes. Within this mass of taxpayers, however, there were significant differences that mirrored the structure of society and the constitution of the state. These divisions distinguished the capital city, the Italian mainland, and the overseas colonies by different legal traditions and economic, social and political structures. Taxpayers of the capital city and taxpayers of the mainland (the so-called *stato da terra*) were registered in different tax lists. The latter, furthermore, were subdivided as city dwellers and peasants. Venetian landowners enjoyed privileges; they were exempted, for example, from the obligation to provide services for the maintenance of the army in peacetime. Beginning in the mid-sixteenth century, following the severe crisis of the League of Cambrai of 1509–16, these differences between taxpayers, however, began to narrow. One of the most significant episodes concerns the imposition of the subsidy of 100,000 ducats in 1529 on the mainland communities.[17] The tax caused complaints and resistance both against the government and, above all, among the provincial bodies, so that only in 1543 was the division of the tax finally established, while the conflict between the cities and rural communities continued for years regarding the definition of their respective shares in relation to the wealth of their taxpayers. With the subsidy, the Venetian ruling class aimed to target the wealth of the local aristocracies, also favouring the traditional separation between citizens' assets and those of the rural population, but the result was, in some respects, partial.

The decades between Lepanto and the great plague of 1630–31, in a scenario of growing difficulties for urban economic structures, saw the subjected city elites suffer severe difficulties, caught on the one hand by the emerging classes in the district, who pushed to gain a space of power that had until then been denied, and on the other by the Venetian ruling group, which through a series of measures both fiscal and judicial, sought to seriously undermine the mainland aristocracy. By intervening in the prerogatives of citizen landholders, the interests of the urban aristocracy, which derived the foundations of its power and social prestige from the land, were primarily affected. The tax immunities enjoyed – both in fact and by right – by the noble landowners constituted one of the supporting elements of the client network in the countryside. The action of the territorial bodies, supported by the Venetian patriciate who were investing substantial capital in the purchase of land properties on the mainland, impacting the condition of citizens' properties, penetrated the complex web of power, privilege and clientele centred around the figure of the nobleman. The city councils were forced to negotiate the traditional role of overseeing fiscal mechanisms with the rural elites. This rebalancing of forces, resulting from significant economic and social change in the state, expanded the involvement in the tax structure to other social groups. Now the various rural notables, through communal and territorial institutions, could regulate the mechanisms of tax allocation, albeit under the vigilant control of Venice. The redistribution of power areas among local elites, encouraged by the Venetian government, thus gained the consent of the district ruling groups, who nevertheless had to more or less willingly acknowledge the possibility of central intervention in financial management at municipal level. Orders and regulations issued by the Venetian authorities for the proper administration of municipalities and territorial bodies, although often disregarded, constituted a normative framework that legitimised governmental action over the district communities. The active participation of sections of subjects was not only manifested in the local division of the tax burden; it was necessary to collect the money as well as manage its flow to the provincial treasuries. City authorities and district notables were therefore the protagonists of basic tax activity, with a substantial difference compared to the past, however, since the background of internal power relations within the *stato da terra* had profoundly changed.

Like the Venetian one, the Florentine state was also formed following the expansion of a city that had progressively conquered a vast territory. Unlike Venice, however, where the republican form persisted until the end in 1797, in the Florentine state the Medici family assumed power and the ducal title in 1530 thanks to the pikes and cannons of the soldiers of Charles V and lost it for lack of heirs in 1734. The period considered in this essay includes few moments in which the Grand Duchy was involved in conflicts: following the War of Siena (1553–59), Cosimo I acquired the Sienese territory as a 'new state' and united it with his dominions; during the Long War between the Ottomans and Imperial forces in Hungary (1593–1606) Florence sent units to the front, with little success; during the so-called War of Castro (1641-44), when Grand Duke Ferdinand II intervened on behalf of the Farnese, supporting the attack of Pope Urban VIII's army. Few wars of little significance – except that against the hated Sienese – thus do not shed light on the relationship between military pressure and state building. Even the subsidies requested by the emperor did not constitute a significant structural factor, although they caused an increase in public debt.

Yet between the mid-sixteenth century and 1670 Tuscan budgets doubled. Precisely in the 1550s, the conflict against Siena exerted considerable pressure that led to a noticeable increase in revenues with effects in the years to come. If in the mid-century the budget recorded an income of 78 tons of silver, in the following decade the amount doubled and, above all, the pre-war levels would never reach again.[18] In 1554, the ducal government imposed new taxes (taxes on flour and meat, an increase in the salt tax) and resorted to borrowing on both the domestic and foreign markets. The taxes decreed for the war became ordinary and, in some cases, lost the characteristic of indirect taxes to instead assume that of a lump sum paid by each community to the Grand Ducal Treasury. This entailed a wide degree of autonomy for the local elites, who could choose various means to collect the necessary money. Moreover, since the agreed amounts were rarely updated, their effective burden decreased over time due to inflation. In short, thanks to limited military commitments and the policy of mediations and compromises, the Tuscan grand dukes and their subjects were able to avoid the enormous problems that distressed most of the governments and taxpayers of Europe.

As for the State of the Church, public finances reflected the dual nature of the pope's power: he relied on the temporal revenues of the territorial state and the spiritual revenues (rights, grants of grace, taxes on clergy, etc.) coming from Catholic territories. The latter had already shown a tendency to decline in the fifteenth century, a trend that was further accentuated by the Reformation. Despite this, the money flows from the various dioceses continued to represent a significant portion of the entire income of the Holy See.[19] By the mid-sixteenth century, the tax system was based on new taxes, which would remain notably important even in the following century. The establishment in 1543 of the *sussidio triennale* was one of the most significant events. After negotiations between the government and provincial institutions, the new tax of 300,000 scudi was introduced on an extraordinary basis for three years but continued to be levied until the end of the Church state. Its collection was delegated to local authorities and, at least theoretically, it affected all subjects. Just as with the Milanese *mensuale*, the triennial subsidy provided the model for subsequent taxes. Between the 1570s and the late seventeenth century, state revenues in terms of silver increased by just one and a half times. Like the Tuscan grand dukes, the popes did not face heavy and prolonged military commitments, but unlike the Medici they took on an international role that had to be supported by financial aid to Catholic powers. Furthermore, the lavish building policy required huge sums of money that had to come from the state budget. It is interesting to note, however, that throughout the seventeenth century the level of revenue reached a plateau that remained almost constant although the general economic framework registered signs of difficulty.

Despite the the relative abundance of state budgets in the Kingdom of Naples, the available documentation does not allow for a clear outline of revenue trends for certain periods. By the mid-sixteenth century, however, revenues grew from about 50 to 116 tons in 1638 and even reached the historic peak of 235 tons in 1646, on the eve of the revolt against Spanish government in the kingdom; by the early eighteenth century, the level was around fifty tons. The pillar of Neapolitan finance was the *donativo*, which became an ordinary tax starting from the 1530s. The divergence between economic health and public finance began to emerge in the late sixteenth century and worsened dramatically in the second quarter of the following century.[20] The revolt of 1647–48 marks a turning point in several respects. Regarding state finance, immediately after the repression, the government decided to reserve a minimal portion (300,000 ducats) of tax revenues for itself, leaving the management of alienated revenues entirely to creditors, to restore its creditworthiness after the stormy years preceding the revolt. Subsequently, the government attempted to recover the alienated taxes, but this only happened around the mid-eighteenth century.[21] The second half of the seventeenth century still saw significant involvement of the Kingdom of Naples in wars. In addition to financial and material aid to garrisons beyond its borders, the Neapolitan budget was called upon to contribute to the maintenance of ships and soldiers for the Messina revolt (1674–78) and for further wars fought in Europe and the Mediterranean. All of this occurred in a situation of severe difficulties for public finance.

By the mid-sixteenth century, Sicily like the continental South had a tax system that was now settled, with the *donativo*, granted by the parliament, now becoming a regularly collected tax and functioning as a matrix for further charges. The amount of money granted by parliament rose from just over two tons of silver in the mid-sixteenth century to 7–8 tons from Lepanto to the early years of the Thirty Years' War and stood at 16 tons in the second half of the seventeenth century. As a result, the share provided by parliamentary taxes grew to about 40 percent of state revenues.[22]

After this brief overview, Table 3.1 summarises some fiscal data.

The data in Table 3.1 Table 1.1 do not show a close relationship between tax levy and constitutional structure. Looking at the amount of silver per capita, republican governments appear to be more effective in obtaining money from their taxpayers than kings and princes. Similarly, the tax burden in city-states is somewhat higher, perhaps because of the high capital intensity of economic activities. It is not surprising that by the mid-sixteenth century, the fiscal resources of the Republic of Venice were far superior to those of other states. Next came the Kingdom of Naples, now consolidated within the Habsburg sphere; the Papal State showed considerable fiscal capacity. This was probably due both to its greater involvement than Genoa in the past Italian Wars and to the contribution of flows from so-called spiritual revenues, *i.e.*, levies, fines, and various duties collected throughout the vast area of Catholicism. At first glance, the position of the State of Milan may seem surprising, given that it had been one of the great powers of the peninsula in the fifteenth century. In fact, just a few decades earlier, the Sforza dukes could count on far greater resources than Charles V. It is therefore plausible to believe that, despite the constant complaints of the Lombard subjects against the imperial court and attempts to reform the means of assessment and introduce new taxes, the new government did not weigh particularly heavily on the taxpayers, although the military demand on the population in terms of the supply of goods and services must be considered. However, it cannot be ruled out that the high levels of taxation in the late fifteenth century put the results of the Habsburg tax system in the early years of their rule in a relatively different perspective.

The picture became quite different in the following years. The second half of the sixteenth century was marked by a significant increase in state revenues of Milan, which tripled its available resources, reaching the level of the papal budget, while Genoa doubled and the Papacy increased by just two-thirds. The seventeenth century was characterised by different trends; Milanese public finances remained apparently high but tended to decline, while the revenues of the Apostolic Chamber increased. It should be noted that papal taxation was not stimulated by military demand, as in Milan, but by enormous spending on public works, with important redistributive effects that have not yet been fully analysed by scholars. At the end of the century, the ratio between the size of the Milanese and papal budgets seems to have returned to the situation of the mid-sixteenth century, with the latter being

Table. 3.1 Central receipts of Italian states and Castile, 1550–1700

	Genoa			*Milan*			*Venice*			*Florence*			*Rome*			*Naples*			*Sicily*			*Castile*		
	1	*2*	*3*	*1*	*2*	*3*	*1*	*2*	*3*	*1*	*2*	*3*	*1*	*2*	*3*	*1*	*2*	*3*	*1*	*2*	*3*	*1*	*2*	*3*
1550	9.4	32.0	8.0	13.8	17.0		51.1	27.0	6.0	13.0	22.0	6.0	25.0	15.0		41.2	14.0	4.0	15.7			107	19.0	4.0
1600	20.4	57.0	12.0	41.9	32.0	4.0	68.2	37.0	5.0	42.0	54.0	7.0	42.4	21.0	3.0	74.6	22.0	5.0	26.6	24.0	4.0	430	63.0	7.0
1650	19.8	49.0	9.0	35.2	39.0	7.0	66.0	46.0	6.0	38.0	53.0	6.0	53.5	29.0	3.0	41.0	15.0	3.0	16.0	14.0	2.0	412	57.0	8.0
1700				19.1	16.0	5.0	90.0	45.0	8.0				65.0	33.0	4.0	37.0	11.0	4.0	20.0	18.0	3.0	219	29.0	5.0

Sources: Italian data derive from several sources that will be presented in my forthcoming monograph entitled *Mars and Pluto*; as for Castilian data, Thompson, 1994: 157; Andrés Ucendo and Lanza García, 2008: 147–90.

1: Tons of silver; 2: Per capita gr. of silver; 3: Man days of unskilled labour much larger than the former. It should also be borne in mind that a considerable portion of state revenues was used to pay state creditors and that between the mid- and late seventeenth century, the Milanese money of account was devalued by 23 percent, while the Roman currency remained remarkably stable.

However, shifting our attention to the second part of the table, the picture changes significantly. Throughout the period shown in the table, Genoa stands out for its high ratio of revenue to population. The explanation for this primacy probably lies primarily in the central role played by the urban economy of the capital and the substantial trade flows affecting the Ligurian territory. About 40 percent of Genoa's revenue came from trade taxes, while the percentage of direct taxes rose from an insignificant 3 percent in 1550 to 9 percent a century later.[23] This was certainly not a long-term trend, since between the late fourteenth and mid-fifteenth centuries, the percentage of direct taxation was higher than in the sixteenth century. It is plausible that direct taxation was strengthened following the sharp decline in the urban population, which fell from 22.5 percent in 1600 to just 14.2 percent a century later.[24] The Milanese budgets do not allow for a detailed analysis of the trends in the various items, but the impression is that, starting in the mid-sixteenth century, taxation became more complex, affecting both real estate and exchange in goods.[25] As for the Papal State, the capital's role as a source of revenue remained limited, providing only 14–18 percent of the total revenue between 1592 and 1633; this percentage rose to around 20 percent in the second half of the seventeenth century, reflecting the growing importance of taxation on trade and consumption.[26] If we estimate taxes on cities and trade as a proxy for the commercialisation rate of the country, then we could argue that Genoa and Milan were able to cope with greater tax pressure than the Papal state. It is interesting to note, however, that a comparison between Milan and Rome at the end of the seventeenth century would confirm that the high wages of Roman building workers made it possible to sustain a considerable tax burden.[27] Furthermore, it is worth noting that the Castilian data are in line with the Italian territories under the Habsburg rule. This reinforces the judgment that the Spanish government did not exert a particularly heavy tax burden on the Italian territories, and that the financial heart of the Monarchy was Castile.

The summary financial data show that the trends in the three countries considered follow a common path but with significant variations, and that a direct relationship can be found between the degree of commercial and financial capital intensity, and the ability to sustain growing fiscal demand. A further element to be considered concerns whether governments have strengthened their ability to levy. According to Peter Lindert, by increasing direct levy, modern democracies decreased collection costs and thus achieved a high level of fiscal efficiency.[28] In the case of the old regime states, the issue takes on rather intricate characteristics,[29] as high collection costs prevented the collection of a direct tax that efficiently affected taxpayers' wealth. The fact that the central government decided on the collection of a tax aimed at hitting the income or wealth of individuals did not imply that the same principle was adopted at the local level. Generally, one was limited to charging a fixed sum, the burden of which had to be distributed among the various local bodies, cities, rural communities, guilds, clergy, feudal areas and peripheral territories (mountain valleys, border communities, etc.). In addition, this mechanism did not allow for timely updating of the share among the various bodies and the changes in their taxable income. It is therefore not surprising that governments avoided intervening in the delicate balances associated with the allocation of taxes at the local level. Thus, the *mensuale* imposed by Charles V in 1537 on Lombard taxpayers was met in the most diverse ways, depending on the political and economic context. The same happened in the Papal State throughout the sixteenth and seventeenth centuries, where the *sussidio triennale* – also conceived in 1543 as an extraordinary tax – was paid according to available local resources (duties and *gabelle*, 'heads', land ownership, etc.). By contrast, the Genoese ruling class was quite reluctant to exploit direct taxation, such as the provincial one. In 1630 the city council of Savona preferred to take on a debt, the interest payments on which would be supported by consumption taxes, rather than resort to direct taxation. The prevalence of direct or indirect taxation, in short, must be evaluated at the time of assessment and collection, being more a political than a strictly fiscal problem.[30]

However, this does not prevent us from proposing some hypotheses to overcome, for example, the republic/prince dichotomy or Habsburg domains vs. independent states. The fiscal geography of states is like a mosaic, whose tiles reflect prerogatives that were negotiated between the prince and the community at the time of conquest. Areas placed in strategic positions, on the borders, inaccessible or endowed with strong local powers (towns and powerful fiefs) were able to obtain substantial judicial and fiscal prerogatives. Although periodically subject to negotiation, these privileges were regarded as the pillars of the system of relations between prince and subjects. City-states do not exhibit a greater degree of homogeneity than princely states. While the latter include large feudal areas, which are by definition special, the former favour subject elites by protecting their areas of exemption in rural districts. However, as we have seen, all governments seek to erode privileges and immunities, albeit cautiously and following a path fraught with obstacles.

Privilege is the symbol of the tax constitution of the old regime, as it epitomises the divisions of class and status that characterise that society. The granting of tax exemptions was a formidable instrument of power for the prince. The privilege emphasised a special relationship between the beneficiary (a noble, a community, a family, clergy, soldiers...) and the grantor; a subtle relationship bound them together. Through the early modern age, governments largely granted tax prerogatives to rural and urban militias, established in the sixteenth century; tens of thousands of men enjoyed exemptions, albeit limited, from direct taxes and especially from the corvées that affected the countryside. It is not appropriate to emphasise the immunities of clergymen, who traditionally enjoyed privileges that constituted one of the hardest knots to untie in conflicts between local bodies. However, it would be wrong to emphasise the clash between state and church around taxation. We could interpret ecclesiastical exemptions as a benefit granted by the government in exchange for cooperation in maintaining control over its subjects, and particularly their consciences; and it is no coincidence that the revenue from taxes on the clergy found its way to both the Roman Curia and the coffers of the state treasury.

In addition to coercion, tax revenues are also the product of consensus, obtained through negotiation and patronage. Indeed, the action of the central power would have little effectiveness if it could not rely on the cooperation of local authorities, not only in collecting taxes but especially in ascertaining taxable wealth. Thus, the enormous amounts of money that governments are able to transfer from taxpayers' pockets to treasury coffers can be interpreted as an indicator of the degree to which subjects conform to the demands of state taxation. A compliance, however, that was forged through tight negotiation between government authorities and local elites, and that must be rediscussed when the government demands new taxes. The negotiation is not only about the amount to be paid but also – and more importantly – about the role of the elites in determining the distribution of the tax and the portion they are able to control. This allows the central government to avoid a significant share of the transaction costs associated with the tax control and management function. This explains the extensive use of the contracting system rather than direct management of taxes.

Although the revenue between the two systems did not change substantially, farming out offered numerous advantages both at the level of managerial foresight and at the more purely political level. This system is generally referred to as one of the most oppresive mechanisms of old regime taxation because it aggravated the relations between taxpayers and tax collectors. But, on closer inspection, from the point of view of government authorities the system represented – as Max Weber wrote – an "outstanding instrument of financial rationalisation".[31] Procurement allowed the authorities to rely on a given sum for a relatively long period, and this opened the possibility of building up a long-term state debt. In addition, taxpayers' anger was focused on the toll collectors rather than government representatives, as was the case during the initial stages of the uprisings in the Mezzogiorno in the 1640s. The contractors represented investors who could be required to make further advances of money – in the form of loans – to the government, which exerted some pressure to draw money from this undoubtedly advantaged group of characters. A local contractor was able to minimise the transaction costs represented by gathering information on the goods and activities to be taxed, controlling the movement of goods, consumption and production. The tangle of different tariffs (between capital, city, county, lay, ecclesiastical, etc.), moreover, dictated the establishment of small-scale tax-farmers that conformed to the social, economic and institutional structure of the state. From the perspective of the patronage system, networks of tax collectors and government officials found themselves mutually supporting each other in the need for control of territory and extraction of monetary resources. Beyond the profits generated by tax-farming activity, the function opened various avenues of access to state and local apparatuses, strengthened the grip on the territory and consequently created client relationships both downward and upward, and allowed for the availability of cash that only later was destined for the state treasury. The social profit could turn out to be far greater than merely economic.

The weight of such characters appears to be much more evident in the Mezzogiorno than in the Papal States and the center-north of the peninsula. This is probably due to greater scholarly attention to the central role of tax-farmers in the kingdom's financial system. Indeed, it is undeniable that they were extremely important in other states as well; however, they were perhaps not as inherent in the public debt system as had come to be the case in the Mezzogiorno. The close link between tax-farmers and public debt, however, also emerges in the State of Milan. Although specific research is lacking – at least to my knowledge – such persons are called upon to provide advances or loans using as collateral the taxes they are contracted to collect. This implies that in both the Neapolitan and Lombard cases, state revenues are severely diminished due to tax alienations.

Debt systems

As is well known, the money that the state was able to obtain from taxpayers was employed, sooner or later, directly or indirectly, in warfare. The need to borrow was obviously widely shared by all governments, but the methods of obtaining it differed.[32] During the late Middle Ages, the major cities of central and northern Italy instituted a system of financing based on the imposition of forced loans on citizens on the tax rolls. As is well known, citizens were forced to lend an amount of money in relation to their assessed wealth or income and in return received interest (usually 5 percent per year) until the principal was repaid. In the state of Milan, on the other hand, the duke sold (or rather, alienated tax revenues) by granting purchasers the right to collect from taxpayers the money equivalent to the interest on the amount paid to the treasury. Alongside the system of compulsory loans, there was also voluntary borrowing, short-term and with an interest rate of around 14 percent, which supplemented the deficit financing. The traditional borrowing constituted by compulsory loans, however, encountered a series of crises throughout the fifteenth century so they gradually became less and less exploited by governments. Naturally, borrowed capital was rarely repaid and debts were consolidated.

Beginning in the early sixteenth century, governments began to enter the free capital market by issuing loans to be placed among voluntary investors. Governments of city-states (Genoa, Venice and Florence) sold bonds whose interest was paid from tax revenues, while in the Habsburg territories of the Peninsula the main route was the alienation of taxes. The case of the papal state is interesting: although it belonged to the category of monarchies and employed as customary the services of merchants and bankers as providers of credit, from the early 1500s it began to sell securities on the market with considerable success, following the model of the large cities.

The two financing systems – the sale of securities and the alienation of taxes – are significantly different. The former generally appeals to the market, considering all potential investors equal; the latter, in addition to securing a financial annuity, also adds an advantage for the buyer, who can – if provided – exercise the right to collect the tax in a place, perhaps where he already owns land and has peasants at his service. In this case, there is a strong attraction to investing in an annuity that can also take on significant political weight. In addition, it is likely that selling shares of annuities disposed of on the secondary market is less smooth than with securities. The regular annuity payment of the former depends first and foremost on the financial capacity of the taxed communities, and despite the government's commitment to support the creditors' arguments, it could happen that they were not regularly paid, while the payment of the latter depended solely on the government's choices.

Figure 3.1 shows the prevailing nominal interest rates at whichthe peninsular governments borrowed.

The data show a trend common to the whole of Europe, already known to scholars. After a rising phase in the sixteenth century, from the second quarter of the seventeenth century the interest rate declined. On the reasons for the decline in the cost of money, various hypotheses can be proposed: from the improvement in the efficiency of financial markets to the increasing imports of American precious metals to Europe, to the institutional framework, which generates positive expectations for the future and thus induces savings. In the specific case of interest rates on government debts, as is well known, there has been an interesting debate that initially focused on England between the seventeenth and eighteenth centuries. The Glorious Revolution would have generated, through the strengthening of property rights and the elimination of Crown discretion, a favourable institutional environment so as to make the English government a credible debtor. On the other hand, some emphasise the role of the government's increased fiscal capacity, which, by means of a harsh tax policy, was able to rake in substantial resources to reassure and satisfy its creditors. The Italian peninsula offers ample case studies to test the two different approaches to the debtor state problem.

Figure 3.1 shows that different governments paid different amounts on their loans. During the Cyprus War Venice paid 8 percent on its loans while in the middle of the following century, during the War of Candia, the rate was 6 percent; the Spanish governor of Milan in the mid-sixteenth century alienated revenues at 10–12 percent and a century later the rate was halved; a similar trend for the kingdom of Naples (9 percent to 4–5 percent) can be seen; while Genoa, Florence and Rome were not involved in significant conflicts. In the seventeenth century, therefore, borrowing proved to be cheaper than in the past. Of course, it must be considered that military apparatuses were expanding, thus nullifying interest rate savings. A further observation concerns the relationship between different interest rates and the economic and financial environment of different states.

Prominent in the picture is the position of Genoa, steadily holding the best position compared to the rest of the governments. The Ligurian city was brimming with money, coming from various marketplaces in Europe, especially Spanish money, which flowed to Genoa thanks to the efficient network of merchant-bankers who controlled the exchange system and strategically occupied the nodes of the money routes. Genoa's secret has been attributed to the House of St George, a

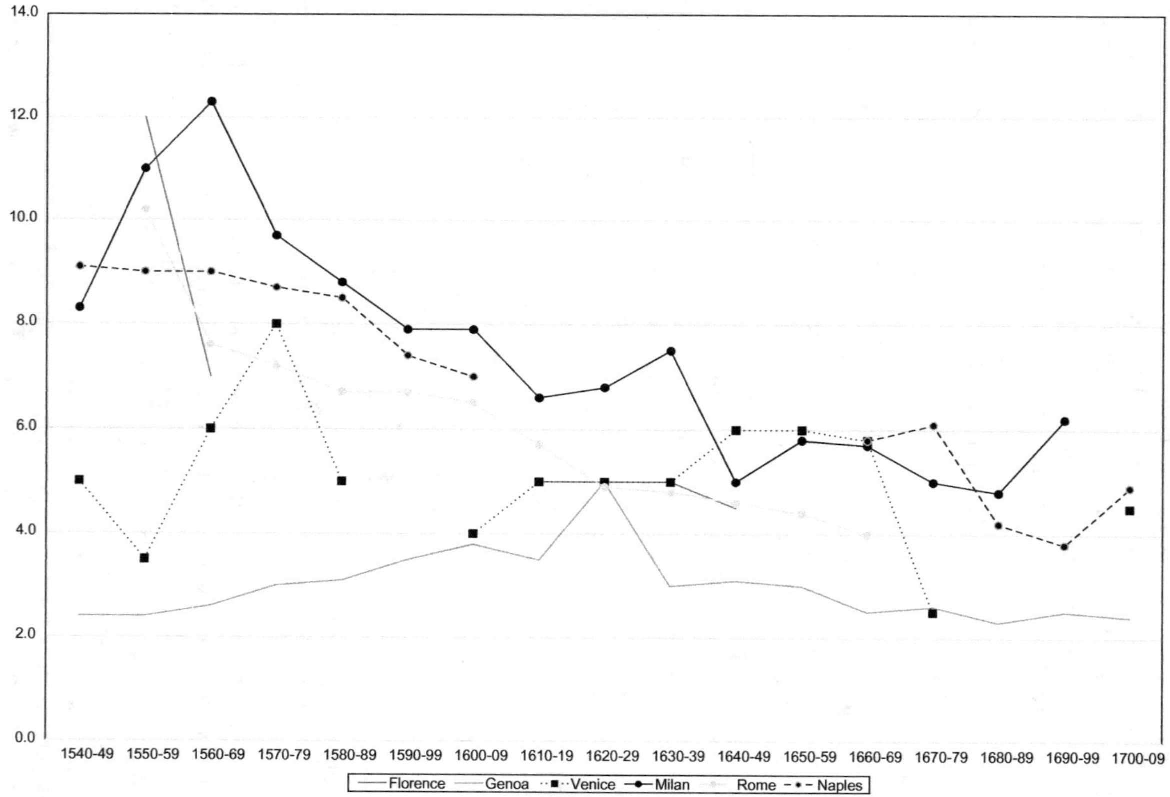

Figure 3.1 Nominal interest rate paid by Italian governments on their securities, 1540–1709.

Source: Author's database.

consortium formed by the state's creditors that managed the bulk of the tax revenues allocated to interest payments. The obvious identity between creditors of the state and controllers of the flow of resources allocated to debt service made Genoa a secure debtor, controlled by its creditor. Genoa's secret was not so much that it was a republic as that it assigned the consortium of creditors to manage the money intended for themselves. It is unlikely, however, that this mechanism would have worked efficiently if Genoa had been involved in long, tiresome conflicts, as happened to other states.

In fact, the case of the papal state, the other most reliable debtor, demonstrates the close relationship between creditors' involvement in debt service management mechanisms and the international political environment. From the mid-1600s onward, the rate of the papal bonds gradually decreased to 4 percent and at the same time attracted foreign investors, particularly from Genoa and Florence. Unlike Genoa, papal finance had to bear both the costs of the popes' grandiose policy of conspicuous consumption and the provision of aid and subsidies to Catholic powers engaged against Protestants in France and Eastern Europe and against the Ottomans in the eastern Mediterranean and the Balkans. As in Genoa, representatives of the investors were assembled in Colleges that were responsible for collecting taxes and distributing the money among all bondholders.

The Apostolic Chamber sold annuities at a relatively modest rate on the open capital market. Although the first issuance was limited, in later years, especially from 1550 onward, the system took off, so that the *Monti* became the bulk of papal financial activity. The *Monti* can be considered an important step towards true public debt: first, the loans were freely subscribed by investors; secondly, interest payments were assigned on clear and reliable tax revenues; and thirdly, the lending system took on the characteristics of true financed debt (low interest rate and long-term bonds). The role of bankers, however, continued to be relevant; they acted as intermediaries between the government and ordinary investors, and could closely monitor financial inflows from the Papal state and Catholic countries. Despite being a monarchy and lacking central representative institutions, the Papacy was considered a reliable debtor. Several factors helped build such creditworthiness. The advantages (including financial benefits) enjoyed by the Holy See as a perpetual, supranational institution; the absence of notable bankruptcies from at least the 1530s onward; the role of bankers as intermediaries while also being involved in the state's fiscal machine as controllers of the health of public finances; and, again, the lack of heavy and lasting military involvement, so that the papal treasury could fully honour its debt.

Venice, on the other hand, maintained the direct management of debt servicing. After the severe difficulties of compulsory loans in the fifteenth century, the government offered securities on the open market, while compulsory loans were not abandoned but played a secondary role. The sixteenth century, marked by numerous conflicts both in Italy and in the eastern Mediterranean, ended with the grandiose elimination of public debt. The absence of debt in the Venetian balance sheets was short-lived, as the early years of the next century saw new war commitments;

however, the repayment of capital had earned the Lion Republic great confidence among potential investors.

As for the Kingdom of Naples, the financial situation precipitated in the early seventeenth century and then reached a state of deep crisis during the final phase of the Thirty Years' War. Although the State of Milan had been heavily involved in Habsburg politics, the consequences of fiscal pressure seem to have been less devastating. Probably military spending largely benefited Lombardy, thus mitigating the impact of taxation.

The Florentine case presents one of the few examples of constitutional change in early modern Italy. Beginning in 1530, at the fall of the last Florentine republic, the Medici dynasty ascended the throne and held it until 1734. The constitutional change represented by the founding of the principality would seem to corroborate the neo-institutional model of degrading the financial market to an autocratic regime. And indeed, in the 1550s Cosimo I turned to foreign companies and private financiers to support the war effort against Siena. Interest rates were quite high, hovering around 12 percent. Within a few years the government launched bonds on the free capital market that offered yields in line with the best markets in the Peninsula. Despite the low level of institutional representativeness, the cost of money in Florence was by no means higher than elsewhere, and, at least until the end of the seventeenth century, the grand ducal finances were not under severe strain.

Conclusions

The Italian cases prompt some general considerations about the links between institutional structure and finance. First, the considerable tax-raising capacity of governments between the sixteenth and seventeenth centuries undoubtedly supported the increase in debt, but did not reassure investors, as in the cases of the Habsburg dominions, where interest rates – both those on alienated revenues and those at the Bisenzone fairs – were generally higher than those paid by other governments. The heavy hand of the exchequer created several serious problems in the relations between subjects and governments and triggered the widespread structural indebtedness of communities, a phenomenon that was common, however, throughout Western Europe. Similarly, the marked decrease in the interest rate throughout the seventeenth century was not the result of greater state fiscal efficiency, but rather a phenomenon in a framework common to the entire continent.

Secondly, the ability to levy taxes was determined not so much by the degree of centralisation of state sovereignty as by the pursuit of policies of negotiation and compromise with local bodies and cooperation with provincial institutions.

Thirdly, the differences between republics and principalities were much deeper in the late Middle Ages than in the Early Modern Age. The former had instituted the system of forced loans, which turned out to be a powerful tool for financing war but then collapsed because of continuing war commitments. In the principalities, the close link between the state treasury and the merchant-bankers who provided financial services was maintained, but the range of debt instruments widened significantly with the mechanism of the sale of tax revenues and, in the Roman case, in the establishment of the *Monti*. The pope's monarchy demonstrates that a well-managed and stakeholder-inclusive debt system was as efficient as the debt system in a republic. The real difference in early modern Italy can be recognised between the territories under the Habsburg Crown and the independent ones, in terms of persistent fiscal demand in the former versus the latter.

Fourthly, the previous point brings us to the question of the Spanish presence in Italy. As far as financial history is concerned, the foundations of fiscal-financial systems were established during the thirteenth and fourteenth centuries, while new taxes were introduced thereafter, but they did not change the previous structural setting. Similarly, the financial instruments of the Crown of Aragon were not exported to the cities of the Mezzogiorno. Likewise, Louis XII of France, having conquered Milan, did not introduce fiscal instruments of his kingdom. The fiscal-financial sphere, in short, was a delicate matter, to be treated with extreme caution so as not to alienate local elites.

Fifthly, the fundamental financial innovations developed in the bustling mercantile world of late medieval Italy did not bring significant improvements to government deficit financing mechanisms, despite the early establishment of consolidated debt. The formation of a secondary market for debt securities offered enormous speculative opportunities for cash holders and facilitated transactions without the use of cash, but this did not represent a consistent benefit to government coffers.

What state emerges from this overview of the Italian peninsula? Regarding the evolution of the domain state to the fiscal state as proposed by Schumpeter and further articulated in Bonney and Ormrod's taxonomy,[33] the Italian cases of the early modern age already show an established fiscal structure that draws limited resources from state property and relies largely on taxes. The close relationship between war and state building is evident in some states, such as the republics of Florence and Venice and the duchy of Milan, but it seems to me that we need to go back to the period between the fourteenth and fifteenth centuries to find some structural connections. The late Renaissance and Baroque periods saw the progressive involvement of the Habsburg territories on the peninsula in imperial politics, with varying effects and only the duchy of Savoy seems to follow the fiscal-military path modelled on Britain. Tuscany retained a rather limited military structure as did the Church state, which increased its revenues due to its grandiose building policy and financial aid to Catholic governments. After all, it is not easy to determine the degree of absolutism of a government by employing parameters such as increased bureaucratic personnel and volume of receipts. What can be said is that negotiation and compromise were the fundamental elements of fiscal relations between governments and elites, urban, rural and feudal, and that the result was a moderate increase in state revenues. The exception to this rule, that is the excessive prevalence of one party over the others, led to riots, fiscal crises and ultimately to a less dynamic society.

Notes

1 Elias, 2000: 268.
2 Clamageran, 1867: I, 483–89; Lassalmonie, 2002.
3 Hintze, 1975: 180–215.
4 Tilly, 1975 and Tilly, 1990.
5 Brewer, 1988; Downing, 1992; Ertman, 1997.
6 Storrs, 2009.
7 Hespanha, 1987.
8 See, in this regard, as early as 1960 the essay of J. Vicens Vives, 'Estructura administrativa estatal en los siglos XVI y XVII', republished in Albareda Salvadó and Janué i Miret, 2011: pp. 31–56; and later, Elliott, 1992: 48–71; and Blockmans, 1993: 1–14.
9 Gamberini and Lazzarini, 2012.
10 For what follows, Felloni, 1999: 199–296.
11 Chabod, 1971: 238 ff.
12 Zappa, 1995: 392.
13 Vigo, 1979.
14 Di Tullio, 2011: 27–28.
15 Rizzo, 2001; Buono, 2009.
16 Pezzolo, 2006.
17 Del Torre, 1986: 68–83.
18 Pezzolo, 2014: 293–305.
19 Bauer, 1928: 457–503; Partner, 1980: 17–62; Stumpo, 1985, Gardi, 1986: 509–57.
20 Calabria, 1991.
21 De Rosa, 1987.
22 Giuffrida, 1999; Cancila, 2001; Ligresti, 1997.
23 Felloni, 1999: I.
24 Malanima, 1998: 91–126.
25 De Luca, 2013: I, 185–95.
26 Piola Caselli, 2012: 330–31.
27 For wages, Rota and Weisdorf, 2020: 931–60.
28 Lindert, 2004: I, 35.
29 Kiser and Kane, 2001: 183–223.
30 See, for example, Stumpo, 19855: 142–43.
31 Weber, 2011: 256.
32 This part summarises some of the findings of my monograph *Mars and Pluto*.
33 Bonney and Ormrod, 1999: 1–20.

Bibliography

Andrés Ucendo, José Ignacio, and Lanza García, Ramón (2008), "Estructura y evolución de los ingresos de la Real Hacienda de Castilla en el siglo XVII", *Studia Historica. Historia Moderna*, 30, pp. 147–90.

Assereto, Giovanni (2007), *La città fedelissima: Savona e il governo genovese tra XVI e XVIII secolo*, Savona: Ferraris.

Bauer, Clemens (1928), "Die Epochen der Papstfinanz. Ein Versuch", *Historische Zeitschrift*, 138, pp. 457–503.

Blockmans, Wim (1993), "Les origins des états modernes en Europe, XIIIe-XVIIIs siècles: état de la question et perspectives", in W. Blockmans and Jean-Philippe Genet, eds., *Visions sur le développement des États éuropéens. Théories et historiographies de lÉtat moderne*, Rome: École Française de Rome, pp. 1–14.

Bonney, Richard and Ormrod, W.R. (1999), "Crises, Revolutions and Self-Sustained Growth: Towards a Conceptual Model of Change in Fiscal History", in Richard Bonney and William R. Ormrod, eds., *Crises, Revolutions and Self-Sustained Growth*, Stamford, CA: Watkins Publishing, pp. 1–20.

Brewer, John (1988), *The Sinews of Power. War, Money and the English State, 1688–1783*, London: Century Hutchinson.

Buono, Alessandro (2009), *Esercito, istituzioni territorio. Alloggiamenti militari e «case herme» nello Stato di Milano (secoli XVI e XVII)*, Firenze: Firenze University Press.

Calabria, Antonio (1991), *The Cost of Empire. The Finances of the Kingdom of Naples in the Time of Spanish Rule*, Cambridge: Cambridge University Press.

Cancila, Rossella (2001), *Fisco, ricchezza, comunità nella Sicilia del Cinquecento*, Roma: Istituto per la storia dell'età moderna e contemporanea.

Chabod, Federico (1971), *Storia di Milano nell'epoca di Carlo V*, Torino: Einaudi.

Clamageran, Jean-Jules (1867), *Histoire de l'impôt en France*, Paris: Guillaumin.

De Luca, Giuseppe (2013), "Milanese Finance, 1348–1700", in Gerard Caprio, ed., *Handbook of Key Global Financial Markets, Institutions, and Infraestructure*, Oxford: Elsevier, I, pp. 185–195.

De Rosa, Luigi (1987), *Il Mezzogiorno spagnolo tra crescita e decadenza*, Milano: Il Saggiatore.

Del Torre, Giuseppe (1986), *Venezia e la Terraferma dopo la guerra di Cambrai. Fiscalità e amministrazione (1515–1530)*, Milano: FrancoAngeli.

Di Tullio, Marco (2011), "L'estimo di Carlo V (1543–1599) e il perticato del 1558. Per un riesame delle riforme fiscali nello Stato di Milano del secondo cinquecento", *Società e storia*, 131, pp. 1–35.

Downing, Brian (1992), *The Military Revolution and Political Change: Origins of Democracy and Autocracy in Early Modern Europe*, Princeton, NJ: Princeton University Press.

Elias, Norbert (2000), *The Civilizing Process: Sociogenetic and Psychogenetic Investigations*, London: Blackwell.

Elliott, John H. (1992), "A Europe a Composite Monarchies", *Past and Present*, 137, pp. 48–71.

Ertman, Thomas (1997), *Birth of the Leviathan: Building States and Regimes in Medieval and Early Modern Europe*, Cambridge: Cambridge University Press.

Felloni, Giuseppe (1999), *Scritti di storia economica*, Genova: Società Ligure di Storia Patria.

Gamberini, Andrea and Lazzarini, Isabella, eds. (2012), *The Italian Renaissance State*, Cambridge: Cambridge University Press.

Gardi, A. (1986), "La fiscalità pontificia tra medioevo ed età moderna", *Società e storia*, 33, pp. 509–57.

Giuffrida, Antonino (1999), *La finanza pubblica nella Sicilia del '500*, Caltanisetta: Sciascia.

Hespanha, Antonio Manuel (1987), As *vésperas do Leviathan. Instituições e poder politico. Portugal, séc. XVII* , Lisboa: Instituto de Ciências Sociais.

Hintze, Otto (1975), *Historical Essays*, Oxford: Oxford University Press.

Kiser, Edgar and Kane, Joshua (2001), "Revolution and State Structure: The Bureaucratization of Tax Administration in Early Modern England and France", *American Journal of Sociology*, 107, pp. 183–223.

Lassalmonie, Jean-François (2002), *La boîte à l'enchanteur. Politique financière de Louis XI*, Paris: Comité pour l'histoire économique et financière de la France.

Ligresti, Domenico (1997), *Governo e territorio nella Sicilia moderna*, Catania: Cooperativa Universitaria Catanese di Magistero.

Lindert, Peter (2004), *Growing Public: Social Spending and Economic Growth since the Eighteenth Century*, Cambridge: Cambridge University Press.

Malanima, Paolo (1998), "Italian Cities, 1300–1800: A Quantitative Approach", *Rivista di storia economica*, 14, pp. 91–126.

Partner, Peter (1980), "Papal Financial Policy in the Renaissance and Counter-Reformation", *Past and Present*, 88, pp. 17–62.

Pezzolo, Luciano (2006), *Una finanza d'ancien régime. La repubblica di Venezia fra XV e XVIII secolo*, Napoli: Edizioni Scientifiche Italiane.

Pezzolo, Luciano (2014), "Note sulla finanza dello stato fiorentino, 1350–1700", in A. Fornasin and C. Povolo, eds., *Per Furio: Studi in onore di Furio Bianco*, Udine: Forum, pp. 293–305.

Pezzolo, Luciano (forthcoming), *Mars and Pluto.* Oxford: Oxford University Press.

Piola Caselli, Fausto (2012), "The Formation of Fiscal States in Italy: The Papal States", in Bartomolé Yun Casalilla and Patrick Karl O'Brien, eds., *The Rise of fiscal States: A Global History 1500–1914*, Cambridge: Cambridge University Press, pp. 285–303.

Rizzo, Mario (2001), *Alloggiamenti militari e riforme fiscali nella Lombardia spagnola tra Cinque e Seicento*, Milano: Unicopli.

Rota, Mauro and Weisdorf, Jacob (2020), "Italy and the Little Divergence in Wages and Prices: New Data, New Results", *Journal of Economic History*, 80, pp. 931–960.

Storrs, Christopher, ed. (2009), *The Fiscal-Military State in Eighteenth-Century Europe*, Farnham: Ashgate.

Stumpo, Enrico (1985), *Il capitale finanziario a Roma fra Cinque e Seicento. Contributo alla storia della fiscalità pontificia in età moderna (1570-1660)*, Milano: Giuffrè.

Thompson, Irving A.A (1994), "Castile: Polity, Fiscality, and Fiscal Crisis", in P. Hoffman and K. Norberg, eds., *Fiscal Crises, Liberty, and Representative Government, 1450–1789*, Stanford, CA: Stanford University Press.

Tilly, Charles, ed. (1975), *The Formation of National States in Western Europe*, Princeton, NJ: Princeton University Press.

Tilly, Charles (1990), *Coercion, Capital, and European States, AD 990–1990*, Oxford: Blackwell.

Vicens Vives, Jaime (2011), "Estructura administrativa estatal en los siglos XVI y XVII", in J. Albareda Salvadó and M. Janué i Miret, eds., *El nacimiento y la contrucción del estado moderno*, Valencia: Universidad de Valencia, pp. 31–56.

Vigo, Giovanni (1979), *Fisco e società nella Lombardia del Cinquecento*, Bologna: Il Mulino.

Weber, Max (2011), *Wirtschaftsgeschichte*, Berlin: Duncker & Humblot.

Zappa, Anita (1995), "Le lotte e i contrasti per la realizzazione dell'estimo generale dello Stato di Milano", in Paolo Pissavino and GianVittorio Signorotto, eds., *Lombardia borromaica, Lombardia Spagnola, 1554–1659*, Roma: Bulzoni, pp. 383–403.

4 Fiscal crisis and public debt in Castile at the end of the reign of Charles V

Sergio Sardone

The imperial decline, between the rise of Philip and the military defeat

The failure of the siege of Metz between October 1552 and January 1553 marked the beginning of the Emperor's decline. Faced with the great difficulties of those years, gout and the spectre of bankruptcy, Caesar seriously considered the possibility of abdicating the thrones of Austria, Burgundy and Spain. The Empire was divided by the extension of the Protestant Reformation, war with France had broken out again, and the Turks were again threatening Hungary and Austria, while Barbary pirates were ravaging the Mediterranean.[1] England was not in a better situation: after the Act of Succession of 1544 by which Henry VIII had created the Anglican Church, there was an economic and social crisis. When he died three years later and his son Edward VI Tudor ascended the throne at the age of ten, the government was left in the hands of John Dudley, Duke of Northumberland, the strongman of England who, with the measures adopted against the Catholic Church, aggravated the recession that hit the country. Edward's early death in the summer of 1553 changed the international political scene in favour of Charles V, who immediately offered his support to his cousin Mary Tudor to overcome the resistance of the nobility led by Dudley and the Duke of Suffolk, Henry Grey, his relative. They tried to place Jane Grey on the throne, but seven days later Mary was crowned Queen of England and soon after her marriage was arranged with Prince Philip, her second cousin, who became king consort the following year. However, the reign ended in November 1558.[2] Through this marriage, the emperor had tried to promote the creation of a new state in northern Europe composed of his possessions in the Netherlands and the Kingdom of England and the British dominions belonging to the Tudors. This would also have helped to strengthen the Habsburg position in the English Channel.

The course of the imperial transition from Charles to his son Philip was rather long and complicated, due to the numerous wars and rebellions that broke out across European and American territories. The transition had begun well in advance, perhaps as early as October 1540 with the "secret" transfer of the Duchy of Milan to the future Prudent King, which had been definitively in Spanish hands following the death without an heir of the last Duke Francis II Sforza in 1535 and the victory over France in the conflict that broke out the following year. However,

DOI: 10.4324/9781003653301-5

Philip's official recognition was delayed until 1548 when he travelled to Italy to take possession of the duchy, while in Castile his sister, Maria of Austria, recently married to her cousin Maximilian, Archduke of Austria who later became emperor,[3] remained as regent. On the occasion of their marriage, Charles had granted them – in addition to titles and assets in the states of Bohemia and Hungary – a dowry of 200,000 Castilian ducats and the legitimate dowry of 100,000 that was due to Mary as heiress of the Empress Isabella of Avis, which were to be paid in the year following the wedding, celebrated in Valladolid on 13 September 1548.[4] However, the emperor had enormous difficulties in fulfilling these commitments, to the point that he extinguished his dowry debt by issuing *juros* at 7.14% in December 1556 and redefined the amounts of the legitimate dowries, distributing them unequally among his three legitimate children.[5]

Meanwhile, the change in the regency of Castile was part of an international political context that had become very complicated since 1548 because of the growing tensions in the Holy Roman Empire, in Italy and in northern Europe, which the King of France, Henry II of Valois, was trying to exploit by provoking a new cycle of wars, and because of the dispute between the Habsburgs over Charles' claim to facilitate the succession in favour of Philip, not only to the kingdoms of Spain, but also to that of the Netherlands and the Empire, at the expense in this case of the interests of Ferdinand and Maximilian.[6] Friction among the Habsburgs therefore grew due to conflicting plans for the division of the imperial inheritance. Maximilian maintained the most rigid position for fear of being left with only the title of archduke and without important territories, so he decided to leave Castile, leaving his wife as governor in Spain and return to the court of Vienna. Tensions were reduced in March 1551 thanks to a first compromise that did not exclude the succession to the imperial throne of Ferdinand, King of the Romans since 1531, leaving the free choice by the Germanic princes still open. Meanwhile, the Spanish inheritance was resolved in favour of Charles and, consequently, of Philip after Queen Joanna's death in April 1555.

His stays in northern Italy and Flanders in 1548–1549 and his brief return to Milan in June 1551 enabled Philip to confirm his recognition as Duke of Burgundy by the States General of Flanders and that of Duke of Milan. In the summer of 1551, the prince returned to Castile to assume the regency again.[7] In October 1553, negotiations for the marriage to Mary Tudor were concluded, culminating in the wedding in July 1554 that made him king consort of England.[8] It took Philip five years to return to Castile in 1559, when he was already king, and once the peace of Cateau-Cambrésis was concluded, which followed the victory of San Quintín in August 1557. With Philip away from Spain, his sister Joanna, dowager queen of Portugal, assumed the regency of the kingdoms of Castile and Aragon. In those five years Joanna had to face serious internal problems, in particular those of a fiscal and financial nature that led to the suspension of payments by the Royal Treasury of Castile on 17 April 1557, the first of the three decreed by Prudent King.[9]

Succession to the thrones and imperial dignity was an additional problem that Charles V had to try to solve. The most pressing were the armed conflicts, which absorbed resources in all territories, particularly in Castile, Naples and Milan, where the *mensuale was* reintroduced, an initially extraordinary tax to finance the war that served to cover the growing deficits of the Milanese state.[10] In Peru, the publication of the New Laws of 1542 provoked a rebellion two years later that would not be resolved until 1548 with the defeat of Gonzalo Pizarro's henchmen and the pacifying mission of the new viceroy of Peru, Don Pedro de la Gasca, who was able to return to Castile in September 1550 with an important treasure that served to meet the Emperor's growing need for silver.

In 1546, war broke out against the Schmalkaldic League formed by some of the Lutheran princes. The imperial victory at Mühlberg in April 1547 and the capitulation of Wittenberg did not prevent the conflict from continuing as a result of the intervention of the troops of Henry II of France in October 1552 and the consequent siege of the city of Metz, which forced the emperor to flee in January 1553 and thus suffer one of the most difficult moments of his reign. The war with the Lutheran princes ended with the Peace of Augsburg in 1555 which recognised the principle "*Cuius regio, eius religio*" according to which the subjects followed the religion of their princes, and they thus achieved the same status as the Catholic states of the Empire.

In Italy, the 1550s were also characterised by tensions and confrontations with alternating results. A first war front opened in 1551 with the War of Parma because of the emperor's claim to take over the duchy after the assassination four years earlier of Duke Pier Luigi Farnese, grandson of Pope Paul III. The imperial army, under the command of the governor of Milan, Ferrante Gonzaga, took Piacenza, provoking the reaction and resentment of Octavian Farnese, the emperor's son-in-law, following his marriage to Margaret of Austria. Contributing to the conflict was the position of the new pope, Julius III, who decided to support Octavian militarily, and the invasion of Piedmont by the army of Henry II of France, with the intention of marching on Milan. The dispute between Charles and Octavian was resolved in May 1552, although official recognition as Duke of Parma took place in Ghent four and a half years later, in September 1556.

The second Italian war front emerged in 1555 with the ascension to the papal throne of Paul IV, the Neapolitan Gian Pietro Carafa, who in September closed a secret military alliance with France, willing to support him with more than 12,000 soldiers. Aware of the danger of these manoeuvres, Charles and Philip decided to send the Duke of Alba, Fernando Álvarez de Toledo, to Italy, first as the new governor of Milan and then, from 1556, as viceroy of Naples to strengthen the defence of the kingdom. In a short time the Spanish army invaded the Papal States, forcing Paul IV to a first armistice – not respected – and a definitive agreement signed at Cave on 13 September 1557, barely a month after the Spanish victory at San Quentin.

There was also no lack of tensions in Aragon, coinciding with the abdication of Charles in 1556, the absence of Philip and the withdrawal of the viceroy, Per Afán de Ribera, which led to a new convocation of the courts in 1559, although they did not disappear completely until 1566.[11]

The African front was in fact sacrificed by the emperor, until it became the most dangerous for the Spanish kingdoms due to the numerous incursions of Barbary pirates on the Spanish coasts. In addition, from 1548 Sultan Suleiman advanced in Barbary with an imposing campaign that allowed the Sa'di occupation of Fez. However, it was not until 1554 that it was decided to undertake a military intervention at the expense of the Castilian treasury, the cost of which had to be added to the 150,000 ducats per year required for the maintenance of the prisons in Africa, from Melilla to Oran, passing through Mazalquivir and La Goleta de Tunisia. This did not prevent Bujía from falling definitively into Ottoman hands in 1555. In August of the following year, Oran suffered a siege that ended with the flight of the Turks and the recovery of Tremecén by the Spanish.[12]

Once tranquillity was restored in the Empire and Queen Joanna died on 12 April 1556, Charles was able to accelerate the abdication process. On 22 October he renounced the sovereign powers of the Order of the "Golden Fleece". Three days later, in the great hall of the castle of Brussels, the official handover of the dominions of the Netherlands to Philip, already seated on the thrones of Naples and England, took place. On 16 January 1556 he also transferred sovereignty over Castile, Aragon, Sicily and the Indies to his son, saying goodbye on 28 August in Ghent, his native city. Charles disembarked in Laredo on 28 September, going slowly through Castile until he reached Jarandilla de la Vera in November. Here he stayed in the castle of the Count of Oropesa, Fernando Álvarez de Toledo, before settling permanently on 3 February 1557 in the house next to the monastery of the Hieronymites of Yuste, where he died on 21 September 1558. On 12 March, six months earlier, his brother Ferdinand had been proclaimed Holy Roman Emperor by the Teutonic prince electors.[13]

The main tax revenues: The role of the treasury of Castile

All of the aforementioned political and military events that occurred between 1548 and 1556 had an enormous impact on the finances of Castile because they caused a growth in public spending and debt in the short and long-term that the two suspensions of payments of 1557 and 1560 entailed. In fact, as early as 1556 all ordinary income was practically mortgaged with the interest on the debt. From then on, Philip II was able to increase revenues by raising the rates of existing taxes and creating new ones, or by alienating public offices, without the authorisation of the Castilian Cortes.[14]

In 1554, the ordinary revenues of Castile, all leased, amounted to about 510 million maravedís, having increased by 1.7% annually from 470 million in 1550. Among the ordinary revenues, the main one was the general heading of *alcabalas* and *tercias* , which contributed 65% of the total with 333.6 million per year, an amount that had been fixed in the Cortes of Madrid in 1551–1552 and to which the contribution of the city of Valladolid was added as of 1553.[15] Despite its importance, this income was almost entirely absorbed by the long-term debt service, i.e. the *situado* or returns of *juros*, which in that year of 1554 reached 329 million and in 1560 70% more with 559 million.[16]

In addition to the ordinary revenues, the Crown could count on the *servicios* (aid) granted by the Cortes, the rents and pastures of the *Maestrazgos* , the papal graces, that is, the Crusade bull and the Ecclesiastical Subsidy, and, finally, the income from the American treasury received by the *Casa de la Contratación* of Seville.

In 1555 there had still been no income from the silver mines of Guadalcanal, discovered in August by two residents of the town who renounced their exploitation in favour of the Crown in exchange for *pensiones*. Agustín de Zárate – who had accompanied Prince Felipe to England – was the first person in charge of the administration of the mines, being assisted by Pedro Luis de Torregrosa, appointed depositary in December of that year. The income from the mines from November 1555 to the first of June 1556 amounted to almost 103 million maravedís, exceeding 135 million by the end of the year.[17]

From 1548 onwards, the Cortes of Valladolid requested the perpetuation of the heading of *alcabalas* or, failing that, a new extension of at least ten years to prevent the value of the contribution from rising in the meantime. In exchange, they granted the king a new extraordinary *servicio* of 154 million for the three-year period of 1549–1551, to which 100 million per year had to be added from the ordinary *servicio*. By accumulated value, the service was the second most important income of the revenues granted by the Cortes, which guaranteed an average annual flow of 150–154 million, as will be explained later.

Among the main revenues of the Crown were those of the papal graces of the Crusade and the Subsidy, to which the *Excusado* – the main tithe house of each parish – was added in 1567. The first two contributed a lot of money to the imperial cause, particularly in the four years from 1552 to 1555. The revenue of maravedís for His Majesty collected in the preaching of the bull of St. Peter and of several jubilees in the triennia of 1552–1554 and 1555–1557 amounted to 298 and 271.7 million in each, which yielded annual averages of 99.3 and 90.5 million maravedis respectively.[18] In the previous years, from 1548 to 1551, the total corresponding to His Majesty could be estimated at 453 million, which, spread over four years, amounts to 113.2 million per year (Table 4.1). According to this trend, the returns from the preaching of the bulls were worsening and yielding less than in the first years of the decade, probably due to the worsening of the fiscal crisis at the end of the reign.

The Ecclesiastical Subsidy provided a cumulative income of more than 102 million maravedís, with the clergy of Seville, Toledo, Cuenca, Tarragona and Aragon contributing the largest share, as noted below (Table 4.5).

The income of the General Treasury

The revenues of the General Treasury governed by Alonso de Baeza reached 217.5 million maravedís in 1549, increasing to 494 million in 1551 and reaching the maximum level with 741.7 million maravedís in 1552. In 1553 they remained at a still high level of 735.7 million, gradually declining to around 229.7 million in 1555 (Table 4.1).

Much of this growth was due, on the one hand, to the collection of extraordinary revenues such as *servicios*, the Crusade and the Ecclesiastical Subsidy. The value of the ordinary and extraordinary *servicios* that entered the treasury of Baeza

Table 4.1 Table summarising the main tax revenues and debt of the Royal Treasury of Castile, 1550–1555 (values in millions of maravedís)

Incomes	*1550*	*1551*	*1552*	*1553*	*1554*	*1555*	*Total*	*Average*
Ordinary revenues	470.6	471.5	476.1	500.5	500.0	500.0	2,918.8	486.5
Servicios (1)	156.5	156.3	160.2	156.5	156.6	161.0	947.0	157.8
Maestrazgos	75.8	89.6	89.6	89.6	89.6	93.9	528.1	88.0
Sales of offices, jurisdictions	7.2	2.6	10.2	59.1	15.0	15.4	109.5	18.3
Casa de la Contratación (2)	62.3	847.5	116.8	250.2	522.4	479.7	2,278.8	379.8
– Forced Loans			2.7		224.8	320.0	547.5	91.3
– Other loans (3)	1.9		5.3	9.2	7.5		23.8	4.0
– Royal treasury of Indies	60.4	847.5	108.9	241.0	290.1	159.6	1,707.5	284.6
Cruzada (4)	113.2	113.2	99.3	99.3	99.3	90.5	615.0	102.5
Subsidio eclesiástico			39.6	55.7	6.2	0.8	102.3	17.1
Total	885.6	1,680.7	991.8	1,211.0	1,389.2	1,341.3	7,499.6	1,249.9
Income of Tesorería General	320.8	494.0	741.7	735.7	405.1	229.7	2,926.9	487.8
Service of Juros (*situado*)	323.7	284.4	299.6	291.9	329.3	330.0	1,858.9	309.8
Asientos (paid or renewed) (5)	273.4	699.2	1,664.8	1,369.1	980.6	562.6	5,549.7	925.0
Asientos (negotiated) (6)	231.0	551.3	1,348.2	851.7	471.9	409.4	3,863.5	643.9

Sources: The data on ordinary incomes, maestrazgos and *asientos* come from Carande, 1970: II and III. The data from the *Casa de Contratación*, including the part of loans and forced loans from American remittances come from AGI, Contaduría, 275, N.1-2; 277, N.1-3 and Sardone, 2019b: 58. The data on the General Treasury, on the sales of offices and jurisdictions and on the Ecclesiastical Subsidy come from AGS, Contaduría Mayor de Cuentas, 1st period, 1233, 1252 and 1492. The data on the Crusade come from AGS, Crusade, 442, 450 and 451. We thank Ramón Lanza García for this valuable information. Data on debt service, or situated, come from Sardone, 2019a: 63 and Ulloa, 1963: 130-131.

Notes: (1) Sum effectively paid by the communities of Castile for "ordinary" and "extraordinary" parts; (2) Includes the values of forced loans, of other loans received and the Royal treasures or properties managed by the officials of the *Casa de la Contratación*; (3) Includes also sums sent or lent by the treasury of Castile; (4) Includes the *Bula de San Pedro* and *Jubileos*; (5) Includes the value paid with interest or other financial costs, or the renegotiated amount; (6) Includes the agreed initial value.

reached in the years 1550 and 1552 the value of 170 and 237 million maravedís respectively, compared to an average annual income recorded by the recipients of between 156 and 161 million maravedís. The income of the General Treasury was cancelled in the following years, due to the fact that the treasurer Baeza had already collected, in the first years, a part of the *servicio* in advance, while between 1553 and 1555 the *servicio* collected was almost completely absorbed by the payments allocated to said revenue. Our analysis has shown that the Royal Treasury received a higher amount for ordinary and extraordinary *servicio* than the value set by the Cortes, probably due to demographic growth that had not been taken into account in advance. This aspect will be detailed later.

In addition, the increase in income was due to the graces of the Crusade and the Subsidy, which allowed the entry of just under 550 million maravedís, of which only a part entered through the General Treasury of Baeza.

Short-term debt

Indebtedness was an important component of the crisis at the end of Charles V's reign. The importance of the debt can be seen in the 1,450 million maravedís – equivalent to 3,867,107 ducats – that the treasurer Baeza received in short-term debt and *juros* sold, 63% of which came entirely through loans from institutions and prelates, and also from *socorros* and *asientos* contracted with Genoese, Castilian, German and Flemish merchants and bankers. These short-term loans increased the income of the Treasury and were recorded in certain tax revenues, mainly in *servicios*, but also in the Crusade, the *Maestrazgos* of Santiago, Alcántara and Calatrava, their pastures and minor incomes such as the *moneda forera*.

The *socorros* (loans from individuals) and *asientos* (contracts between the king and the merchants) earned interest of between 11% and 14% per year and went from nothing in 1550 – when it seems that the treasurer Baeza did not receive money for this item – to 70 million in 1551 and 173.7 million in 1552. In the same two years, the Crown was also able to count on another 3.75 million and 69.6 million in loans from ecclesiastical corporations and prelates.[19] In the biennium of 1553–54 the sums received by Baeza for *socorros* and *asientos* reached 327 and 198.9 million, decreasing to 76 million in 1555.

This short-term debt that entered the General Treasury represents a small part of that which the Crown contracted, extinguished or renewed during the period. Carande, after a systematic analysis of the *asientos* of the Caroline reign, indicates a minimum value of 231 million maravedís in *asientos* contracted in 1550 and a maximum of 1,348.2 million maravedís in 1552, compared to 231 and 1,665 million maravedís that in these two years constituted the paid or renewed *asientos*, including the financial costs of interest and exchange.[20]

On the whole, the amount of short-term loans (*socorros*) and *asientos* paid into the Treasury, which was very far from the cumulative amount negotiated, reached maximum levels in 1553 and 1554 with values of 327 and almost 199 million respectively. These values represented 44.5 and 49% of the General Treasurer's revenue in those years (Table 4.1). Very significant is the fact that the difference with respect to the total volume of *asientos* negotiated widened, with the *asientos* linked to bills of exchange sent abroad to support the Crown's expenditure. This growing difference is a symptom of the great financial effort that was being made in Castile to carry out the imperial policy.

Another part of the short-term loans was classified by the Treasury as "loans of grandees and prelates" and, unlike the *asientos*, they did not always produce an additional cost for interest. These were voluntary loans that, according to the initial agreements, were to be repaid in the short term, charged to the kingdom's revenues, basically *servicios* and the Ecclesiastical Subsidy. However, in very specific cases, such as that of the Duke of Escalona, Diego López Pacheco y Enríquez, creditor of 30 million maravedís (80 thousand ducats), the loan would be repaid with the delivery of *juros al quitar*.

In 1551 and 1552, when this type of short-term loan can be detected, the Treasury received a sum of 73.3 million maravedís from 3,750,000 and 69,632,500 maravedís in each of those years. The money came from nobles (54%), political-administrative institutions (15%) and religious institutions (3%), and also from prelates (24%) and from a private individual named Rodrigo Mejía, who contributed 3 million maravedís.

In the first group of lenders, the most prominent was the aforementioned Duke of Escalona, Diego López Pacheco y Enríquez, with 30 million maravedís. He was one of the four members of the nobility who responded to the call of Philip and the Council of Finance, together with the Duchess of Calabria, Mencía de Mendoza with 10,000 ducats, the Count of Ureña, Juan Téllez-Girón, with the same amount, and the Count of Siruela, Gabriel de la Cueva, with 5,000 ducats.

Among the prelates were the archbishops of Toledo and Zaragoza and the bishop of Cuenca with 10,000 ducats each,[21] the archbishop of Valencia with 8,000 ducats and the bishop of Salamanca with another 5,000. There is also evidence of the contribution of 3,800 ducats in two instalments by Diego de Zúñiga, abbot of Santa María Párraces (Segovia), but it has not been possible to clarify whether this sum came from his patrimonial assets or from those of the abbey. On the other hand, more modest were the loans from the three ecclesiastical institutions found, the monastery of Nuestra Señora de Prado in Valladolid, the convent of Las Cuevas in Seville and the chapter of the Church of Seville, which contributed 1,000 ducats, 3,000 and 2,000 respectively.

In addition to prelates and religious institutions, there are also some loans from corporations or persons linked to them. This was the case of the city of Seville and its regions, which advanced 10,000 ducats,[22] the universities of Salamanca and Valladolid, with 8,000 and 1,500 ducats respectively, and the Royal Chancelleries of Valladolid and Granada, whose participation took place through their respective general depositories, Alonso López de Calatayud with 7,387 ducats and Diego de Soria with 3,000 ducats.

Long-term debt

The income from the sale of *juros* was substantial, although less than other items. At the same time that the Crown sold new *juros*, it tried to extinguish some long-term debts previously incurred also through the sale of *juros*. In the following table we summarise the data that refer to the income from the sale of *juros* of different interest rates and the amount reached by the redemption or amortisation of securities by the Crown in the years 1550–1555. The difference between the two items is the outstanding debt, the amount of which ranged from a maximum of 146 million in 1552 to a minimum of 4.8 million in the previous year (Table 4.2). The sale of consolidated debt securities underwent significant increases, especially in the years 1552 and 1553 when it exceeded 182 million maravedís, with an annual average in the six-year period of just over 89 million maravedís, including both the *juros al quitar* in cash, perpetual and for life and the *juros* paid in grain and the "*accretions of juros*".

At the same time, the value of the redemption of *juros*, that is, the amortisation of securities that were cancelled, grew. Accordingly, the year with the highest amortisation was 1551 in which almost 50 million maravedís were recorded in performances, while in 1555 nothing was redeemed. As a result of these two incoming and outgoing movements of *juro* values, the net income of the General Treasury related to the sale of *juros* was on average above 65.6 million maravedís in this period, with maximums in 1552 and 1553.

The extraordinary servicio

Throughout the reign of Charles V, the request for extraordinary aid from the Cortes became more frequent. The ordinary *servicio* was added to the extraordinary

Table 4.2 The sale and redemption of juros made by the treasurer Alonso de Baeza, 1550–1555 (values in millions of maravedís)

	1550	*1551*	*1552*	*1553*	*1554*	*1555*	*Total*	*Average annual*
Position (sale and "accretion" of *juros*)								
Al quitar en dinero								
14,000 el millar (7.14%)	11.9		135.9	81.2	50.1	52.6	331.7	55.3
18,000 el millar (6.25%)			2.7	30.6			33.3	5.5
20,000 el millar (5%)	40.2	23.8					63.9	10.7
25,000 el millar (4%)		29.1	33.4				62.4	10.4
Perpetuos								
30,000 el millar (3.3%)			7.9				7.9	1.3
Al quitar de pan (*)				0.7			0.7	0.1
De por vida en dinero	0.4	0.2		22.7	0.1		23.3	3.9
Acrecimiento de juros	2.5	1.4	2.5	4.7	0.2	0.2	11.6	1.9
Total	55.0	54.5	182.3	139.8	50.4	52.9	534.8	89.1
Disclaimer								
Juros desempeñados	34.3	49.6	35.7	3.6	17.6		140.8	23.5
Juros pendientes	20.7	4.8	146.5	136.2	32.8	52.9	393.9	65.7

Sources: AGS, Contaduría Mayor de Cuentas, 1st period, 1233, 1252 and 1492.

Notes: (*) *Juros* in kind that were usually issued during periods of famine and that guaranteed, instead of payment in cash, annuities of bushels of bread corresponding to the value indicated. On these issues, see Toboso Sánchez, 1987: 36–38 and Sardone, 2018: 237.

servicio and both were converted by the Cortes of Toledo into regular concessions in 1525. In addition to the 154 million maravedís for three years of the former, another 150 million from the latter were collected between 1526 and 1529. The Cortes of Madrid in 1528 granted the emperor, in addition to the 154 millions of ordinary *servicio*, another 50 million of the extraordinary *servicio* that was collected between 1530 and 1532. The Cortes of Madrid in 1534 and those of Valladolid in 1537 did not grant extraordinary *servicios*, although the amount of the ordinary *servicio* rose to 204 million maravedís in each concession, to be collected in three years. The collection took place in the first case between 1535 and 1537 and in the second in 1538 and 1539. From this moment on, the Cortes of Toledo in 1538, those of Valladolid in 1542, 1544 and 1548, and those of Madrid in 1551 established the amount of this contribution at 100 million per year on account of the ordinary *servicio* and another 154 million, divided over the three years, for that of the extraordinary *servicio*.

The collection of these tributes was in the hands of an extensive network of tax collectors distributed throughout the kingdom. In most cases, these were agents or persons linked to the General Treasury who received directly from the local authorities the amount due from the district for which they were responsible. In this regard, it has been possible to identify up to 26 main tax districts, some of them, such as those of Burgos, Castilla and Alcaraz, Galicia, Jaén-Calatrava or Valladolid, divided into minor districts, later called *partidos*.

The average values of the ordinary and extraordinary *servicio* for the period 1550–1555 are shown in Table 4.3. The Crown received values between 156 and 160 million per year for ordinary and extraordinary *servicio*, respectively. The province of Seville was the main contributor, with almost 17 million on average annually, followed by the province of Trujillo with almost 10.7 million, Salamanca with 9.7 million, León with 8.9 and Toledo with 8.8 million.

The data we have managed to collect are generally greater than those calculated by José Manuel Carretero Zamora in his study on ordinary and extraordinary *servicio.*[23] The difference is between 6.5 and 11 million, depending on the year considered, likely due to the different timing and accounting of the sources taken into account.[24] The one we use here is a charge and discharge account, with the resulting balance, made after the collection of the *servicio*. It includes numerous references to lawsuits and disputes raised by some communities that believed they had contributed more than what was established and distributed by the Cortes because the investigation that was carried out revealed a higher number of *pecheros*, who were then subject to taxation.

Regarding the collection of the *servicio* and the part that entered the Baeza Treasury, it should be noted that the general treasurer received almost 45% of the total volume of this tax, specifically the part of the extraordinary *servicio* that was being collected was sent to him – in some cases even in advance – in addition to some amounts from the part that was not pledged. The bulk was received between 1551 and 1552 with almost 145/148 million maravedís that the treasurer Baeza received for this item (Table 4.4).

Table 4.3 The distribution of ordinary and extraordinary *servicios* in Castile, 1550–1555 (average data in maravedís)

	Value		*Value*		*Value*
Ávila	5,574,675	Tuy	708,000	Toledo (Mesa arzobispal)	4,419,267
Burgos	7,201.283	Lugo	2,940,783	Toledo	4,377,242
Trasmiera	374,567	Mondoñedo	759,383	Ciudad Real	255,700
Tierra del Condestable	1,447,850	La Coruña-Betanzos	1,543,667	Campo di Calatrava	2,335,117
Zamora	2,959,200	Orense	2,215,528	Murcia	3,715,425
Castilla (O. de Santiago)	2,566,917	Guadalajara	5,441,325	Salamanca	9,702,808
Campo de Montiel	1,041,150	Jaén	5,658,542	Segovia	6,854,392
Alcaraz	946,692	Calatrava de Andalucía	1,331,800	Sevilla	16,909,775
Cuenca	5,146,533	León	3,594,700	Soria	6,059,858
Huete	1,935,317	Asturias	765,533	Toro	1,532,700
Córdoba	7,185,324	Ponferrada	624.800	Trujillo	10,588,050
Palencia-Carrión-Saldaña	5,950,625	León (Orden de Santiago)	5,457,032	Valladolid	5,185,875
Santiago de Compostela	2,843,383	Madrid	2,922,058	Benavente	1,580,333

Sources: AGS, Contaduría Mayor de Cuentas, 1st period, 821 and 892.

Table 4.4 The collection of the *Servicio* and its payment to the General Treasury, 1550–1555 (values in millions of maravedís)

	1550	*1551*	*1552*	*1553*	*1554*	*1555*	*Total*	*Average*
Servicio ordinario	106.5	106.3	106.2	106.5	106.6	107.0	639.0	106.5
Servicio extraordinario	50.0	50.0	54.0	50.0	50.0	54.0	308.0	51.3
Total	156.5	156.3	160.2	156.5	156.6	161.0	947.0	157.8
Income in the *Tesorería General*	54.0	144.6	147.5	52.7	10.6	14.9	424.3	70.7
% of Total income in *Tesorería*	*34.50*	*92.53*	*92.09*	*33.67*	*6.77*	*9.26*	*44.80*	

Sources: AGS, Contaduría Mayor de Cuentas, 1st period, 1233, 1252 and 1492.

Crusade and Subsidy

Apart from some estimates offered in his time by Ramón Carande, the income produced by the graces of the Crusade and the Ecclesiastical Subsidy in the final years of Charles V's reign is not well known. However, the revenues of the General Treasury provide important information on both, that show a significant increase in these years of fiscal crisis.

For the period from 1548 to 1551, there were two *asientos*. One referred to the preaching of the bull of San Pedro and a buleta and four jubilees in the years 1548, 1549 and 1551 and was in the hands of Domingo de Orbea, servant of His Majesty, and Francisco de Artiaga or Arteaga, a resident and alderman of Segovia. The other was signed by them together with Luis Falaguer and Rodrigo de Lerma and referred to the bull of the jubilee of Rome in 1550. In the first *asiento* they undertook to help and pay the king 420,000 ducats at the May and October fairs in Medina del Campo. In the second, they offered another 74,000 ducats, plus 30,000 escudos of 350 maravedís, specifically "in the exchange of Álvaro de Benavente and Fernando Ochoa in the payments of the present fair of Medina de Rioseco [May 1547] that must be paid for the costs and work that have been done in bringing and dispatching the jubilee, and the rest to the terms agreed with the nuncio of his holiness".[25]

In the triennium of 1552–1554, the Crown signed an *asiento* with Francisco de Arteaga and Miguel de Zamora, a resident of Burgos, who undertook to pay 551,000 ducats for the bull of San Pedro and 94,000 for several buletas on the agreed terms. Miguel de Zamora signed the *asiento* of the jubilee bull (*bula de caja*) of the Purification of 1555.[26] During the triennium of 1555–1557, the *asiento* was signed with Gerónimo Candiano, Camilo Brevia and Juan Antonio Pinelo, who undertook to pay 894,000 ducats in various instalments at fairs. Paul IV suspended the preaching of the Crusade on 8 May 1556 and the king responded by stopping the transfer of 20,000 ducats due to the St. Peter's Factory (Table 4.5).

In his income Baeza recorded more than 44.3 million maravedís in 1550 and 152.7 million in 1551, while in 1553 he received only 3.75 million and almost 13 million in 1555. On the other hand, no money was recorded for this purpose in 1552[27] and 1554, years in which Baeza was also able to count on 39.5 and 6.2 million maravedís respectively for the Subsidy, in addition to another 59 million in 1553 and only 817,000 maravedís for this item in 1555.

At first glance these flows were not regular. This irregularity, in the case of the Crusade, depended mainly on the income advanced by a group of *asentistas* who agreed with the Crown to collect the sums advanced from the collection of

Table 4.5 Values of Crusade and Subsidy and what was paid into the General Treasury, 1550–1555 (values in millions of maravedís)

	1550	*1551*	*1552*	*1553*	*1554*	*1555*	*Total*	*Average*
Valor de Cruzada y jubileos	113.2	113.2	99.3	99.3	99.3	90.5	615.0	102.5
De lo cual, ingresado en Tesorería General	44.3	152.7		3.8		12.9	213.7	35.6
%	*39.13*	*134.85*		*3.77*		*14.27*	*34.74*	
Subsidio ingresado en Tesorería General			39.6	55.7	6.2	0.8	102.3	17.1

Sources: AGS, Contaduría Mayor de Cuentas, 1st period, 1233, 1252 y 1492, y Cruzada, 451.

the proceeds of the preaching of the bulls. On some occasions, interest rates of 14% per year are indicated. The 36.4 million maravedís (94,000 ducats) out of the 44.3 million entered in 1550 came from the four treasurers of the Holy Jubilee, Juan de Orbea, Francisco de Arteaga, Luis Falaguer and Rodrigo de Lerma, according to the *asiento* taken with them. Another 7.5 million consisted of *socorros*, that is, money advanced, for the change of Hernando de Ochoa.[28] The alderman of Segovia Arteaga appears linked to Francisco de Zamora, a resident of Córdoba, in different collections of the bulls of San Pedro and jubilees.

The General Treasury recorded income from the Ecclesiastical Subsidy from 1552, the year in which it was particularly substantial, as well as in 1553. The payments came from the dioceses of all the kingdoms of Spain, plus Sardinia. Between 1552 and 1555 a total of up to 102 million maravedís were received, of which 99.5 million came from ecclesiastical institutions and 2,791,447 maravedís from two payments made by the Genoese Felipe Spínola and Hernán Pérez Mejía, deputy of the compositions. Of particular relevance are the contributions from Seville and Toledo, of 12 and 11 million maravedís respectively; those of the ecclesiastical states of Tarragona and the kingdom of Aragon, with another 6 and 4 million respectively; that of the church of Cuenca, with 4.2 million, and those of Córdoba, Burgos, Ávila, Calahorra, León and Osma, with more than 3 million (Table 4.6). There are also contributions to the Subsidy of the military orders of Alcántara, Calatrava, with 2.4 and 2.1 million maravedís respectively, and that of the Order of Preachers of Santo Domingo, which contributed 204,000 maravedís.

The income and main expenses of the *Casa de la Contratación*

The situation in the 1550s was perhaps the most critical of Charles V's reign for the city of Seville and the merchants to the Indies, characterised by successive difficulties and bankruptcies of the public banks. The banks of the Genoese Pedro Juan Leardo and the Basque Domingo de Lizarraras went bankrupt, respectively, in August 1552 and March 1553. That of the company formed by the Basque Juan de Íñiguez and the Genoese Octaviano Negrón entered a deep crisis in the spring of 1554.[29] A situation that was also characterised by a continuous export of the American treasure to Europe, as the English financier Thomas Gresham, an agent in the service of the Queen of England Mary Tudor, was able to verify directly, being involved in the transport of sacks of precious metals from Seville and Cádiz to England and Flanders.[30] Gresham himself spoke, in the context of the crisis of the Íñiguez-Negrón bank, of a certain scarcity of precious metals and of the fear that this would cause more important bankruptcies.

However, the preceding months to which Gresham refers were characterised by important arrivals of gold, silver and pearls received by the *Casa de la Contratación* of Seville, as can be seen in the records and books of the treasurer Francisco Tello. Its revenues, without considering the annual balances, went from the minimum of 62 million maravedís in 1550 to the maximum of 847 million in 1551 and then 522.4 million in 1554 and 480 million in 1555.[31] These sums correspond not only to the royal treasury, because they also include some payments received by money

Table 4.6 Amounts of the Ecclesiastical Subsidy paid into the General Treasury, 1550–1555 (values in maravedís)

	Value		*Value*
Iglesia de Sevilla	12,004,000	Iglesia de Badajoz	1,788,000
Iglesia de Toledo	10,920,000	Iglesia de Coria	1,761,000
Estado eclesiástico de Tarragona	6,120,000	Iglesia de Salamanca	1,629,000
Iglesia de Cuenca	4,241,000	Iglesia de Astorga	1,506,000
Estado eclesiástico de Aragón	4,114,000	Iglesia de Orense	1,407,985
Iglesia de Córdoba	3,469,000	Iglesia de Oviedo	1,362,000
Iglesia de Burgos	3,300,000	Iglesia de Granada	1,000,000
Iglesia de Ávila	3,292,000	Iglesia de Pamplona	1,000,000
Iglesia de Calahorra	3,283,000	Estado eclesiástico de Mallorca	843,750
Iglesia de León	3,141,000	La Seo de Callar (Cagliari)	816,000
Iglesia de Osma	3,102,000	Iglesia de Ciudad Rodrigo	809,000
Iglesia de Santiago	2,750,000	Iglesia de Cádiz	724,000
Iglesia de Sigüenza	2,640,000	Iglesia de Tuy	583,000
Iglesia de Palencia	2,605,000	Iglesia de Canaria	428,485
Iglesia de Zamora	2,522,000	Iglesia de Lugo	425,000
Orden de Calatrava	2,437,500	Iglesia de Mondoñedo	414,000
Iglesia de Plasencia	2,408,000	Orden de Santo Domingo	204,000
Iglesia de Valencia	2,343,175	Iglesia de Ágreda	158,500
Orden de Alcántara	2,125,000	Iglesia de Alfaro	92,000
Iglesia de Cartagena	2,004,000	Total	99,522,395
Iglesia de Jaén	1,889,000	Other income (*)	2,791,447
Iglesia de Segovia	1,861,000	Total	102,313,842

Sources: AGS, Contaduría Mayor de Cuentas, 1st period, 1233, 1252 and 1492.

Note: (*) There are 750,000 maravedís from Hernán Pérez Mejía, receiver of the compositions and applications made by the Commissary General at the Court, and 2,041,447 maravedís from Felipe Spínola in payments of the October fair of the 4,082,896.

orders from another treasurer or from individuals, such as the Consulate of Seville, from private lenders and also from the requisitions of remittances that took place between 1552 and 1555.

The main revenues of the *Casa de la Contratación* in the years 1550 and 1551 came from the great treasure brought from Peru by the fleets of the Licentiate Don Pedro de la Gasca, appointed Bishop of Palencia after his return to Castile, and by the fleet of Sancho de Biedma that arrived the following year. The treasure began to be paid into the coffers of the *Casa de la Contratación* on 28 September 1550.[32] A later report, signed by Agustín de Zárate on 29 July 1552, puts the total treasure brought from Peru and what was paid in 1551 by Biedma at 667,128,841 maravedís, equivalent to 1,779,010 ducats.[33] This amount was paid by Tello in 1551, together with another from the fleets, to exceed the amount of 847.5 million maravedís at the end of the same year (Tables 4.1 and 4.7).

In November 1552, the treasure brought by the fleet of Captain General Francisco de Mendoza, son of the viceroy of Peru Antonio de Mendoza, began to be deposited in the treasury of the *Casa de Contratación*, with an important treasure, which in the first months of 1553 was still being minted.[34] A large part of the income recorded that year came from this treasury, which amounted to almost 117 million maravedís (Tables 4.1 and 4.7), including loans and carryover balances.

The 552.4 million maravedís in 1554 are the result of the income from the fleet of Bartolomé Carrero, which arrived in Sanlúcar on 24 October 1554, and from the other fleet from New Spain that arrived in February of that year, with treasure brought from the provinces of *Tierra Firme*, Cartagena and New Spain. In addition to the part belonging to the king and voluntary loans received, the charge includes 224.8 million that came in after the order, issued by Philip on 15 December 1553, to seize up to 600,000 ducats.

The income of 1555 amounted to almost 480 million maravedís, of which 320 came from requisitioning private metal precious. These revenues were due to the arrival of large fleets, such as that of Cosme Rodríguez Farfán who arrived from the *Tierra Firme* in January, that of Diego Felipe, who arrived from New Spain in the summer, as well as the fleet of Juan Tello de Guzmán, from the Caribbean. The first two fleets also brought cargo from two important shipwrecks. The first occurred in 1554 in the Gulf of Mexico, in the area near the current Texas city of Corpus Christi, also called "Florida shipwreck" or "Padre Island", with the rescue of the cargo that, brought to Veracruz, was sent mostly to Spain in the aforementioned fleet that arrived in the summer. The second occurred in January 1555 in the waters of Zahara de los Atunes, which included the cargo of Cosme Buitrón's ship, rescued in several phases and then brought at different times to Seville.[35]

Loans received in Seville

The General Treasury of Alonso de Baeza was not the only institution to receive the amount of loans to the Crown. The *Casa de la Contratación*, thanks to its control over the precious metals of individuals and the king that arrived in Seville, was also able to exercise this important function when it came to requiring merchants or wealthy individuals to lend amounts of money that could be disbursed within short periods of time.

In 1550, the treasurer of the *Casa de la Contratación*, Francisco Tello, registered on 13 July the 1,875,000 maravedís (5,000 ducats) received from the Genoese Nicolás Ragio, for a bill of exchange that he would pay in Medina del Campo to Juan Jácome Spínola and Nicolás Cataño and Ángelo de Marín during the May fair, plus the "1.5 [per cent] of interest and 6 per thousand for cash payment",[36] and another 20,000 ducats received, half of it from the bank of Domingo de Lizarraras, and the other half from the bank of Pedro de Espinosa. The 25,000 ducats were repaid plus interest on 28 July.[37]

In the revenues of 1552, the treasurer Francisco Tello received 5.2 million maravedís (14,000 ducats) as a loan from Lope de Mendieta, through the bank of Alonso and Pedro de Espinosa, which were extinguished with a *juro* of 1,000 ducats at 7.14%. Tello then sent the sum to the treasurer Baeza, through the German intermediary Cristóbal Raizer.[38] Not included in Tello's accounts, however, were the almost 8.3 million maravedís received through the Asistente of Seville, Count of Coruña, Lorenzo Suárez de Mendoza, and which Tello disbursed on 25 August to 118 people. The sum was received by the Asistente and sent to the treasurer Baeza by royal order, through Raizer.[39] Nor are included the 27 million taken as a forced loan from the warehouse of the deposit of the individuals,[40] to be sent to Málaga, with the exception of the 1,617,768 maravedís of the heirs of Rodrigo Gallego, which Tello registered by virtue of an executory letter.[41] This money was part of a larger mobilisation of the "deposit" of the warehouse of the *Casa de la Contratación* of 39.5 million maravedís, all recorded in the discharge of 1553, but only the difference was returned to the warehouse.

The charges of 1553 show some loans received to prepare the fleet of Alonso Pejón, which was headed to the Azores for the escort of the convoys of the Carrera de Indias. Approximately up to 30,000 ducats were needed, and between June and August the treasurer Tello received more than 7.5 million maravedís, and specifically up to 5,000 ducats in three payments by Hernando de la Fuente and Rodrigo de Illescas, prior and consul of the University of Merchants of Seville, which were repaid to him between February and April 1554 along with another 2,000 ducats received in the same month of February, adding interest and costs of the exchanges carried out in the Azores, in Lisbon, Valencia and Seville.[42] For the same purpose on 22 June, he received another 300 ducats from Octaviano Negrón, banker of Seville, plus 15,000 ducats from Hernando de Sarabia de Hoyo sent by the treasurer Baeza, that is, from the accounts of the General Treasury.[43]

In 1554 Tello received up to 7.5 million in money that was not the king's own. In addition to the aforesaid 750,000 maravedís (2,000 ducats) obtained in February from the prior and consul of Seville to prepare the navy of Pejón, he received on 19 September another 3,516,790 maravedís to pay the costs of the fleet of Juan Tello de Guzmán, which had returned from the Azores,[44] and another 8,500 ducats for two bills of exchange addressed to Juan Moreno in Valencia, to be paid in the month of November.[45]

In addition to this, the treasurer Tello received other resources from the requisition of remittances from the Indies to individuals. These were substantial forced loans from merchants and individuals who, instead of their gold and silver, received from the officials of the *Casa de Contratación* some credit certifications that, after months, were converted into long-term debt securities, as *juros al quitar* at different rates, or, exceptionally, *libranzas* and payments charged to the colonial royal treasuries.

As we have already pointed out in other works dedicated specifically to the subject of Charles V's forced loans,[46] the Crown carried out the requisition of American funds from private individuals in 1552, December 1553 – whose accounts were included in the following year – and on several occasions in 1555. These were not the first occasions on which the emperor resorted to this extraordinary financing measure, which was much criticised by the merchants of the Carrera de Indias, having been previously adopted in the years 1523, 1534, 1535, 1536 and 1545, at which time Prince Philip, during his first regency, issued the main instructions to the Sevillian officials and tried to reduce the negative impact of the expropriation of gold and silver. Despite the repeated fears expressed to the king, his father, of a possible collapse of transatlantic trade, Philip also resorted during his reign to requisitioning American precious metals, even more aggressively than his predecessor, and so did his successors Philip III and Philip IV.[47]

Between 13 and 29 May 1552, prince Philip, having resumed the governance of Castile, issued several letters to request the sending to Malaga of some money that had been seized in the deposit of the *Casa de la Contratación*. Ninety different items were entered in this first requisition for a total value of 26,783,479 maravedís, the largest of which belonged to Hernando Pizarro, already imprisoned in the castle of La Mota de Medina del Campo after the civil war and the rebellion in Peru.[48] On 24 October 1553, Bartolomé Carreño's fleet arrived in Sanlúcar, without the admiral ship Santa Catalina, whose cargo had been recovered in the Azores and brought to Seville by the fleet of Juan Tello de Guzmán in August 1554. On 15 December 1553, the prince ordered the officials of Seville to borrow precious metals worth 600,000 ducats, two-thirds of them from merchants and the remaining part from private individuals, and the treasurer Tello registered in 1554 the charge of 224,853,750 *maravedís*.[49]

The payments of the Casa de la Contratación

In 1550, against a net income of just over 62 million maravedís, almost 10 million were spent on *asientos*. Of these, the 37.5 million were passed to the treasurer Baeza and the rest were used to prepare ships of the navy of Captain General Bernardino de Mendoza and other usual expenses of the *Casa*, such as salaries, the travel expenses of religious and American officials, etc. The *asientos* and exchanges amounted to almost 14 million maravedís, including the 9.3 million (25,000 ducats) received from the banks Lizarraras and Espinosa and the Genoese Nicolás Ragio and the interest incurred, and the 4.2 million maravedís due to the Genoese Andrea Lomelín and Cristóbal Centurión.[50]

In 1551 the revenues – which shot up to 847.5 million maravedís – made it possible to sustain a significant volume of payments for *asientos* allocated to the royal revenues of the *Casa de la Contratación*, with a third of them, that is, for 266.5 million. The main group of *asentistas* was that of the Genoese, who were mainly granted an interest of 14% per annum. There are also other Italian, Flemish and German bankers, including the Affaitati , the Schertz and the Fuggers, who received payments that included interest of 12%. That same year, more payments were made, specifically in favour of Alonso de Baeza for 141 million and two important remittances abroad (Table 4.7). The first, under the item of a loan, was for 37.5 million maravedís (100,000 ducats) and consisted of a remittance to Italy in favour of His Holiness the Pope. The second was a large delivery of 100,096 marks and 2 ounces of silver paste, valued at 210,000,330 maravedís (600,000 escudos), in favour of Alonso del Castillo, the King's chamberlain, who managed it in Flanders, having moved to the emperor's court.[51]

In 1553 the income amounted to 250 million, which was mainly used for the payment of *asientos* amounting to 135 million, for payments to Baeza of 50 million and for the restitution of remittances taken from the warehouse, for almost 40 million maravedís.

Table 4.7 The income and main expenses of the *Casa de la Contratación* , 1550–1555 (values in maravedís)

	Treasurer's Positions (1)	*Treasurer's Disclaimers*				
		To Alonso de Baeza	*Asientos*	*Direct remittances abroad*	*To the paymaster Diego de Cazalla*	*For the Almacén de la Casa*
1550	62,259,077	37,500,000	13,933,972			
1551	847,485,902	140,803,125	266.542.183	247,582,337		
1552	116,784.094	30,750,000	136,791,847		6,680,094	10,581,571
1553	250,197.059	50,524,515	135,497,347			39,467,769
1554	522,426.218	71,153,068	77,625,000	284,030,477	14,437,500	9,000,000
1555	479,661.402	58,495,210		251,527,700	52,737,000	
	2,278,813,752	389,225,918	630,390,349	783,140,514	73,854,594	59,049,340

Sources: The data on charges, entries, remittances and warehouse come from AGI, *Contaduría*, 275 and 277; Alonso de Baeza's data come from the General Treasury.

Note: (1) The values shown are the net of the scopes of the corresponding years.

In 1554, once 225 million had been received from the forced loan ordered at the end of 1553, preparations were made for Prince Philip's trip to England for the marriage of Queen Mary I Tudor. To prepare the fleet assembled in La Coruña for the crossing to London, 114,500 ducats were allocated, with 50,000 received by Baeza directly from the *Casa de la Contratación.* In mid-January 1554 Philip asked the officials in Seville to finish minting the treasure of Carreño's fleet in the Atarazanas by mid-February. Contrary to what had already been ordered – the minting of a third of the metal in two-real coins and two-thirds in four-real coins – he asked that half be minted in eight-real coins and the other half in two- and four-real coins in equal parts. It was also agreed to satisfy the Royal Treasury for other payment orders issued at that time. Specifically, 5,000 of the 10,000 ducats owed to the former ambassador in Rome, Don Diego de Mendoza. Finally, it was recommended to reserve sufficient resources to cover the expenses of preparing four ships, a *patache* and a caravel to add to Alonso Pejón's navy. All the gold and silver, minted or in ingots, belonging to the King or seized from private individuals, would be delivered to the accountant Agustín de Zárate to take them to La Coruña and from there to Flanders and England. Zárate brought with him a large cargo of 284,030,477 maravedís (757,415 ducats), of which 167,096 were gold escudos and the rest were reales and silver paste. One part was used to mint the new coins with the image of Philip and Mary Tudor, kings of England.[52] In the same 1554, 77.6 million maravedis were paid, and up to 71 million were delivered to Baeza, according to his accounting record, while 9 million were returned to the deposit from the treasury taken from private individuals.

In 1555, with the income having increased thanks to the different extractions of precious metals, the treasury of the *Casa de la Contratación* was able to make important payments to servants of the Crown such as Alonso del Castillo and Agustín de Zárate, who were in charge of taking the aforementioned treasure to Flanders. In 1555 Agustín de Santander, Alonso de Fonseca and Commander Verastegui were entrusted with these tasks for a cumulative amount of almost 229 million maravedís, to which another 22,252,700 maravedís received by Antonio de Almaguer should be added to take them to Valladolid. Santander received in May 200,000 ducats for the emperor and 2,500 ducats to cover transport costs, plus 2,500 for the principal courier Raimondo de Tassis. Alonso de Fonseca received, on 30 September, another 200,000 ducats to send to Genoa to the Duke of Alba, who was then viceroy of Naples, with more than 2,000 ducats in costs for shipping with the galleys from Cartagena. Finally, on 5 October, Commander Verastegui received 204,400 ducats to send to Flanders.[53]

In addition to these main costs, the *Casa de la Contratación* spent in 1552, 1554 and 1555 almost 74 million maravedís on successive shipments to the paymaster of the galleys of Cartagena, Diego de Cazalla, to support the navy of Cartagena and the garrison of Oran, including the six payments due to 1,000 soldiers stationed there[54].

Conclusions

The last five years of Charles V's reign were characterised by a deep fiscal crisis in Castile due to the foreign policy carried out by the emperor, who was already close to his abdication in favour of Philip, the "Prudent King". There were various emergencies that the sovereign attempted to address. First, the war against France and the Lutheran princes, which ended with Caesar's flight from Innsbruck and the siege of the imperial troops in Metz from the end of 1552 to the beginning of 1553. The following year, Prince Philip moved from Spain to England with his large court for his marriage to the Queen of England, Mary I Tudor. Finally, the return of the emperor and his court to Castile, which ended with his retirement and death in the monastery of Yuste. In between, another war had broken out in Italy, first over the possessions of Parma and Piacenza, and then over disputes with Pope Paul IV Carafa, who was adverse to the Habsburgs, with the sending to Italy of the Duke of Alba and an important army. The African possessions, and especially Oran, would also require increasing support from the finances of Castile.

On the one hand, the lack of resources was addressed with large-scale borrowing, both in the long and short term, and, on the other, with increased tax revenues, thanks in particular to extraordinary taxation. The income of the *Casa de la Contratación* was of great importance thanks to the American treasure that arrived with the fleets of Pedro de la Gasca, Sancho de Biedma, Francisco de Mendoza, Bartolomé Carreño and Cosme Rodríguez Farfán and Diego Felipe, which would allow the Crown to use the part belonging to merchants and private individuals in the years 1552, 1553 and 1555.

The importance of the services of the Cortes of Castile and the graces of the Crusade and the Subsidy granted by the Pope of Rome in this fiscal crisis has also been highlighted. Our analysis of the *servicios* has shown a growth in tax revenues, on average from 6.5 to 11 million maravedís per year more than the previous study by José Manuel Carretero Zamora. The Crusade, on the other hand, has shown a significant reduction in tax collection in the final years of the reign, an obvious sign of the fiscal and economic crisis that was to spread in Castile, particularly between 1554 and 1555.

The accounting analysis has shown that only part of the sums collected in taxes entered the General Treasury of Castile, while the bulk of the debt issued was in the form of *juros* or long-term income and floating debt. However, the high volume of *asientos* contracted, paid for or renewed by the Crown that year far exceeded the level of taxes collected, forcing the emperor to alienate a part of the royal patrimony through the sale of offices, jurisdictions and noble titles, and to pledge future revenues with the large issue of public debt.

Acknowledgement

The research has been supported by the STAR program, L.1, 2018, within the “ForcedLoans” Research Project, funded by the Università degli Studi di Napoli “Federico II” and Compagnia di San Paolo and by "Under Uncertainty. Coping with Risks in the Mediterranean Martime Business (Italy, 16th-19th centuries)" Research Project, funded by the Italian Ministry of University and Reseearch (MUR) and the European Union -NextGenerationEU (CUP: E53D23000340006).

Appendix 4.1

Appendix 4.1 Revenues deposited in the *"Tesorería General de Castilla."* (*"Síntesis del cargo de la Tesorería General de Castilla: distribuciones por principales conceptos, 1550-1555"*)

Maravedís	*1550*	*1551*	*1552*	*1553*	*1554*	*1555*	*Total*	*Average*
Debt								
Juros	55,018,264	54,451,140	182,251,028	139,834,790	50,372,578	52,862,084	534,789,884	89,131,647
Juros of oil	0	0	0	11,005,000	12,065,000	0	23,070,000	3,845,000
Loans	0	73,775,000	243,310,605	327,009,750	198,905,000	76,125,000	919,125,355	153,187,559
Taxes								
Contratación	37,500,000	140,803,125	30,750,000	50,524,515	71,153,068	58,495,210	389,225,918	64,870,986
Crusade	44,306,732	152,682,500	0	3,750,000	0	12,916,448	213,655,680	35,609,280
Extraordinary	169,912,561	63,204,187	226,754,419	78,959,022	15,838,585	9,317,355	563,986,129	93,997,688
Subsidy	0	0	39,564,735	55,698,410	6,234,697	816,000	102,313,842	17,052,307
Others								
Libranzas	6,270,525	4,397,166	4,475,000	0	28,761,715	0	43,904,406	7,317,401
Licences	0	0	1,239,867	4,252,985	4,379,640	234,486	10,106,978	1,684,496
Sales*	7,156,875	2,632,875	10,174,500	59,115,551	15,006,448	15,446,600	109,532,849	18,255,475
Balances	647,755	2,045,036	3,135,728	5,544,533	2,358,218	3,484,749	17,216,018	2,869,336
Total	320,812,712	493,991,029	741,655,882	735,694,556	405,074,949	229,697,932	2,926,927,059	487,821,176
Percentages	**1550**	**1551**	**1552**	**1553**	**1554**	**1555**	**Total**	**Average**
Debt								
Juros	17.15	11.02	24.57	19.01	12.44	23.01	18.27	18.27
Juros of oil	0.00	0.00	0.00	1.50	2.98	0.00	0.79	0.79
Loans	0.00	14.93	32.81	44.45	49.10	33.14	31.40	31.40

(*Continued*)

Appendix 4.1 (continued)

Maravedís	*1550*	*1551*	*1552*	*1553*	*1554*	*1555*	*Total*	*Average*
Taxes								
Contratación	11.69	28.50	4.15	6.87	17.57	25.47	13.30	13.30
Crusade	13.81	30.91	0.00	0.51	0.00	5.62	7.30	7.30
Extraordinary	52.96	12.79	30.57	10.73	3.91	4.06	19.27	19.27
Subsidy	0.00	0.00	5.33	7.57	1.54	0.36	3.50	3.50
Others								
Libranzas	1.95	0.89	0.60	0.00	7.10	0.00	1.50	1.50
Licences	0.00	0.00	0.17	0.58	1.08	0.10	0.35	0.35
Sales*	2.23	0.53	1.37	8.04	3.70	6.72	3.74	3.74
Balances	0.20	0.41	0.42	0.75	0.58	1.52	0.59	0.59
Total	100.00	100.00	100.00	100.00	100.00	100.00	100.00	100.00

Sources: AGS, Contaduría Mayor de Cuentas. 1ª época. 1233, 1252 and 1492.

Notes: Sales*: sales of public offices, jurisdictions and *hidalguías; Data in maravedís and percentages.*

Notes

1 Rodríguez Salgado, 1992: 49–71; Pardo Molero, 2001: 33–81; Parker, 2019: 583–619; Sardone, 2019b: 324–328.
2 The persecutions of heretics and Anglicans earned her the nickname "Bloody". Erickson, 1998: 303–407.
3 Rodríguez Salgado, 1992: 66–67, 75.
4 AGS, Patronato Real, 57, 121, 1. Marriage contract between Prince Maximilian of Austria and the Infanta Maria.
5 The reserved share of 900,000 *Portuguese doubloons* was redistributed in 1555, leaving most of it to Philip, as heir to the throne and leaving Maria and Joanna 148,532 *doubloons*, equivalent to 54,214,277 maravedís or 144,571 Castilian ducats. AGS, Patronato Real, 50, doc. 117.
6 In 1548, exercising his imperial powers, Charles created the new state of the Netherlands, uniting the inherited territories, for a time belonging to Charles I of Burgundy, the Bold, to those conquered, including the fiefs of Utrecht and Gelderland. Rodríguez Salgado, 1992: 66–67, 75.
7 Álvarez-Ossorio Alvariño, 2001 and 2002.
8 Erickson, 1998.
9 De Carlos Morales, 2004 and 2016. The 1560 Revolution is considered an extension of the first.
10 Introduced occasionally in 1536, to guarantee a monthly flow of 20,000 escudos, between 1547 and 1553 the *monthly guaranteed* annual income between 260,000 and 300,000 escudos. From 1600 it became a permanent income of 300,000 escudos. Chabod, 1971: 118–121; D'Amico. 2012: 126; De Luca, 2013.
11 Buyreu Juan, 2000: 79–80.
12 Rodríguez Salgado, 1992: 379–444.
13 García Simón, 1995: 33–47.
14 In 1558 Philip II established a new right on exported wool, the following year he introduced the "dry ports" of Portugal and, on the death of the Constable of Castile in 1559, he incorporated the "tithes of the sea" ("*diezmos de la mar*") into the Crown. Two years later, the Cortes accepted a 37% increase in the value of the *alcabalas*. Ulloa, 1963; Fortea Pérez, 2008: 123–159; Álvarez Nogal, 2009.
15 Ulloa, 1963: 105; Fortea Pérez, 2008:115.
16 Ulloa, 1963: 89, 113–114, 172; Toboso Sánchez, 1987: 89.
17 González, 1831: 168–169; Hernández Esteve, 1986: 121–124.
18 AGS, Cruzada, files 442, 450 and 451. We thank Ramón Lanza García for this information.
19 The 3,750,000 maravedís indicated by 1552 refer to the 10,000 ducats received from the Archbishop of Cuenca and which came within the scope of Baeza of the same year, as they were effectively received only in 1553.
20 Carande, 1990: III, in his appendix distinguishes, on the one hand, "*amounts taken*", i.e. the value of what is borrowed or negotiated in entries, and, on the other hand, "*amounts due or paid*", which also include financial costs.
21 The contribution of the bishop of Cuenca was registered within the scope of the treasurer Baeza of 1551, being received at the beginning of the following year.
22 It is probably part of the loan, of greater quantity, which was collected in Seville through the assistant, the Count of Coruña, which the *Casa de la Contratación* disbursed in 1552.

23 The values of Carretero-Zamora, 2016: 472–476, are as follows: 144,648,900 (1550); 144.491.800 (1551); 153.735.550 (1552); 149.754.190 (1553); 149.754.190 (1554); 154.086.050 (1555). Our totals, based on AGS, CMC, 1a ápoca, 812 and 892, are shown in Table 4.4.

24 The analysis of Carretero-Zamora, 2016: 472–476 is based mainly on the source of the *Escribanía Mayor de Rentas* (EMR), files 364, 372, 408 and 415. The author also indicates the source of CMC, 1st period, 892, which will have served him to include the data of 1555 and 1556. Our data come, in addition to the latter source for the year 1555, from AGS, CMC, 1st period, 812. It is likely that the source of the *Escribanía Mayor de Rentas* includes only the values set at the time of the distribution made by the Cortes of Castile and does not consider, on the other hand, the definitive data results to the *Escribanos Mayores* (Senior Accountants), once the accounts of each fiscal district have expired.

25 AGS, Cruzada, 450.

26 Jubilees of the box preached on All Saints' Day in 1552 and 1553, that of Santo Tomé in 1552 and that of Santiago in 1554 of the first triennium, and on All Saints' Day in 1555 and 1557, that of the Purification in 1555 and that of the Magdalene in 1556 in the second triennium. AGS, Cruzada, 451.

27 In fact, in 1552 62,250,000 maravedis were received from Jerónimo Candiano and Alejandro Cataño, which had to be returned through the Crusade and jubilees of 1554 and were charged under the account of the *socorro*. AGS, Contaduría Mayor de Cuentas, 1st period, 1252.

28 From Alberto Coon, 183,732 maravedis were received, by the bishop of Lugo, general commissioner, with the intention of collecting them in the Subsidy of 1550, 1551 and 1552; while Francisco Yáñez and the heirs of Diego de Gamarra received 248,000 maravedís, from the position of the jubilee of 1548 of the bishoprics of Calahorra and Pamplona. AGS, Contaduría Mayor de Cuentas, 1st period, 1233.

29 Carande, 1990: I, 299–321; Otte, 2008: 263–66; Sardone, 2015: 268–271; Álvarez-Nogal and Sardone, 2026.

30 Carande, 1990: I: 315–316; II: 139 y III: 410-419; Guy, 2019: 81–82.

31 Estimates similar to ours are those of Haring, 1939.

32 AGI, Contaduría, 275, N.2, fol.3.

33 AGS, Cámara de Castilla, Diversos, 46, 36.

34 AGI, Contaduría, 277, N.2.

35 Sardone, 2019b: 58, 125–141.

36 AGI, Contaduría, 275, N.1, fol. 74.

37 AGI, Contaduría, 275, N.1, fol. 283.

38 AGI, Contaduría, 275, N.2, fols. 163, 265.

39 AGI, Contaduría, 275, N.2, fols. 274–278.

40 In addition to the Crown treasury, the *Casa de la Contratación* managed the treasury of individuals entered for different items: remittances addressed to persons or institutions indicated in the registers of ships or in powers of attorney, assets of the deceased, assets contested in lawsuits, etc. When these remittances were subject to requisition and forced loan, physical and accounting operations (charges and discharges) took place between the chest and book of the "deposits" and the treasurer's chest and book.

41 The sum was not returned to the deposit chest, paying the heirs 225,000 maravedís. AGI, Contaduría, 277, N.1, fol. 53.

42 AGI, Contaduría, 277, N.1, fols. 46; N.2, fols.1 and 35–36 (Sardone 2019b, 496–497)

43 AGI, Contaduría, 277, N.1, fols. 46 and 54.

44 The breakdown financed the protection of the fleets of the *Carrera de Indias*. Its cost was shared among the recipients of the remittances. In the case of Tello de Guzmán's fleet, the cost-sharing tariff amounted to 5% of the value of the remittances brought. AGI, Contaduría, 277, N.2, fol. 19.
45 The first bill of 1,687,500 maravedís was taken with Diego Núñez de Toledo, the second of 1,500,000 maravedís with Pedro Luis de Torregrosa, both residents of Seville. AGI, Contaduría, 277, N.2, fol. 20.
46 Sardone, 2015, 2019a, and 2019b.
47 Sardone, 2017; Álvarez-Nogal, 1997: 174–211; Marcos Martín, 2024.
48 Sardone, 2019b: 52 and 58.
49 AGI, Contaduría, 277, N.2, fol.15v. Sardone, 2019b: 124.
50 AGI, Contaduría, 277, N.1, fol. 283.
51 AGS, Cámara de Castilla, Diversos, 46, 36; AGS, Contaduría Mayor de Cuentas, 1st period 1589.
52 Sardone, 2019b: 326–328, 497–498. See algo, De Francisco Olmos, 2005.
53 Sardone, 2019b: 499–500.
54 Sardone, 2019b: 496–500; AGI, Contaduría, 275, N.2.

Bibliography

Álvarez-Nogal, Carlos (1997), *El crédito de la monarquía hispánica en el reinado de Felipe IV*, Valladolid: Junta de Castilla y León.

Álvarez-Nogal, Carlos (2009), *Oferta y demanda de deuda pública en Castilla: Juros de Alcabalas (1540–1740)*, Madrid: Banco de España.

Álvarez-Nogal, Carlos and Sardone, Sergio (2026), "La crisis de la banca pública sevillana a mediados del siglo XVI. La quiebra de Domingo de Lizarraras en 1553", in Angela Orlandi, ed., *Gestione del rischio, insolvenza e bancarotta nel mondo premoderno (secc. XIII-XVIII)*, Firenze: Firenze University Press, pp. 309–330 .

Álvarez-Ossorio Alvariño, Antonio (2001), "Ver y conocer. El viaje del príncipe Felipe (1548–1549)", in *Carlos V y la quiebra del humanismo político en Europa (1530–1558)*, Madrid: Sociedad Estatal para la Conmemoración de los Centenarios de Felipe II y Carlos V, vol. 2, pp 53–106.

Álvarez-Ossorio Alvariño, Antonio (2002), "Una forma di consiglio unito di Napoli et Milano: la corte de Felipe II en Londres y el gobierno de Lombardía", Madrid: Universidad Autónoma de Madrid, vol. 1, pp. 301–406.

Buyreu Juan, Jordi (2000), *La corona de Aragón de Carlos V a Felipe II. Las instrucciones a los virreyes bajo la regencia de la princesa Juana (1554–1559)*, Madrid: Sociedad Estatal para la Conmemoración de los Centenarios de Carlos V y Felipe II.

Carande, Ramón (1990), *Carlos V y sus banqueros*, Barcelona: Crítica, 3 vols.

Carretero-Zamora, Juan Manuel (2016), *Gobernar es gastar. Carlos V, el servicio de las Cortes de Castilla y la deuda de la monarquía hispánica, 1516–1556*, España: Sílex.

Chabod, Federico (1971), *Lo Stato e la vita religiosa a Milano nell'epoca di Carlo V*, Torino: Einaudi.

D'Amico, Stefano (2012), *Spanish Milan: A City Within the Empire, 1535–1706*. London: Palgrave Macmillan.

De Carlos Morales, Carlos (2004), *Felipe II: el Imperio en Bancarrota. La Hacienda Real de Castilla y los negocios financieros del Rey Prudente*, Madrid: Dilema.

De Carlos Morales, Carlos (2016), *El precio del dinero dinástico: endeudamiento y crisis financieras en la España de los Austria, 1557–1647*, España: Banco de España, 2 vols.

De Luca, Giuseppe (2013), "Milanese Finance, 1348–1700", in Gerard Caprio, ed., *Handbook of Key Global Financial Markets, Institutions, and Infrastructure*, Oxford: Elsevier Inc., vol. 1, pp. 185–195.

De Francisco Olmos, José María (2005), "Las primeras acuñaciones del Príncipe Felipe de España (1554-1556): Soberano de Milán, Nápoles e Inglaterra", *Documenta and Instrumenta*, 3, pp. 155–186.

Erickson, Caroly (1998), *Bloody Mary*, New York: St. Martin's Griffin.

Fortea Pérez, José Ignacio (2008), *Las Cortes de Castilla y León bajo los Austrias*, Valladolid: Junta de Castilla y León.

García Simón, Agustín (1995), *El ocaso del emperador: Carlos V en Yuste*, San Sebastián: Nerea.

González, Tomás (1831), *Noticia histórica documentada de las célebres minas de Guadalcanal, desde su descubrimiento en el año de 1555, hasta que dejaron de labrarse por cuenta de la Real Hacienda* , Madrid: Miguel de Burgos, 2 vols.

Guy, John (2019), *Gresham's Law: The Life and World of Queen Elizabeth I's Banker*, London: Profile Books Ltd.

Hernández Esteve, Esteban (1986), *Establecimiento de la partida doble en las cuentas centrales de la Real Hacienda de Castilla (1592): Pedro Luis de Torregrosa, primer contador del libro de caja*, Madrid: Banco de España.

Haring, Clarence H. (1939), *Comercio y navegación entre España y las Indias en la época de los Habsburgos*, México: Fondo de Cultura Económica.

Marcos Martín, Alberto (2024), "Formas extraordinarias de financiación de la Monarquía Hispánica en los siglos XVI y XVII. Las incautaciones de las remesas americanas de plata para particulares", *Anuario de Estudios Americanos*, 81, 2, pp. 1–19.

Otte, Enrique (2008), *Sevilla, siglo XVI: Materiales para su historia económica*, Sevilla: Centro de Estudios Andaluces.

Pardo Molero, Juan Francisco (2001), *La defensa del imperio. Carlos V, Valencia y el Mediterráneo*, Madrid: Sociedad Estatal para la Conmemoración de los Centenarios de Felipe II y Carlos V.

Parker, Geoffrey (2019), *Carlos V: Una nueva vida del emperador*, Madrid: Planeta.

Rodríguez Salgado, María José (1992), *Un imperio en transición. Carlos V, Felipe II y su mundo*, Barcelona: Crítica.

Sardone, Sergio (2015), "El aporte vasco a las requisas de remesas indianas durante el reinado de Carlos I", *Revista de la Historia de la Economía y de la Empresa*, 9, pp. 247–294.

Sardone, Sergio (2017), "Lo sviluppo del commercio coloniale spagnolo. Il ruolo della Casa de la Contratación e del Consulado di Siviglia, 1503-1650", *RISES. Ricerche di storia economica e sociale,* 3, pp. 61–93.

Sardone, Sergio (2018), "El 'Maluco'. La financiación de las expediciones, 1518–1529", in Carlos Martínez Shaw, ed., *Congreso Internacional de Historia "Primus circumdedisti me"*, Valladolid: Ministerio de Defensa-Junta de Castilla y León, pp. 225–259.

Sardone, Sergio (2019a), "Forced Loans in the Spanish Empire: The First Requisition of American Treasures in 1523", *Economic History Review,* 72, 1, pp. 57–87.

Sardone, Sergio (2019b), *Los préstamos forzosos de Carlos V. El tesoro privado americano al servicio del Imperio (1523–1555)*, Sevilla: Fundación González-Abreu-Instituto Hispano-Cubano de Historia de América.

Toboso Sánchez, Pilar (1987), *La deuda pública castellana durante el antiguo régimen (juros)*, Madrid: Instituto de estudios fiscales.

Ulloa, Modesto (1963), *La Hacienda Real de Castilla en el reinado de Felipe II*, Roma: Librería Sforzini.

5 State coercion, negotiation and predation

The political economy of the Spanish Empire and the taxation of the *Carrera de Indias*, *c.* 1570–1700

Xabier Lamikiz

5.1 Introduction

For much of its history, the *Carrera de Indias*, the trade and navigation system connecting Spain with its American domains, operated under various institutions established before 1570. This chapter examines how these institutions shaped the nature and extent of state coercion over the transatlantic trade during the long seventeenth century – a period when the monarchy desperately required substantial resources to finance costly wars in Flanders and elsewhere. My starting point is that to achieve tax compliance, there needs to be state coercion, with the imposition of penalties for non-compliance. However, coercion can also become predatory. In Spain's colonial trade during the seventeenth century, negotiation and predation both played a role in state coercion, with the relative importance of the two approaches fluctuating over time. Moreover, coercion was applied unevenly in the Spanish and Spanish American ports. What factors caused these temporal and geographical differences? What mechanisms of coercion did the Spanish Crown employ to ensure fiscal obedience, and were those mechanisms conducive to state predation?

The numerous partial seizures of American silver imports belonging to private individuals were blatant predatory acts. The first occurred in 1523 and the last in 1652. Charles I (r. 1516–1556) ordered silver requisitions in 1523, 1534, 1535, 1536, 1538, 1545, 1553 and 1555, and Philip II (r. 1556–1598) in 1556, 1557, 1558, 1566, 1577, 1583, 1587, 1590 and 1596.[1] Philip III (r. 1598–1621) did not order any requisitions, but Philip IV (r. 1621–1665), as the empire crumbled, retained silver belonging to private individuals in 1621, 1625, 1629, 1630, 1635, 1637, 1641, 1642, 1649 and 1652.[2] Typically the Crown did not seize all the precious metals imported but just a specific portion. In 1620, for instance, it retained 800,000 ducats (equivalent to 1,102,941 silver pesos) of privately owned silver, approximately an eighth of all the precious metals imported that year. After long negotiations with the merchants, that particular seizure was turned into a loan of sorts in 1621.[3] Indeed, on paper, all seizures were forced loans, as the owners of the silver had to be compensated either with *vellón* (billon coinage) plus interest or with redeemable annuities known as *juros* (which were backed by earmarked revenues).[4] The Crown's willingness, at least initially, to reimburse the silver it

DOI: 10.4324/9781003653301-6

seized has led Sardone to challenge the view that these requisitions violated property rights.[5] However, this argument is hardly tenable, as a violation of property rights was an intrinsic characteristic of these loans, which were made against the will of the "lenders" and often involved resorting to violence.[6] Furthermore, merchants had never considered repayment in *vellón* and *juros* adequate compensation, and during Philip IV's reign these forms of restitution gradually lost any remaining credibility.[7] As the Crown's finances worsened, particularly in the first half of the seventeenth century, repayments were made with heavily devalued *vellón* coinage, *juros* of questionable quality, or not at all. Unsurprisingly, the forced loans are considered "one of the causes most directly responsible for the decline of the Indies trade" in the 1630s and 1640s.[8]

The question of whether the silver requisitions were an attack on property rights is part of a broader debate about political institutions and economic development. In an influential article examining the relationship between Atlantic trade, political institutions and economic growth in the early modern period, Acemoglu, Johnson and Robinson assert that "in countries with highly absolutist institutions such as Spain", where "the power of the Crown was relatively unchecked", trade was regulated to serve the interests of the Crown and its allies, preventing the adoption of institutional changes that would have favoured economic growth.[9] At its core, this interpretation originated in a seminal article by North and Weingast, which I discuss in Section 5.2.[10] However, historians working on Spain and its empire emphasise that the Hispanic Monarchy (*Monarquía Hispánica*) was a composite entity rather than an absolutist one. The Crown's authority was not without limits, and Spanish political institutions were not highly absolutist. Crucially, to increase revenue, the king had no option but to negotiate with and secure the approval of the parliaments, territories, cities and corporations that formed the dynastic conglomerate under his rule. This was the case even in the kingdom that served as the Habsburg Empire's fiscal backbone, Castile, which was more amenable to royal direction than other territories.[11]

Taken to extremes, both the absolutist and composite interpretations of the Hispanic Monarchy fail to account for the full range of royal political action. How can flagrant violations of property rights, such as the silver seizures, be reconciled with the non-absolutist, negotiation-oriented nature of the Hispanic Monarchy? I contend that in their emphasis on negotiation, historians working on Spain and its empire have not sufficiently acknowledged the use and abuse of coercion.[12] Within specific areas and institutional frameworks of the Castilian economy, the monarch wielded significant power, enabling the implementation of measures that, as this chapter reveals, might be deemed absolutist.

The forced loans ended in 1652 because the Crown feared its predatory actions might have gone too far. The transatlantic trade had declined, and fraud, which was merchants' only possible response to the king's rapacity, had increased to such an extent that it jeopardised the very existence of the colonial trade system. But the difficulties faced by the Royal Treasury did not disappear after 1652, and the allure of American precious metals did not fade. Coercion over silver imports remained significant in the second half of the seventeenth century but took on less overt, more subtle forms. It is important to emphasise that the varying levels of state coercion did not correspond to changes in investment. Indeed, the consistently limited investment in coercive measures led to a highly inefficient system of taxing the transatlantic trade. As I explain in this chapter, the same institutional framework that enabled silver seizures and the implementation of effective coercive measures to secure silver belonging to private individuals was also responsible for a leaky taxation system. Both the structure of trade and the institutional set-up account for the apparent paradox of a monarchy capable of coercing silver owners but incapable of efficiently taxing Spanish exports to the Indies.

In addition to this introduction, the chapter comprises four sections and a conclusion. Section 5.2 places the discussion within the debate on economic institutions, property rights and state coercion in the early modern period. The Hispanic Monarchy and its political economy play a prominent role in this debate. The effectiveness of state coercion depends both on the resources available and on the specific institutional framework within which it operates. Nonetheless, this section emphasises that the state could often rely solely on the latter to increase coercion to the point of predation. I examine two well-known cases of property-rights infringements that had severe adverse effects not only on transatlantic merchants but also, more broadly, on the Castilian economy: the devaluation of *vellón* and *juros* interest detractions. Section 5.3 explores the taxation of the Spanish colonial trade on the outbound leg, demonstrating that the fleet system and the goods exported rendered the ad valorem method impracticable. As its ordinary fiscal revenue decreased, the Crown chose to impose extraordinary contributions on transatlantic merchants. How these extraordinary contributions were collected is analysed in Section 5.4, which deals with the return leg and the institutional set-up that facilitated the implementation of stricter coercive measures. Section 5.5 delves into state coercion in the second half of the seventeenth century. After that, I draw some conclusions.

5.2 Institutions, property rights and state coercion

For very different reasons, England (Great Britain after 1707) and the Spanish Monarchy have featured prominently in debates about the institutions that promoted economic development and those that hindered it in the early modern period. In a well-known article based on the postulates of new institutional economics, North and Weingast argue that "for economic growth to occur, the sovereign or government must not merely establish the relevant set of rights, but must make a credible commitment to them".[13] In their view, the key moment was the 1688 Glorious Revolution, as the institutions that emerged from the parliamentary system led to "a marked increase in the security of private rights", which in turn produced "the drive toward British hegemony and dominance of the world".[14] Good economic performance requires institutions that limit government intervention and allow private rights and markets to prevail in large segments of the economy. The Glorious Revolution spurred a financial revolution with significant results: the greater legitimacy of the parliamentary system enabled greater net tax revenue with less coercion and helped to stabilise public finances by controlling the budget and reducing the cost of sovereign debt.

In North and Weingast's narrative, while post-1688 England – and, later, Great Britain – serves as the paradigmatic example of an optimal institutional framework and a government's credible commitment to respect property rights, the Spanish Monarchy plays the role of the absolutist villain.[15] However, as indicated above, historiography in recent decades has emphasised that it is incorrect to describe the Spanish Monarchy as an absolutist regime. It was not absolute but composite, the result of a dispersed dynastic conglomerate composed of territories, cities and corporations with different institutional and legal frameworks.[16] The king was obliged to negotiate with them if he wanted to increase his tax revenues. In fact, as Grafe points out, "the legacy of this dynastic unification without political or territorial integration was nowhere more obvious than in the fiscal system".[17] The dual and often conflicting nature of the dynastic conglomerate is emphasised by Yun-Casalilla. On the one hand, there was the imperial political economy (that is, the way in which resources were distributed and allocated through the institutional framework), driven by the dynastic aspirations of the Habsburgs; on the other hand, there was the political economy of the empire's various kingdoms and regions, which aimed to protect their local and corporate institutions. The tension between these two forces was constant and, ultimately, decisive for the imperial system's trajectory.[18]

Since the key to understanding the Spanish Empire lies in the negotiations between the monarch and the various kingdoms and regions under his rule, it is worth asking what role coercion played in those negotiations. In a thought-provoking essay examining the limited revenue-raising capacity of the Spanish Monarchy under the Habsburg and Bourbon dynasties, and comparing them with the British case, Irigoin and Grafe argue that the relationship between tax collection and the state's coercive efforts was not linear but rather an inverted U-shape. In their model, coercion is plotted on the *x*-axis and net revenue on the *y*-axis.[19] Initially, increased coercion is followed by higher tax revenue, which continues to increase until it reaches its peak, the apex of the inverted U, which Irigoin and Grafe call point A. Beyond point A (moving along the *x*-axis), increased coercion becomes counterproductive because it encourages fraud. Net tax revenue therefore begins to decrease – first slowly, then precipitously – until the inverted U is complete. A vertical line passing through point A divides the inverted U into two halves that are crucial to Irigoin and Grafe's central argument: in the left half, increasing coercion stems from improvements in state coordination for tax collection; in the right half, beyond point A, coercion results from the state's predatory impulse, which ultimately leads to rampant fraud. According to Irigoin and Grafe, North and Weingast's article would place post-1688 England on the right half of the model, but close to point A – which is to say, near the potential peak of tax revenue. In contrast, Spain would be located much further to the right of England, at the end of the inverted U, far from point A, with reduced revenue as a direct consequence of the fraud provoked largely by the monarchy's predatory policies. However, Irigoin and Grafe see it very differently: they place Spain on the left half of their model, in the first third of the inverted U, where the essential problem is the state's capacity for coordination, not its predatory actions. They assert that "Spain was throughout the Early Modern period on the left half of the graph, where states combined revenue collection capacity with low degrees of investment in coercion".[20]

Is it true that the Spanish monarchs refrained from predatory measures and based the political economy of their empire on negotiation? That there was a high degree of negotiation is undeniable. However, it is also the case that, on occasion, the Spanish monarchs resorted to absolutist forms of predation. The king possessed *regalías* (royal prerogatives) that allowed him to make unilateral decisions with significant economic impacts. This fact, which Irigoin and Grafe overlook, reduces the utility of their inverted U-shaped model. In fact, the Habsburgs, under pressure from costly military campaigns in Europe, carried out flagrant violations of property rights in Castile, especially in the seventeenth century. Two breaches, with severe consequences, were the recurrent manipulations of the billon coinage (the fractional currency of Castile, much more widely used than silver coinage) and the systematic confiscations of substantial portions of the interest on the consolidated debt in the form of *juros*. Irigoin and Grafe mention these transgressions only briefly and attach little importance to them.[21]

It is useful to briefly recall how the manipulations of the billon were carried out and the extent of the confiscations of interest on *juros*. Both examples show that state plunder did not require significant investments, but simply an institutional and legal framework that facilitated it.

Since minting coins and altering their characteristics (weight, fineness and face value) were a *regalía*, the king could be tempted to resort to currency manipulations in times of need. It was easy for him to increase the currency's face value relative to its real value and pocket the difference.[22] There were two ways to do this: by minting new billon coins or by restamping coins already in circulation. The second option was more attractive because it was cheaper. It simply required Castilians to take their billon coins to the mints for restamping. There, a mark was applied, increasing the face value. Then the owners received the same face value they had handed over to the mint, now contained in fewer coins with a higher extrinsic value. With the remaining coins, the Royal Treasury could pay the king's creditors.[23] In a book published in Germany in 1609, a Jesuit and historian from Toledo, Juan de Mariana, explained the ultimate meaning of the counterstamps (*resellos*) with a perspicacious analogy: "Would it be lawful for the king to enter the granaries of private individuals and take half of all the wheat for himself and want to satisfy them by having them sell the other half for double what it was before?"[24] Such short-term, inflationary practices, more frequent during the reign of Philip IV (with counterstamps in 1641, 1643, 1651, 1654, 1658 and 1661), were followed by deflationary measures – decreasing the face value of *vellón* – that in practice amounted to a second blow to property rights. The problems caused by these measures far outweighed any short-term gains.[25] The issuance and restamping of coins generated inflation while simultaneously increasing the silver premium (the premium demanded for exchanging copper coinage for silver coinage). Subsequent deflationary measures, intended to counteract the billon inflation, severely damaged urban economies and, by extension, reduced tax revenue.

Monetary problems worsened in the 1670s. In January 1680, the silver premium reached 275 per cent. The *vellón,* used in most domestic transactions and for tax payments, had undergone its most severe historical depreciation. The following month, a 75 per cent reduction in the face value of the billon coinage was decreed. This and other, similar measures caused a monetary contraction that "paralysed credit and trade, plunging the Castilian economy into a depression that could not be fully overcome in the following two decades".[26] In light of the *vellón* manipulations, Santiago Fernández, an expert on Spanish monetary history, considers the abuse of Castilian monetary legislation a manifestation of "seventeenth-century political absolutism".[27]

The confiscation of a portion of the interest on *juros* was another predatory measure employed by the Crown to generate revenue, thereby breaching the commitment made to *juro* holders. These confiscations, known as *valimientos* and *descuentos*, began to be applied in 1625. Initially selective and temporary, they soon became general and permanent. From 1635 the deduction of the annual interest on *juros* was 50 per cent (the so-called *media anata de juros*); from 1660 onwards it exceeded 65 per cent. In fact, from 1637 the deductions of interest on *juros* represented the most regular and reliable source of income for the Royal Treasury of Philip IV.[28] Álvarez Nogal contends that they "actually became confiscations or partial suspensions of debt, thereby infringing upon the property rights that their holders had acquired when purchasing the annuities".[29] The systematic confiscations of interest on *juros* destroyed the reputation of consolidated public debt and, with it, the Spanish Monarchy's capacity to issue debt securities until the second half of the eighteenth century.[30]

The *vellón* devaluations and the *juros* interest confiscations show that low investment in the means of coercion did not necessarily mean there were no predatory practices. During the seventeenth century, state predation was accompanied by meagre investment in improving tax-collection efficiency. How was it possible that a monarchy which had relatively limited coercive resources and was forced to negotiate with regional and urban governments could nevertheless implement predatory measures with profound economic impact? The answer lies in the arbitrariness permitted by the institutional framework in some respects. On the one hand, the monarch was obliged to negotiate tax increases, the creation of new levies or the renewal of subsidies, such as the *millones*, with the parliament or *Cortes* of Castile, and, from 1665, with individual cities.[31] But on the other hand, monetary policy and public debt posed few obstacles to taking unilateral and arbitrary measures. This observation is not intended to endorse the North and Weingast thesis, which has been vigorously challenged even in its claims about the British Empire's respect for property rights.[32] What I want to emphasise is that simply characterising the Hispanic Monarchy under the Habsburgs as either absolute or composite is insufficient to fully grasp its political economy. The lack of a long-term fiscal and financial masterplan, coupled with the large number of heterogeneous, contradictory and short-term decisions adopted, is clear evidence of this complexity. Rather than fully subscribing to one of the customary characterisations of the monarchy, it is more illuminating to analyse the levels and forms of coercion that the state employed in certain institutional spheres. The *Carrera de Indias* provides an example of state coercion that moved between negotiation and predation. Here, too, the institutional framework played a key part.

5.3 Taxing the fleet system: The outbound leg

The *Carrera de Indias* was organised around a series of laws and institutions enacted during the first decades of transatlantic communication. Firstly, participation in trade with the Indies and the right to travel there were exclusively reserved for Spaniards. Secondly, all transatlantic navigation was channelled through Seville, home to the *Casa de la Contratación* or House of Trade, the official supervisory body created in 1503. Ships could also depart from the adjacent ports of Sanlúcar de Barrameda and Cadiz. Thirdly, in 1543, Seville's transatlantic merchants obtained royal permission to establish a mercantile court: the *Consulado de Cargadores*. The *Consulado* also fulfilled guild, administrative, financial and fiscal functions. The merchants themselves elected the leaders of their institution (a *prior* and two *cónsules*) from among the most prestigious members of the merchant community. The fourth key institution of the Indies trade was a system of regular fleets that transported the bulk of trade between Spain and the Americas. Before 1560, convoy navigation had been a wartime defensive measure. However, the system of armed fleets, which would operate for more than two centuries, was created and regulated between 1561 and 1565. From then on, all trade with the Americas would be conducted using two annual fleets, one for New Spain (destined for the port of Veracruz) and another for Tierra Firme (for Cartagena and Nombre de Dios/ Portobelo). For their military defence, the *Armada de la Guarda* (Guard Fleet) was created. Although the departure dates varied slightly, the voyages needed to avoid the most dangerous seasonal periods in the Caribbean and the Gulf of Mexico. In particular, the New Spain fleet had to avoid sailing through the Gulf of Mexico at the end of summer, when hurricane risk was higher.

The single-port policy sought to increase the Crown's control over the transatlantic trade and migration, and the House of Trade implemented it. The fleet system, for its part, responded to the need to protect the transatlantic trade militarily, particularly the enormous quantities of silver that arrived in Seville from the 1560s onwards. Equally important, the regularity of the fleets reduced uncertainty in the transatlantic trade and was therefore a factor highly valued by merchants. However, did the fleets facilitate taxation?

From its inception, the House of Trade maintained a *registro*, or register, of all ships, goods and people crossing the Atlantic. Although the *registro* initially had no fiscal purpose, the creation of the *avería* (a tax levied to cover the defence costs of the transatlantic trade) in 1523 and the *almojarifazgo de Indias* (the main ordinary tax on the transatlantic trade in Seville and Cadiz) in 1543 demonstrated that it also served as a means of tax collection. In Haring's view, fiscal control became the register's primary function from the mid-sixteenth century onwards.[33] Likewise,

García-Baquero asserts that the register enabled the rigorous collection of all taxes.[34] Yun Casalilla states that "from the sixteenth century onwards, a system of convoys was organised to increase fiscal efficiency and repel corsair attacks".[35] For Álvarez Nogal, the rigidity of the fleet system and the maintenance of the single port are "examples of the Spanish Crown's predatory attitude, whereby, in exchange for greater ease in controlling merchants and collecting taxes from them, more productive alternatives were sacrificed".[36]

However, to determine whether the fleet system facilitated tax collection and exemplified, as Álvarez Nogal indicates, the Crown's predatory disposition, it is essential to distinguish between the outbound leg to America and the return voyage to Spain. Elsewhere, this distinction has proven extremely useful for delving into two fundamental aspects of the colonial trade in the seventeenth century. Firstly, it has allowed me to refine my analysis of the evolution of tax evasion and reveal that it was subject to very different incentives on the outbound and return legs.[37] Secondly, it has allowed me to observe that the net ordinary tax burden on trade moved further away from the nominal tax rate throughout the seventeenth century, which resulted in a significant decrease in the tax burden on the outbound leg, particularly after 1660.[38] In this chapter, I want to show that there was a considerable contrast between the level of coercion applied on the outbound and return voyages, and that at the root of this contrast lay the institutional framework and the nature of the goods transported. Regarding the outbound leg, the fleet system severely hampered fiscal oversight.

Spain's most important export was textile manufactures (generically called *ropas*), which travelled packed in bales, bundles and crates. From 1524 onwards the Crown never allowed these packages to be opened or inspected at the customs houses. Instead, merchants were required to declare the market value of their cargo. This was an easy way to evade taxes: the merchants could merely declare a value lower than the goods' actual worth. When the measure was approved, at a time when Spain's transatlantic trade was still in its infancy, fraud through false declarations was limited. However, with the growth of the transatlantic trade and the establishment of the fleet system from the 1560s onwards, the decree preventing the inspection of packages created a widening gulf between what would have been collected through the effective application of the nominal ad valorem tax and what was actually collected at the customs houses of Seville and Cadiz. This difference generated numerous disputes between merchants and customs officials, especially during the periods when the collection of the *almojarifazgo de Indias* was farmed out. The conflicts at the customs houses delayed fleet preparations to the point of jeopardising the expeditions themselves. Faced with this dilemma, the Crown always sided with the merchants. It preferred to sacrifice tax revenue rather than put at risk the departure of the fleets.[39] The consequence was the progressive decrease in ordinary tax revenue.

Tax-collection problems also affected American customs houses upon the arrival of the fleets. There, tax revenue was hampered by a worrying resource shortage. Royal officials complained about this every time the fleets arrived. The treasurer of Veracruz, Andrés de Aramburu, succinctly summarised the situation in a letter to the king in January 1649. The problem of tax evasion had to be solved in Seville and Cadiz because

> The remedy is more straightforward in Spain, where Your Majesty's ministers have more influence and are more readily obeyed than in the Indies, where our defence consists of four guards, and against this power, there are two thousand or more people who come in the fleet, all or most of whom are involved in commerce.[40]

The customs houses of Veracruz and Nombre de Dios/Portobelo operated independently of those in Seville and Cadiz. The duties levied on the two sides of the Atlantic were neither the same nor had the same rate, although in the case of the *almojarifazgo* they shared the same name. Furthermore, in the seventeenth century, the management of Peninsular customs houses was mainly in the hands of tax farmers (for 85 years between 1595 and 1700), while royal officials continuously administered those in the Americas. Despite these differences, and despite the parallel worlds in which the customs houses on opposite sides of the Atlantic seem to have existed, their tax systems maintained a little-studied connection. Although initially the royal officials of Veracruz and Portobelo were tasked with appraising the tax base (the appraisal was known as *avalúo*) of goods arriving from Spain, by the 1580s it was clear that this was an arduous task, due to the scarcity of resources and the considerable size of the shipments.[41] From then on, customs officials used the merchandise appraisals made at the customs houses of Seville and Cadiz, to which they added a percentage *crecimiento* (increase) that, theoretically, was supposed to reflect the price increase of European goods in the Americas. The first increase I know of was applied to the Tierra Firme fleet *registro* at Nombre de Dios in 1582, amounting to 65 per cent.[42] The average increase applied to the 13 fleets that arrived at Portobelo between 1601 and 1621 was 68.4 per cent.[43] In Veracruz, during the middle decades of the seventeenth century, a 50 per cent increase was commonly applied to bales and crates containing *ropas*.[44] Once the tax base was assessed in this way, customs officials applied the 10 per cent *almojarifazgo* duty and other minor taxes. As a result, revenue in the Americas also fell considerably throughout the seventeenth century.[45]

Why didn't the Crown take more effective coercive measures to increase revenue? Part of the answer lay in the service of the *juros* on the *almojarifazgo de Indias*. By the beginning of the seventeenth century, its entire revenue was tied up in servicing *juros* interest.[46] From the 1630s onwards, revenue from the *almojarifazgo de Indias* began to decline rapidly, and *no cabimiento* (non-payment of a varying number of *juros* due to insufficient tax revenue) became a permanent situation. By the 1660s, non-payment reached 95 per cent of the annual annuity service. The literature highlights two reasons to explain the drop in customs revenue. On the one hand, the "reduction and discontinuity" of Spain's transatlantic trade;[47] on the other hand, the increase in fraud.[48] Outbound fraud was prevalent in the middle decades of the century but it decreased from 1660 onwards: the decrease in ordinary-tax pressure discouraged it, leaving it as a residual phenomenon.[49] The decreased frequency of fleet voyages was undoubtedly a significant factor, though it did not necessarily imply a decrease in trade value. My interpretation is that other, more decisive factors influenced the drop in revenue. Firstly, there was a structural transformation in the quality of goods exported to the Americas, with an increase in the proportion of higher-value goods relative to their volume and a decrease in relatively low-priced, bulky goods. This transformation began at the start of the century and continued beyond 1650. A lower volume of trade should not have affected revenue if a strict ad valorem method had been applied, but this was not the case. Secondly, and related to the above, a series of measures sanctioned by the Crown itself, which sought to put an end to the problems caused by false declarations from merchants, considerably reduced the tax burden. These included the introduction of two methods for calculating the tax base, approved in 1629 and 1680 respectively – the first appraised goods by weight, and the second by volume. And lastly, in 1661, the Crown ordered a one-third reduction in the tax base for goods shipped to the Americas. These measures led to a growing discrepancy between the goods' customs valuations and their market prices. The limited private documentation available indicates that by the end of the seventeenth century, the tax base calculated by Spanish customs officials did not exceed 5 per cent of the market price of the textile products shipped to the Indies.[50]

Would the Crown have increased tax revenue if it had allowed packages to be opened at the customs houses and if market prices had determined the tax base? Besides the substantial interest on annuities that the increased revenue would have had to cover before generating net income, the undertaking would not only have required a massive investment in personnel and encountered strong opposition from merchants, but it would also have had to adapt to the increasingly irregular and infrequent departures of the fleets. In the period 1660–1699, there were 19 fleets to New Spain and 11 to Tierra Firme; no fleet sailed in 15 of the 40 years, and the two fleets sailed only in five of those years.[51] The cost of maintaining a larger number of customs staff, who were idle for long periods, would have been prohibitive both for the king and even the most daring tax farmer.

In short, the fleet system itself, the composition of products exported to the colonies and the pledging of the entire *almojarifazgo de Indias* revenue on servicing *juros* interest discouraged any attempt to increase the level of coercion in ordinary taxation. The cost would have been enormous and the results uncertain. The Crown opted, primarily from 1635 onwards, for an alternative, less costly way to tax the transatlantic trade and raise more substantial revenue: it began demanding extraordinary contributions from merchants in the form of *indultos* (agreed fines or pardons), *donativos* (monetary "gifts") and *servicios* ("voluntary" subsidies). These contributions became the proper taxation of the *Carrera*. As they were free of the *juros* service, they went directly to the king's coffers. This process, which was neither linear nor premeditated, was guided by a combination of the Crown's constant economic needs and a logic that sought to marginalise the *almojarifazgo de Indias* revenue and the *juro* holders. To understand what prompted merchants to pay the extraordinary contributions, it is necessary to look first at the return leg.

5.4 The return leg and the 1660 reform

The return voyage allowed for strict fiscal control at low cost. Silver, which accounted for a relatively small volume, represented more than 80 per cent of the value of goods imported from the Americas in the seventeenth century.[52] The silver was not subject to the *almojarifazgo*, but rather to the *avería*, a levy intended to finance the military defence of the fleets. The possibility of more rigorous taxation on the return leg was made available through the process for collecting the *avería*. Upon the fleet's return, all the registered silver was taken to the Treasure Chamber in the House of Trade in Seville and held there until the total cost of the transatlantic expedition's military defence was known. Only then could the *avería* rate be calculated.[53] This procedure offered the king the tempting opportunity to appropriate private silver. He only needed to give the order to the House of Trade officials. As already seen, excesses of this kind were relatively frequent between 1523 and 1652. However, the silver seizures ordered by Philip IV from 1621 onwards spurred tax evasion to unprecedented levels. Furthermore, the lower amounts of registered silver arriving were an additional incentive for fraud, because the less silver entered the Treasure Chamber, the higher the *avería* rate. The so-called "*avería* crisis" forced the Royal Treasury to assume the bulk of the fleets' defence costs.[54] It was paramount to find a new way to finance the military protection of the transatlantic trade. Fortunately for the Spanish Monarchy, with the Franco-Spanish (1635–1659) and Anglo-Spanish (1654–1660) wars at an end, a solution to the *avería* problem became possible due to lower fleet-protection costs.

The solution consisted of suspending the mandatory registration of silver and, therefore, its temporary storage in the Treasure Chamber. This measure was ordered by a royal decree issued on 31 March 1660. Following the Crown's recurrent excesses since 1621, the loosening of governmental control over silver shipments became a necessary institutional adjustment. This measure was meant to strengthen the credibility of the Crown's commitment to respecting property rights, as highlighted by the Council of the Indies in a summary report presented to the king in August 1661:

> It seemed that the most effective means there could be to eradicate [the fraud committed on the return leg] would be to grant the merchants the liberty they had always desired to bring their silver freely without being obliged to get it into the House of Trade, for it was [in the Treasure Chamber] that they suffered the greatest anguish.[55]

Freedom of registration marked a turning point in the history of the Spanish colonial trade. It has been debated whether the recovery of the transatlantic trade began at that moment or a couple of decades later.[56] What is beyond doubt is that it brought about a profound reconfiguration of the rules of the game. It is true that most of the silver had already arrived unregistered before 1660 and would continue to do so thereafter, only now legally. However, there was more to it than that. On the one hand, the silver would no longer be held in the Treasure Chamber of the House of

Trade. The king had agreed to dispense with this mechanism, which was intended to facilitate the collection of the *avería* once the cost of military defence had been calculated. Dispensing with the Treasure Chamber was interpreted by merchants as a guarantee that their silver would be respected. On the other hand, the suspension of mandatory registration meant the defence of the fleets would have to be financed differently. The *consulados* on both sides of the Atlantic pledged to contribute a fixed new *avería* of 640,000 silver ducats (882,353 pesos) to the defence of the *Carrera*. The Royal Treasury, for its part, would contribute 150,000 silver ducats. The amount allocated to each *consulado* or merchant community was set out in a 1667 *asiento* or contract. Peruvians were to pay 350,000 ducats each time the Tierra Firme fleet crossed the Atlantic, and the merchants of Cartagena were to pay 40,000 pesos. The Mexican merchants were to pay 125,000 pesos for each New Spain fleet. The Seville *Consulado* was to pay 150,000 pesos for the New Spain fleet and 83,750 pesos for the Tierra Firme fleet. Following an agreement between the *consulados* of Mexico and Seville, the peninsular Spaniards were responsible for collecting the quotas from both communities.[57]

Merchants initially doubted that the Crown would honour the agreement. The fact that silver no longer had to be taken to the Treasure Chamber was intended to reduce the king's predatory power and, consequently, reassure the merchants. However, the government in Madrid had learned its lesson. In 1664, the House of Trade suggested to the Council of the Indies that some control measures should be adopted so that fleet commanders would know the quantities of silver brought to Spain. The Council rejected the suggestion, explaining that such an order could "interfere with the freedom granted to merchants".[58] Nothing should be done without first consulting the Seville *Consulado*.

Although the royal decree of 1660 established general guidelines for collecting the new *avería*, the *consulados* retained some discretion. The Seville *Consulado* appointed three deputies on each fleet to apportion their quota among all those who had loaded goods. Typically, *repartimientos* (apportions) were carried out in Veracruz and Portobelo by assessing each fleet's cargo on a pro rata basis. The deputies received instructions on the procedure to follow. The royal decree of 4 July 1667 ordered, in its fifth chapter, that the three deputies should make the distribution "as they deemed convenient, justified and easy for collection, [...] assigning specific value to each pitcher, cask, bale, crate or barrel".[59] It is important to emphasise that the *repartimientos* also served to collect extraordinary contributions, either previously negotiated with the Royal Treasury or imposed at the last minute by the king. On occasion the negotiation between the *Consulado* and the Crown was kept secret from the merchants, as for example in the case of the 1695 New Spain fleet.

Seven months before the fleet's departure, in December 1694, the Seville *Consulado* committed to the Crown to collect in Veracruz, in addition to the 275,000 pesos for the new *avería*, an *indulto* of 308,000 pesos for the shipment in Cadiz of French textiles, which were prohibited due to the war with France. The merchants were aware of these payments, but the deputies received secret orders from the *Consulado* to collect more money. Just before the return to Spain, to everyone's surprise, the deputies announced that the amount they had to prorate actually totalled

1,409,800 pesos, a sum that included the new *avería*, the *indulto* and the money needed to redeem a loan the *Consulado* had taken out in 1694 to pay the king an extraordinary contribution. The merchants were to pay 375 pesos for each *frangote* (bale) they had imported to Veracruz. The deputies managed to raise 831,162 pesos, a figure below the required amount. The *Consulado* made another attempt in Cadiz upon the fleet's return in the spring of 1697. In the Bay of Cadiz, the deputies used the apportionment carried out in Veracruz to collect 400,000 pesos for a "voluntary" *donativo* and 600,000 pesos to redeem the 1694 loan taken out by the *Consulado* on behalf of all the merchants.[60] As a result, the merchant community split into two factions: those who supported the *Consulado* authorities, and those who considered the contributions to be excessive. The amounts demanded and collected, as well as the tension generated within the merchant community, suggest that the *Consulado* had assumed the role of a fiscal agent in the service of the Royal Treasury. I examine the factors that explain this transformation in Section 5.5.

The full amount paid as extraordinary contributions after 1660 is not yet known. Attempting to identify all the payments is a very complex task.[61] Díaz Blanco estimates, based on data from García Fuentes, that the Crown received a total of 9,319,091 silver pesos from the Seville *Consulado* as extraordinary contributions during the second half of the seventeenth century. However, 79 per cent of that amount pertains to the period 1680–1700.[62] Díaz Blanco admits that the total figure must have been higher.

To understand the importance of extraordinary taxation, it is very illustrative to look at the 1695 New Spain fleet. Table 5.1 presents the tax-base appraisals of

Table 5.1 Tax bases, tax revenues and *crecimientos* of the 1695 New Spain fleet's outbound cargo (silver pesos of 272 maravedis)

Fleet cargo	*Tax base (avalúo) in Cadiz and Seville*	*Tax revenue in Cadiz and Seville on departure (9.14%)*	*Crecimientos added to the Cadiz and Seville tax base in Veracruz*	*Tax base (avalúo) in Veracruz*	*Tax revenue in Veracruz on arrival (12%)*
Merchandise (textiles, iron, haberdashery...)	563,666 ps	51,519 ps	60%	901,866 ps	108,224 ps
Raw materials and foodstuffs	23,686 ps	2,165 ps	45%	33,160 ps	3,979 ps
Wine	83,971 ps	7,675 ps	35%	109,609 ps	13,153 ps
Total	671,323 ps	61,359 ps	---	1,044,636 ps	125,356 ps

Source: Own elaboration from "Resumen de lo que ymportan los costos y afueros de las mercaderías", Veracruz, 11 January 1696, AGI, México, 64, R.2, N.22.

Note: I calculated the nominal tax rate on departure from Cadiz (9.14 per cent) based on the customs manifest of one of the fleet ships: "Registro del navío *Nuestra Señora de las Mercedes*", AGI, Contratación, 1254, N.4. The rate included the *almojarifazgo de Indias* (5 per cent) and minor duties. The 12 per cent corresponding to arrival in Veracruz included the *almojarifazgo* (10 per cent), the Mexico *Consulado* duty (1 per cent) and the Windward Fleet tax (1 per cent).

the fleet's outbound voyage in 1695, carried out in Cadiz and Veracruz, as well as the taxes collected in both ports and the percentage increases applied in Veracruz. The tax farmers of the *almojarifazgo de Indias* collected 61,359 pesos at departure from Cadiz.[63] What remained after covering expenses was used to pay the interest on a few lucky *juros* that still received it. The Crown did not retain even one of those pesos. Through ordinary channels, the Crown received the 125,356 pesos from the import *almojarifazgo* in Veracruz.[64] In contrast, the double apportionment carried out by the deputies of the Seville *Consulado* in Veracruz and Cadiz raised 1,583,000 pesos, adding the new *avería*, the *indulto*, the *donativo* and the part destined for the repayment of debts.

However, it is useful to put the amount collected by the deputies in perspective. Although 1,583,000 pesos was a substantial figure, constituting a 12-fold increase in the fleet's ordinary revenue, it does not appear to have translated into high fiscal pressure, at least if we are to believe Morineau's estimates. The French economic historian places the value of the precious metals carried to Spain by the 1695 fleet at between 23 and 30 million pesos.[65] This wide band, however, suggests that his figures must be taken with a pinch of salt.

The contributions demanded by the Crown were not constant either in their frequency or their magnitude. They were the result of unforeseen emergencies. What is surprising is that the *Consulado* was able to collect considerable sums with such limited resources. This suggests that merchants granted greater fiscal legitimacy to the institution that represented them than to customs officials or tax farmers. Something that merchants valued above all, due to their "perpetual scruples and misgivings", was that their business dealings and the funds they handled remained secret.[66] The *Consulado* guaranteed this.

5.5 State coercion after 1660

Could simply granting the *Consulado* the power to levy taxes, and ensuring the secrecy of business dealings, persuade merchants to agree to pay the sums demanded by the king? These were significant adjustments that could hardly contribute to increasing Crown revenues without an adequate level of coercion.

According to the minutes of the meetings held at the *Consulado*, negotiations with the Crown were largely uneventful during the 1660s, primarily because the extraordinary contributions demanded were minimal. The first point of tension appears to have arisen in 1670, when the Council of the Indies requested that the merchants cover the costs of reinforcing the New Spain fleet with two galleons. This fleet, which typically sailed protected only by the *capitana* (flagship) and the *almiranta* (rear-flagship), was about to depart. The Count of Peñaranda, who was the president of the Council, believed that the payment would not be a significant burden on the merchants, as they were reaping considerable profits thanks to the 1660 decree.[67] The requested amount was 80,000 ducats (110,294 pesos). The *Consulado* presented the request at the trade general meeting, where the attendees voted on whether or not to comply with the king's demand. With 18 votes against and 10 in favour, those present decided that the hundreds of merchants of the *Carrera* should not bear the cost of reinforcing the fleet, as it exceeded the 275,000 pesos agreed upon in the 1667 contract for the new *avería*.[68] Predictably, this response was not well received in Madrid. In mid-May, the secretary of the Council of the Indies wrote to the House of Trade about what to do. The tone was very different from that used by Peñaranda a few weeks earlier. It was no longer a request directed to the *Consulado*, but a firm order accompanied by a veiled threat: "And because it is necessary to know the persons who attended the meetings held by the *Consulado*, and the opinion they held, Your Lordship and those gentlemen [the *Consulado* authorities] will send testimony of this with all distinction and clarity".[69]

As on other occasions, the minutes of the meetings do not indicate whether the merchants ultimately assumed the expense of reinforcing the fleet or whether the *Consulado* sent the list of attendees to the Council. As for what the Council could do with a blacklist of merchants, I can only speculate. Besides enriching themselves, we know that merchants sought to improve their social standing and gain ennoblement. Becoming a member of one of the main military orders (Santiago, Calatrava and Alcántara) was an established goal among the wealthiest merchants of the seventeenth century. The granting of membership to Seville transatlantic merchants began in the 1620s and reached its peak in the 1640s. Afterwards, the number declined significantly. Perhaps it is no coincidence that, in the 12 years following 1670, the time of the Council's threat, no Sevillian merchants joined the military orders.[70] Furthermore, the 1670 meeting was not the only time the Council sought the names of the attendees. It was one of the first orders the Duke of Medinaceli issued shortly after assuming the presidency of the Council of the Indies in 1679. The *Consulado* refused to provide the list because "if the names of those attending the general trade meetings were mentioned, it would be much more difficult to convene them".[71]

Merchants could avoid attending the meetings, and indeed, hundreds of them did. The leaders of the *Consulado*, however, could not hide. Therefore the Crown directed its pressure towards them, and one way to ensure this had an effect was to make sure the *Consulado* leaders most receptive to royal demands remained in their positions beyond the term prescribed by the institution's ordinances.

In accordance with the ordinances, the election of the prior and the second consul (the first consul was the second consul of the previous year) was to be held annually. The procedure consisted of electing 30 electors every two years to choose the prior and the second consul each year. However, the frequency of the elections was not always as stipulated. Between 1618 and 1646, they were suspended on 10 occasions.[72] It was usually the Council of the Indies that sanctioned the election. Sometimes the Council had an interest in maintaining the same *Consulado* interlocutors during negotiations on matters such as the settlement of the *avería* or an *indulto*, which could be particularly arduous and lengthy. However, between 1675 and 1700 there were only six elections.[73] It cannot be a coincidence that the elections were frequently suspended in the same period during which the extraordinary contributions demanded by the Crown proliferated. As shown in Figure 5.1, the direct consequence of cancelling more elections than in previous periods was

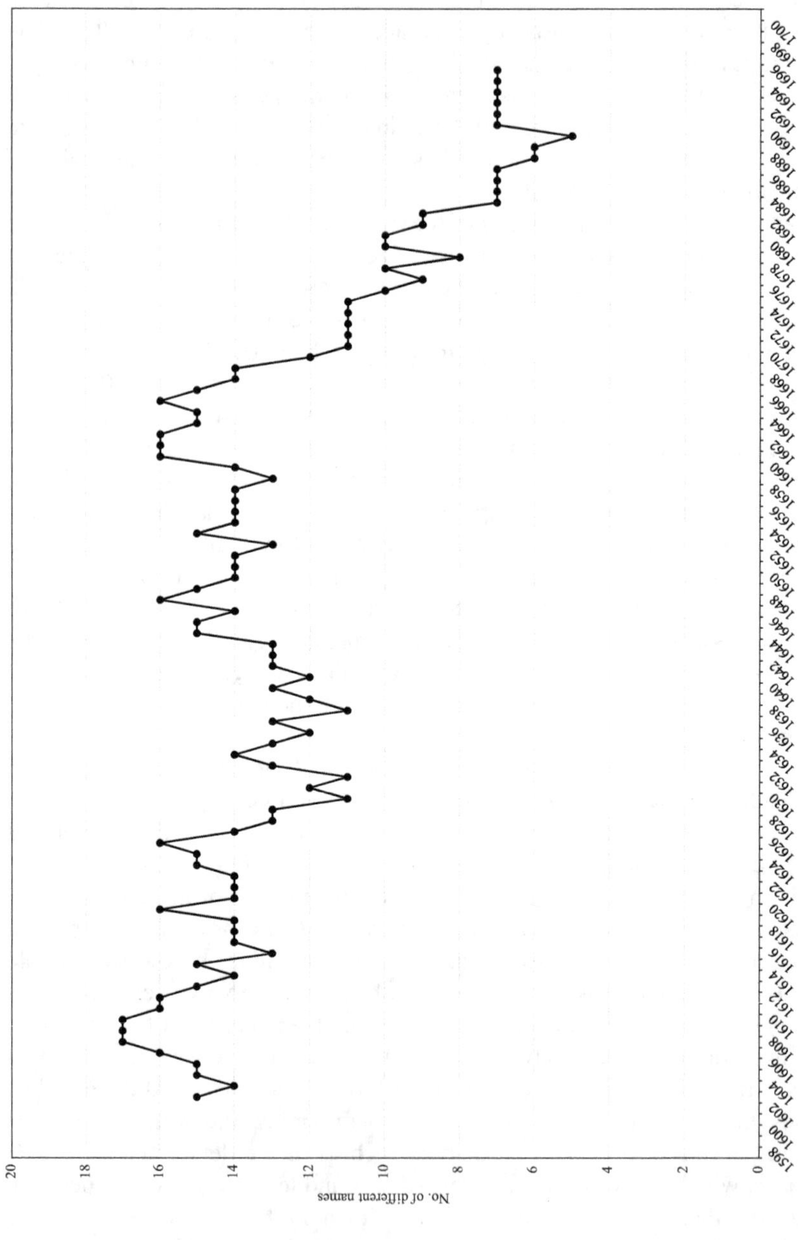

Figure 5.1 Number of different individuals in the governing body of the Seville *Consulado*, 1598–1701 (11-year moving totals of prior and consul names).

Source: Own elaboration from Díaz Blanco, 2012: 297–301.

the reduced number of different individuals leading the *Consulado*. The figure displays the 11-year moving totals of different prior and consul names from 1598 to 1701. In accordance with the electoral system, which kept consuls in office for two years, a theoretical maximum of 23 different people could have led the *Consulado* in an 11-year period. Until the 1660s, the number ranged between 11 and 17. From then on, it decreased to between five and seven.

The Crown retained the leaders who were most accommodating towards its monetary demands, and when a prior or consul seemed unwilling to cooperate, their tenure was brought to an end. This was the case with Francisco de Contreras Chaves. After four consecutive years as prior, from 1674 to 1677, he was re-elected in 1678. However, the appeals judge (the king's representative who oversaw the election process) annulled the re-election, stating that Contreras had served too many terms. But was that the real reason? According to Díaz Blanco, "Contreras's great sin was defending the interests of the merchants with more fervour than could be tolerated in Madrid".[74] The longest-serving *Consulado* triumvirate of the century, elected in January 1685, was composed of Lorenzo López de Ezeiza (prior), Luis de Torres y Monsalve (first consul) and Martín del Ollo (second consul). They remained at the helm of the *Consulado* for eight years, which would have been impossible without the Crown's approval. They were succeeded by a triumvirate that stayed together for three years, then another that remained in place for seven years. Furthermore, the two priors of the 1690s, the Basques Antonio de Legorburu and Ramón de Torrezar, were first cousins.

An important aspect that remains understudied, but which I can only briefly mention here, is the loans that the Seville *Consulado* took out to pay for extraordinary contributions to the king. The example of the 1695 New Spain fleet, cited above, is very illustrative of how these loans acted as an incentive for the *Consulado*'s leaders to include in the new *avería* apportionments that far exceeded what had been agreed in 1667. The creditors were the wealthiest merchants, who maintained the closest ties with the *Consulado*. The 600,000 pesos included in the *repartimiento* carried out in the Bay of Cadiz upon the fleet's return in 1697 were intended to redeem a loan with which, at the king's request, the *Consulado* had covered the expenses of shipping mercury to Veracruz in the summer of 1694. The loan yielded interest of 12 per cent for the creditors.[75] This helps explain why the merchant community split in two following the 1697 *repartimiento*.

The coercive mechanisms discussed so far had nothing to do with the silver seizures ordered by Philip IV. However, it would be naive to think that blacklists and the maintenance of amenable consular officials were sufficient on their own to ensure payment of the considerable monetary contributions the Crown demanded. Silver had ceased to enter the Treasure Chamber, but the fleet system and single-port policy could still facilitate the seizure of silver if that is what the king wanted. This threat loomed over the port of Cadiz in the 1680s and 1690s. An improved commercial environment allowed the Crown to seek funding in Seville for its wars against France. Hence, in those years, there was "a very significant reactivation of the tax pressure on colonial trade, to the point of not falling far short of the intensity applied during the government of the Count-Duke [of Olivares]".[76] The Crown began to take more aggressive coercive measures, and what happened in the mid-1680s is highly illustrative.

The War of the Reunions (1683–1684) against France broke out in October 1683. Shortly afterwards, on 15 December, the New Spain fleet, returning from Veracruz, entered the Bay of Cadiz. From Cadiz, the Seville *Consulado* prior wrote to his colleagues in Seville about "the great and urgent efforts that the Duke of Guastalla is making to extract five hundred thousand silver pesos belonging to the French from the fleet".[77] If the king's order was not obeyed, the duke threatened to remove all the treasure from the fleet and deposit it in Puntales Castle (located in the Bay of Cadiz), so that the king could command "whatever was in his best interest".[78] The transatlantic merchants, gathered in a meeting in Seville, requested that the king instruct the *Consulado* to seize the funds belonging to the French merchants, rather than let the Duke do so. Guastalla ignored the Sevillians' plea and seized 500,000 pesos from the fleet. The confiscation was so swift that there was no time to verify whether the silver truly belonged to the French; the *Consulado* asserted that it did not. In June 1684 it transpired that the Spanish merchants would recover the 500,000 pesos, plus 8 per cent interest, but not from the silver the Crown had seized: the king had authorised the *Consulado* to recover this amount from the French merchants' silver. However, no one knew how long this would take or whether it could be carried out. Meanwhile, the *Consulado* apportioned the 500,000 pesos seized by Guastalla among all the merchants, hoping to collect later what belonged exclusively to the French. Finally, the *Consulado* raised half a million pesos, but the matter remained unresolved.

In July 1684 the *Consulado* offered the king a subsidy of 250,000 pesos so that the Tierra Firme fleet, which was about to depart for Cartagena, could freely load French goods and that the money from the sales would return to Spain without suffering a new confiscation.[79] The Crown accepted the offer. Peace arrived in August, and with it a demand from the king of France that the 500,000 pesos seized in January be returned to the French merchants. But who should make the repayment, the Spanish merchants or the Crown? The answer to that question would become clear upon the return of the Tierra Firme fleet in the summer of 1686. In June, the king ordered that "the sum of said five hundred thousand pesos be divided and taken from the treasure coming on the galleons expected shortly from the province of Tierra Firme".[80] The merchants could scarcely believe the king's audacity. He was the one who had ordered the confiscation in January as retaliation and who had kept the money for himself. The funds subsequently raised by the *Consulado* had served to compensate the Spaniards. Now the Crown wanted to evade any responsibility and burden its subjects with the cost of reimbursing the French.

In August, when there was still no news of the fleet, unverified reports began to circulate in Seville and Cadiz that sent shivers down the spines of the merchants. The rumour was that the king had chosen to instruct the fleet soon arriving from Tierra Firme to be redirected to La Coruña or Santander, in northern Spain.[81] The arrival in Santander of three of the king's ministers, with a secret commission, indicated that he was preparing to carry out another silver seizure. The *Consulado* hastened to write to the monarch to remind him of the importance of scrupulously respecting the 1660 agreement for the smooth functioning of trade. The king had given unequivocal assurances that under no pretext would he interfere in the examination or inspection of private assets. If the king chose to disregard the 1660 agreement, "past risks" – probably a reference to Philip IV's reign – would re-emerge, all because of a "fleeting, temporary interest".[82]

The rumour about the king ordering the fleet to divert to northern Spain turned out to be false. The 18 ships of the convoy entered the Bay of Cadiz on 16 September 1686. However, it was only a brief respite for the merchants. Representatives of the *Consulado* discovered in Cadiz that the 250,000 pesos paid upon the fleet's departure two years earlier had been for nothing. Guastalla now had orders from the king not only to take 500,000 pesos from the silver that had just arrived from Tierra Firme and return it to the French, but also to demand from the *Consulado* "a very considerable subsidy, without precedent, and that if it was not done, all the treasure would be seized and minted into coins of greater value, and the reales would be restamped".[83] Ten days remained for a new royal decree to conclude the period of monetary reform that had begun in 1680 with the 75 per cent devaluation of *vellón*. The final measure, adopted on 14 October 1686, devalued the silver coinage minted in Spain (an expedient not implemented in the Americas), aligning it with the value of other European silver coins in an attempt to stem the outflow of Spanish pesos to other European countries. The decree mandated that eight-real coins (i.e. pesos) in circulation would be worth 10 silver reales in Spain, while the intrinsic value of eight-real coins minted thereafter would be reduced by 20 per cent.[84] The Crown's use of the new coinage and counterstamps as a threat to force merchants to pay a considerable contribution was reminiscent of the *vellón* manipulations that had generated so much revenue for the Royal Treasury at the expense of private individuals. The message was understood by the merchants, and the *Consulado* reluctantly agreed to pay a "gracious *donativo*" of 800,000 pesos.[85]

The 1684 incident was not the only time the Crown forcibly seized silver during the reign of Charles II. Another instance was when the president of the House of Trade took 589,000 pesos from the flagship of the Tierra Firme fleet upon its return in July 1698.[86] The most egregious coercion was driven by the Crown's pressing financial needs and facilitated by the institutional framework of the colonial trade, which, even after the abolition of mandatory silver registration, continued to offer the king the opportunity to adopt predatory measures without having to invest in the means of coercion. Necessity and opportunity combined throughout the century to tempt the Crown to take a share of the silver imports.

5.6 Conclusions

Some American economic historians consider the Hispanic Monarchy a paradigmatic example of a highly absolutist regime, in which the monarch prioritised dynastic interests over the economic development of the territories under his rule. In contrast, Hispanists of recent decades have insisted that the Hispanic Monarchy was not absolute but composite, with the king obliged to negotiate with the various regions, cities and corporations of the Spanish Empire to increase his tax revenues.

However, the absolutist-composite dichotomy contributes little to improving our understanding of the political economy of the Hispanic Monarchy during the Habsburg era. The Crown negotiated with the *Cortes* of Castile to obtain greater tax revenues, but also enacted predatory measures that had profound economic effects. How could it do so, if investment in the means of coercion was always low? My answer is that, in certain areas, the institutional framework facilitated state predation without requiring increased spending on coercion. Three of these areas were the minting of *vellón* coins, the payment of interest on *juros* and the colonial trade. In this chapter I have focused on the last one.

The institutional framework established before 1570 greatly influenced the taxation of the transatlantic trade in the seventeenth century. The monopoly of the western Andalusian port complex over trade with Spanish America, adopted at the beginning of the sixteenth century, was complemented in the 1560s by a system of regular fleets with predetermined dates and destinations. However, in terms of the efficiency of tax collection, there was a significant difference between the outbound and return legs.

The most essential goods on the outbound leg, textile products, were also the most difficult to tax ad valorem. The Crown prohibited the opening and examination of bales and crates at the customs houses because inspection of a fleet's cargo before its departure was complex and time-consuming, and threatened to delay the departure. However, speeding up departure procedures negatively impacted tax revenue. The level of tax enforcement was even lower in the American customs houses, where the means of coercion were scarce. Around 1580, it was decided that the royal officials at Veracruz and Nombre de Dios (Portobelo, from 1598) would calculate the tax base of goods arriving from Spain based on the values established at Seville and Cadiz.

In contrast, the return leg offered the possibility of more rigorous taxation. Silver represented the most valuable Spanish import. Upon arrival, it was deposited at the House of Trade. There, the *avería*, a levy intended to finance the fleets' military defence, was deducted. The deposit of large quantities of silver at the facilities of a royal institution proved to be an irresistible temptation for the Spanish monarchs. The silver seizures incentivised tax evasion during the return voyage, especially under Philip IV. The drastic decrease in registered silver in the 1640s and 1650s forced the Royal Treasury to cover most of the *Carrera*'s military-defence costs. To solve the problem, the Crown decided to eliminate compulsory registration on the return leg in March 1660. The silver no longer had to be deposited at the House of Trade, and the Crown would have no way of knowing how much was coming or to whom it belonged. In return, merchants on both sides of the Atlantic pledged to contribute to the defence of trade through a fixed quota. With this new agreement, the Crown succeeded in getting merchants to once again contribute to the financing of military defence.

A key fact was that the distribution method used by the Seville *Consulado* to collect the new *avería* also served to gather the extraordinary contributions (*indultos*, *donativos* and *servicios*) demanded by the Crown. As these demands became more frequent and substantial in the 1680s and 1690s, the Crown had to resort to a series of coercive measures to ensure merchants paid the required amounts. While the fleet system, due to its cumbersome nature, had contributed to reducing the revenue-collecting efficiency of Spanish and American customs on the outbound leg, on the return leg it had the opposite effect: it continued to facilitate the state's coercive actions without requiring additional investment.

Notes

1 Lorenzo Sanz, 1977.
2 Domínguez Ortiz, 1983 [1960]: 271–278.
3 Díaz Blanco and Hernández Rodríguez, 2020.
4 Díaz Blanco and Hernández Rodríguez, 2020: 268–269.
5 Sardone, 2019.
6 Lorenzo Sanz, 1977: 283–284.
7 Marcos Martín, 2024.
8 Domínguez Ortiz, 1983 [1960]: 270.
9 Acemoglu, Johnson and Robinson, 2005: 550–551 and 563.
10 North and Weingast, 1989.
11 Elliott, 1992; Fortea Pérez, 1990 and 2008; Jago, 1981.
12 This view is also held by Yun-Casalilla, 2015: 55.
13 North and Weingast, 1989: 803.
14 North and Weingast, 1989: 804 and 830.
15 North and Weingast, 1989: 808.
16 Some historians prefer to describe the Spanish Monarchy as polycentric. See, for instance, Grafe, 2013.
17 Grafe, 2013: 247.
18 Yun-Casalilla, 2012 and 2018.
19 Irigoin and Grafe, 2013.
20 Irigoin and Grafe: 223.
21 Irigoin and Grafe: 209 and 215.
22 Lanza García, 2023: 382.
23 García Guerra, 2003: 17.
24 Mariana, 2017 [1609]: 75.
25 Andrés Ucendo, 2022: 476.
26 Lanza García, 2023: 431.
27 Santiago Fernández, 2008: 9.
28 Toboso Sánchez, 1987: 179.
29 Álvarez Nogal, 2009: 34.
30 Dedieu, 2018: 25–41.
31 Fortea Pérez, 2008: 321–363.
32 See Hoppit, 2011.
33 Haring, 1918: 67.
34 García-Baquero, 1992: 31.
35 Yun-Casalilla, 2012: 143.
36 Álvarez Nogal, 2004: 40–41.
37 Lamikiz, 2023.
38 Lamikiz, 2024.
39 Antúnez Acevedo, 1797: 239.

40 Andrés de Aramburu to the king, Veracruz, 15 January 1649, Archivo General de Indias (hereafter AGI), México, 37, N.2.
41 Council of the Indies to Martín de Irigoyen, Madrid, 21 July 1570, AGI, México, 1090, L.6, f. 98r; Juan Vivero to the king, Panama, 20 May 1580, AGI, Panamá, 12, R.19, N.111.
42 Royal officials to the king, Nombre de Dios, 11 October 1582, AGI, Panamá, 33, N.125.
43 Juan López de Cañizares to the king, Panama, 15 December 1621, AGI, Panamá, 34A, N.55.
44 Viceroy of New Spain to the Veracruz officials, Mexico City, 4 December 1671, Archivo General de la Nación-México, General de Parte, vol. 12, exp. 90, f. 109v.
45 Vila Vilar, 1982.
46 Lamikiz, 2024.
47 Pulido Bueno, 1993: 146.
48 Alloza Aparicio, 2019: 203.
49 Díaz Blanco, 2024; Lamikiz, 2023 and 2024.
50 Díaz Blanco and Hernández Rodríguez, 2022: 119–120; Lamikiz, 2024: 187–188.
51 García Fuentes, 1980: 165–166.
52 Chaunu and Chaunu, 1955–1960, VI-1: 474.
53 Veitia Linaje, 1672: 72–73.
54 Álvarez Nogal, 1998.
55 Lamikiz, 2024: 185.
56 Oliva Melgar, 2004: 68; Díaz Blanco, 2012: 239.
57 Lamikiz, 2023: 234–241.
58 Juan del Solar to the president of the House of Trade, Madrid, 31 July 1668, AGI, Consulados, L.7, f. 214r.
59 Lamikiz, 2023: 239.
60 Lamikiz, 2023: 242.
61 See, for instance, Díaz Blanco, 2012: 268–282; García Fuentes, 1980: 116–134; Sánchez Belén, 1996: 270–275; Storrs, 2006: 137–143.
62 Díaz Blanco, 2012: 276.
63 The *almojarifazgo de Indias* was farmed out to Juan Francisco Eminente for 4,730,080 maravedis (17,390 pesos) a year from 1692 to 1697. Archivo General de Simancas, Contadurías Generales, 2948.
64 As for the return leg, the accounts of the 2.5 per cent *almojarifazgo* collected at Veracruz on departure and the 5 per cent collected upon arrival at Cadiz have not been preserved. However, both revenues are likely to have been very small due to the suppression of compulsory registration and the fact that silver never paid *almojarifazgos*.
65 Morineau, 1985: 236. Only a small part of the silver belonged to the king. In the second half of the seventeenth century, as the cost of imperial defence in the Americas increased, the Crown gradually received smaller silver consignments. See Díaz Blanco, 2013.
66 President and judges of the House of Trade to the king, Seville, 2 June 1676, AGI, Indiferente, 2369.
67 Count of Peñaranda to the Seville *Consulado*, Madrid, 29 April 1670, AGI, Consulados, L.8, ff. 18v-19r.
68 Junta general de comercio, Seville, 13 May 1670, AGI, Consulados, L.8, f. 28r-v.
69 Francisco Fernández de Madrigal to the president of the House of Trade, Madrid, 18 May 1670, AGI, Consulados, L.8, ff. 31v-32r.
70 Domínguez Ortiz, 1976.

71 Duke of Medinaceli to the Seville Consulado, Madrid, 16 May 1679, AGI, Consulados, 135.
72 Heredia López, 2022.
73 Heredia Herrera, 1985: 220.
74 Díaz Blanco, 2018: 84.
75 Seville *Consulado* to the Duke of Montalto, Seville, 22 June 1694, AGI, Consulados, L.58, ff. 32v-33v.
76 Díaz Blanco, 2012: 269.
77 Junta general de comercio, Seville, 2 January 1684, AGI, Consulados, L.11, f. 139r.
78 Junta general de comercio, Seville, 2 January 1684, AGI, Consulados, L.11, f. 139r.
79 Junta general de comercio, Seville, 7 July 1684, AGI, Consulados, L.11, f. 162v.
80 Junta general de comercio, Seville, 11 September 1686, AGI, Consulados, L.11, f. 273v.
81 The Seville *Consulado* to the king, Seville, 29 August 1686, Archivo de la Casa Zavala, 40.9, f. 1r.
82 Archivo de la Casa Zavala, 40.9, f. 2r.
83 Junta general de comercio, Seville, 4 October 1686, AGI, Consulados, L.11, f. 278r.
84 Lanza García, 2023: 403–404.
85 Díaz Blanco, 2012: 271.
86 Junta general de comercio, Seville, 19 July 1698, AGI, Consulados, L.13, ff. 188v-192r.

Bibliography

Acemoglu, Daron, Johnson, Simon and Robinson, James (2005), "The Rise of Europe: Atlantic Trade, Institutional Change, and Economic Growth", *American Economic Review*, 95, 3, pp. 546–579.

Alloza Aparicio, Ángel (2019), *Sistema aduanero en la Corona de Castilla, 1550–1700*, Valladolid: Universidad de Valladolid.

Álvarez-Nogal, Carlos (1998), "Finanzas y comercio en la España del siglo XVII: la crisis de la avería", in José Antonio Armillas Vicente, coord., *Actas del VII Congreso Internacional de Historia de América*, Zaragoza: Gobierno de Aragón, vol. 3, pp. 1365–1374.

Álvarez-Nogal, Carlos (2004), "Instituciones y desarrollo económico: la Casa de la Contratación y la Carrera de Indias, 1503–1790", in Antonio Acosta Rodríguez, Adolfo Luis González Rodríguez and Enriqueta Vila Vilar, coords., *La Casa de la Contratación y la navegación entre España y las Indias*, Sevilla: CSIC/Universidad de Sevilla, pp. 21–51.

Álvarez-Nogal, Carlos (2009), *Oferta y demanda de deuda pública en Castilla: juros de alcabalas, 1540–1740*, Madrid: Banco de España.

Andrés Ucendo, José Ignacio (2022), "Mariana tenía razón: Las manipulaciones del vellón y la Hacienda de la Corona de Castilla en el siglo XVII", in Ángel Galán Sánchez, Ramón Lanza García and Pablo Ortego Rico, coords., *Contribuyentes y cultura fiscal, siglos XIII-XVIII* , Sevilla: Universidad de Sevilla, pp. 459–482.

Antúnez Acevedo, Rafael (1797), *Memorias históricas sobre la legislación y gobierno del comercio de los españoles con sus colonias en las Indias Occidentales*, Madrid: Imprenta de Sancha.

Chaunu, Huguette and Chaunu, Pierre (1955–1959), *Séville et l'Atlantique, 1504-1650*, Paris: Armand Colin and S.E.V.P.E.N, 8 vols.

Dedieu, Jean-Pierre (2018), "De la merced a la deuda: la Monarquía española y el crédito en el siglo XVIII", in Michel Bertrand and Zacarías Moutoukias, coords., *Cambio institucional y fiscalidad: Mundo hispánico, 1760–1850*, Madrid: Casa Velázquez, pp. 25–41.

Díaz Blanco, José Manuel (2012), *Así trocaste tu gloria: Guerra y comercio colonial en la España del siglo XVII*, Madrid: Marcial Pons.

Díaz Blanco, José Manuel (2013), "La sombra de Proteo: transformación del tesoro americano durante el siglo XVII", *Tiempos Modernos*, 27, pp. 1–41.

Díaz Blanco, José Manuel (2018), "Elección y representación: Itinerarios de una cultura política mercantil en el siglo XVII", in Jean-Philippe Priotti and Bertrand Haan, dirs., *Une Europe des affaires (XVIe-XVIIIe siècles): Mobilités, échanges et identités*, Brussels: Peter Land, pp. 73–97.

Díaz Blanco, José Manuel (2024), "El cálculo del infrarregistro en la Carrera de Indias: Una propuesta basada en la comparación de fletes y registros de navíos", *Magallánica. Revista de Historia Moderna*, 10, 20, pp. 99–131.

Díaz Blanco, José Manuel and Hernández Rodríguez, Alfonso Jesús (2020), "La negociación asimétrica en la Carrera de Indias: ¿cómo interpretar el octavo de la plata de 1620?", in Guillermina del Valle Pavón, coord., *Negociación, lágrimas y maldiciones: la fiscalidad extraordinaria en la Monarquía Hispánica, 1620–1814*, Mexico City: Instituto Mora-CONACYT, pp. 27–74.

Díaz Blanco, José Manuel and Hernández Rodríguez, Alfonso Jesús (2022), "La muerte del mercader. Una ventana a los negocios de Indias a fines del siglo XVII", *Revista Complutense de Historia de América*, 48, pp. 103–132.

Domínguez Ortiz, Antonio (1976), "Comercio y blasones: concesiones de hábitos de órdenes militares a miembros del Consulado de Sevilla en el siglo XVII", *Anuario de Estudios Americanos*, 33, pp. 217–256.

Domínguez Ortiz, Antonio (1983 [1960]) *Política y hacienda de Felipe IV*, Madrid: Pegaso.

Elliott, John H. (1992), "A Europe of Composite Monarchies", *Past and Present*, 137, pp. 48–71.

Fortea Pérez, José Ignacio (1990) *Monarquía y Cortes en la Corona de Castilla: Las ciudades ante la política fiscal de Felipe II*, Salamanca: Cortes de Castilla y León.

Fortea Pérez, José Ignacio (2008), *Las Cortes de Castilla y León bajo los Austrias: Una interpretación*, Valladolid: Junta de Castilla y León.

García-Baquero, Antonio (1992), *La Carrera de Indias: Suma de la contratación y océano de negocios*, Sevilla: Algaida.

García Fuentes, Lutgardo (1980), *El comercio español con América, 1650–1700*, Sevilla: Diputación Provincial de Sevilla.

García Guerra, Elena María (2003), *Moneda y arbitrios: Consideraciones del siglo XVII*, Madrid: CSIC.

Grafe, Regina (2013), "Polycentric States: The Spanish Reigns and the 'Failures' of Mercantilism", in Philip J. Stern and Carl Wennerlind, eds., *Mercantilism Reimagined: Political Economy in Early Modern Britain and Its Empire*, Oxford: Oxford University Press, pp. 241–262.

Haring, Clarence H. (1918), *Trade and Navigation between Spain and the Indies in the Time of the Hapsburgs*, Cambridge, MA: Harvard University Press.

Heredia Herrera, Antonia (1985), "Los dirigentes oficiales del Consulado de Cargadores a Indias", in Bibiano Torres Ramírez and José J. Hernández Palomo, coords., *Actas de las III Jornadas de Andalucía y América*, Sevilla: EEHA, vol. 1, pp. 217–236.

Heredia López, Alfonso Jesús (2022), "Las elecciones a prior y cónsul del Consulado de Sevilla en la visita de Juan de Góngora, 1618–1648", *Temas Americanistas*, 48, pp. 288–311.

Hoppit, Julian (2011), "Compulsion, Compensation and Property Rights in Britain, 1688–1833", *Past and Present*, 210, pp. 93–128.

Irigoin, Alejandra and Grafe, Regina (2013), "Bounded Leviathan: Fiscal Constraints and Financial Development in the Early Modern Hispanic World", in D'Maris Coffman, Adrian Leonard and Larry Neal, eds., *Questioning Credible Commitment: Perspectives on the Rise of Financial Capitalism*, Cambridge: Cambridge University Press, pp. 199–227.

Jago, Charles (1981), "Habsburg Absolutism and the Cortes of Castile", *American Historical Review*, 86, 2, pp. 307–326.

Lamikiz, Xabier (2023), "Fiscalidad y fraude en la reactivación de la Carrera de Indias, 1660-1700", in Ramón Lanza García, coord., *Los dineros de la corona: Finanzas y cambio fiscal en la Monarquía Hispánica, siglos XVI-XVII*, Granada: Comares, pp. 213–248.

Lamikiz, Xabier (2024), "The Fiscal Transformation of the Spanish *Carrera de Indias* in the Seventeenth Century: A Reinterpretation", *Revista de Historia Económica/Journal of Iberian and Latin American Economic History*, 42, 2, pp. 171–192.

Lanza García, Ramón (2023), "La reforma monetaria de 1680-1686 y la depresión económica de Castilla a finales del siglo XVII", in Ramón Lanza García, coord., *Finanzas y crisis financieras en la Monarquía Hispánica, siglos XVI-XVII*, Madrid: Marcial Pons, pp. 379–436.

Lorenzo Sanz, Eufemio (1977), "La requisición de las remesas de oro y plata de mercaderes y particulares por la corona en el siglo XVI", *Anuario de Estudios Americanos*, 34, pp. 271–293.

Marcos Martín, Alberto (2024), "Formas extraordinarias de financiación de la Monarquía Hispánica en los siglos XVI y XVII: Las incautaciones de las remesas americanas de plata para particulares", *Anuario de Estudios Americanos*, 81, 2, pp. 1–19.

Mariana, Juan (2017 [1609]), *Tratado y discurso sobre la moneda de vellón*, Barcelona: Deusto.

Morineau, Michel (1985), *Incroyables gazettes et fabuleux métaux: Les retours des trésors américains d'après les gazettes hollandaises (XVIe-XVIIIe siècles)*, London: Cambridge University Press.

North, Douglass C. and Weingast, Barry R. (1989), "Constitutions and Commitment: The Evolution of Institutional Governing Public Choice in Seventeenth-Century England", *Journal of Economic History*, 49, 4, pp. 803–832.

Oliva Melgar, José María (2004), *El monopolio de Indias en el siglo XVII y la economía andaluza: la oportunidad que nunca existió*, Huelva: Universidad de Huelva.

Pulido Bueno, Ildefonso (1993), *Almojarifazgos y comercio exterior en Andalucía durante la época mercantilista, 1526–1740*, Huelva: Universidad de Huelva.

Sánchez Belén, Juan Antonio (1996), *La política fiscal en Castilla durante el reinado de Carlos II*, Madrid: Siglo XXI.

Santiago Fernández, Javier (2008), *La moneda castellana del siglo XVII: Corpus legislativo*, Madrid: Editorial Complutense.

Sardone, Sergio (2019), "Forced Loans in the Spanish Empire: The First Requisition of American Treasures in 1523", *Economic History Review*, 72, 1, pp. 55–87.

Storrs, Christopher (2006), *The Resilience of the Spanish Monarchy, 1665–1700*, Oxford: Oxford University Press.

Toboso Sánchez, Pilar (1987), *La deuda pública castellana durante el Antiguo Régimen (Juros) y su liquidación en el siglo XIX*, Madrid: Instituto de Estudios Fiscales.

Veitia Linaje, José de (1672), *Norte de la contratación de las Indias Occidentales*, Sevilla: Juan Francisco de Blas.

Vila Vilar, Enriqueta (1982), "La feria de Portobelo: apariencia y realidad del comercio con Indias", *Anuario de Estudios Americanos*, 39, pp. 275–340.

Yun-Casalilla, Bartolomé (2012), "Las instituciones y la economía política de la Monarquía Hispánica, 1492–1714: Una perspectiva trans-'nacional'", in Fernando Ramos Palencia and Bartolomé Yun Casalilla, eds., *Economía política desde Estambul a Potosí: Ciudades estado, imperios y mercados en el Mediterráneo y en el Atlántico ibérico,* c. *1200–1800*, Valencia: Universitat de València, pp. 139–162.

Yun-Casalilla, Bartolomé (2015), "Imperio español, entre la monarquía compuesta y el colonialismo mercantil. Metodologías, contextos institucionales y perspectivas para el estudio de la fiscalidad y la movilización de recursos", in María Pilar Martínez López-Cano, Ernest Sánchez Santiró and Matilde Souto Mantecón, coords., *La fiscalidad novohispana en el Imperio Español: Conceptualizaciones, proyectos y contradicciones*, México: Instituto Mora, pp. 29–67.

Yun-Casalilla, Bartolomé (2018), *Iberian World Empires and the Globalization of Europe, 1415–1668*, Basingstoke: Palgrave Macmillan.

6 Merchants of Mexico City and the *Bula* of Crusade in New Spain, 1590–1659

María del Pilar Martínez López-Cano

Introduction

The objective of this chapter is to show the advantages obtained by a group of wealthy merchants of Mexico City from their involvement in the collection of royal taxes in New Spain through the analysis of the *Renta de Cruzada*, one of the main revenues of the Crown in the Viceroyalty between 1590 and 1659. To that end, I will analyse the role played by the city merchants who sold the *Cruzada's* bulls for the Crown (*Tesoreros de Cruzada* or treasurers), the conditions of the contracts they signed with the representatives of the Crown, and the main economic, political and social benefits obtained from the office. The period 1590–1659 was characterised by the demographic decline of the indigenous population, strong oscillations in silver production and the Atlantic trade,[1] plus the growing demand for resources to pay for the defence of the Indies and the Philippine Islands, as well as wars and rebellions in Europe.[2] From 1649, the Crown also sold some posts of the *Cruzada* Court (*Tribunal de Cruzada*) of Mexico and some local *tesorerías*.[3] Between 1649 and 1654, it obtained little more than 167,000 pesos from the sale of the Yucatan *tesorería* (14,900 *pesos*), the offices of main accountant and bailiff of the *Tribunal de Cruzada* (70,000 and 82,205 *pesos*, respectively), plus the half *anata* levied on the latter two.[4]

The treasurers and contracts that I will analyse are those of Luis Núñez Pérez (1590–1598), who also served as moneyer and assayer at the Mexico City Mint, and Don Francisco de la Torre, in charge of the *Tesorería de Cruzada* between 1606–1625 and the royal monopoly levied on playing cards (*asiento de naipes*) between 1627 and 1636. They were followed by the priors of the *Consulado* Juan de Ontiveros Barrera and Juan de Alcocer, treasurers of *Cruzada* between 1625–1635 and 1635–1647 respectively (the latter was also holder of the *asiento de naipes* between 1618 and 1627). The last treasurer analysed will be Antonio Millán, treasurer of *Cruzada* between 1647 and 1659, who also served as factor in the drainage of the Valley of Mexico (1643–1649) and administrator of the stamp paper (1644–1652). All of them were wealthy merchants, settled in Mexico City, involved in domestic trade with a strong presence in transatlantic and transpacific commerce.[5]

DOI: 10.4324/9781003653301-7

The context

From the last decades of the 16th century and driven by the rise of silver production and the economic growth of New Spain, it is possible to find in the city of Mexico a group of rich merchants, who controlled the trade with the Iberian Peninsula and the Philippines.[6] It is important to bear in mind that communication between the metropolis and the Asian archipelago went through New Spain and that from the end of the 16th century the Crown forbade the rest of its American colonies to trade with the Philippines, so the northern viceroyalty became the hub of the route which linked Spain and America, through Manila, with the Asian market, which was avid for silver.[7]

In exchange for the silver, whether in the form of silver *reales* or bars, the great merchants of Mexico City monopolised the imports from Seville and Manila and their distribution in the interior of New Spain. Their solvency and liquidity allowed them to control Mexican internal and external trade and become a source of financing for a large part of the local economy, from mining and agriculture to artisanal production and transportation. In 1592, a merchants' guild, the *Consulado*, was founded in Mexico City, the only one in New Spain until 1795, which enabled local merchants to defend their commercial interests and negotiate with the Crown various privileges. This happened between 1644–1661, 1668–1676 and 1694–1708 with the royal sales tax levied in the capital (*alcabala*) whose collection was transferred to the corporation in return for a lump-sum paid to the Crown.[8] These merchants diversified their interests with investments in agriculture and cattle raising. They also owned houses and real estate in the viceregal capital and a large number of slaves. To obtain silver, they developed relationships with the mining districts and silver merchants of the viceregal capital, purchased offices in the Mint of Mexico City, the only one in New Spain and until 1737 under private administration, and were in charge of collecting royal, municipal and ecclesiastical taxes.[9]

The economic growth of New Spain made it possible to increase the revenues of the Crown, which underwent an important upturn from the last quarter of the 16th century. The taxes levied on mining (smelting, assaying, *quintos* and tithes), the coining of silver pieces (*señoreaje* and *braceaje*), internal and foreign trade (*alcabala* and *almojarifazgo*) plus the tribute paid by Indian communities and some royal monopolies (in particular those levied on quicksilver and playing cards) became the pillars of New Spain's taxation.

In 1574, the *alcabala* was introduced in New Spain, although the indigenous people were excluded from paying this tax. In the same year, the sale of Crusade Bulls (*Bulas de Cruzada*), previously restricted to Spaniards, was extended to the entire population. Years before, there had been a rise in the rate at which the *almojarifazgo*, a customs tax, was levied. The tribute paid by Indian communities was converted into a *per capita* tax, also extended to mulattos and free blacks, and was increased by four reales more per year in 1592. In the first half of the 17th century, new taxes were introduced and adjustments were made to some of the existing ones. In 1625, the papacy granted the Crown a subsidy (*Subsidio*

Eclesiástico); in 1631 the Viceroyalty began to collect the *media anata*, which in 1638, was extended to ecclesiastics.[10] In the decade of 1630 the *alcabala* increased from the 2 percent established in 1574 to 6 percent, with a 2 percent surcharge for the *Union de Armas* (1633) and another 2 percent for the *Armada de Barlovento* (1639). In the same year, the *almojarifazgo* levied in Veracruz and Acapulco was increased by another 2 percent for the same purpose. At the same time, card decks were surcharged with three *reales*.[11] In 1644, stamp paper (*papel sellado*) became obligatory in the viceroyalty.[12] From the end of the 16th century until 1660, judging by the summaries of charge and date of the Royal Treasury of New Spain, the *Cruzada* could have amounted to 7 percent of the total revenues of the Treasury in New Spain.[13] Undoubtedly, the revenue from the sales of bulls was the main ecclesiastical income obtained by the Crown in these years in America.[14]

Royal officials were in charge of collecting various taxes, particularly those levied on silver mining. They were supported, in some cases, by local authorities such as the *alcaldes mayores* for example, were tasked with distributing quicksilver in the mining centres, an input that, coming from Almaden, was indispensable for the amalgamation of silver ore.[15] The *alcaldes mayores* were also in charge of tax collection in Indian towns, which granted them a commission of 6 percent of what was collected.[16] In other areas, agreements were made with corporations, such as in the case of the *alcabalas*, collected by the Consulate of merchants in the viceregal capital, or by the city councils of Puebla (1601–1697), Mexico (1602–1643, 1661–1667) and Zacatecas.[17] Likewise, private individuals were in charge of collecting some branches of the royal treasury, such as the *asiento de naipes*, plus municipal and ecclesiastical revenues, the Church tithes and, of course, the *Cruzada*.

It was decided at the end of the 1570s to place the sales of crusade bulls in the hands of private individuals. This was probably because in 1579, the Archbishop of Mexico, Pedro Moya de Contreras, at that time Deputy General Commissioner of the Crusade in New Spain, opposed its administration by Crown officers to emphasise its religious character. In those years, the bulls were just beginning to be sold in the Indian communities and every effort was made to prevent the Indians from assimilating the Crusade Bull with the tribute already paid by their communities to the Crown. Because of this, the names of those parishioners who acquired bulls were never recorded, nor were the *alcaldes mayores* tasked with collecting the Crusade, as was done with the tribute.[18] Instead, to facilitate the control and auditing of accounts, a single contract (*asiento general*) was preferred, which was called general since it included the entire viceroyalty (New Spain, New Galicia, Yucatan, Guatemala and the Philippines).[19] It should be noted that at the time the term *asiento* was synonymous with contract and did not necessarily imply an advance of money, and that the big merchants of Mexico City enjoyed great social prestige in New Spain. As the Viceroy Marquis of Mancera recognised in 1673, "Merchants and dealers [...] are very close to the nobility [...] so that it can be assumed that, in these provinces, for the most part, the gentleman is a merchant, and the merchant is a gentleman".[20]

The Cruzada treasurers

The Cruzada treasurers who took charge of the *asiento de Cruzada* between 1590 and 1659 were wealthy merchants settled in Mexico City, although some had been born in the Iberian Peninsula. This was the case with Luis Núñez Pérez de Meñaca, who came from a family of merchants from Seville. At the time he obtained the *asiento de Cruzada* in 1590, aged 45 or 50, Pérez had been residing in the viceroyalty for about 20 years;[21] and with Don Francisco de la Torre, a native of Zamora, who arrived in New Spain at a young age.[22] The rest were creoles: Juan de Ontiveros Barrera, Juan de Alcocer and Antonio Millán, all born in Mexico City.[23] I do not know the birthplace of Jerónimo de Soto, who held the post in the early years of the 17th century.

The *peninsulares* married rich Creole women. Luis Núñez Pérez married twice: his first marriage was with Doña Inés de Aguilar, daughter of a local family and granddaughter of the conquistador Gonzalo Rodríguez Ocano, and his second was with Doña Catalina de Mendoza Zaldívar, daughter of the wealthy Zacatecan miner Vicente de Zaldívar.[24] Upon his arrival in New Spain in 1606, Don Francisco de la Torre was supported by his uncle, Pedro de la Torre, who introduced him into the collection of the *Cruzada*. Pedro de la Torre was a merchant, member of the *Consulado*, and had bought the post of Secretary of the Government of New Spain for 86,500 *pesos*. This secretaryship was auctioned in the second decade of the 17th century for 126,000 *pesos*.[25] He lived next to the convent of Santa Clara and owned other houses and small shops on the same street.[26] At his death, in 1619, his fortune was valued at more than 400,000 pesos and he left his niece Isabel de la Torre, married to a prominent merchant, Juan del Castillo, as his heir.[27] Don Francisco de la Torre helped his uncle in the collection of the *Cruzada*. Three years after his arrival in the New World, he married Doña Ana Amado de Melo, widow and heiress of one of the great merchants of the viceregal capital, Don Gaspar de Peralta. Doña Ana contributed to the dowry with some pieces of urban real estate, houses and stores, *censos*, credits and merchandise, for more than 150,000 pesos.[28] Don Francisco made repairs and investments in these properties, sold some pieces and bought others and acquired an urban patrimony valued at around 200,000 pesos.[29] He remained in New Spain until his death in 1648, although he expressed his wish to be buried in the convent of San Benito de Valladolid, where the only son of the couple, Fray Diego de la Torre, had taken vows as a monk. He left his son and the convent as his heirs. In spite of his great fortune, he died in jail because of the debts he owed to the royal treasury, which derived precisely from his involvement with the collection of the Crusade and the *asiento de naipes*, and his lawsuits with royal officials and the Consulate of Merchants of Mexico.[30]

As for the creoles, they came from merchant families. Juan de Ontiveros Barrera took up the post of Cruzada Treasurer when he was about 31 years old. He had previously been consul and prior of the *Consulado*, being the only one of the treasurers who opted for celibacy. He belonged to a powerful family of merchants and stockbreeders. His paternal uncle, Clemente de Ontiveros, in addition to being consul and prior of the *Consulado* in the last decade of the 16th century, owned extensive cattle ranches in the north. On his mother's side, his cousin, Doña Catalina de la Barrera[31] was the niece of Gil de la Barrera, *racionero* of the cathedral, and married Esteban del Real, who became consul of the *Consulado*. The daughter of the marriage and niece of Juan de Ontiveros, Doña Isabel de la Barrera y Escobar, married Simón de Haro, a rich silver merchant, who served many terms as *prior* of the Consulado and was very active in the trade with Castile and the Philippines. He was also a great benefactor of ecclesiastical institutions. Juan de Ontiveros had a very close relationship with Haro, who would become the executor of his will.[32] Captain Juan de Ontiveros became a priest at the end of his contract, being ordained to a chaplaincy that he had founded with the interest obtained from a 1,500-peso *censo* on the two pairs of houses of his dwelling on the central street of Celada in Mexico City.[33] These properties would later pass to Simón de Haro, who would rebuild them and free them from any encumbrances. Upon Ontiveros' death, his fortune was valued at 300,000 pesos and distributed among pious donations. As a presbyter, he became part of the prestigious Congregation of San Pedro. He died in 1652, aged 58.[34]

He was succeeded in the *Tesorería de Cruzada* by Juan de Alcocer, son of the merchant Alonso de Alcocer Berlfert, a native of Seville, who had settled in Mexico City and married Doña María de Herrera Contreras, a native of San Martín de Sombrerete, in the district of Zacatecas, daughter of a well-connected family.[35] For 17 years, Alonso de Alcocer was in charge of municipal tax collection for Mexico City, in particular the so-called *renta del desagüe* and the excise (*sisas*) on wine, which in the last decade of the 16th century and first decade of the 17th, amounted to around 100,000 pesos a year.[36] Alcocer also owned a farm, orchard and mills near the city and cattle ranches in Michoacán with 9,000 head of large cattle and 60,000 small, as well as houses, slaves, tools and other livestock, which his son would inherit and expand.[37] Juan took part with his father in the collection of the municipal taxes of Mexico City and settled the accounts upon his death. Captain Juan de Alcocer married Doña Guiomar de Bocanegra y Avalos, who was related to notable families of New Spain on both sides.[38] When he became *Cruzada* Treasurer, he had previously obtained the *asiento de naipes* and served as *consul* and *prior* of the Consulate of Mexico. He was also an accountant of the Tribunal of the Holy Office, and he must have been between 42 and 44 years old.[39] He died in 1649, with heavy debts, which had to be settled by his relatives, who had secured him for the position of treasurer.[40]

Antonio Millán started very early in the mercantile activity and was proud of having made his fortune in commerce.[41] He was born in 1595 in Mexico City, from the marriage of Francisco Millán, master stonemason from Castilleja de la Cuesta, and Doña Beatriz Hernández de Cuadros, from Seville.[42] On his father's side, he was connected to a prestigious local family, the Millán Poblete family, whose members held positions and dignities in the cathedral of Mexico and the Inquisition. Some of them became bishops in the Philippines.[43] Antonio Millán traded with New Spain, Castile and the Philippines, owned rich sugar *haciendas* and an impressive urban patrimony.[44] He was the first administrator of the *papel sellado*, from January 1644, when the tax was introduced in the viceroyalty, until December 1652, with a yearly salary of 2,000 *pesos*.[45] From the end of 1647, he alternated this post with the *Tesorería de Cruzada* and was also factor of the drainage of the Valley of Mexico in the 1640s. At the time he obtained the *Tesorería de Cruzada*, he was already a lay member (*familiar*) of the *Inquisición* and accountant of the Mexican Court of the Holy Office.[46] In addition to being alderman of Mexico City while at the *Tesorería*, he became ordinary mayor of the viceregal capital in 1660,[47] which speaks to his reputation and good relations. When he took over the *Cruzada* Treasury, at the age of 52, his fortune amounted to more than 400,000 pesos.[48] He died in 1661 at the age of 65.

All of the treasurers traded with the Iberian Peninsula and, in the 17th century, the Philippines. Some were electors, consuls and priors of the Mexico City Consulate, such as Juan de Ontiveros Barrera[49] and Juan de Alcocer.[50] Others were linked to the city mint. Luis Núñez Pérez held the post of assayer and moneyer of the mint, for which he paid almost 60,000 pesos in 1584, which earned him an annual income of 8,000 to 12,000 pesos in the last decade of the 16th century and the beginning of the 17th century.[51] Juan de Alcocer was interim treasurer of the mint between 1629 and 1635.[52] Three of our treasurers, Don Francisco de la Torre, Juan de Alcocer and Antonio Millán, lent money in 1630 to Juan Lorenzo de Vera to purchase the office of permanent treasurer of the mint.[53] On the other hand, Juan de Alcocer and Antonio Millán served simultaneously as *Cruzada* treasurers and accountants of the *Santo Oficio*; Alcocer for more than 20 years (1626–1648),[54] also served as interim accountant of taxes and *azogues*,[55] and in 1629 he requested a position as chief accountant in the Court of Accounts.[56] His brother-in-law, Martín de Rivera, was one of the accountants of the Court.[57] Millán held the post of accountant of the Holy Office from 1641 until his death in 1661.[58]

Another trait shared by the *Cruzada* treasurers was their interest in royal monopolies and the collection of royal and municipal taxes. In addition to the Crusade, Don Francisco de la Torre and Juan de Alcocer were in charge of the *asiento de naipes*. This granted them the monopoly for the production of playing cards and their distribution in all the provinces of the viceroyalty. The holder of the *asiento* undertook to pay a fixed amount: 80,000 pesos in the contract of Juan de Alcocer (1618–1627), and 100,000 in that of Francisco de la Torre (1627–1636), and to sell the deck at five *reales*, a price that rose as of 1 January 1633, to six *reales*. On the same date, the amount of the contract rose to 120,000 *pesos*.[59] The holder of the *asiento* had to pay the costs involved in the production of *naipes*, particularly the paper, imported from the Iberian Peninsula, as well as those of their distribution and marketing.[60]

Antonio Millán was the first administrator of stamp paper. Years later, his first-born son, Don Félix, would alternate the administration of the *Cruzada* bull in the archbishopric of Mexico and the playing cards in New Spain.[61] Luis Núñez Pérez, in addition to being assayer of the Mint, became in charge, after leaving the *tesorería*, of distributing quicksilver in Taxco, a task was given to him as mayor of a mining district (1608–1610).[62] Some treasurers were also linked to the collection of taxes granted to Mexico City for funding public works, such as the drainage of the Valley of Mexico to tackle the town's frequent floodings. Alcocer helped his father in the collection of the *sisa* and *quartilla* of wine at the beginning of the 17th century.[63] Between 1643 and 1649, Antonio Millán took an active part in the works of the Huehuetoca drainage and in the collection of the taxes allocated to that end (*quartilla* of wine in Mexico City, 25 pesos per pipe of wine in Veracruz, plus the taxes levied on the butcher shops of the viceregal capital).[64]

Cruzada treasurers enjoyed the status of royal officials and became temporary aldermen to the Mexico City municipal council for the duration of their tenure. The only exception was Juan de Ontiveros, who waived that privilege at a time when the town council was fighting a hard battle to prevent royal officials from being part of the municipal corporation.[65] Their ancestry and social prestige are also evidenced by their noble status (Luis Núñez)[66] and the fact that they were elected ordinary mayors of the city, as was the case with Juan de Alcocer and Antonio Millán. The latter, in addition, was offered the *corregimiento* of the capital under the condition of continuing as *Tesorero* at the end of his contract, an offer that he turned down.[67]

Finally, they all were well-connected. Luis Núñez was able to go to the Indies thanks to the support of Juan de Ovando, president of the Council of the Indies[68] and, once in New Spain, he kept a close relationship with Archbishop Pedro Moya de Contreras, who became interim viceroy.[69] Don Francisco de la Torre was very close to the viceroy Marquis of Gelves.[70]

All of them owned substantial urban assets and had their homes on the central streets of the city. Their training was usually received while assisting their fathers or relatives in their trade dealings and tax collection, as Juan de Alcocer did with his father. Others were involved in the *Cruzada* before they became treasurers. Thus, Luis Núñez Pérez was commissioned between 1575 and 1585 by the treasurers of the time, Diego Becerril, Juan Alonso Medina and Francisco Martínez,[71] to sell the bulls, and Don Francisco de la Torre worked in the same capacity for his uncle since 1606. Antonio Millán would introduce his son Don Félix, who would eventually take over the collection of the Crusade in the archbishopric of Mexico, in the *asiento*.

We have little information about their studies, although some treasurers received university degrees. Juan de Alcocer confessed to having given up his literary inclinations to help his father, but received bachelor's degrees in Arts (1608), Theology (1611) and Canons (1621) at the University of Mexico.[72] His education allowed him to apply first for the post of notary of the Holy Office in Michoacán and later for that of accountant of the Inquisition Court in Mexico City, a position he held for more than 20 years.[73] Towards the end of his days, Captain Juan de Ontiveros is recorded as holding a university degree (*licenciado*) and, as noted, at the end of his contract joined the Church, becoming a presbyter.[74] Although we do not know if Don Francisco de la Torre ever obtained any degree, everything indicates that he must have at least passed through the university classrooms, given his great facility for writing, often in his own hand, as he did with his inventory of goods and his will.[75]

Special features of the asiento de Cruzada

Although Crusade bulls had been circulating since the incorporation of New Spain into the Spanish Empire, everything indicates that until 1573 only Spaniards bought them, and that their preaching was forbidden in Indian villages.[76] The situation changed in 1573, when it was decided to preach the Bull of the Crusade to the entire population and, for that reason, the amount of the contract was considerably increased. Although at the beginning the preaching was annual, as in peninsular Spain, from 1578 it was extended to two years, so the time period taken as reference for the duration of the contract (pontifical concession) lasted 12 years, divided into six preachings or bienniums.[77]

Another peculiarity of the *asiento de Cruzada* was the broad demarcation it encompassed, since it included New Spain and the provinces of the viceroyalty, from the wide northern borders of Spanish rule in the American continent to Yucatán and, by the 17th century, Guatemala and the Philippines.[78] In particular, the inclusion of the Philippines in the *asiento* offered good opportunities to the treasurers by allowing them to take part in a trade that, in principle, was reserved for Spaniards living in Manila. From 1593, Mexican merchants were licensed to send one ship annually and 600 tons of merchandise to the islands. The maximum amount of money that could be sent there was 500,000 pesos and the cargo that could be shipped from the archipelago to New Spain in the return trip was limited to 250,000 pesos.[79] The implementation of the Bull of the Crusade was later in the Philippines than in New Spain and it was not until 1610 that the archipelago was included in the contract signed by Pedro de la Torre and his nephew Don Francisco de la Torre.[80]

Table 6.1 General treasurers of Cruzada in New Spain (1590–1659)

Treasurer	*Years*	*Other offices and posts held*
Luis Núñez Pérez de Meñaca	1590–1599	Assayer and moneyer at the Mint (1584–1610) Mayor of the Taxco mines and quicksilver distributor (1608-1610)
Pedro de la Torre (up to 619) D. Francisco de la Torre	1606–1625	Pedro: Member of the *Consulado* and Secretary of the Government of New Spain D. Francisco: holder of the *asiento de naipes* (1627–1636)
Juan de Ontiveros Barrera	1625–1635	Consul and Prior of the Consulate
Juan de Alcocer	1635–1647	Holder of the *asiento de naipes* (1618–1627) Acting Treasurer of the Mint (1629–1635) Tribute and Azogues Accountant Accountant of the Holy Office (1626–1648) Consul and Prior of the *Consulado* (1625...) Mayor of Mexico City
Antonio Millán	1647–1659	Administrator of the *Papel Sellado* (1644–1652) Factor of the works of the Huehuetoca drainage (1643–1649) Accountant of the Court of the Holy Office (1642–1661) Ordinary Mayor of the City of Mexico (1660)

Sources: See Text.

Unlike other contracts of this kind, the holders of the *asiento de Cruzada* did not have to pay the Treasury an annual fixed amount of money. The treasurer was given the bulls in Mexico City and had to pay the amount resulting from their sales there. The unsold copies were returned to the authorities. On the amount of the bulls sold (plus the proceeds from fines, compositions, and the granting of licenses for erecting chapels and oratories), he received a commission, which in the years studied went down, although not in a linear way, from the 14 percent that Luis Núñez Pérez enjoyed in the last decade of the 16th century to the 11 percent that Antonio Millán agreed to in 1647 (Table 6.2). At the beginning of the 17th century, in Jerónimo de Soto's *asiento*, 16.75 percent was agreed upon, a commission that dropped in the following contract to 13.5 percent. To guarantee their compliance with the terms of the contracts, the treasurers offered bonds and mortgaged goods and credits in their favour, which in the 17th century reached more than 200,000 *pesos*.[81]

The first *asiento* was granted in Madrid, in 1573, to three peninsular merchants who were to take care of all the Indies through some deputies. In 1586, two *Tesorerías de Cruzada* were created – for New Spain and Peru – and a peninsular, Gaspar de Soto, was sent to the former. The authorities must not have been very satisfied with these arrangements. The income derived from the Crusade was already an important source of revenue for the treasury, so in 1590, before it ended, the *asiento* was abrogated and its holder was compensated with 8,000 pesos. A new contract was signed with an important merchant of Mexico City, Luis Núñez Pérez, and the Crown managed to reduce the commission by 6 percentage points, from 20 to 14 percent.[82] From then on, the *asiento* was negotiated in New Spain, although it continued to be subject to the approval of the king and the Crusade Council in Madrid, and the *asentistas* came from people with roots in New Spain (although, as we saw, some were born in the Iberian Peninsula).

As for the costs involved in the whole operation, the Crown paid for the printing costs of the bulls (in the Hieronymite convent of Buenavista in Seville) and their transportation to Mexico City from 1590. Once there, they were taken by the treasurer. The latter was in charge of the cost of distributing the copies and collecting the revenues resulting from the bulls sold until the proceeds were deposited in the royal treasury's dependences in the viceregal capital. The Crown also paid for the

Table 6.2 Average gross income per biennium of the Cruzada Treasures of New Spain 1590–1659 in common gold pesos (272 maravedís)

Years	*Treasurer*	*Amount collected*	*Commission*	*Gross income*
1590–1596	Luis Núñez Pérez de Meñaca	290.466	14.0%	40.665
1611–1623	Pedro and Francisco de la Torre	272.645	13.5%	36.807
1625–1635	Juan de Ontiveros Barrera	276.663	11.5%	31.816
1635–1645	Juan de Alcocer	246.442	10.0%	24.644
1647–1659	Antonio Millán	242.477	11.0%	26.672

Source: Accounts of the second, fourth, fifth, sixth and seventh grants: AGS, Cruzada, 556 and 557.

transport of the bulls to the cities of Mérida (for the bishopric of Yucatán), Santiago de Guatemala (for the Central American bishoprics) and Manila (for the Philippine archipelago). The amounts collected in these distant provinces had to be taken to Mexico City at the treasurer's expense and risk.

Both the Crown and the treasurers had to pay an additional amount (*regalo extraordinario*). The *regalo* had its origins in the 1,000 ducats that the treasurer Luis Núñez Pérez offered to disburse among the priests in charge of the Indian parishes so they would become more enthusiastically involved in the preaching of the *Cruzada* every biennium. Subsequently, the Crown committed itself to allocating 2,000 ducats per biennium and the treasurer another 1,300 to the priests and the authorities of the Indian towns that helped in the preaching and distribution of the bulls.

Some treasurers offered monetary advances to obtain the contracts. Juan de Alcocer, for example, promised to advance 150,000 pesos for the first biennium and the first fleet that left for Spain after the bull was published in Mexico City. In the following bienniums, he would pay only 120,000 pesos of the first instalment, the payment of which was scheduled a year after the bull was published.[83] Almost all of them did some kind of service to the Crown, by paying some amounts of their contracts in advance to provide the authorities with funds for the dispatch of the fleets to Seville or the Manila galleon. Don Francisco de la Torre lent 58,000 pesos in 1620 for the latter and, the following year, he served with 6,000 *pesos*. Then, in 1622, he supplied funds for the equipment of the soldiers (*gente de guerra*) that went to the islands, plus 10,000 pesos for the port of Veracruz and 7,000 for biscuit and supplies (*bastimentos*). In the same year he also lent another 32,000 pesos for the dispatch of the fleet.[84] Lastly, Don Francisco de la Torre contributed with 10,000 pesos to the loan of 204,000 to the Crown in 1623. His successors Juan de Ontiveros and Juan de Alcocer also took part in the operation with 4,000 and 2,000 pesos, respectively.[85] Nevertheless, the general trend was to agree on long instalments, which would allow for a delay in collection of proceeds before taking them to the dependences of the royal treasury in Mexico City.

This was because the treasurer could use the money and goods obtained from the sales of the Bulls in his own dealings before the payment of the proceeds of the sales to the Royal Treasury. The first instalment was a year after publication of the Bull of the Crusade in Mexico City, and the second at the end of the biennium. In 1611, it was agreed to pay two thirds of the biennial amount in the first year, but the exact amount of the payment was not specified, which caused tensions between the authorities and the Crusade treasurer.[86] In the following contracts (1625–1635, 1635–1647) this amount was settled at 130,000 *pesos*,[87] reduced to 100,000 for the asiento of 1647–1659. In the last contract, an additional payment of 40,000 pesos was agreed upon at the end of the biennium, and it was also decided to grant an additional year for the treasurer to pay the Crown the biennial amount.[88] These were generous terms that made it possible for the treasurers to easily pay their first biennial instalment, as most bulls were sold at the beginning of the first year. We know little about the treasurers' agreements with the local receivers working for them, although the data suggest that the latter sold the bulls between three and six months after the beginning of the preaching. For example, in 1636, the treasurer Juan de Alcocer agreed with the authorities of the town of Atitalaquia in the archbishopric of Mexico to a 3 percent commission on the amount of the bulls sold in their district. The proceeds of the sales would be taken to Mexico City, where Atitalaquia's representatives had gone to obtain the bulls allocated to them and sign the corresponding receipt, in two and a half months.[89] As the treasurer had a year for the first instalment, Alcocer enjoyed a nine-month differential to invest the money in his own dealings. The three percent commission granted to the authorities of Atitalaquia paid for the distribution, collection and transportation costs of the bulls and their proceeds, since the community would take them to the viceregal capital. Of course, there was no shortage of defaults among local receivers and in these cases the treasurer requested the intervention of the *Tribunal de Cruzada* to collect the debt.[90] Generally speaking, however, the payment terms were usually extended, especially as the treasurers agreed to retain the money if there was no fleet or ships bound for the Iberian Peninsula, and between 1590 and 1659 the fleets lost their annual frequency.[91] After all, this offered them an excellent opportunity for profit in a cash-strapped economy.

The faithful could pay the amount of the bulls in kind. When this happened, the goods collected were exempt from the *alcabala* (and the surcharges imposed in the 1630s on this tax), and (in the district of Yucatán) the *almojarifazgo* levied on the sea route between the ports of Campeche and Veracruz. Of course, these exemptions were a cause of fraud and abuse. The treasurer marked with a cross the bundles of goods to indicate that they belonged to the Crusade, with no other proof other than his oath, and they became tax-exempt. As was common in areas with a high density of indigenous population and little access to currency, such as Yucatan, the bulls were apportioned among local communities through a *repartimiento* and, months later, the towns paid the amounts owed with goods. The use of this method in the province of Yucatan was denounced, and there were frequent requests to enforce the Cedula of 1 August 1633, which strictly forbade it.[92] The *repartimientos* were highly profitable for treasurers. Unlike most other *repartimientos* where raw materials or money were involved, here treasurers distributed bulls convertible into money or goods. Such bulls had been advanced by the Royal Treasury to treasurers who paid the amount of their sales to the Crown one or two years later. As usual in these cases, the goods delivered by the towns to pay for the bulls (cotton and wax blankets) were priced below market prices with the consequent profit for the holder of the *asiento*.[93]

There are data on the distribution of *bulas de Cruzada* in the Philippines among the aboriginal population in charge of the *alcaldes mayores*.[94] The bulls were paid for by the chronically cash-starved local communities in goods and then taken to Acapulco in the return trip of the Manila Galleon. To this end, the treasurers were allocated four tons per biennium in the cargo of the ship. Although they tried to have these goods exempt from the *almojarifazgo* they were unsuccessful.[95] Once the galleon docked at Acapulco, the next step was to pay the Crown in Mexico City. From the treasurers' perspective, the possibility of using the merchandise brought from Manila for their own dealings was the main incentive offered by the inclusion of the islands in the contract. Proof of that is that in 1736, after the end of the general *asientos*, one of the bidders for the Crusade *tesorería* of the Philippines offered to lower his commission by three points if instead of depositing the proceeds of the sales of bulls in the royal dependences of Manila, he was authorised to send goods to Mexico to sell them in the viceroyalty.[96]

Regardless of how the payment had been made (in money or goods), the treasurer deposited the money in the royal treasury in silver bars, money or payment orders of the Crown (*libranzas*). Silver bars were admitted by the Crown at their legal value. As the market price of silver bars was 3.5 percent less than the legal one, this constituted an additional source of profit for the treasurers.[97] Since they could pay in silver bars or coins, treasurers usually claimed a discount from the amounts paid in coin (for example, the salaries of the members of the Tribunal de Cruzada). Thus, during his term of office (1647–1659), Antonio Millán was paid 5,608 pesos, since he had paid 157,139 pesos in *reales*, i.e. an average discount rate of 3.5–3.6 percent of the amounts paid.[98]

Other than silver bars and coins, treasurers could resort to the payment orders traditionally issued by the Crown for paying wages and gifts (*libranzas*). As these orders were not always honoured by the Treasury, they circulated below par, but when used by the treasurers they were admitted for their nominal value; at least until the mid-17th century. In 1646–1647, the *libranzas* circulated 70–50 percent below par, with the subsequent loss to the Royal Treasury and in the last year it was decided to limit to 20 percent the amount of the *asiento* that can be paid to the Crown in this way.[99] This enabled Antonio Millán to use *libranzas* worth 400,000 pesos to pay his 2,000,000 pesos contract. The other 1,600,000 pesos were paid in silver bars.[100]

Treasurers also enjoyed a special set of legal privileges (*fuero*). They were judged by a special Court (*Tribunal de Cruzada*). The sums privately owed to them were considered as owed to the Crown itself, which enabled Don Francisco de la Torre to request the Crusade Court to collect 200.000 pesos for him.[101] This caused great controversy and clashes with the local authorities and courts of the viceroyalty, particularly because the appeals to the rulings of the Crusade Court had to be submitted to the Cruzada Council in Madrid. For this reason, it is not strange that, during the negotiations between the City Council of Mexico City and the viceroy on the funding of the *Armada de Barlovento*, the former asked to limit these privileges.[102]

Finally, being temporary royal officials for the time of their tenure, treasurers enjoyed a seat as aldermen in the Cabildo of Mexico City, like the three officials of the royal treasury of Mexico (treasurer, accountant and factor), the main courier and the treasurer of the local mint.[103] This gave them voice and vote in the local council, plus precedence over the other members of the corporation, immediately after the *Corregidor*. In the 1610s, the *alguacil mayor* disagreed with this disposition and enlisted the support of the rest of the aldermen, but after a long lawsuit the Council of the Indies ruled in favour of the treasurer of *Cruzada*, Don Francisco de la Torre.[104] Some treasurers took an active role in the affairs of the corporation, such as Juan de Alcocer, who participated in the negotiations between the city and the viceregal authority on the ways of funding the *Armada de Barlovento* during the 1630s,[105] while there is hardly any trace left of others in the minutes of the Cabildo.

Other privileges enjoyed by the treasurers included a prominent place in the procession and the ceremony in the cathedral the day of the publication of the Bull of the Crusade and the right to be escorted by two black slaves with daggers and swords, a privilege enjoyed by some other authorities, but that was limited over the years, as happened to the sheriff of the viceregal capital.[106]

The most obvious benefit of the *asiento* was the commission received by the treasurer for the bulls sold, which left him with a gross income of between 10 and 16.75 percent, depending on the terms of the *asiento* (Table 6.2). The treasurer had to bear the bull distribution and collection costs, which included the payment of all those who helped him in the whole operation. Therefore, it is not surprising that all the treasurers were wealthy merchants who resorted to their own networks of agents to distribute the bulls. They also enlisted the help of the officials of indigenous communities (*repúblicas de Indios*) who distributed the bulls in their districts or even in Mexico City in return for a 3 percent commission.

Based on the accounts they rendered, the gross income derived from the commissions for the treasurers in the bishoprics of the royal audiences of Mexico and Guadalajara (Mexico, Puebla, Michoacan, Oaxaca, Guadalajara and Durango), excluding Merida, ranged from an average of 24,644 pesos per biennium enjoyed by Juan de Alcocer (1635–1645) to the 40,665 obtained by Luis Nuñez Pérez in 1590–1596 (Table 6.2). Undoubtedly, this drop reflects the decline of the indigenous population, which constituted the majority of the population and which continued to fall in the first half of the 17th century.

The gross income of the treasurers increases by 90–100,000 pesos per biennium when taking into account other districts (Guatemala, Yucatan and the Philippines), which rendered separate accounts (Table 6.3). Most of the increase came from the bulls sold in the districts of Guatemala and Yucatan. In contrast, in the Philippines, revenues rarely exceeded 10,000 pesos per biennium (Table 6.3).

Table 6.3 Average gross income per biennium of the Cruzada Treasures (New Spain, Guatemala, Yucatan and the Philippines)

Treasurer	*New Spain*	*Guatemala*	*Yucatan*	*Philippines*	*Total collection*	*Gross income*
Luis Núñez Pérez	290.466					
Pedro and Francisco de la Torre	272.645	42.441	38.546	9.370	363.002	49.005
Juan de Ontiveros	276.663		38.303	10.506		
Juan de Alcocer	246.442	50.857	43.174	6.586	347.059	34.706
Antonio Millán	242.447	58.373	30.719	5.561	337.130	37.084

Source: AGS, Cruzada, 556, 557 and 560.

Note: Data common gold pesos (272 maravedís).

The vast range of other sources of profit previously mentioned (the possibility of dealing with the proceeds of the sales until they were deposited in the royal treasury's dependences; the potential profits from the sales of goods; the possibility of paying the royal treasury in silver and *libranzas*; the involvement in the trade with the Philippines and the substantial advantages derived from the *Fuero de Cruzada* for the *asentista*), although far from negligible are difficult to quantify.

In short, because of the amounts collected, the commission rates granted, the demarcation it covered and the privileges and opportunities it offered, the *asiento de Cruzada* became in the first half of the 17th century one of the main contracts to which any private individual could aspire in New Spain. Other branches of the treasury were administered directly by the Crown (taxes, mining rights), transferred to local communities in return for the payment of a lump sum (*alcabalas*) or, more simply, could not compare with the Crusade (such as the *estanco de naipes*).

Those wanting to collect the *Cruzada* had to mobilise a vast network of relationships to win the contract, first, and to reduce the costs involved in the sales of the bulls, second. This was something only within reach of the wealthy merchants of Mexico City, who, as Antonio Millán pointed out, were the best candidates for the post, since "in this kingdom, no [wealth] is safe except that of merchants and members of the consulate, whom the viceroys always seek when looking for revenues and candidates for the royal *asientos*".[107]

Notes

1 An overview of the economy of New Spain in: von Mentz, 2010; Hausberger and Mazín, 2010, as well as Calderón, 1988.
2 On the pressure of war expenses on the Indies in the 17th century: Serrano Hernández, 2020; on the remittances, via *situados*, from New Spain, for the defense of the Caribbean: Reichert, 2012, and for the Philippines, Alonso Álvarez, 2009 and 2012. On the loans and donations requested by the Crown: de Nardi, 2018.
3 Royal Decree of 12 January 1649.
4 Martínez López-Cano, 2019.
5 I have not found data on Jerónimo de Soto, who was in charge of the *Cruzada* in the early years of the 17th century. He accumulated heavy debts and died before the end of his contract.
6 For 1590–1660 the most complete study on this merchant group remains that of Hoberman, 1991.
7 The regulations of the traffic with the Philippines in Yuste, 1984.
8 See del Valle Pavón, 1997.
9 The investments of the merchants in Hoberman, 1991, and de la Peña, 1983.
10 On the origin and introduction of these taxes in the viceroyalty, de Fonseca and de Urrutia, 1845–1853.
11 On the negotiations and increases to the levies during the 1630s, Alvarado Morales, 1983, and Sánchez Santiró, 2012.
12 de Fonseca and de Urrutia, 1845–1853.
13 We do not have figures for the income and expenditures of the Royal Treasury of New Spain for these years, only the summaries or abstracts of the charge and data accounts of the Royal Treasury, compiled by TePaske, 1976, which, as Sánchez Santiró, 2013, has

emphasised, must be taken with caution, since charge and data are not synonymous with income and expenditures. From these summaries it is possible to see the relative weight of the different sources of revenue in the long term. According to the data recorded in the source, between November 1576 and April 1598, the Crusade would have represented 5.6% of the charge; in the reigns of Philip III, 6.8%: Martínez López-Cano, 2017: 177. Based on the summaries of the royal coffers for New Spain, the average annual income of the Royal Treasury stood at more than two million *pesos* annually between 1600 and 1659, with oscillations that could range from almost nine million to slightly more than 16 million *pesos* per quinquennium. Serrano Hernández, 2020: table 4.1, 525.

14 On the weight of the *renta de Cruzada* within the ecclesiastical contributions in the viceroyalties of New Spain and Peru: Serrano Hernández, 2020: tables, 2.11, 2.12 and figures 2.20, 122, 123 and 128.

15 Regarding the mechanisms for the collection and accounting control of income: Gordoa de la Huerta, 2024.

16 Gordoa, 2024.

17 About the *alcabalas* in Mexico City, del Valle Pavón, 1997; for Puebla, Celaya Nández, 2010a; about the modalities of collection, Celaya Nández, 2010b; about the *superintendencia de alcabalas* in Mexico City between 1576 and 1698, Gordoa de la Huerta, 2024.

18 Martínez López-Cano, 2017: 180–182.

19 Martínez López-Cano, 2017: 180–181.

20 Relación del marqués de Mancera a su sucesor, in *Instrucciones y memorias de los virreyes novohispanos*, 1991: 1, 583.

21 Hillerkus and Quiñones, 2015. The authors consider that he must have been born between 1545 and 1549.

22 This is what he declared in 1622 in the inventory of his goods: Archivo General de Indias (AGI thereinafter), México, 263, N. 191.

23 About Juan de Alcocer, this is recorded in the information of cleanliness of blood (*limpieza de sangre*) that he presented before the Holy Office of the Inquisition in Mexico, Archivo General de la Nación (AGN hereinafter), Inquisición, vol. 351, exp. 3 and in the *Información de oficio y parte* that he presented before the Real Audiencia, AGI, México, 237, N. 13; Juan de Ontiveros said so in his will. Archivo de José María Basagoiti Noriega (AHJMBN hereinafter), Estante 5, Tomo 5, exp. 5. 13, and Antonio Millán, in his *limpieza de sangre*, Arhivo Histórico de la Nación (AHN hereinafter), Inquisición, legajo 1186, exp. 16.

24 Hillerkus and Quiñones, 2015.

25 He obtained the office at auction and mortgaged it to guarantee the *Asiento de Cruzada* in 1611: Archivo General de Simancas (AGS hereinafter), Cruzada, 578. He was a member and elector of the Consulado: Rojas Cruz, 2018: 98, 238. The value of the office at his death, in: Ayala Tafoya, 2021: 80.

26 AGS, Cruzada, 578.

27 The amount of his estate was recorded by his nephew, Don Francisco de la Torre, in the inventory of goods that he presented in 1622: AGI, México, 263, N. 191. The designation of his niece Isabel as heir: Ayala Tafoya, 2021: 79.

28 Among his properties there were 20 pairs of houses with stores on San Juan Street, valued at 85,000 or 90,000 *pesos*; another three pairs of houses that he sold for 13,500 pesos with which he bought houses with a store in the merchants' portal, plus two *censos* for 21,000 pesos in principal, 12,040 pesos from a deed against Francisco de Quintadueñas and his wife, merchandise and deeds for more than 20,000 *pesos*; jewelry, clothing and

household goods for another 18,000 pesos. These possessions were encumbered with 19,000 *pesos* of *censos* for masses for the soul of the deceased Gaspar de Peralta: inventory of goods of 16 July 1622: AGI, Mexico, 263, N. 191.

29 The first figure is mentioned by Don Francisco in the inventory of 1622; the second, in his will (AGI, Escribanía, 170B *Pleitos Audiencia de México*) and in *Memorial del pleito que el convento real de San Benito de la ciudad de Valladolid litiga....*, Biblioteca Nacional de España (BNE hereinafter), VC/201/1.

30 The first figure is mentioned by Don Francisco in the inventory of 1622; the second, in his will (AGI, Escribanía, 170B *Pleitos Audiencia de México*) and in *Memorial del pleito que el convento real de San Benito de la ciudad de Valladolid litiga....*, Biblioteca Nacional de España (BNE hereinafter), VC/201/1.

31 Isabel's brothers were religious. One of them, Alonso, would be prior of the convent of Santo Domingo in Mexico City: Rojas Orzechowski, 2017.

32 With 6,000 *pesos*, Simón de Haro was among the 42 guarantors of Ontiveros when the latter obtained the *Asiento de Cruzada*: AGI, Mexico, 30, N.5. On the family relations of Juan de Ontiveros, see his will in AHJMBN, Estante 5, Tomo 5, exp. 5, and Rojas Orzechowski, 2017.

33 AGN, Bienes Nacionales, v. 494, exp. 5.

34 Testament of Juan de Ontiveros: AHJMBN, Estante 5, Tomo 5, exp. 5; Rojas Orzechowski, 2017, and Guij, 1986: I, 197–198.

35 The family was related to Pedro Gómez de Contreras, treasurer in the royal treasury of Zacatecas and to Pedro Moya de Contreras, general inquisitor, archbishop of Mexico, interim viceroy and general commissioner of the Crusade of New Spain: Genealogy information and cleansing of Juan de Alcocer: AGN, Inquisición, vol. 351, exp. 3.

36 AGI, México, 237, N.13.

37 Alvarado Morales, 1979: 502.

38 AGN, Inquisición, vol. 379, exp. 2.

39 I have calculated his age based on the date he received his Bachelor of Arts degree (1608). I am grateful to Enrique González and Rodolfo Aguirre for the information on the age at which the students of the University used to obtain the degree.

40 de Guijo, 1986: 59–60.

41 As he personally stated when he applied for the *asiento*: AGS, Cruzada, 583.

42 See his information in: AGN, Inquisition, vol. 417, part one, exp. 3, and AHN, Inquisición, 1737, exp. 13.

43 AGN, Inquisición, vol. 417, first part, exp. 3, and AHN, Inquisición, 1737, exp. 13.

44 AGS, Cruzada, 583; AGN, Tierras, v. 1272.

45 AGI, Indiferente, 156, N. 43.

46 AGN, Inquisición, vol. 417, part one, exp. 3.

47 de Guijo, 1986: II, 131; Pazos, 1999: 388. His son, in addition to being an alderman, would be elected ordinary mayor in 1661: de Guijo, 1986: 143.

48 AGS, Cruzada, 583.

49 In 1624 he appears as prior of the corporation: Rojas Cruz, 2018: 183.

50 He was first consul, and in 1629 prior of *Consulado*: AGI, Mexico, 237, N. 13.

51 Quality and merit information from 1591 and 1594–1595: AGI, México, 220, N.13 and AGI, Mexico, 221, N. 20; Hillerkus and Quiñones, 2015.

52 AGI, Contaduría, 810.

53 Rojas Cruz, 2024: 14.

54 In those years the revenues of the *Inquisition* increased considerably as a result of the *autos de fe*, persecutions and confiscation of goods of the defendants accused of Judaizing, particularly those of Simón Báez de Sevilla.

55 AGI, Contaduría, 788.
56 AGI, México, 237, N. 13.
57 AGI, México, 36, N.33.
58 AGN, Inquisición, vol. 417, part one, exp. 3.
59 Correspondence of Viceroy Cerralbo, year 1634: AGI, Mexico, 31, N. 29.
60 AGI, Philippines, 42, N. 16; AGI, Mexico, 237, N. 13. The profits and characteristics of the *asiento*, Martínez López-Cano, 2013a and 2013b. See also, Cuello, 1966.
61 AGS, *Cruzada*, 556; AGN, General de Parte, vol. 112, exp. 183, f. 1511 and vol. 12, exp. 396, f. 288.
62 Hillerkus and Quiñones, 2015.
63 AGI, México, 237, N. 13.
64 AGN, Desagüe, vol. 6, exp. 1.
65 Rojas Cruz, 2018: 101.
66 Hillerkus and Quiñones, 2015: 161.
67 AGI, Mexico, 38, N. 81.
68 Hillerkus and Quiñones, 2015: 161.
69 AGI, Mexico, 220, N.13 and AGI, Mexico, 221, N. 20.
70 *Brief of the lawsuit*: BNM, VC/201/1.
71 See their information in: AGI, Mexico, 220, N.13 and AGI, Mexico, 221, N.20.
72 Information: AGI, *Mexico*, 237, N. 13.
73 In 1614 he proved his cleanliness of blood, required for the post of notary of the Tribunal in the province of Michoacán: AGN, *Inquisition*, vol. 351, exp. 3. In 1626 he obtained the post of permanent accountant of the Holy Office, which he held until 1648. The position had no assigned salary and he served it through a servant: AGN, *Inquisición*, vol. 560, exp. 16.
74 See his will: AHCV, E5, T5, v. 5.
75 AGI, Mexico, 263, N. 191, and AGI, Escribanía, 170 B.
76 Part of this section is based on Martinez López-Cano, 2013a and 2017: Chapter 6 and 2023.
77 On these changes, Martinez López-Cano, 2017.
78 In the information provided by the treasurer Luis Núñez in 1591 and 1594–1595, Guatemala and the Philippines are not mentioned as part of the asiento: AGI, México, 220, N.13 and AGI, México, 221, N.20.
79 Yuste, 1984: 13–14.
80 AGS, Cruzada, 578. Still in 1608, Governor Rodrigo Vivero stopped its publication among the indigenous people of the islands due to the protests of the religious orders and the city council of Manila: AGI, *Filipinas*, 20, r.2, n. 21.
81 See Martínez López-Cano, 2017: 205.
82 AGS, Cruzada, 555 and 556.
83 Letter of the Viceroy Marquis of Cadereyta of 17 April 1636: AGI, Mexico, 31, N.39, and AGN, Mexico, 237, N.13.
84 AGI, México, 263, N. 191.
85 Reproduced in de la Peña, 1983: 257–260.
86 AGS, Cruzada, 578.
87 AGI, México, 30, N.5.
88 AGS, Cruzada, 583.
89 AGN, Bulas de la Santa Cruzada, vol. 2, exp. 17.
90 AGN, Bulas de la Santa Cruzada, vol. 2, exp. 17.
91 In the decade 1611–1620 there were 10 fleets; in 1621–1630, 9; in 1601–1610, 8; in 1591–1600, 1631–1640, 1641–1650, 7; and in 1651–1660, 6: Calderón, 1988: 527.

92 Resolution of the Council of the Indies of 17 June 1642, requesting respect for the cedula of 1633: AGI, Mexico, 3046.
93 Although of later date, an idea of the magnitude of the operations, the treasurer's profits, the vexations caused to the towns and the fraud to the Royal Treasury in these transactions, in: AGN, *Escribanía*, 327. Martínez López-Cano, 2014: 165–170.
94 AGI, Indiferente, 3006 and AGS, Cruzada, 560.
95 AGS, Cruzada, 560.
96 AGI, Indiferente, 2868, L.7.
97 The difference could range from 1.5 reales per mark which was recorded between 1611 and 1613, to 2 reales between 1615 and 1619, or to 2.5 reales/mark, as recorded in the accounts of 1613–1615, 1619–1625, 1635–1637, 1641–1645 or 1647–1659. Rendición de cuentas de los asientos de la cuarta, quinta, sexta y séptima concesiones: AGS, Cruzada, legajo 556.
98 AGS, Cruzada, 56 (accounts of the seventh asiento).
99 AGS, Cruzada, 583.
100 AGS Cruzada, 556.
101 AGS, Cruzada, 578.
102 Alvarado Morales, 1983.
103 Alvarado Morales, 1979.
104 AGI, 168 A.
105 Alvarado Morales, 1983; AGI, México, 237, N. 13.
106 AGI, 168 A.
107 AGS, Cruzada, 583.

Bibliography

Alonso Alvárez, Luis (2009), *El costo del Imperio asiático. La formación colonial de las islas Filipinas bajo dominio español, 1565–1800*, Mexico: Instituto Mora/Universidade da Coruña.

Alonso Alvárez, Luis (2012), "La ayuda mexicana en el Pacífico: socorros y situados en Filipinas, 1565–1816", in Carlos Marichal and Johanna von Grafenstein, coordinators, *El secreto del Imperio español: los situados coloniales en el siglo XVIII*, México: El Colegio de México/Instituto Mora, pp. 251–293.

Alvarado Morales, Manuel (1979), "El cabildo y regimiento de la ciudad de México en el siglo XVII. Un ejemplo de oligarquía criolla", *Historia Mexicana*, 112, 284, pp. 489–514.

Alvarado Morales, Manuel (1983), *La ciudad de México ante la fundación de la Armada de Barlovento. Historia de una encrucijada (1635–1643)*, Mexico: El Colegio de México/ University of Puerto Rico.

Ayala Tafoya, Eduardo (2021), "Patronazgo en la corte virreinal novohispana: los criados, allegados y paniaguados del marqués de Guadalcázar (1612–1621)", *Histórica*, XLV, 2, pp. 51–100.

Calderón, Francisco R. (1988), *Historia económica de la Nueva España en tiempos de los Austrias*, Mexico: Fondo de Cultura Económica.

Celaya Nández, Yovana (2010a), *Alcabalas y situados. Puebla en el sistema fiscal imperial 1638–1742*, México: El Colegio de México.

Celaya Nández, Yovana (2010b), "La cesión de un derecho de la Real Hacienda: la administración del impuesto de la alcabala novohispana en el siglo XVII. Tres estudios de caso", *América Latina en la Historia Económica*, 17, 1, pp. 93–125.

Cuello Martinell, María de los Ángeles (1966), *La renta de naipes en Nueva España*, Sevilla: Escuela de Estudios Hispanoamericanos.

de Fonseca, Fabián and de Urrutia, Carlos (1845–1853), *Historia general de la Real Hacienda* , Mexico: Vicente G. Torres, 5 vols.

de Guijo, Gregorio Martín (1986), *Diario*, México: Editorial Porrúa, S.A., Edition and prologue by Manuel Romero de Terreros, 2 vols.

de la Peña, José (1983), *Oligarquía y propiedad en Nueva España, 1550–1624*, Mexico: Fondo de Cultura Económica.

de Nardi, Loris (2018), "Voluntary Donations: An Understudied Aspect of Spanish Habsburg American Politics (16th–17th Centuries)", *Latin America in Economic History*, 25, 1 pp. 7–35.

del Valle Pavón, Guillermina (1997), *El Consulado de comerciantes de la ciudad de México y las finanzas novohispanas, 1592–1827*, PhD Thesis, Mexico: El Colegio de México.

Gordoa De La Huerta, Rodrigo (2024), *Norma, estilo y arbitrio. 'Cuenta y razón' y jurisdicción contenciosa en la Real Hacienda de Nueva España (siglos XVI-XVII)*, PhD Thesis, Mexico: Instituto Mora.

Hausberger, Bernd and Mazín, Oscar (2010), "Nueva España. Los años de autonomía", in various authors, *Nueva Historia General de México*, México: El Colegio de México.

Hillerkus, Thomas and Quiñones Flores, Georgina Indira (2015), "El testamento de Luis Núñez Pérez de Meñaca, tesorero de la Casa de Moneda de la ciudad de México (1610)", *Relaciones*, 36, 142, pp. 159–191.

Hoberman, Louisa Schell (1991), *Mexico's Merchant Elite, 1590–1660: Silver, State and Society*, Durham, NC: Duke University Press.

Instrucciones y memorias de los virreyes novohispanos (1991), Mexico: Porrúa, 2 vols. Coordination, preliminary study, bibliography and notes by Ernesto de la Torre Villar, compilation and indexes by Ramiro Navarro de Anda.

Martínez López-Cano, María del Pilar (2013a), "La administración de la bula de la Santa Cruzada en Nueva España (1574–1659) ", *Historia Mexicana*, 62, 3, pp. 975–1017.

Martínez López-Cano, María del Pilar (2013b), "El Galeón de Manila, las bulas de Cruzada y las barajas de cartas. Las oportunidades de los asientos generales en la primera mitad del siglo XVII", in Salvador Bernabeú Albert and Carlos Martínez Shaw, eds., *Un océano de seda y plata: el universo económico del galeón de Manila*, Sevilla: CSIC, pp. 203–227.

Martínez López-Cano, María del Pilar (2014), "La Bula de la Santa Cruzada en Yucatán. Las pecualiaridades y oportunidades de su administración", *Jahrbuch für Geschichte Lateinamerikas*, 51, pp. 151–175.

Martínez López-Cano, María del Pilar (2017), *La Iglesia, los fieles y la Corona. La bula de la Santa Cruzada en Nueva España, 1574–1660*, Mexico: UNAM.

Martínez López-Cano, María del Pilar (2019), "Nuevos espacios. La venta de oficios del tribunal de Cruzada de México en la conformación y consolidación de las elites y oligarquías en la segunda mitad del siglo XVII", in Francisco Javier Cervantes Bello and María del Pilar Martínez López-Cano, coords., *La Iglesia en la construcción de los espacios urbanos*, Puebla: BUAP/UNAM, pp. 195–220.

Martínez López-Cano, María del Pilar (2023), "Antonio Millán y la tesorería general de Cruzada de Nueva España y sus provincias (1647–1659) ", in María del Pilar Martínez López-Cano, Guadalupe Pinzón Ríos and Javier Sanchiz, coords., *Nueva España y el Pacífico hispánico. Un homenaje a Carmen Yuste* , Mexico: UNAM, pp. 69–94.

Pazos, María Luisa (1999), *El Ayuntamiento de la ciudad de México en el siglo XVII: continuidad institucional y cambio social*, Sevilla: Diputación de Sevilla.

Reichert, Rafal (2012), "Entre la paz y la guerra, el gasto militar novohispano en la región del Gran Caribe (1609–1648)", in Angelo Alves Carrara and Ernest Sánchez Santiró, coords., *Guerra y fiscalidad en la Iberoamérica colonial (siglos XVII-XIX)*, Juiz de Fora-México: Editora Federal de Juiz de Fora /Instituto Mora, pp. 39–64.

Rojas Cruz, Ana Consuelo (2018), *Cabildo de comerciantes. El sustento material de la autonomía de la ciudad de México, 1600–1624*, México: UAM/Iztapalapa, Tesis de Maestría.

Rojas Cruz, Ana Consuelo (2024), "Mercaderes tesoreros de la casa de moneda de México: poderes locales y lazos trasatlánticos de autoridad (1585–1630)", *Anuario de Estudios Americanos*, 81, 1, pp. 1–20.

Rojas Orzechowski, Alan (2017), "Juan Ontiveros, Simón de Haro e Isabel de la Barrera: la continuación de un capital y su aplicación piadosa", in María Cristina Torales Pacheco, coord., *Empresarios, sociedad y cultura, siglos XVI al XVIII. De la Europa del Renacimiento al México nacional*, México: Universidad Latinoamericana/El Colegio de San Luis, pp. 63–79.

Sánchez Santiró, Ernest (2012), "La Armada de Barlovento y la fiscalidad novohispana (1636–1749)", in Angelo Alves Carrara and Ernest Sánchez Santiró, coords., *Guerra y fiscalidad en la Iberoamérica colonial (siglos XVII-XIX)*, Juiz de Fora-México: Editora Federal de Juiz de Fora /Instituto Mora, pp. 65–90.

Sánchez Santiró, Ernest (2013), *Corte de caja. La Real Hacienda de Nueva España y el primer reformismo fiscal de los borbones (1720–1755). Alcances y contradicciones*, Mexico: Instituto Mora.

Serrano Hernández, Sergio Tonatiuh (2020), *Building an Empire in the New World. Taxes and Fiscal Policy in Hispanic America during the Seventeenth Century*, PhD Thesis in Economic History, Madrid: Universidad Carlos III.

TePaske, John J., with the collaboration of José Hernández Palomo and Mari Luz Hernández Palomo (1976), *La Real Hacienda de Nueva España: la Real Caja de México (1576–1816)* , México: INAH.

von Mentz, Brígida (2010), "La plata y la conformación de la economía novohispana", in Sandra Kuntz Ficker, coordinadora, *Historia económica general de México. De la colonia a nuestros días*, Mexico: El Colegio de México/Secretaría de Economía, pp. 113–141.

Yuste, Carmen (1984), *El comercio de Nueva España con Filipinas, 1590–1785*, Mexico: INAH.

7 Cardinal Portocarrero, the Cathedral Chapter of Toledo and the Papacy in the negotiations of the 1707 loan to Felipe V

Roberto López Vela

Introduction

At the critical moments of the War of the Spanish Succession, the administrations of Philip V and Charles III showed the greatest interest in accessing the treasures and silver of the churches. It was a last resort to obtain immediate liquidity but using the silver of jewels and sacred objects without papal licence and without even the explicit consent of the ecclesiastical state and the prelates constituted, at the very least, a crime against ecclesiastical immunity condemned with the highest canonical penalties.[1] It was a legally demanding framework and, except for the proposal to take possession of the churches' silver, Austracists and Bourbons acted differently, revealing the unequal relations that Charles III and Philip V maintained with the prelates, *cabildos* (cathedral chapters) and clergy of the territories loyal to them.

In his classic work on the government of Archduke Charles in Barcelona, Voltes Bou (1963: 1, 88) collected information from Francisco Castellví, a direct witness to the events (Alcoberro, 2025), on the Junta created on 31 October 1713 at the request of the Diputaciò. At this time Barcelona was under siege by Bourbon troops. By then, Charles III had been Emperor Charles VI for two years and his court was residing in Vienna; moreover, the Empress and the allies had abandoned the city, leaving it in a critical state (Albareda Salvadó, 2010: 362). The aim of the Junta was delicate and, as Castellví wrote, it summoned "the best theologians of the religious orders and University professors to decide whether, on that solemn occasion, they could use the churches's silver, with the obligation to repay it to its owners".

The prelate of Barcelona, Benet y Sala, a recognised Austracist summoned to court in 1704, had been imprisoned or exiled in France since then (Alabrús, 2013: 172). Innocent XI named him cardinal in the consistory of 30 January 1713, in an obvious nod to Austracism and Emperor Charles VI. At last, Austracism had a cardinal who was an active prelate of a Hispanic diocese. Benet y Sala returned to Barcelona in April 1713 and in early July, he left for Genoa with the intention of taking possession of his cappellum in Rome. He was absent, therefore, when the churches' silver was requested. In the meantime, his ecclesiastical chapter was going through a difficult situation, which led most of its canons to give allegiance

DOI: 10.4324/9781003653301-8

to Philip V in December 1713 (Albareda Salvadó, 2010: 378). Therefore, neither the prelate nor the ecclesiastical state of Barcelona were in a canonically adequate position to hand over the silver to the secular power. The Diputaciò drew upon the opinion of a Junta, but this could not supplant the powers of the head of the city's church, still less those of the pope.

The Junta of 31 October considered it legitimate to use the silver, on the condition that the secular resources of the "lay people" were spent first. Afterwards, if necessary, they could resort to the churches′ silver, excluding the sacred vessels. With this opinion, the Diputació and the city of Barcelona took the silver to the Casa de la Moneda (Mint), but it was not used. In line with what Catalan Austracism had done since the beginning of the conflict (Alabrús, 2014: 214), the Diputació tried to safeguard orthodoxy and give its decision a veneer of canonical legitimacy, but it was not ignorant of canon law and perhaps for this reason preferred not to use the silver. Given the situation facing the city, the absence of the prelate, the monarch and the nuncio (who by then had left the city), and the fact that the silver was not used, the papacy was prevented from intervening in the matter. The capture of the city by the Bourbon armies in September 1714 helped bury the affair in oblivion.

Something quite different happened in Philip V's Castile in early 1707, when the Bourbon administration urgently needed resources to finance the campaign to recover the territories dominated by Charles III. Unlike what happened in Barcelona in 1713, the King and the papal nuncio were in Madrid and many of the prelates of the Castilian dioceses resided in their (bishoprics) or at court. This reality demonstrates the great difference that existed between the ecclesiastical universes of the Austracist and Bourbon territories. Despite the abundant complaints about the situation of the churches that justified the 1707 loan, the Castilian ecclesiastical hierarchy remained operative during the conflict and, together with the ministers of the monarchy, negotiated the loan. This took place in parallel with the renewal of the agreements (Concordias) with the royal ministers for the payment of the new five-year subsidy and *excusado* (a part of the church tithes transferred by the former to the Crown). Unlike what happened in Barcelona in 1713, the negotiations in Castile over the monarchy's requests had an unmistakable institutional character, with the participation of figures from the French and Spanish monarchies, together with Cardinal Luis Manuel Fernández Portocarrero and the Toledo chapter.

The monarchy's initial plan was to obtain silver resources from the churches, however a tradition had developed in Castile around the Congregation of the Clergy of negotiating with the royal ministers over the payment of the subsidy and *excusado* and appeals against the extraordinary impositions.[2] Louis XIV pressed for silver from the churches, but the 1707 loan was negotiated between Madrid and Toledo with an eye on Rome. The first objective of this paper is precisely to analyse the attitude of the papal curia and the pope regarding the Spanish conflict and its implications in the religious sphere. The dealings between Madrid, Paris and Toledo resulted in the request for silver from the churches being transformed into a loan. The second objective of this work is to study the novel characteristics of this request and the way in which it was handled by Cardinal Portocarrero and his cathedral chapter. These facts demonstrate the cardinal's unequivocal adherence to the cause of Philip V, at least in those months, which rules out any question of his supposed Austracist leanings. The third part studies the legal mechanisms through which the cardinal committed the ecclesiastical state of the archdiocese to the loan and how it was transferred to the rest of the churches. Lastly, we analyse the reaction of the nuncio and the pope when they became aware of these resolutions.

The ambassador of the Spanish monarchy in Rome and the "partiality" of Clement XI

The war of succession to the Spanish monarchy had multiple fronts and involved a large number of European political actors and their overseas possessions. It had previously unseen universal dimensions, which affected the Church, the most universal institution of the time, with particular intensity. The papacy did its best to maintain an equidistant position in the diplomatic arena in the face of the succession dispute, which did not, however, prevent it from participating in or, at least, being closely involved in the political games. According to Cardinal Portocarrero, the position adopted by Innocent XII in support of the French option was of great importance in convincing Charles II definitively in favour of the Bourbon candidate. Innocent XII died shortly before Charles II and on 23 November 1700 Clement XI was elected. On 6 February the following year, the new pope addressed a breve to Philip V wishing him well, that is, he recognised him as the new king of the Spanish monarchy.[3]

While the war raged in Central Europe, the Spanish Church was able to live out its loyalty to the Bourbon king without too much tension, but that changed with the proclamation of Charles III in Barcelona in the autumn of 1705 and a few months later in Valencia. Charles III gained control of two important peninsular kingdoms and support in other kingdoms, as demonstrated by his successful campaign for Aragon in the first half of 1706. These events had great repercussions on the churches and religious orders of the peninsula and profoundly affected the loyalty of the clergy. The tensions in the Hispanic clergy were clearly expressed through the correspondence of the Duke of Uceda—a person of long standing during the reign of Charles II, who was appointed ambassador to Rome in 1699.[4]

The appointment of Philip V as king of Spain and the pope's refusal to give him the investiture of the kingdom of Naples had already led Uceda to distrust the pope's attitude towards Philip V (Martín Marcos, 2011: 44–50). Throughout 1706, Uceda's letters insisted on pointing out Rome's heightened awareness of the implications of the War of the Spanish Succession for the Italian peninsula and, in particular, for the pope and the Universal Church. The abundant circulation of Bourbon and Austracist propaganda in the city from very early on is evident from the records of the Spanish embassy in Rome that were not burned in 1738. Some memorials spoke of the Portuguese King D. Pedro and his instructions to introduce heretical books into Spain.[5] That is to say, of the complicity of the Catholic princes allied with the archduke with the English and Dutch heretics. On the other hand, in other papers translated into Italian and therefore more widely distributed, it was argued that the Spanish monarchy would end up united with France by the

Salic law, despite the testamentary dispositions of Charles II. Louis XIV wanted universal dominion.[6]

As was the case in the Iberian Peninsula, one of the main axes of Bourbon propaganda, if not the main one, was the vision of war as a crusade against heretics, while the Austracist considered Philip to be a mere instrument of Louis XIV to achieve universal dominion (Pérez Picazo, 1966: 1; García-Badell Arias, 2005, and 2008). Aware of the political debate in Rome and the latent war that was taking place there, José Grimaldo, head of the Secretariat of the Office of War and Finance of the Bourbon monarchy, sent regular reports to the Spanish ambassador denouncing the heretics' attempts to introduce banned books into Spain. As in the years of the confessional conflict, the Inquisition redoubled its efforts under the new Inquisitor General Vidal Marín and ordered the control of libraries, bookshops and anyone who handled books[7].

In a letter dated on 18 November 1705, Philip V announced to the Duke of Uceda that he was putting himself at the head of the armies to reconquer Barcelona and preserve in those territories "the obedience to Rome". Since the contributions of his secular subjects were not sufficient to pay the costs of the campaign, he had ordered the Duke of Veragua, president of the Council of Orders, to sell up to three hundred thousand escudos coming from the "the real estate of the religious orders, tithes, pastures, in the understanding that H.M would reimburse that amount of money to the orders concerned", when the king overcame these difficulties. Philip V ordered Uceda to request the necessary authorization from the pope (*breve*), pointing out that something similar had been done in the reigns of Charles I and Philip II. The papal secretary of breves told the ambassador that he was unaware of the breves adduced by Philip V, and that other concessions to those kings had been made, but to fight infidels, not heretics.[8]

On 5 January 1706, Uceda informed the Council of State that he had met twice with the pope about the sale of property belonging to the Orders. He had told him that heretics were the same as infidels and that in the invasion of Catalonia, the enemy were rebels "against their legitimate king, who had not only maintained their old laws and privileges, but had even expanded them" and he had the right to freely dispose of that property. In other words, the campaign in Catalonia was a new war by the King against the heretics. However, the pope had not admitted such reasoning and had replied that he himself would look for precedents in the Vatican Archives. In a subsequent interview, the pope informed him that no precedent enabled the grace requested by the King. In view of this, it seemed to Uceda that there was no point in making further requests, "especially given the partiality of the pope for the emperor". He also noted that, on 2 January, he had received another letter from the King asking him to urge the pope to issue a breve to sell the offices of notaries (escribanos) of the orders, but he had not submitted this request "since he would have the same answer".[9]

On 5 January 1706, Uceda wrote Grimaldo a letter in which he stated with "great sorrow" that the pope treated the affairs of the King of Spain "so that the King of Romans and the Archduke do not have any cause for complaint. In his answers, there is nothing that favours us and much that does favour the enemies". He added that the Archduke had many followers among the Spaniards residing in Rome and among the natives of the Papal States, "being publically acclaimed as king Charles III". He had made representations to the pope and the authorities denouncing these facts, but no punishment had been imposed, and he gave details. He said that in the house of the Bolognese senator Casali, 24 gentlemen of the city's high nobility had celebrated a banquet for the victory of Charles III in Barcelona, shouting in favour of the Queen of England and Charles III.[10]

During 1706 and 1707, Grimaldo maintained close correspondence with the monarchy's ambassador in Rome, who insisted "that the pope would not make any concession to the detriment of the Archduke and to the displeasure of the King of the Romans". For this reason, he told Grimaldo to forget the idea of obtaining any kind of papal support.[11] With a curia and a city in which Charles III and his supporters were strong, he warned of the difficulty of obtaining any favour, knowing that their refusal would be seen as a sign of weakness. From the beginning of 1706, if not earlier, Philip V's government knew that the pope would not help him with anything that would cloud his relations with the emperor and Charles III.

Aware of the tensions between the pope and the Spanish monarchy, Louis XIV on repeated occasions instructed Cardinal de La Trémoille, his ambassador in Rome, to mediate between Uceda and the pope, or to advise the Spanish ambassador to show greater restraint. However, as the conflict intensified in Spain (and especially in Italy), Louis XIV began to take on board Uceda's assessments of the pope's partiality towards Charles III and the mistreatment of his grandson. Likewise, the depiction of the war in Spain as a religious war became increasingly relevant.[12]

Philip V's decree of 6 April 1707 demonstrated how intensely the Spanish conflict was being felt in Rome. The decree denounced the "many Cathalans, Mallorcans, Valencians and Aragonese settled in Rome who spoke against the Crown". It ordered all agents of Spanish institutions to withdraw the powers given to them and to suspend all correspondence with them. In their place, "they were to appoint exclusively Castilians", although they first had to have the approval of the Duke of Uceda.[13] The monarchy was aware of the presence of Austracism in Castile. The decree accused the natives of some kingdoms of the monarchy of infidelity, but not of heresy. Philip V's ministers knew that for Clement XI and the Roman Curia, what was happening in Spain was a war between Catholic princes and nothing more.

Cardinal Portocarrero, a curial at the Spanish court

The Austracist armies' rapid advance as far as Madrid in the spring and early summer of 1706 had demonstrated the weaknesses of Philip V's armies, which managed to reverse the situation with the support of France. When the Bourbon administration returned to Madrid, the priority was to reorganise the army with the prospect of a campaign against the Austracist troops. Of course, it was essential to raise large sums of money to finance it, and thought turned to the "treasures" of the Castilian church (Castro, 2004: 203).

Amelot, the French ambassador in Madrid, informed Louis XIV on 10 January 1707 of the efforts being made in Madrid to obtain resources from the large amounts of superfluous silver immobilized in the religious institutions of the country. The King replied on the 30th of that month, saying that he doubted that "such wealth amounted to the sums commonly imagined", although it would be of great use for preserving religion. He did not doubt that, "were Austracists masters of the situation", they would appropriate these riches without consideration, because the Germans were doing this in Milan. To this end, he commissioned Amelot to convince Portocarrero to overcome "his refusal to grant the King of Spain consent to take the churches′ silver by way of a loan under due guarantees" (Iñurritegui and Viejo, 2012: 351–352). The pressure on the cardinal must have been very intense and, as will be seen, the nuncio in Madrid, the archbishop of Damascus, Antonio Felice Zondadori, informed the pope of the cardinal's opposition to using the silver. It was very difficult, if not impossible, for the cardinal and the ecclesiastical hierarchy (or failing that a board of theologians and ecclesiastics) to approve the use of silver and gold from sacred objects without a papal breve. Portocarrero and the Toledo chapter therefore proposed a different route, in the belief that it would be quicker and more profitable.

Portocarrero's role in the succession of the monarchy and in the early years of Philip V's government has often been emphasised, which has overshadowed his career as a cardinal and diplomat in Rome during the 1670s, as well as his work in the archdiocese of Toledo.[14] After the fall of Everardo Nithard, John Joseph of Austria pressed for Portocarrero's cardinalate and in November 1669, when he was no more than dean, Clement IX named him cardinal *in pectore* shortly before his death. His first task that year was to attend the conclave to elect Clement X, the new pope. During this pontificate, Portocarrero took part in the work of various congregations, yet not without significant friction with Cardinal Nithard, closely linked to Mariana of Austria, who acted as the monarchy's representative in Rome from 1671 (Marqués, 1983). Portocarrero played an important role in the canonisation of new Hispanic saints during those years (King Ferdinand III the Saint, Saint Rose of Lima, Saint Louis Beltran and Saint Francis Borgia). Aware of his influence in Rome, the queen also asked him to become involved in the election of new prelates (Muñoz Rojo, 2019: 135–145).

Together with Nithard, Portocarrero took part in the conclave of 1676 from which Innocent XI was elected a year later, and during the *valimiento* of D. Juan José de Austria, he was appointed councillor of state, interim viceroy of Sicily and archbishop of Toledo. In 1678, he returned to Rome as ambassador extraordinary of the monarchy and shortly afterwards returned to Spain. As the French ambassador (who met the cardinal as soon as he arrived in Rome) pointed out, his manners, his courtesy and his ability did not seem very Spanish (Muñoz Rojo, 2019: 125). Indeed, during his Roman years, he demonstrated his great social and negotiating skills, as well as his discretion. This allowed him to carve out a place for himself in the difficult world of the curia and to carry forward petitions from the Spanish churches, despite the resistance or lack of collaboration from Nithard.[15]

From Rome, he returned to the peninsula as archbishop of Toledo and Primate ("primado de las Españas"), a post of limited juridical power which, nevertheless, gave him undisputed preeminence over the rest of the prelates by tradition and by the amount of his income (Rodríguez González, 2006). Throughout his political career at the court of Charles II, Portocarrero asserted the weight that came with being archbishop of Toledo and demonstrated in his political actions how much he had learned in Rome. Aware of the importance and weight of the chapter of Toledo (Sánchez González, 2000), the cardinal always maintained active correspondence and exercised his powers in the archbishopric through his Council of Government, including the first years of the monarchy of Philip V, when he had the highest responsibilities of government (Sánchez González, 2004: 299–310). During the more than 30 years that he ruled the archbishopric, he was aware of the importance of keeping an smooth relation with the Cathedral´s chapter for the government of the archbishopric.

Portocarrero was always careful in his relations with the nunciature and even more so when he distanced himself from the government of Philip V and when the effects of the war heightened the conflicts between the royal jurisdiction and the papacy. In the 1705 correspondence between the papal Secretary of State and the nuncio in Madrid, references to Portocarrero were commonplace. The nuncio hardly ever dealt with an important ecclesiastical matter without consulting him, and the pope appointed him to address the most complex matters, such as the jurisdiction included in the breve to punish seditious and tumultuous ecclesiastics, whose execution he granted to Portocarrero.

In the autumn of 1705, the Vatican Secretary of State sent successive letters to the nuncio informing him that the Duke of Uceda's request to expand the range of crimes covered by the *breve* on seditionists had been rejected. By the end of 1705, this was an extremely delicate matter in which the monarchy was trying to exert maximum pressure on Rome. On 26 December, the Secretary of State informed the nuncio of the pope's audience with Uceda to clarify the exact terms of the breve. The pontiff hoped that the ministers of the monarchy would respect his decisions and, above all, "would cease always trying to violate and offend the Church". Regarding the prison that had been established at court for religious offenders included in the breve, they warned him that the only judge was Portocarrero and not "his advisers". Moreover, the pope was very displeased to hear from royal ministers that the ecclesiastics were the main source of unrest.[16]

As a curial and trusted servant of the papacy, the cardinal combined in his person his political relevance, his pre-eminence as archbishop of Toledo and his closeness to the papacy. It is true that when Toledo swore allegiance to Charles III in July 1706, Portocarrero also did so and that, 20 days later, following in the city's footsteps, he returned to the allegiance of Philip V. However, this exchange of allegiances does not seem to have broken his relationship with the Bourbons (García Fernández, 2013: 1148), not even when, in 1709, shortly before his death, diplomatic relations with the Holy See were severed. Portocarrero firmly opposed the decision, because whatever the political conflict, including the recognition of

Charles III by the pope, relations with the head of the Church were unbreakable (Egido, 2004: 924).

In the winter of 1707, the cardinal had to draw on his knowledge of the functioning of the monarchy and the Vatican curia to channel the desires of the Spanish and French monarchies to avail themselves of the churches' treasures, knowing that Rome would not allow it. Cardinal Portocarrero, assisted by his chapter and a Junta set up by the King, drew on the negotiating experience of the Castilian clergy, which differed from the French, to explore the possibilities of providing liquidity to the monarchy without having to resort to the silver goods of religious institutions.[17]

The Toledo chapter and the king´s Junta

The pressures of the French and Spanish monarchy on Portocarrero took place in parallel with the negotiations between the monarchy and the Toledo chapter about the new concordías for the renewal of the subsidy and *excusado* (Artola, 1982: 59–62). The Toledo chapter acted on behalf of the Castilian bishoprics, assuming the functions previously exercised by the Congregation of the clergy. The Congregation of the Holy Churches and Clergy of Castile and León ("La Congregación de las santas Iglesias y Clero de Castilla y León"), as it signed its documents, had medieval roots and its functioning had a complex trajectory derived from its adaptation to the new burdens that the monarchy was able to impose on the clergy, with prior papal consent. From being a congregation that sporadically brought together the capitulars of the 36 Castilian dioceses when the pope granted the King a levy on the clergy, it gradually took on a more regular character after the papal concession of the subsidy in 1560 and the *excusado* in 1567 (Carpintero Aguado, 1988: 15–21; 1996a: 147–168). Its convenings followed a regular procedure: once the King received the breve renewing these impositions, he communicated it to the Commissary General of the Crusade and the latter to the chapter of Toledo which, as the primate church, summoned the rest of the bishoprics.

The last Congregation was convened in 1664, and from the 1680s onwards, it was the Toledo chapter that managed with the royal ministers the negotiations for the payment of the subsidy and *excusado* (Carpintero Aguado, 1989 and 1996b). In the proceedings of the chapter, there is evidence of this task and also of its centralising role in dealing with complaints from the Castilian bishoprics, usually requesting the support of the Toledo chapter to present a complaint to the monarchy or the papacy through the Congregation's agents in Madrid or Rome. The chapter of Toledo was also in charge of appointing and paying these agents, and of maintaining correspondence with them. Many matters that had nothing to do with the subsidy and the excusado passed through its hands[18] and, therefore, its relations with the rest of the Castilian diocesan chapters were quite fluid, as were those of the Toledo chapter with the ministers of the royal treasury, which had been remodelled in recent years.[19]

At its session of 21 January 1707, the Toledo chapter, which was in charge of signing the agreement with the royal ministers for the payment of the subsidy and *excusado*, stated that it had received a large part of the letters from the bishoprics of Castile and León with their powers and proposals. Its deliberation focused on whether for this negotiation it was better to resort to the agent of the Castilian churches at Madrid, as had been done in 1673, or to send two commissioners from the Toledo chapter to the capital. In view of subsequent events, the question was not a secondary one, and the chapter decided to send two of their most renowned canons, Bartolomé Cernuda and Diego Ossorio, reinforcing their negotiating capacity with two others: Andrés Murillo and Pedro Hereña. Their first mission was to inform the chapter of what the Castilian bishoprics had requested so the former could "give them the instructions" they had to follow in their negotiations with the royal ministers.[20] They worked quickly and, on 7 February, they sent their report: they had included all the proposals, except for one from Santiago, which was difficult to accommodate. The chapter congratulated them for their diligence It then approved the instruction to the commissioners and agreed to send it to the archbishop "in case he wished to remove or add anything".[21] All the decisions and formalities were carried out with great speed.

The day after approving the instruction to the commissioners, on 8 February, the chapter saw a letter from the procurator general of the Churches at court, stating that the King had set up a junta with some ministers to discuss "about the possibility of using some of the deposits and some silver of the churches".

At the same session, they saw a memorial (supposedly anonymous), denouncing this attempt as a violation of ecclesiastical immunity which would be carried out through "special committes (Juntas)".[22] Surprisingly, the chapter decided to communicate "the main points of such memorial" to the cardinal. In reality, the decision had been taken before the Junta was formed. At the session of 12 February, the chapter saw the letter that the King had sent to Portocarrero two days earlier, accompanied by another from the War Secretary ("Secretario Universal de Guerra"), Grimaldo. Philip V was not asking to the Church of Leon and Castile for silver, but for a loan of two million escudos. In his communication to the chapter, the cardinal urged "it to serve the Crown". The chapter immediately convened a session two days later, including fines for those who did not attend.[23]

The Toledo chapter and the nuncio referred to a junta convened by the King, which met at Portocarrero's rooms to discuss all matters relating to silver. We know its members thanks to a list that the nuncio sent to the pope.[24] Among them, we find representatives of the highest echelons of the ecclesiastical hierarchy at court, starting with the Inquisitor General Vidal Marín, the Commissioner General of the Crusade, as well as the royal confessor, several canons of Toledo, the Provincial of the Society of Jesus, that of Santo Domingo, and other prominent ecclesiastics. In all likelihood, one of the purposes of the Cardinal's trip to the court, as reported in the proceedings of the Chapter of 16 February, was to put himself at the head of the Junta.

It is not easy to follow the deliberations of a Board that acted with the utmost discretion. They were aware that the request for "superfluous" silver from the churches without a papal breve, as Louis XIV wanted, would be met with a resistance difficult to overcome among the religious hierarchy and, above all, it would cause a dangerous division in the clergy at a time when it was essential to ensure their fidelity. Of course, they knew that Clement XI would not do anything that would put him at odds with Charles III. Thanks to the nuncio it is known that the Junta was against the King's request to obtain the silver from the churches,[25] and based on the minutes of the Toledo chapter, we also know of their doubts about the powers of Portocarrero and the chapter to force the ecclesiastical state of the archdiocese to contribute to the loan. It seems very plausible that the Junta, with Portocarrero and his chapter, devised a complex strategy to have the nuncio approve the resolution adopted by the Toledo chapter on 14 February, which had nothing to do with the silver of the churches.

The Toledo´s chapter and the granting of the loan

In his letter to Portocarrero dated 10 February, Grimaldo supplemented the King's request by offering a framework for negotiation on the issue of the loan. He explained the monarchy's efforts to raise the resources for the forthcoming campaign against the Austracists, who had destroyed towns and villages in the kingdom. The monarchy "had returned to the Crown the jewels and assets that had previously been alienated", reducing the expenses of the state and forcing the secular state to contribute. Yet all this proved insufficient, and it was necessary to ask the ecclesiastical state for a loan "that could be considered as a natural debt, since above the common good there is the highest need to ensure the purity of the religion and the preservation of the temples from plunder and destruction" in towns and villages. Without saying so explicitly, he also understood borrowing as an obligation to the urban common good, a point on which the privileges of the clergy were more limited and debatable (Artola, 1982: 61). The two million were needed "promptly, and the loan would be issued using as collateral the jewels and financial assets chosen by all those interested in subscribing it", including the subsidy and *excusado*. In other words, fresh funds were urgently required.

To arrange for the apportionment of the two million among the churches, Grimaldo suggested using the rule followed for the distribution of the subsidy and *excusado*.[26] Knowing that the devastation of the war would prevent some churches from contributing, it was necessary for the others to make an extra effort. He gave the greatest guarantees regarding their restitution and proposed, that "since the commissioners of the Holy Church of Toledo were about to come to this court to negotiate on behalf of all of them the concordías for the renewal" of the subsidy and *excusado*, "it would seem to be a task well-suited to ecclesiastics who have the confidence of the Castilian bishoprics (Holy Churches), if it were in Your Majesty's interest, to be entrusted with the task of raising the loan".[27]

Around this time, the monarchy sent the letters from the King and Grimaldo to each prelate so that, with the agreement of their respective chapters, they could proceed to grant the loan. However, the monarchy's negotiating strategy was based on a quick agreement with Portocarrero and the Toledo chapter. It is clear that before these letters were sent, Grimaldo and Amelot had negotiated and agreed on the matter, including the concordias and the rest of the details, with the cardinal and the Toledo chapter. This complicity was manifested in the following weeks through correspondence that showed their accord,[28] which allows us to understand that two days after the arrival of the letters from the King and Grimaldo, the Toledo chapter adopted a resolution that, with the agreement of the cardinal, established the conditions and demands of the ecclesiastical state of the archdiocese and admitted the quota of the loan allocated to the archbishopric. This resolution established the framework for the monarchy's negotiations with the churches.

In the resolution of 14 February, the chapter took up Grimaldo's arguments on the critical situation of the monarchy and his suggestion to apportion the amount of the loan allocated to each bishopric on the basis of the criterion followed in the subsidy and excusado. The sum allocated to the secular clergy of Toledo amounted to 254,192 escudos, although their available liquidity was reduced to 70,000 escudos of ten reales de vellón from Obras Pías, that is, from trusteeships "administered by the chapter" which could not dispose of them to "grant loans or in any other way that constituted alienation". Nevertheless, given the urgency and inability to request a breve from the pope to use these funds and to ensure that

> the public cause might be aided with goods from the Church, it was agreed that the bishops, each one in his diocese, with the consent of the clergy represented in their chapters, can undertake the alienations they judge convenient and necessary for the purpose of the said loan, and the chapters can give consent in the name of all the clergy.[29]

In other words, with the chapter's prior agreement, each prelate could resort to any kind of resource they deemed necessary to raise the part of the loan allocated to them and establish the conditions for its repayment by the monarchy.

The Toledo chapter was aware of the problem of resorting to the funds of Obras Pías without papal authorisation and by all means tried to obtain the surest guarantees for the restitution of these funds by the monarchy, stating this in the new concordias for the subsidy and *excusado* and with the guarantee of the General Commissioner of the Crusade. From January 1708, although there were changes on this date, the bishoprics could reimburse the loan by deducting it from their annual payments due to the monarchy for these contributions. To this could be added "their other obligations owed to the monarchy that His Eminence [Portocarrero] might choose". The chapter also demanded that the letters of payment sent by the Treasury to attest that the bishoprics had paid their quota of the subsidio and excusado to the Crown should be drawn up

> stating that, even although some payment orders on the Cruzada and Subsidy levied in each district have been given previously to other parties, they are not to have any force or action whatsoever, it being the obligation of His Majesty to satisfy those parties with other effects of his patrimony.[30]

If the monarchy could not repay the loan, the obligation to do so would fall on the archbishop, the canons and all the clergy of the archdiocese, at an annual rate of 1.5% from 1 January 1708 "until the repayment of the deposits". The chapter also asked the King that, until the arrival of the papal breve, "it would be necessary to obtain the approval from the papal nuncio in Madrid". The loan would become effective when Portocarrero issued the corresponding payment decree. The cardinal issued the decree on 16 March and the Count of Moriana issued the corresponding receipt.[31] One week remained before the nuncio gave his approval, with conditions, to the whole operation.

The chapter's agreement was surprisingly unanimous. In the first half of 1707, the Toledo´s chapter and "His Eminence" ("Su Eminencia") exhibited in their correspondence huge amounts of trust and courtesy ("fineza") with which they negotiated, since the chapter and "the archbishop must proceed together and without separation, both in the granting of the loan and in the choice of the ways to raise the money, remaining equally exposed to all contingencies that might arise". All parts concerned "should sacrifice their own interests to the Royal Service and the common good". This relationship could also include Grimaldo, with whom communication was equally smooth.[32] This collaboration made it easier for the churches of Castile and León to see the loan as an advance on the payments of the subsidy and *excusado* which, as was customary, could be managed through the Toledo chapter and the bishoprics´ procurator in Madrid.

The profanations of the "sectarians" and the approval of the loan by the nuncio

The Board of ecclesiastical dignitaries set up by the King, which met at Portocarrero's rooms, made a number of suggestions which were taken up by the Toledo chapter in some cases, as noted on 21 February, incorporating minor nuances regarding the loan conditions. The proceeds of 22 March noted the Junta's congratulations to the Toledo chapter for having responded promptly to the royal request and instructed one of its members, the royal confessor, to "impress upon the King how much effort this Holy Church had made in his service", recording the amount of its contribution and the work of the archbishop.[33]

By decree of 2 March, the cardinal appointed two people of his utmost confidence: Rodrigo Cordero de Ledesma, vicar of the choir and canon of Toledo and member of the Archbishopric's Governing Council, together with the ecclesiastical prosecutor of Madrid, Alejo López Caldid. He commissioned them to deal about the urgent need of resources for the royal treasury, without papal authorization. The decree incorporated the chapter's decision of 14 February, including the amounts pledged and the commitment that "if necessary, any sum missing to complete the amounts offered would be borrowed by the clergy at a 1.5 per cent". Moving within the framework set up by the Congregation of the Clergy, Portocarrero sought to demonstrate that there were good reasons to grant funds to the King without awaiting a papal breve.

Acting as if it were a procedural inquiry, Cordero summoned parish priests from different bishoprics in Madrid and ecclesiastics from territories that were or had been under the Austracist government. He also interrogated other individuals, some of them linked to the army, such as the Marquis of Santiago, supplier to the armies of the Spanish and French monarchy.[34] On the same date of 2 March, he summoned Manuel de Ayala, parish priest of St. Ginés in the capital, and in response to his questions, the latter said that the "secular state was bled dry, unable to pay the ordinary taxes", let alone the extraordinary expenses of the King's campaign to defend the kingdom and religion from the enemy armies, largely made up of "sectarians" ("sectarios"). The urgency of the loan was such that there was no time to turn to the pope, "nor to apportion it, nor to collect it from each individual".[35]

Another witness, Alfonso Castellano, lawyer to the Royal Councils, claimed that, without the loan, Philip V's army could not be paid and would desert in the face of the enemy.[36] Díaz de Batres, parish priest of the church of S. Pedro el Real in Madrid, pointed out that without the "expedient devised by the Holy Primate Church of Toledo it would be impossible to provide the necessary assistance to defeat the armies of English and Dutch heretics".[37]

All the witnesses insisted on the large presence of "sectarios" in the enemy armies and some Valencian ecclesiastics documented it. Pedro de Rocha, of the Order of Alcántara and parish priest of Santa María de la Encarnación in that capital, said that when the English and Dutch troops entered, "there was no image, altarpiece, sacred vessel or ornament that they did not break or take away". The Portuguese had been more numerous in that army, but could not prevent the English from dragging and smashing the image of Our Lady of Mercy. Pedro Ortega, also of the Order of Alcántara and a resident of Valencia, narrated similar episodes. Another witness from Gibraltar recounted the smashing of "the prodigious image of Oulr Lady of Europe", which was later collected by the locals and "today is venerated in Cádiz".[38]

Testimonies abounded regarding the critical situation of the Bourbon monarchy, while at the same time denouncing the sacrileges of the heretical troops. It is true that during the English penetration of Cadiz and its surrounding areas, images were destroyed, but most of the sacrileges were due to the search for booty, rather than religious motivations, given the habit of hiding jewels and valuable objects in the tombs and sacred places of the churches (González Cruz, 2002: 163). However, no witness pointed to the "ingleses" ("the English") spreading heretical doctrines in the Hispanic territories, something that is corroborated by the inquisitorial sources of those years (López Vela, 2014: 311–352).

Once the inquiry was concluded, Canon Cordero and Alejo López sent it to Portocarrero and on 9 March, he submitted the file to the ecclesiastical prosecutor, who considered the procedures carried out to be valid and, with his approval, sent it back to the cardinal, who formally declared the ecclesiastical state of the archbishopric to be obliged to comply with the commitment made by the Toledo chapter with the granting of the loan. He also sent very precise powers to the chapter's commissioners in Madrid. The commissioners appointed by the chapter on behalf of the Castilian bishoprics to negotiate the concordias of the subsidy and the *excusado* therefore negotiated the loan requested by the King at the same time.[39] This confusion between *concordias* and *empréstito* (loan) proved very effective and ensured that most of the churches of Castile did not see the difference.

All the documents in this procedure were sent to the nuncio on 11 March, and on 23 March, the nuncio replied that, in view of the information received, he "approved and confirmed the said order of His Eminence, with the proviso that within six months, the confirmation of His Holiness must be obtained".[40] His only condition was that it should be proved to him "that the million os silver reales reales de a ocho and the other funds that had recently arrived from the Indies in the Barlovento flagship and other ships" was not enough to cover the needs of the Crown.

The next day, Portocarrero commissioned Canon Cordero and Alejo López again to investigate about the amount of money arrived from the Indies and they immediately questioned officers from the war treasury. In their statements, they referred to the army of 50,000 men that the King was raising to fight the enemy. Between 15 and 16 million escudos were needed, while the ship indicated by the nuncio had barely brought a million reales. To this had to be added another half a million coming from the royalties due to the King for the cargo carried by the rest of the ships of the fleet.[41] As the Toledo chapter had requested, the nuncio approved what the church had done so far. It is clear that the inquiry made by order of the cardinal into the urgency of the defence of the monarchy and the faith lacked propagandistic intention. His aim was to create a legal basis to reinforce the obligations of the ecclesiastical state of the archdiocese and its loyalty to the Bourbon cause. From that time onwards, the pulpits of Toledo likely preached more intensely against Austracism and the heretics.

The strategy devised by Portocarrero, together with his chapter, was that of a consummate curialist. He had managed to have the monarchy request the loan instead of the silver, and to secure the nuncio's approval before receiving the breve. It is difficult to imagine that the complex process that led to this solution could have been achieved without the silent work of Portocarrero, whose steps can be glimpsed from the writings of others and from the proceeds of the chapter. He was careful not to leave a written record of what he had said and negotiated in interviews and meetings.

The chapter, Portocarrero and the churches of the kingdom

Without a papal breve, there could be no general framework for negotiation between the monarchy and the bishoprics of the kingdom, only a specific one for each case. Grimaldo's letter and the resolution of 14 February of the Toledo chapter established the conditions: it was up to each bishopric to agree with the royal agents the conditions under which each one should contribute to the two million, based on the rules followed in the apportionment of the subsidy and excusado. Moreover, if it was necessary to resort to the endowments of the Obras Pías without a breve, the strategy followed by Toledo seemed the best alternative. After all, Toledo's lack of liquidity to meet the immediate payment of the loan was not exceptional.

As soon as "the circular letters His Majesty" informing about the loan arrived, the Segovia chapter wrote to its Toledo counterpart asking for its opinion. The Toledo chapter replied indicating their willingness to grant it. A few days later, the *cabildos* of Guadix, Jaén and Cádiz wrote to Toledo with the same question, but the chapter decided not to answer them and to delay the answer to Segovia until Portocarrero's opinion arrived. After several letters from the commissioners sent to the court, including the cardinal's opinion, the chapter decided on 5 March to answer to these and other bishprics ("iglesias").[42]

On 5 April, the chapter of Toledo replied to a letter dated on 21 March from the chapter of Lugo in which they stated that they would follow Toledo's example and considered "advisable that, in accordance with the subsidy and *excusado*, the security of reimbursement of the loan be taken for all churches". They replied that this had already been foreseen and that the assurances that Toledo had obtained would be given to all the others. However, Toledo reminded them of the need to send special powers to the commissioners and the attorney general of Madrid "for all the arrangements and adjustments pertaining the apportionment of their quota". On the same day, other letters from Guadix and Osma were replied to in the same vein. The commissioners of Toledo in Madrid were receiving more letters like these and answered that if they remained in the capital until "the negotiations of the details pertaining the loan with each bishopric of the country were finished, it would be costly for all, as many would not be able to arrange it for many days, and some might want to resort to other expedients".

Given the complexity of the matter, the chapter postponed the decision, although it did adopt a transitional solution that proved successful. While the commissioners were in Madrid, "they would assist the bishoprics that requested their assistance, and afterwards the Attorney General might continue with it by sending [the churches] the powers". At the same time, the chapter wrote to the churches informing them of the state of the negotiations.[43] The commissioners' return to Toledo had to be delayed for a few weeks, because some of the resources provided by the chapter to meet the payment of the 245,192 escudos were not available. This was the case with the 20,000 escudos coming from the interests of census owned by the Tranciscan third order and with other funds. Portocarrero had to resort to the "endowments of some parishes of small villages and hamlest surrounding Madrid".[44]

To find out Portocarrero's position after the resolution of the Toledo chapter of 14 February, we must refer to its proceeds. On 16 February, the chapter sent the report requested by the cardinal on the loans previously granted to the Crown by the Church of Toledo. In their records, they found several examples: on 17 June 1591, on 18 February 1639, on 29 January 1640, on 1 February 1641, on 20 March 1643, on 4 March 1645 and even the one made by Archbishop Carrillo in 1474. However, the report did not indicate the nature of these loans, nor the reasons behind their granting, nor whether they had papal licence. That same day, the chapter recorded the archbishop's request for information on the funds available in the chapter for the payment of the subsidy and *excusado*, as well as Portocarrero's departure for the court, together with the commissioners of the chapter, where negotiations regarding the loan would now take place.[45]

There was continuous communication between Portocarrero and the chapter through the commissioners appointed by the latter to deal with the concordias. The royal ministers' priority was to conclude as quickly as possible with all the dealings with Toledo about its participation in the loan, before the signing of the concordias, and they even suggested the city of Toledo to advance the money offered by the chapter. The latter thanked Portocarrero for his efforts, but said that it had been able to get out "of the trouble by other means", which were, precisely, what Portocarrero resorted to at the last moment. Faced with this pressure, Toledo's commissioners forced the royal ministers to close the agreements before raising the quota of the loan allocated to the archbishopric.[46]

The proceeds of 15 March mention that the commissioners had received the powers pertaining to the loan and had signed the concordías of the subsidy and *excusado* for the following five-year period, plus the deadline for the first reimbursement of the loan, scheduled on 1 January 1709.[47] The chapter congratulated the General Commissioner of the Crusade for his work in the negotiation and received the cardinal's letter of 16 March to deliver to the Count of Moriana, Chief Accountant of the Treasury and Chief Treasurer of War, the 70,000 escudos from the Obras Pías.[48]

The pope's rejection of the loan

On the same day that the Chapter decided in favour of the King's request, on 14 February, the nuncio wrote to the Secretary of State about the unrest at court, reporting on the meeting convened at Portocarrero's rooms to discuss the King's project. This Junta had considered opposed to Gods´s law ("contrario al onore Divino") the King's desire to use the silver of the churches as *annata* or subsidy to be paid by the ecclesiastics. It said that Portocarrero had pointed out to the King that "he did not have the power to oblige his archbishopric, much less those of the kingdom" to come into the loan and wanted to consult His Beatitude on the matter. The King, however, "seemed satisfied with these proposals" and asked the cardinal to write a minute. The nuncio expected to receive it from Portocarrero and send it to Rome in the next post.

As the nuncio pointed out in the same letter, the feeling of the majority of the ecclesiastical hierarchy was to help the King, and there were even some in favour of resorting to the church´s silver to that end, such as the archbishop of Seville who "had his silver melted down to send the King a thousand doblones". While the situation was being clarified, the King's representatives negotiated with the court merchants to obtain a loan with the guarantee of what they would receive from the churches. However, the merchants would not grant it until the arrival of the fleet.[49] It is surprising that the nuncio was not up to date about the details of the loan at such an advanced date. It is clear that the monarchy's first option was to ask for the silver from the churches, but no doubt upon the advice of Portocarrero and a very small circle of ecclesiastics, the option of serving the king with a loan on the terms set Toledo´s chapter prevailed. This was undoubtedly more acceptable to the religious hierarchy and the Castilian clergy than handing over the silver. Moreover, as events showed, this enabled them to delay the pope's reaction for several months.

The fierce fighting between the Bourbon and Austracist troops between late winter and early spring of 1707 must have hampered the mail between Madrid and Rome. Correspondence from these months alludes to these issues. The first explicit order from the Secretary of State to the nuncio about the loan is dated 12 April. It asked him to inform Portocarrero, the monarchy and the representatives of the Churches present at court of the need to request the pope's approval to satisfy this operation. Without it, no contribution of any kind could be demanded from the clergy.[50]

The details of the negotiation of the loan took some time to reach Rome, but on 18 April the pope summoned "with great haste" the representative of the bishoprics of the country (Procurador General de las Iglesias de los reinos de Castilla y León), and read ~~to~~ him the letter sent by the nuncio in Madrid on 14 February, together with the reply from the Secretary of State sent on 12 April. He now knew that Portocarrero and the chapter were moving in unison and that they had already disbursed a large part of their quota of the loan. The pope did not "doubt that a similar effort would be made with the other castilian bishoprics" to commit them to the loan. In his letters, the nuncio had noted the active participation of Amelot, the French ambassador. The pope was convinced that the nuncio had opposed the loan because it was "so directly contrary to ecclesiastical immunity and canon law". He instructed the Procurador de las Iglesias "to endeavour with the utmost vehemence and determination to hinder the loan, so that it would be a failure, and to tell not only to the deputies of Toledo´s chapter, but to all agents of the other churches and bishops, that His Holiness was greatly surprised that such violence, never before practised in these kingdoms, was used.[51]

The pope issued a breve on 1 July condemning the loan and forcing the bishoprics to pay back the funds of the Obras Pías already disbursed in the loan without delay.[52] Portocarrero, with the help of the Junta and the Toledo chapter, had achieved a margin of about five months. In those months, the monarchy had received nine million reales (Castro, 2004: 202). This was far short of the 20 million expected, but it was still a considerable sum and, above all, it had arrived in the royal coffers at the opportune moment, when the costs of the campaign that led to the victory at Almansa and the capture of Valencia and Zaragoza had to be met. It was an achievement that Philip V's monarchy would not have attained without the involvement of the Toledo chapter and Cardinal Portocarrero. The role of the latter was fundamental as an intermediary with the monarchy, with Amelot, the nuncio and the prelates of the kingdom. Without his reputation and credibility, it would have been difficult for the nuncio to have endorsed the loan, nor would most of the prelates have participated in it. However, it should not be forgotten that, beyond his political skills, the cornerstone of the success of the whole operation was the Toledo chapter. The loan would not have been possible without its tradition of representing the ecclesiastical state of Castile, without the decisions it adopted, without the work of its commissioners at court, and without its continuous correspondence with the rest of the churches of the country.

The granting of the loan was an important financial contribution to Philip V's cause on the part of the Church and, above all, a political success. It is true that it provoked the most important conflict between the Bourbon administration and the papacy before the rupture of diplomatic relations in 1709. It was an inevitable consequence. However, thanks to the loan, Philip V had achieved what Charles III had always lacked: the backing of the bulk of the Castilian religious hierarchy, to which should be added, outside the kingdom, the archbishops of Saragossa and Valencia. The majority of the Spanish ecclesiastical hierarchy firmly defended, at least from 1707 onwards, the cause of Philip V, with a programme that identified the Bourbons with the defence of the faith and the Habsburgs with complicity in heresy.

Notes

1 "Señor, la Congregación de las santas iglesias y clero de Castilla y León, dize que su Magestad fue seruido mandar publicar una ley y pragmática sanción dando nueva forma al papel sellado a los instrumentos y demás actos judiciales y extrajudiciales, su fecha 15 de diciembre de 1636", Biblioteca Nacional de España, Sala Cervantes, PORCONES/ 1454
2 Carpintero Aguado, 1988: 15–21; 1996a: 147–168; 1997: 747–756.
3 Martín Marcos, 2007, and 2011: 55.
4 Barrio Gozalo, 2013: 57–76; Huerta García, 2003–2004: 57–76.
5 Roma, Iglesia Nacional Española, Fondo de códices de la Biblioteca contigua al archivo a la Embajada ante la Santa Sede (hereinafter BEESS), 90, *Mogiganga de mojiganga, papelón de papelones, manifiesto de manifiestos, idea de ideas, reflexión de reflexiones, cuento de cuentos, miscelanea de todo surtimiento, fiesta de capa y espada, tramoyas y cascabel gordo, sueño fantástico, histórico, pronostico y jurídico en que se representa lo que fue, es y será con distinción de lo que es y lo que no es. Dormianlo entre gallos y medianoche a la pierna suelta de sus sabanas un descosedor de baraundas, que duerme no más de quando le da la gana y cuenta lo solamente a los que quisieren oyrlo.*
6 BEESS, *109, Fogli tradotti dall'idioma Portoghese nell'italiano. Risposta d'un gentilhumo spagnolo ritirato della corte ad'un ministro del Consiglio di Stato di Madrid sopra la sucessione della Spagna. Tradotta dal francese in lingua portughese da Antonio Homen Pares Ferreyra, anno 1697.*
7 Egido López, 1984: 1227–1246; López Vela, 1988: 63–122.
8 AGS (hereinafter Archivo General de Simancas), Estado, leg. 4751.
9 AGS, Estado, leg. 4751.
10 AGS, Estado, leg. 4751.
11 AGS, Estado, leg. 4751, letter of 6 February 1706.
12 Iñurritegui and Viejo, 2012: 317, 371.
13 ACT (hereinafter Archivo Capitular de Toledo), Acts, 50, ff. 76v-77r.
14 Muñoz Rojo, 2019; Peña Izquierdo, 2004; de Bernardo Ares, 2013.
15 Lozano Navarro, 2010 and 2013.
16 AAV (hereinafter Archivio Apostolico Vaticano), Nunz. Mad. 53, f. 209r, 252r, 314r-v.
17 Fortea Pérez, 2019; 2022.
18 ACT, Acts, 50, 31v,40r.
19 Sánchez González, 2022; de Castro Monsalve, 2004; Dubet, 2008; Dubet and Solbes Ferri, 2019.
20 ACT, Acts, 50, f. 13v.
21 ACT, Acts, 50, f. 26r-v.
22 ACT, Acts, 50, f. 27v-28r.
23 ACT, Acts, 50, f. 31r, 32r-v.
24 AAV, Nunz. Mad. 68, f. 251r-v.

25 AAV, Nunz. Mad. 197, ff. 51r-52r.
26 ACT, Acts, 50, f. 33v.
27 ACT, Acts, 50, ff. 32v-34r.
28 ACT, Acts, 50, 49r-v.
29 ACT, Acts, 50,34v-35r.
30 ACT, Acts, 50, 35r-v.
31 ACT, Acts, 50, ff. 34r-36v; 63v-64r.
32 ACT, Acts, 50, ff. 44v-45r, 49r-v, 52r-v.
33 ACT, Acts, 50, ff. 45r, 62r.
34 The decree and the inquiry form part of the folder "Copia de autos e informaciones hechos por el cardenal mi señor y de comisión de su Eminencia sobre el empréscito secular de este arzobispado de Toledo hace el rey nuestro señor Phelipe V, que Dios guarde", AAV. Nunz. Mad. 68, ff. 225r-250r.
35 AAV, Nunz. Mad. 68, ff. 227r-v.
36 AAV, Nunz. Mad. 68, ff. 230r.
37 AAV, Nunz. Mad. 68, f. 231r.
38 AAV, Nunz. Mad. 68, f. 232v-233r; 234r; 235r-236r.
39 AAV, Nunz. Mad. 68, f. 237v ff.
40 AAV, Nunz. Mad. 68, f. 245r.
41 AAV, Nunz. Mad. 68, ff 246r-ss.
42 ACT, Acts, 50, ff. 43v, 48v, 51v.
43 ACT, Acts, 50, ff. 73r-74r.
44 ACT, Acts, 50, ff. 75v.
45 ACT, 50, Acts, ff, 38v-39r.
46 ACT, 50, Acts, f. 39r.
47 ACT, 50, Acts, f. 58r.
48 ACT, 50, Acts, ff. 62r, 63v-65v.
49 AAV, Nunz. Mad. 197, ff. 51r-52r.
50 AAV, Nunz. Mad. 60, f. 1777r-v.
51 ACT, Acts, 50, ff. 99r-100v.
52 ACT, Acts, 50, ff. 133.

References

Alabrús, Rosa M. (2013), "El caso Benet Sala: ¿un problema en las negociaciones de Utrecht?", *Cuadernos de Historia Moderna*, 12, pp. 153–172.

Alabrús, Rosa M. (2014), "El clero catalán en la Guerra de Sucesión", *Estudis. Revista de historia Moderna*, 40, pp. 213–233.

Albareda Salvadó, Joaquín (2010), *La Guerra de Sucesión de España (1700–1714)*, Barcelona: Crítica.

Alcoberro, Agustí (2025), *Francesc de Castellví i Obando. Memoria de la Guerra de Sucesión*, Valencia: Ediciones Albatros.

Artola Gallego, Miguel (1982), *La hacienda del Antiguo Régimen*, Madrid: Alianza Editorial.

Barrio Gozalo, Manuel (2013), *La embajada de España en Roma durante el reinado de Carlos II (1665–1700)*, Valladolid: Universidad de Valladolid.

Carpintero Aguado, Lucía (1988), "La Iglesia Primada y el poder político en el siglo XVII", in Junta de Comunidades de Castilla-La Mancha, ed., *I Congreso de Historia de Castilla-La Mancha*, Vol. 8 *(Conflictos sociales y evolución económica en la Edad Moderna)*, Toledo: Junta de Comunidades de Castilla-La Mancha, pp. 15–21

Carpintero Aguado, Lucía (1989), "Iglesia y Corte castellana en el siglo XVII: contribución y tributos", *Hispania Sacra*, 41, pp. 547–567.

Carpintero Aguado, Lucía (1996a), "La congregación del clero en Castilla: un organismo mediatizado por la fiscalidad", in Pablo Fernández Albaladejo, Virgilio Pinto Crespo, and José Martínez Millán, eds., *Política, religión e Inquisición en la España moderna, homenaje a Joaquín Pérez Villanueva* , Madrid: Universidad Autónoma de Madrid, pp. 147–168.

Carpintero Aguado, Lucía (1996b), "La contribución del clero castellano a los servicios de Millones", *Revista de Historia Moderna*, 15, pp. 271–298.

Carpintero Aguado, Lucía (1997), "Las décimas eclesiásticas en el siglo XVII: un subsidio extraordinario", in Pablo Fernández Albaladejo, coord., *Monarquía, imperio y pueblos en la España Moderna*, Alicante: Universidad de Alicante, pp. 747–756.

de Bernardo Ares, José Manuel, coord. (2013), *El Cardenal Portocarrero y su tiempo (1635-1709), biografías estelares y procesos influyentes*, León: Csedhistoria.

de Castro Monsalve, Concepción (2000), "El Estado español en el siglo XVIII: su configuración durante los primeros años del reinado de Felipe V", *Historia y política: Ideas, procesos y movimientos sociales*, 4, pp. 137–170.

de Castro Monsalve, Concepción (2004), *A la sombra de Felipe V. José Grimaldo, ministro responsable (1703–1726)*, Madrid: Marcial Pons.

Dubet, Anne (2008), *Un estadista francés en la España de los Borbones. Juan Orry y las primeras reformas de Felipe V (1701–1706)*, Madrid: Biblioteca Nueva.

Dubet, Anne and Solbes Ferri, Sergio (2019), *El rey, el ministro y el tesorero: El gobierno de la Real Hacienda en el siglo XVIII*, Madrid: Marcial Pons.

Egido López, Teófanes (1984), "La inquisición en la España borbónica, el declive del Santo Oficio (1700–1808): los hechos y las actividades inquisitoriales: la Inquisición de una España en guerra", in Joaquín Pérez Villanueva and Bartolomé Escandell Bonet, dirs., *Historia de la Inquisición en España y América*, Madrid: BAC, vol. I, pp. 1227–1246.

Egido López, Teófanes (2004), "El discurso teologizante del antirregalismo (1709)", in Eliseo Serrano Martín, coord., *Felipe V y su tiempo. Congreso internacional*, Instituto Fernando el Católico: Zaragoza, vol. I, pp. 915–932.

Fortea Pérez, José Ignacio (2019), "Le roi et le fisc en France et en Castille au temps des troubles. Quelques réflexions sur deux modèles à confronter", in Martine Acerra and Bernard Michon, coords., *Horizons atlantiques: Villes, négoces, pouvoirs*, Rennes: Presses Universitaires de Rennes, pp. 277–292.

Fortea Pérez, José Ignacio (2022), "El clero y el fisco regio: un ensayo comparativo entre los reinos de Francia y de Castilla en el siglo XVI", in Cristina Borreguero Beltrán, Ángela Pereda López, Asunción Retortillo Atienza, and Óscar Raúl Melgosa Oter, coords., *Piedra a piedra: la construcción de la Historia Moderna a la sombra de las catedrales*, Burgos: Fundación Española de Historia Moderna/Universidad de Burgos, pp. 179–230.

García-Badell Arias, Luis María (2005), "Felipe V, la nobleza española y el Consejo de Castilla. La Explicación jurídica e histórica de la consulta que hizo el Consejo Real de Castilla, atribuida a Macanaz", *Cuadernos de Historia del Derecho*, 12, pp. 125–149.

García-Badell Arias, Luis María (2008), "Los primeros pasos de Felipe V en España: Los deseos, los recelos y las primeras tensiones", *Cuadernos de Historia del Derecho*, 15, pp. 45–127.

García Fernández, África (2013), *Toledo entre Austrias y Borbones: su aportación a la guerra de sucesión (1690-1706),* Tesis doctoral inédita, Universidad Complutense: Madrid.

González Cruz, David (2002), *Guerra de religión entre príncipes católicos. El discurso del cambio dinástico en España y América (1700–1714)*, Madrid: Ministerio de Defensa.

Huerta García, Florencio (2003-2004), "El duque de Uceda Francisco Tellez Girón: un político entre dos siglos", *Archivo Hispalense*, 86–87, pp. 57–76.

Iñurritegui, José María, and Viejo, Julián (2012), *Correspondencia de Luis XIV con M. Amelot, su embajador en España. Publicada por el señor barón de Girardot*, Alicante: Universidad de Alicante.

López Vela, Roberto (1988), "La Inquisición a la llegada de Felipe V. El proyecto de cambio en su organización y bases sociales", *Revista Internacional de Sociología*, 46, pp. 63–122.

López Vela, Roberto (2014), "Inquisición y cambio dinástico: la defensa de la constitución católica de la monarquía (1696–1715)", in Marina Torres Arce and Susana Truchuelo García, eds., *Europa en torno a Utrecht*, Santander: Universidad de Cantabria, pp. 311–352.

Lozano Navarro, Julián José (2010), "La Monarquía española y la sede vacante de 1676". *Tiempos Modernos. Revista Electrónica de Historia Moderna*, 7, pp. 1–27.

Lozano Navarro, Julián José (2013), "Valido defenestrado, embajador despreciado. Algunas reflexiones sobre la deslegitimación política en torno al cardenal Juan Everardo Nithard", *Kripton*, 2, pp. 19–31.

Marqués, José María (1983), *La Santa Sede y la España de Carlos II: la negociación del nuncio Millini 1675–1685*, Roma: Iglesia Nacional de España.

Martín Marcos, David (2007), "Roma ante el cambio dinástico a la Monarquía española. La consulta de Carlos II a Inocencio XII", *Hispania*, 65, 225, pp. 255–276.

Martín Marcos, David (2011), *El papado y la Guerra de Sucesión española*, Madrid: Marcial Pons.

Muñoz Rojo, Manuel (2019), *Un hombre para la Historia: el cardenal Portocarrero (1635–1709)*, Córdoba: Universidad de Córdoba.

Peña Izquierdo, Antonio Ramón (2004), *La Casa de Palma. La familia Portocarrero en el gobierno de la monarquía hispánica (1665–1700)*, Córdoba: Universidad de Córdoba/ Publicaciones Caja Sur.

Peña Izquierdo, Antonio Ramón (2009), "Crisis de sucesión: Felipe V y el cardenal Portocarrero a través de la publicística. La opinión de sus coetáneos (1700–1746)", in José Manuel de Bernardo Ares, coord., *La sucesión de la monarquía hispánica 1665–1725. Lucha política en las Cortes y fragilidad económica-fiscal en los reinos*, Córdoba: Universidad de Córdoba/Caja Sur Publicaciones, pp. 191–253.

Pérez Picazo, María Teresa (1966), *La publicística española en la Guerra de Sucesión*, Madrid: CSIC, 2 vols.

Rodríguez González, A. (2006), *Los primados de Toledo 1666–1709*, Toledo: Ediciones Parlamentarias de Castilla-La Mancha.

Sánchez González, Ramón (2000), *Iglesia y sociedad en la Castilla moderna. El cabildo catedralicio de la Sede Primada (siglo XVII)*, Cuenca: Universidad de Castilla-La Mancha/ Ediciones de la Universidad de Castilla-La Mancha/Ayuntamiento de Toledo.

Sánchez González, Ramón (2004), "Eco de la Guerra de Sucesión en el cabildo de la catedral de Toledo", in Jaime Contreras Contreras, Alfredo Alvar Ezquerra, and José Ignacio Ruiz Rodríguez, coords., *Política y cultura en la época moderna (Cambios dinásticos. Milenarismos, mesianismos y utopías)*, Madrid: Universidad de Alcalá, pp. 299–310.

Sánchez González, Ramón (2022), "Burgos y Toledo: relaciones entre sus cabildos catedralicios", in Cristina Borreguero Beltrán, Ángela Pereda López, Asunción Retortillo Atienza, and Óscar Raúl Melgosa Oter, coords., *Piedra a piedra: la construcción de la Historia Moderna a la sombra de las catedrales*, Burgos: Fundación Española de Historia Moderna/Universidad de Burgos, pp. 251–266.

Voltes Bou, Pedro (1963), *Barcelona durante el gobierno del Archiduque Carlos de Austria (1705–1714)*, Barcelona: Ayuntamiento de Barcelona/CSIC.

8 Changing hands

Debt management, credible commitment, and the market for public debt in Portugal (1520–1760)

Leonor Freire Costa

8.1 Introduction

In the context of early modern state formation, only a limited number of sovereign debts exhibited the hallmarks of robust public credit – specifically, minimal political risk and widely held, highly liquid bonds that were serviced consistently. The convergence of these attributes enabled states to access debt financing at relatively low costs, thereby allowing them to smooth out taxation while building the basis of a strong fiscal state. The issue of when and by what mechanisms public debts attained these qualities is intrinsically linked to the liquidity of securities, supported by an active and impersonal secondary market (Neal, 2000; Coffman and Neal, 2013: 13). Nonetheless, the precise direction of causality remains ambiguous: while credibility may enhance bond turnover, increased market activity can equally reinforce credibility. As such, the essential components underpinning sound debt credibility do not easily coalesce.

Against this broader backdrop, this chapter turns to the case of Portugal, examining how and to what extent its financial system developed the features associated with credible public debt and liquid securities markets. It critically reviews the relevant literature on Portuguese public debt within the wider context of European fiscal states and secondary market activity. Furthermore, it contributes an updated view of Portugal's financial history by using newly developed and expanded databases made available through the DEBT.PT project since 2022.[1]

This investigation acknowledges the substantial body of research on the credibility of public debt. One major strand of the literature links investors' perceptions of political risk – such as the danger of expropriation through sovereign default – to the nature of political constitutions and regimes (North and Weingast, 1989; Dincecco, 2011). The earliest trajectories towards credible public debt management were identified by scholars studying the Italian city-states from the medieval period onward (Stasavage, 2011; Pezzolo, 2003 and 2013; Chilosi, 2014; De Luca, 2015). A complementary line of research, while not in direct opposition to the former, stresses that the specific characteristics of financial instruments and the composition of the bondholding base were equally crucial to the development of financial markets, shaping governments' capacity for debt-restructuring operations (Dickson, 1967; Quinn, 2006; Chamley, 2011; Fritschy, 2003 and 2017). Overall,

DOI: 10.4324/9781003653301-9

studies in European financial history illustrate that Italian cities, and British and Dutch governments were able to establish impersonal credit transactions within a dynamic market system, which preserved the strong reputation of their debt.

The timing and conditions of the take-off towards fiscal credibility remain subjects of considerable debate, and disentangling the various interpretations lies beyond the scope of this paper. It is, however, broadly accepted that sovereigns with established reputations for repayment stand in marked contrast to the more troubled financial trajectory of the Habsburg monarchy in Castile, especially after 1625 (Domínguez Ortiz, 1960; Alvarez-Nogal, 1997 and 2009). There, the crown relied on a complex system of short-term credit agreements with bankers' consortiums, collateralised by *juros de resguardo – al quitar –* and closely tied to intricate tax negotiations within the *Cortes* (Alvarez-Nogal, 2008; Toboso, 1987). This mechanism demonstrated considerable resilience, although it was periodically interrupted by royal decrees suspending debt service. Although American silver represented only a minor share of the collateral itself, expectations of its arrival from the Indies played a critical role in shaping negotiations and enabling debt restructurings after such suspensions (Alvarez-Nogal and Chamley, 2014). In this sense, colonial resources indirectly underpinned the stability of Castile's financial system, often involving the same Genoese financiers who had previously experienced defaults (Drelichman and Voth, 2014). The role of colonial resources in debt management thus emerged as a distinctive feature of the Iberian kingdoms, a theme that will be revisited, but through Portugal's experience during the boom of the Brazilian economy.

Beyond the Iberian world, the functioning of credit systems downstream depended on the liquidity provided by secondary securities markets, although transaction patterns remain difficult to analyse systematically. Following episodes of distrust, markets often rebounded with remarkable speed. A recent study of the 1672 Stop of the Exchequer shows that investor confidence in sovereign credit was swiftly restored (Li, 2019). Similarly, in cities such as Milan and Lisbon, public bonds commonly served as collateral, reflecting widespread trust in the consistent servicing of public obligations and enhancing the liquidity of government securities through their circulation in private credit markets (De Luca, 2015; Costa, Rocha and Brito, 2018). Nevertheless, the concentration of debt holdings among a small number of corporations constrained governments' flexibility to pursue debt-restructuring operations (Dickson, 1967; Quinn, 2006). Therefore, the distribution of debt is likely central to understanding public bond turnover and the overall efficiency of financial markets (Neal, 2000).

This dynamic is particularly evident in seventeenth-century Castile. Scholars of Castilian finance have highlighted several factors influencing the operation of the *juros* market, which functioned through successive issuances of *juros de resguardo* and *juros al quitar* serving as collateral within the system of *asientos*. Most of these securities traded at a discount rather than at par value (Toboso, 1987). After the 1620s, however, returns on *juros* declined as the crown reduced interest rates on outstanding bonds to mitigate debt-service costs. As risk increased and yields fell, public investment waned, and market liquidity deteriorated. In response, many *juros* holders increasingly bequeathed their securities to religious and charitable institutions, further reducing market depth and liquidity (Álvarez-Nogal, 2009).

While the existing literature provides valuable insights into market liquidity, it often treats this element in isolation from the fiscal contexts in which it evolves. Few studies have connected the development of vibrant securities markets to the scale of public indebtedness, even though market depth and broad participation depend on an ample supply of government paper (Gelderblom and Jonker, 2006). On the other hand, the size of the debt stock itself is constrained by the institutional frameworks that governed the expansion of public borrowing. This disconnection obscures how fiscal constitutions and patterns of capital distribution jointly shaped both the credibility and liquidity of *juros*.

Portugal's experience provides an instructive example of how these dynamics operated in practice. The following discussion therefore seeks to integrate these dimensions by examining the underpinnings of Portugal's public debt system, which challenges the notion that mortmain institutions acquired securities solely because private bondholders had lost confidence in *juros*. Instead, Portuguese evidence suggests that the pursuit of consistent returns and reliable debt servicing encouraged buy-and-hold investment strategies. Religious corporations accumulated these securities within their portfolios partly through donations from bondholders – who entrusted the institutions with pious obligations – and partly through the Crown's capacity to implement debt-restructuring operations. In either case, once held by mortmain institutions, these securities were effectively withdrawn from market circulation.

Drawing on an expanded database of *padrões de juro* issued between 1520 and 1800, this chapter examines the social and institutional structure of Portugal's public debt. It treats debt-management operations as key moments of securities transfer. They relied heavily on funds supplied by major creditors – such as the Church and lay brotherhoods – who provided the Crown with the resources to address holdouts by subscribing to newly issued *juros* at reduced interest rates. These operations entailed large-scale transfers of debt, yet the transfers themselves were not accompanied by any loss of debt credibility.

Building on this empirical foundation, the chapter advances the hypothesis that the functioning of the *juros* market depended fundamentally on the social distribution of wealth. The study of Portugal's sovereign debt yields three main conclusions, which together form the pillars of the slow development of its capital market: (a) the formation of the debt stock was constrained by a fiscal constitution that monarchs respected in order to consolidate political legitimacy; (b) the social and institutional composition of debt holdings contributed to the gradual drying up of the securities market; and (c) during periods of rising state indebtedness, debt credibility rested on the sovereign's access to colonial trade revenues. Taken together, these features support the argument that public debt in Portugal functioned as a mechanism for redistributing the returns of the colonial empire to mortmain institutions.

The remainder of this chapter addresses these aspects in turn, examining how credibility, fiscal prudence, and the market for securities were interrelated. The first section reviews the current state of research on Portugal's public debt, drawing on findings published since 2022 as part of the DEBT.PT project (Costa and Miranda, 2023; Costa, Miranda and Nogues-Marco, 2024; Costa and Henriques, 2024; Miranda, Rodrigues and Lopes, 2024). The second section analyses the dynamic aspects of debt distribution across social groups based on cross-sectional snapshots. The third explores the relationship between debt distribution, debt servicing, and the tax revenues that underpinned the monarch's credible commitment to repayment.

8.1.1 Portugal's fiscal constitution, debt stock, and interest rates, 1529–1800

The evolution of Portugal's public debt between 1529 and 1800 must be understood within the constraints and opportunities created by its fiscal constitution – a framework that balanced domestic taxation with the extraordinary revenues generated by the maritime empire. Previous studies have provided valuable insights into the kingdom's fiscal capacity and expenditure patterns (Hespanha, 1994; Costa, Henriques and Palma, 2024). Comparative analyses suggest that the colonial economy played a decisive role in strengthening Portugal's fiscal position without impeding key fiscal innovations during periods of conflict, such as the War of the Portuguese Restoration, 1640–1668 (Costa and Brito, 2018).

In both the sixteenth and eighteenth centuries, revenues derived from the empire accounted for a substantial share of total tax receipts managed by the central government, with no parallel in Castile. In the sixteenth century, fiscal monopolies on commodities such as pepper, provided around 53 percent of total state income. Even amid international threats, between 1600 and 1650 – when in Castile the silver from the *Flota de Indias* accounted for around 14 percent of total revenue (Andrés Ucendo and Lanza García, 2008: 157) – the Habsburgs still derived about 34 percent of their income in Portugal from the kingdom's colonial trade, mainly through taxes on sugar imports and *asientos* connected to the slave trade and supply contracts with Spanish America. The half-century following the Restoration (1640–1690) marked a distinct conjuncture: colonial rents contributed no more than 12 percent of central revenues, since the monarchy relied primarily on domestic taxation. Despite its long-standing dependence on external income, the crown demonstrated the institutional capacity to mobilise internal revenue, when necessary, as was the period of the Restoration war (1640–1668). This pattern suggests that the empire was not responsible for later institutional weaknesses in Portugal's fiscal system; rather, it alleviated the domestic tax burden and provided leverage for managing royal debt, as discussed bellow.

In the eighteenth century, the empire once again became central to royal finances. The Brazilian gold boom and the colony's rapid economic growth raised the empire's contribution to roughly 25 percent of total revenues. During this period, the assembly of the *Cortes* ceased to convene. Portugal's institutional trajectory diverged again from that of Castile: while the Castilian crown suspended the *Cortes* to bypass protracted fiscal negotiations that still required the assent of 18 cities, in Portugal the monarchy discontinued these assemblies altogether.

The abundance of colonial revenues reduced the need to negotiate taxation with municipalities or other represented estates (nobility and church) facilitating a more absolutist form of governance (Henriques and Palma, 2023).

Taxation – whether derived from imperial trade or domestic sources – was not the only instrument available to the Portuguese crown for financing expenditure. The project *Sovereign Debt and Private Credit Markets in Portugal* (DEBT.PT) examined how monarchs employed credit within the constraints of the fiscal constitution to which they adhered. It analysed the long-term relationship between taxation and debt, estimating the debt-to-gross domestic product (GDP) ratio and documenting a historical case of an absolutist, low-debt monarchy that nonetheless maintained consistent creditworthiness.

Our understanding of this distinct regime relies on chancellery records documenting the issuance of *padrões de juro* (*juros al quitar*). Portugal's debt levels were shaped by the fragmented organisation of its tax system: monarchs leveraged fiscal authority delegated across tax districts – particularly *almoxarifados* collecting the *sisa* excise tax – while benefitting from significant imperial revenues, and customs duties. Rather than depending primarily on domestic taxation, new debt issuance was determined by the flexibility provided by fiscal monopolies and expected yields from colonial trade. Consequently, the stability and predictability of revenue streams became the decisive factor in sustaining debt service. This fiscal probity strengthened investor confidence in the crown's commitment to honour its obligations; however, it also capped total indebtedness.

These self-imposed fiscal constraints functioned as a mechanism of political legitimacy, particularly after the *coup d'état* of 1640. Following independence from the Habsburgs, consistent debt servicing became a cornerstone of the Braganza dynasty's fiscal policy as deliberate strategy for accumulating political capital and marking a clear departure from Habsburg financial management (Costa and Miranda, 2023). Figure 8.1 illustrates the outcomes of this fiscal prudence: while brief surges in indebtedness occurred during the early sixteenth century and first half of the seventeenth century under the Habsburg rule – primarily to fund military strongholds in North Africa and later Asia or to defend Brazil from Dutch incursions – the subsequent War of Restoration was largely financed through taxation. A newly introduced income tax that, although conceived as a temporary wartime levy, evolved into a permanent source of revenue after the end of hostilities. Initially approved by the Cortes to service floating debts arising from *asientos* with financiers who had advanced funds for the army, the *décima* was retained even after these obligations were settled, eventually becoming a standard component of the fiscal system until 1820. Portugal thus emerged as one of the earliest European polities to implement an income tax – levied on wages, rents, and interest – anticipating the fiscal modernisation later adopted by nineteenth-century liberal states. The rate of the *décima* remained at the monarch's discretion, typically set at 4 percent in peacetime and raised to 10 percent during war (Costa, Lains and Miranda, 2016: 117–119).

Although the *décima* tax provided substantial fiscal revenue, Portugal's participation in the War of the Spanish Succession required additional financing through

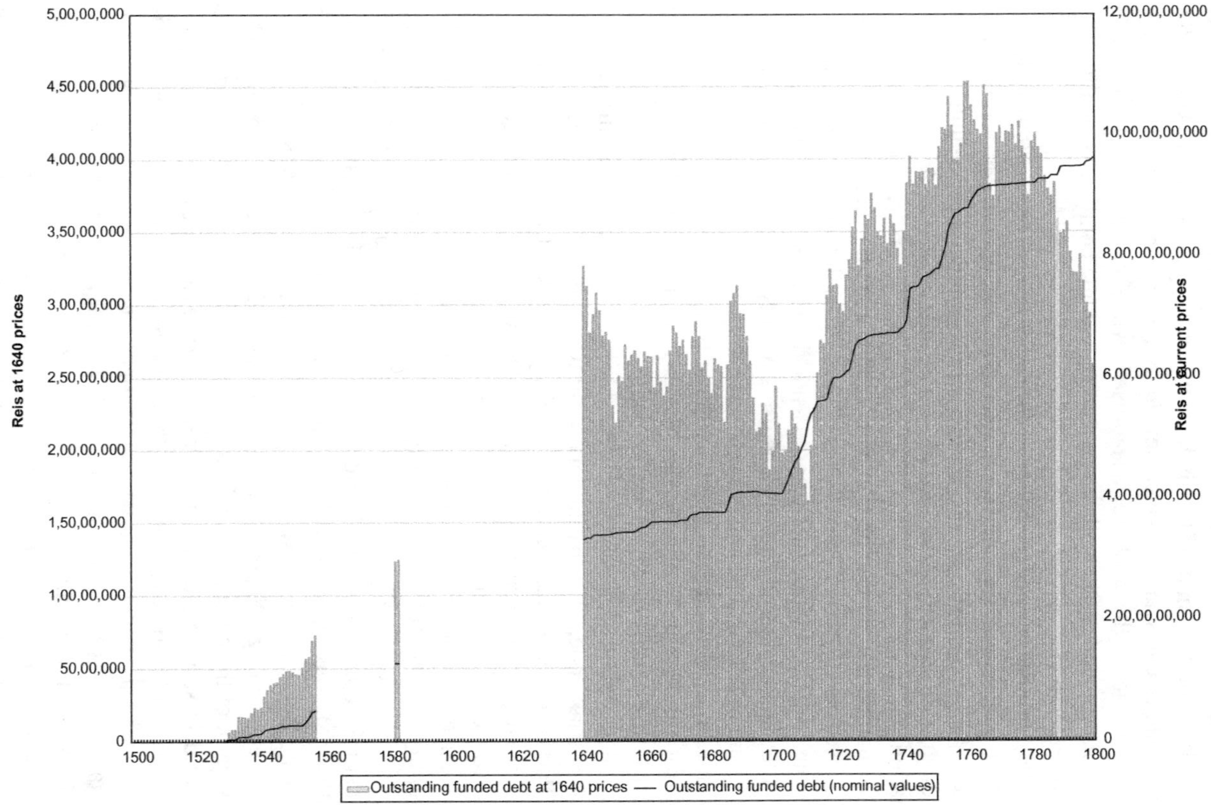

Figure 8.1 Debt stock, real, and monetary values, 1529–1799.

Sources: DEBT.PT – Sovereign debt and private credit in Portugal (Dívida Soberana e Crédito Privado em Portugal 1668–1797); (www.debt.pt) First published, Costa and Henriques, 2024

short-term floating debt and *juros* bearing high interest rates (6.25 percent). Following the Peace of Utrecht (1713), effective debt management operations enabled King João V to consolidate short-term liabilities by issuing new *juros*. Debt-management operations thus accounted for the sharp increase in total debt observed during the first half of the eighteenth century (Figure 8.1). After 1760, however, the monarchy scarcely issued new *juros,* some at the 3.5 percent interest. The nominal value of the debt stock stabilised, while inflation during the final decades of the century – especially amid the Napoleonic conflicts – significantly reduced its real value.

The policy limiting new debt issuance from the 1760s to the 1780s reflected the structural constraint that had historically bounded the Braganza monarchy. As a result, the state financed the growing militarisation of expenditure after 1790 through a different type of security – no longer *padrões de juro* but low-denomination paper instruments not backed by specific tax revenues, designed instead to maintain liquidity through circulation. For this reason, the present chapter focuses on the period between 1560 and 1760 – the core phase of *padrões de juro* issuance and management. It leaves aside the late eighteenth century, when rising debt levels and altered fiscal mechanisms marked a departure from the constitutional framework that had once underpinned the credibility of *juros*.

The institutional foundations of that credibility were laid well before 1760. Since the restoration of political independence in 1640, Portugal's financial history reveals a defining trait: during moments of political or diplomatic strain, the crown could issue debt only by leveraging long-established fiscal revenues embedded in the kingdom's tax code. This institutional rigidity sharply distinguished the credibility of Portuguese *juros* from Castilian bonds. Whereas in Castile fiscal revenues became increasingly debt-driven, in Portugal debt issuance remained firmly tied to existing revenue streams (Costa and Henriques, 2024).

This fiscal discipline, while strengthening creditworthiness, also limited the crown's ability to expand borrowing. Portugal's persistent restraint in issuing funded debt resulted in exceptionally low debt-to-GDP ratios, the lowest yet estimated in early modern Europe (Costa and Henriques, 2024: 21–22). During the Restoration War (1640–1668), consolidated debt reached only about 11 percent of GDP, in contrast to the Dutch Republic, whose Eighty Years' War (1568–1648) ended with debt levels approaching 100 percent of GDP (Fristchy, 2017: 165, Figure 3.4). The growing weight of the colonial empire in the eighteenth century further reinforced this pattern: debt service increasingly depended on revenues from Brazilian gold taxes – the *quinto* (20 percent levy on extraction) and the 1 percent duty on private remittances – as well as from the fiscal monopoly on tobacco, while ordinary domestic taxes such as the *sisa* (but not the *décima*) played a secondary role.

Regardless of the specific tax used to service interest payments on *juros*, Portugal's debt credibility is reflected in the steady decline of interest rates (Figure 8.2). Portugal's experience thus supports the view that political regime type was not the decisive factor behind sovereign debt credibility or interest-rate trends (Sussman and Yafeh, 2006). During the eighteenth century, under absolutist rule, the monarchy kept honouring its debt (Rodrigues, 2019 and 2024).

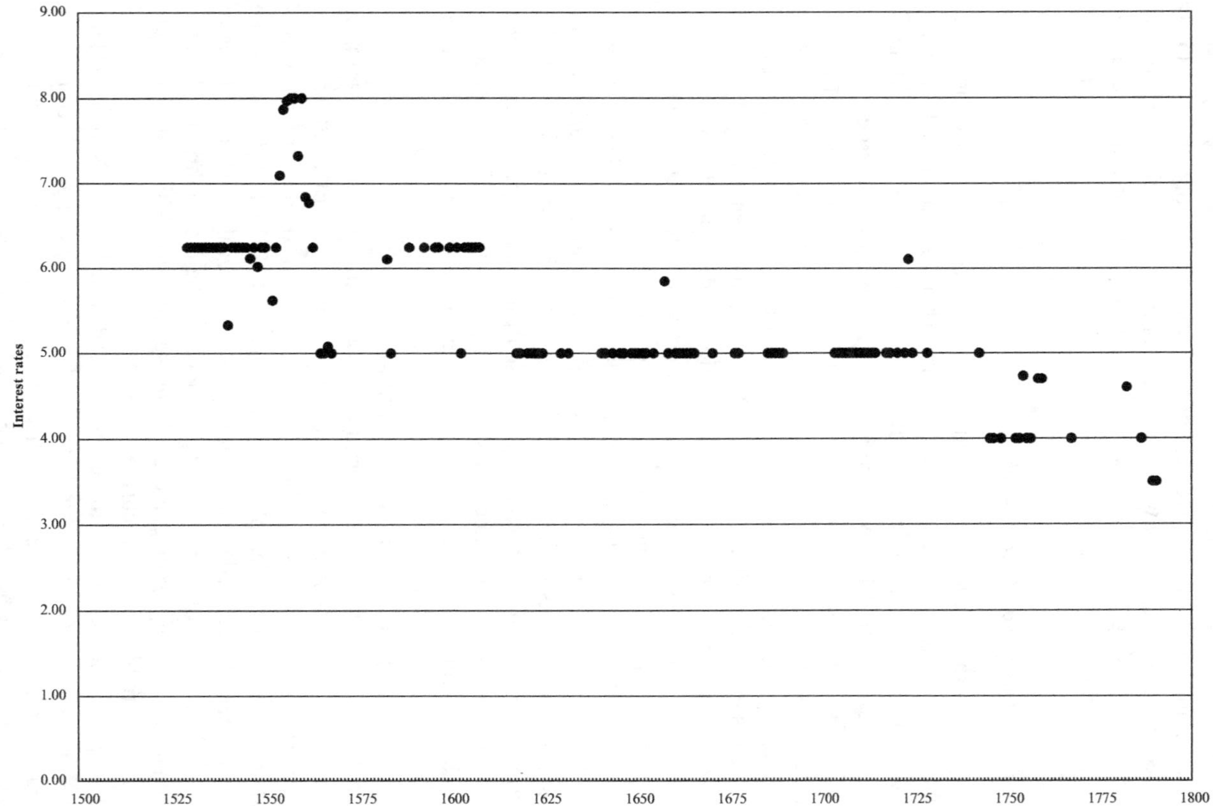

Figure 8.2 Public debt interest rates 1527–1799.

Sources: Costa, Miranda and Nogues-Marco (2024); DEBT.PT – Sovereign debt and private credit in Portugal (Dívida Soberana e Crédito Privado em Portugal 1668–1797); (www.debt.pt).

The kingdom's distinctive combination of limited domestic taxation, substantial imperial revenues, and a cautious fiscal stance sustained low levels of highly credible debt. Yet these same characteristics also constrained market participation: low indebtedness curtailed market depth and liquidity. When holdings became concentrated among a few large investors or institutions, this concentration likely compounded the effect. The following section examines the social dimension of Portugal's debt, focusing on how ownership patterns and the transfer of securities shaped market liquidity over time.

8.1.2 The social structure of the debt stock

Although *juros* were reliably serviced and therefore potentially attractive investments, their scarcity limited market activity. Therefore, the development of secondary markets was not hindered by fiscal instability but rather by the institutional configuration of debt ownership itself. This dynamic diverges from the assumptions of institutional economics, which often attribute underdeveloped capital markets in absolutist regimes to weak property-rights enforcement or arbitrary state decisions. In Portugal, historical evidence shows that the Crown's reliable debt service fostered investor confidence, which eventually encouraged the concentration of *juros* in corporate religious institutions and *propriedades vinculadas* (entailed estates). This section explores whether and how such accumulation occurred, and the institutional mechanisms through which it became entrenched.

Each issuance of *juros* included a buy-back clause granting the Crown the right to redeem the bonds. As a result, *juros* effectively had indefinite maturities, comparable to the British consols introduced in the mid-eighteenth century. During debt-restructuring operations, monarchs exercised this clause, requiring affluent creditors to provide the funds necessary to manage holdouts. These operations reduced debt-servicing costs and created fiscal space for new borrowing. Crucially, all such transactions followed contractual terms and did not involve coercive "haircuts", preserving the reputation and credibility of *juros*.

The analysis bellow draws on a series of cross-sectional snapshots capturing pivotal phases in debt management: the foundational decades of 1520–1550, the period between 1640 and 1699 of political consolidation of the Braganza dynasty, and the final major redemption cycle of 1738–1744, when *juros* bearing 6.25 percent interest were redeemed. These junctures reveal which categories of creditors – private or institutional – were engaged by the crown through the buy-back mechanism, thereby tracing the evolving social composition of holders of Portugal's most credible public securities.

The first phase, covering the initial three decades of Portugal's funded debt, highlights the formative relationship between the monarchy and its creditors – a relationship that established the credibility of *juros* and defined the patterns of investment that persisted in subsequent centuries. Officials of the royal treasury maintained comprehensive records regarding the identities of potential lenders, which included individuals, municipalities, and financially endowed charitable organisations such as the *Misericórdias* (see Table 8.1). The *juros* records

Table 8.1 Social profile of creditors (1529–1557)

Social category of creditors	*Principal (million réis)*	*Principal %*	*N° Padrões*	*N° creditors*
Nobility	343.4	67.63	244	195
Royal officials	53.2	10.49	50	42
Merchants	51.7	10.18	7	7
Religious institutions	22.8	4.50	47	32
Lay brothehoods	2.7	0.54	7	5
Clergymen	0.6	0.13	3	3
Municipalities	0.5	0.10	1	1
Crafstmen	0.25	0.05	1	1
Military	0.25	0.05	1	1
No information	32.2	6.34	45	42
Total	507.6	100	406	329

Source: Miranda, Rodrigues and Lopes 2024: 45.

frequently note that bonds were issued following the monarch's acknowledgment of a creditor's available funds, subsequently requesting their purchase of a *padrão de juro* (Miranda, Rodrigues and Lopes, 2024: 45). This information allowed monarchs to effectively secure funding for military operations in North Africa from 1540 to 1557.

The large share of capital invested by the nobility illustrates the personal nature of such lending ties (Table 8.1). When combined with investments from royal officials, the Crown's social circles accounted for roughly 78 percent of total capital invested in debt (Miranda, Rodrigues and Lopes, 2024: 44). The nobility's primary motive in purchasing *juros* was to establish entailed property (*morgadios*) within family trusts. From the outset, therefore, holding *juros* was perceived as a secure and prestigious form of investment. By tying *juros* to these trusts, aristocratic families not only ensured their economic stability through fiscal revenues earmarked for debt service, but also reinforced the social order in which financial securities were treated as equivalents to real estate – commonly included in dowries among the highest ranks of the nobility (Costa, 2018).

Although *juros* served the social reproduction of the upper elite, their appeal also rested on their competitiveness with land investments. To attract lenders, the monarchy raised the interest rate to 8 percent in the 1550s, as shown in Figure 8.2. This rise does not signal public distrust in *juros* but rather reflects the need to offer returns higher than land rents to keep wealthy nobles interested in financing military campaigns in North Africa. When monarchs exercised the buy-back clause, the redemption of these assets increased liquidity among trustees, who were legally required to reinvest in assets of comparable risk. These institutional constraints on managing entailed wealth often fostered transactions within the nobility itself. Consequently, while *juros* were deeply embedded in the institutional fabric of seigneurial society, their concentration within elite networks limited the prospects for a dynamic capital market to emerge (Magalhães, 2012: 96–98).

The Dynastic Union (1580–1640) transformed the context of Portugal's public debt through administrative and financial integration with the broader Habsburg system. Merchant financiers became heavily involved in the *asientos* network, where *juros* served as collateral. This framework was extended to the financing of the Cape Route trade, as creditors advanced capital to the Crown, which maintained a monopoly over the shipment and import of pepper. Eventually, the resulting credit was consolidated into *juros* serviced by revenues from the *Casa da Índia*.

Sparse evidence suggests that the rise in public debt during this period was accompanied by a marked decline in the credibility of *juros*. Those backed by *Casa da Índia* revenues, for instance, were declared officially non-payable as early as 1607 (Falcão, 1607 [1859]). By the mid-1630s, when the Crown urgently required funds to defend the empire, it struggled to find willing creditors. Municipalities were coerced into issuing local debt – backed by their own tax revenues – to purchase *juros* from the central government in Lisbon, effectively allowing the Crown to service them only irregularly (Santos, 2006). Although a comprehensive study of public debt under the Dynastic Union remains to be undertaken, existing evidence indicates that, from around 1600 onward, the credibility of *juros* steadily eroded. As a result, investors seeking secure placements increasingly directed their savings towards lending to aristocratic households, particularly to the Duchy of Braganza (Costa and Miranda, 2023: 808).

The snapshot of creditors in 1640 (Table 8.2) provides a glimpse of those involved in public credit operations under Habsburg rule and those potentially exposed when the new monarch, formerly Duke of Braganza, assumed power. While the nobility continued to dominate the creditor landscape, religious corporations and lay brotherhoods appear to have expanded their shares.

Table 8.2 Social profile of creditors in 1640

Social group	*Principal of juros (million réis)*	*Principal of juros (percent)*	*Number of juros*
Nobility	292.38	56.57	162
Ecclesiastical institutions	110.79	21.43	168
Lay brotherhoods	35.81	6.93	46
Local élites	29.50	5.71	23
Merchants	12.69	2.45	14
Clergy	5.39	1.04	3
Military personnel	1.20	0.23	1
Municipal councils	0.42	0.08	1
Liberal professions	0.14	0.03	1
No information	28.56	5.52	33
Total	516.88	100.00	453

Sources: Costa and Miranda, 2023. The social background of bondholders was determined through a targeted investigation of archival funds, available at https://digitarq.arquivos.pt/: Habilitações às Ordens Militares; Familiaturas do Santo Ofício; Leitura de Bacharéis and Registo Geral de Mercês.

Recognising that many bondholders belonged to the aristocracy and the Church – key factions that supported the Restoration coup – King John IV saw honouring the sovereign debt as both a political necessity and a means to consolidate alliances. He also decreed that the assets of the Braganza duchy contribute to the war effort through taxation, as required of all nobles under the resolutions of the Cortes assembled in 1641. By refusing any form of partial default or coercive interest reduction that could damage the crown's reputation, the Braganza monarchs transformed public debt into a political instrument – a symbol of legitimate and responsible rule. Yet, this same commitment constrained the monarchy's supply of juros: ordinary revenues were already encumbered by the obligations inherited from Habsburg debt. To regain fiscal space, the crown could only pursue debt-restructuring operations by redeeming the claims of holdout creditors, which demanded significant liquidity. The success of these operations therefore depended on attracting new investors willing to exchange cash for newly issued *juros* at lower rates.

The Crown carried out three debt-restructuring campaigns between 1650 and 1695. The fourth major operation occurred in the 1740s, combining refinancing through principal repayment with a reduction of interest rates on outstanding *juro*. The campaign lasted about three years, though the crown continued issuing a limited number of new *juros* during the 1750s to redeem older ones paying 6.25 percent. After 1750, however, only a small volume of new *juros* was created (Rodrigues, 2024), suggesting that the monarchy financed Portugal's participation in the Seven Years' War (1756–1763) through alternative means – specifically, by raising the *Décima* tax rate from 4 percent to 10 percent and by reforming colonial administration to secure greater fiscal transfers through the Overseas Council.

Even amid rising GDP per capita (Palma and Reis, 2019), the limited issuance of debt shaped the pattern of debt ownership. *Juros* mainly changed hands during state-driven debt-management operations recorded in the royal chancery, rather than through routine private trading. Each round of debt restructuring reinforced the position of institutional creditors, particularly ecclesiastical corporations and lay brotherhoods, which reinvested surpluses derived from leasing their rural and urban properties into public debt. Consequently, these operations further concentrated ownership in mortmain institutions. Hence, the evolution of Portugal's market for public debt cannot be explained solely by constitutional or political constraints. Patterns of wealth distribution emerge as crucial to understanding why financial markets across early modern Europe diverged in depth and liquidity. Building on this interpretation, the following analysis focuses on the outcomes of these campaigns, covering the period from 1640 to 1760. It examines how these debt management operations reshaped the social composition of creditors (Table 8.3).

For this analysis, a comprehensive collection of *padrões de juro* that changed ownership (Table 8.3) was classified into two broad categories – private and institutional lenders – and divided into two periods: the first bounded by the Restoration era (1640–1699), and the second period encompassing the *juros* issued after the War of the Spanish Succession at 6.25 percent, which were subjected to the debt restructuring of the 1740s. The data reveal the relative importance of each lender

Table 8.3 Institutional structure of the public debt

Bondholder	*1640–1699*		*1640–1760s*	
	percent	*Number of lenders*	*percent*	*Number of lenders*
Private creditors	77.2	520	82.8	1,279
Institutional creditors	22.3	152	17.2	266

Sources: DEBT.PT – Sovereign debt and private credit in Portugal (Dívida Soberana e Crédito Privado em Portugal 1668–1797); (www.debt.pt).

Table 8.4 Social and geographic distribution of the public debt

Panel A: Stock hold (percent) by the 1st decile of each category		
	1640–1699	1640–1760s
Private creditors	60.0	63.0
Institutional creditors	68.4	80.0
Panel B: Distribution of the debt stock: stock hold (percent) by the 1st decile of creditors		
	1640–1699	1640–1760
Private creditors	79.4	62.8
Institutional creditors	20.6	37.2
Panel C: Geographic distribution (percent of the stock in 1760)		
Institutional creditors	Geographic distribution	
Lisbon	60.0	
Rest of the country	40.0	

Sources: DEBT.PT – Sovereign debt and private credit in Portugal (Dívida Soberana e Crédito Privado em Portugal 1668–1797); (www.debt.pt).

category based on *juros* held. The number of private lenders more than doubled, confirming that the crown's expanded borrowing in the first half of the eighteenth century enabled wider market participation. The parallel increase in institutional creditors reflects, in part, the transfer of securities to these bodies through pious bequests from private bondholders.

The preliminary conclusions drawn from this broader participation must be assessed considering distributional patterns (Table 8.4). Panel A of Table 8.4 examines the degree of debt concentration within each category of creditors. For the first period, the results indicate no significant differences between private and institutional holders. However, a marked change occurred in the second period: while private creditors did not experience a notable shift toward greater concentration, institutional creditors did. By the mid-eighteenth century, the top decile of institutional holders accounted for approximately 80 percent of the total debt stock within that category.

When the data are organised independently of the creditor categories, focusing instead on the top decile of the whole lenders (Panel B of Table 8.4), we find that institutional creditors increased their share of total wealth held in public debt from 20.6 percent to 37.2 percent, while private creditors correspondingly reduced theirs from 79.4 percent to 62.8 percent. Viewed from different angles, both Panels A and B of Table 4 point to the growing prominence of religious corporations and lay brotherhoods as the monarchy's principal creditors. Both the Patriarchal See of Lisbon and the Misericórdia of Lisbon were called upon by the crown to participate in the debt restructuring campaign of 1740s. In particular, the Patriarchal See contributed approximately two thousand million réis – equivalent to one-third of the annual state budget – to redeem *juros* paying 6.25 percent and buy *juros* at 5 percent serviced by new taxes.

While institutional investors today are a significant feature of modern financial systems, their participation in asset markets in early modern Europe has been regarded as the outcome of strategic management decisions by institutional trustees aimed at ensuring financial sustainability. In Netherlands, charitable institutions could sell real estate during periods of crisis and reinvest the proceeds in securities during more favourable times. In short, in historical cases of financial modernisation as in the Netherlands, the concentration of public bonds in the hands of Amsterdam's institutional investors was a clear response to market conditions in which financial markets offered liquid paper assets. As Gelderblom and Jonker note, "Profitable real estate opportunities became scarcer; in addition, Holland's debt almost tripled between 1670 and 1720, creating a flood of bonds which left investors with few options but to buy" (Gelderblom and Jonker, 2009: 82).

In contrast to the Dutch case, in Portugal the concentration of public debt in institutional hands did not reflect deliberate management strategies but rather the lack of opportunities for religious corporations and lay brotherhoods to invest their surpluses. This situation effectively turned them into quasi-banks from which monarchs borrowed at decreasing interest rates. The concentration of wealth had two further implications. The first was geographical: as shown in Panel C, Lisbon accounted for 60 percent of public debt, partly because the largest religious corporations were based there. The second was institutional: since these major creditors were mortmain bodies, their extensive portfolios remained effectively immobilised and, as the Crown reduced the issuance of new *juros* towards the end of the eighteenth century, opportunities for further investment in public debt diminished. Because these institutions were legally barred from engaging in productive economic activity, their accumulated funds either remained idle or were redirected into private credit markets. Ultimately, the concentration of public debt in institutional hands shaped Portugal's distinctive financial structure: an illiquid market for state securities and a dynamic private credit market that made use of *juros* as collateral, yet with limited capacity to channel capital into productive investment (Costa, Rocha and Brito, 2018).[2]

Finally, as discussed in the following section, because *juros* were punctually serviced, the large portfolios of these institutions effectively channelled substantial portions of tax revenue into their accounts.

8.1.3 Taxes and debt service

The credibility of public debt ultimately depended on the fiscal revenues that guaranteed timely payments. Understanding this link between taxation and debt servicing is crucial to explaining why institutions continued to regard *juros* as safe assets. The portfolio of the monarchy's largest creditor in the eighteenth century (Patriarchal See of Lisbon) provides a revealing example. This ecclesiastical institution alone held about one-fourth of the debt stock, largely as a result of its decisive participation in the last major debt restructuring campaign (DEBT.PT, file A _ DEBT). Investing in public debt represented a viable way to employ the income accumulated from land rents originally endowed by the Crown.

The exceptional feature of this campaign was the participation of a single creditor capable of underwriting the redemption of approximately 2,800 million réis of outstanding debt.[3] The fiscal effects for the Crown were comparable to those of previous successful operations: the reduction of interest rates created fiscal space to issue new bonds at lower rates (4 percent and 5 percent), which were then acquired by the Patriarchal Church. Consequently, the monarchy channelled to the Patriarchal See a variety of tax revenues from diversified sources. As shown in Table 8.5, the colonial empire played a central role in sustaining the credibility of the newly issued *juros* acquired by this leading ecclesiastical body.

At the end of the debt-restructuring operation, the Patriarchal See held approximately 2,860 million *réis* of capital stocked in *juros* (equivalent to about 90 tons of silver), generating 143.4 million réis in annual interest payments. Of this total, 44.4 percent was serviced by income derived from the Brazilian economy and from fiscal sources administered by the Overseas Council. Yet, domestic taxation was not insignificant: the Décima tax contributed more than the Lisbon customs duties. Thus, by the mid-eighteenth century, the credibility of Portuguese public debt rested on two interrelated factors that structurally limited liquidity: first, a high concentration of debt holdings, with nearly one-fourth of the total debt held by a single creditor; and second, this creditor was an ecclesiastical institution. The Patriarchate stands as a revealing example of how ecclesiastical wealth could reinforce rather than transform Portugal's financial order. It was an institution without any program of productive investment, devoted instead to political representation and diplomatic expenditure, and functioning as a particular delegation of the Holy See in Lisbon.

Table 8.5 Juros purchased by the Patriarchal See of Lisbon (1743–1748)

Tax base allocated to debt service	*Nº of Juros*	*Annuity (million réis)*	*Share of the tax base on the total (percent)*
Colonial empire*	406	63.5	44.4
External flows ++	252	24.0	16.7
Domestic economy #	459	55.9	38.9
Total	1.117	143.4	100.0

Sources: DEBT.PT – Sovereign debt and private credit in Portugal (Dívida Soberana e Crédito Privado em Portugal 1668-1797); (www.debt.pt). _ *Chancelaria de D. João V*, Livros 10, 12, 14,15,18, 20, 21, 22, 23, 24, 26, 27.

* One percent tax on gold shipments, Overseas Council, Tariffs on Brazilian sugar; Fiscal monopolies; Tariffs on Brazilian Tobacco. ++ Lisbon and Porto Customs; salt exports from Setubal. # Excise taxes throughout the country; tolls paid in Lisbon and Decima income tax.

8.1.4 Taking stock and forging ahead

The project "Sovereign Debt and Private Credit in Portugal (1500–1797)" (DEBT.PT) offers a perspective on Portugal that challenges the established assumption of a positive correlation between the credibility and liquidity of financial instruments. The Portuguese crown managed to maintain a credible commitment while keeping sovereign debt at relatively low levels, both in terms of GDP and fiscal revenues. These characteristics are closely connected: limited debt levels strengthened the credibility of Portuguese *juros*.

A central question arises regarding why the crown did not utilise its strong reputation to smooth out taxation through increased borrowing. One explanation is that the colonial empire supplemented the domestic fiscal base, financing regular government expenditures. Additionally, the resources provided by the empire meant the crown had less need to negotiate with local constituents over tax increases. On the other hand, *juros*' credibility aligned with creditor strategies to hold or transfer these secure assets to mortmain institutions. Consequently, this analysis underscores the importance of the social and institutional structure of public debt for understanding the development of capital markets in early modern states. Portugal's case indicates that there was no shortage of capital; rather, its high concentration among large, politically influential mortmain institutions may have contributed to market illiquidity, as these entities tended to hold assets offering reliable but non-transferable returns.

In the long run, the most significant consequence of this concentration of financial capital was the transformation of major creditors into quasi-banking entities. This allowed the Crown to rely on a narrow group of institutional lenders, resorting at times to forms of financial repression (Costa and Henriques, 2024), in contrast with the British case described by Quinn (2006). In Britain, between the 1690s and 1750, the corporate securitisation of public debt – that is, the consolidation of government bonds under institutional umbrellas like the Bank of England – simultaneously reduced debtor coordination costs while enhancing the collective bargaining power of creditors. The power dynamics between debtor and creditor thus appear inverted in the two systems: in Britain, debt concentration strengthened creditors; and in Portugal, it reinforced sovereign control, enabling the Crown to draw on the wealth of ecclesiastical institutions for debt-restructuring operations or for the limited issuance of new *juros* after 1760, often yielding as little as 3.5 percent, comparable to British consols.

Overall, these findings highlight that the composition of the bondholding base was at least as consequential as the features of the debt instruments or the constitutional framework in shaping long-term financial development. Future comparative research should therefore investigate why some markets favoured buy-and-hold investors while others evolved toward more liquid, tradeable securities.

Notes

1 www.debt.pt, Sovereign debt and private credit in Portugal, 1640–1800, Project funded by FCT, Portuguese Foundation for Science and Technology (PTDC/HARHIS/28809/2017).

2 The use of *juros* as collateral in short-term private obligation does not necessarily indicate that the market for these securities was liquid. Rather, it reflects the perception that the income generated by a *juro* was secure enough to make it acceptable as collateral for loans. This broadens the discussion of the conditions for market liquidity and the different uses of securities according to institutional settings. For a contrasting case in Holland, see Gelderblom and Jonker (2006).

3 Earlier authors have examined the establishment of the Patriarchate of Lisbon and its institutional role in the early eighteenth century. de Azevedo, 1973; Brazão, 1943: 54, and Pimentel, 2009: 7–22, discuss the creation of the Patriarchate in connection with the enlargement of the Royal Chapel and provide indicative figures for the institution's participation in financing the public debt. Yet it is only with the evidence gathered through the DEBT.PT Project that this participation can now be precisely quantified, based on the original records of debt issuances.

Bibliography

Álvarez-Nogal, Carlos (1997), *El Crédito de la Monarquía Hispánica en el reinado de Felipe IV*, Valladolid: Junta de Castilla y León/Caja Duero.

Álvarez-Nogal, Carlos (2008), "The Role Played by Short-Term Credit in the Spanish Monarchy", in Fausto Piola Caselli, ed., *Government Debts and Financial Markets in Europe*, London: Routledge, pp. 82–95.

Álvarez-Nogal, Carlos (2009), *Oferta y demanda de deuda pública en Castilla. Juros de Alcabalas (1540–1740)*, Madrid: Banco de España.

Álvarez-Nogal, Carlos and Chamley, Christophe (2014), "Debt Policy under Constraints: Philip II, the Cortes, and Genoese bankers", *Economic History Review*, 67, 1, pp. 192–213.

Andres Ucendo, José Ignacio and Lanza García, Ramón (2008), "Estructura y evolución de los ingresos de la Real Hacienda de Castilla en el siglo XVII", *Studia Historica: Historia Moderna*, 30, pp.147–190.

Brazão, Eduardo (1943), *Contributions to the History of the Patriarchate of Lisbon*, Porto: Livraria Civilização.

Chamley, Christophe (2011), "Interest Reductions in the Politico-Financial Nexus of Eighteenth-Century England", *Journal of Economic History*, 71, 3, pp. 555–588.

Chilosi, David (2014), "Risky Institutions: Political Regimes and the Cost of Public Borrowing in Early Modern Italy", *Journal of Economic History*, 74, 3, pp. 887–915.

Coffman, D'Maris and Neal, Larry (2013), "Introduction", in D'Maris Coffman, Adrian Leonard and Larry Neal, eds., *Questioning Credible Commitment: Perspectives on the Rise of Financial Capitalism*, Cambridge: Cambridge University Press, pp. 1–20.

Costa, Leonor Freire (2018), "Entre Investimento e Consumo: a estrutura do património da casa de Bragança no século XVI", in Jessica Hallett and Nuno Senos, coords., *De Todas as Partes do Mundo. O Património do 5° Duque de Bragança, D. Teodósio I*, Lisboa: Tinta da China, Vol. I, pp. 71–84.

Costa, Leonor Freire and Brito, Paulo Brasil (2018), "Why did people pay taxes? Fiscal innovation in Portugal and state making in times of political struggle (1500–1680)", GHES (WP 59). www.repository.utl.pt/bitstream/10400.5/17980/1/WP_59_2018.pdf

Costa, Leonor Freire and Henriques, António Castro (2024), "Different Indeed: Portuguese Sovereign Debt from 1500 to 1796", *e-Journal of Portuguese History*, 22, 1, pp. 5–28.

Costa, Leonor Freire, Henriques, António and Palma, Nuno (2024), "Anatomy of a Premodern State", *European Review of Economic History*, 28, 4, pp. 453–474.

Costa, Leonor Freire, Lains, Pedro and Miranda, Susana Münch (2016), *An Economic History of Portugal*, Cambridge: Cambridge University Press.

Costa, Leonor Freire and Miranda, Susana Münch (2023), "Reputational Recovery under Political Instability: Public Debt, Portugal, 1641–1683", *Economic History Review*, 76, 3, pp. 871–891.

Costa, Leonor Freire, Miranda, Susana Münch and Nogues-Marco, Pilar (2024), "Early Modern Financial Development in the Iberian Peninsula", in Leonor Freire Costa, Regina Grafe, Alfonso Herranz-Loncán, David Igual-Luis, Vicente Pinilla and Heminia V. Vilar, eds., *An Economic History of the Iberian Peninsula, 700–2000*, Cambridge: University Press, pp. 335–357.

Costa, Leonor Freire, Rocha, Maria Manuela and de Brito, Paulo Brasil (2018), "Os Impactos do Terramoto de 1755 no Mercado de Crédito de Lisboa", *Ler História*, 72, pp. 77–102.

de Azevedo, João Lúcio (1973), *Épocas de Portugal Económico*, Lisboa: Livraria Clássica Editora, 3rd ed.

De Luca, Giuseppe (2015), "Government Debt and Financial Markets: Exploring Pro-cycle Effects in Northern Italy During the Sixteenth and the Seventeenth Centuries", in Fausto Piola Caselli, ed., *Government Debts and Financial Markets in Europe*, London: Pickering & Chatto, pp. 45–66.

Dickson, P. G. M. (1967), *The Financial Revolution in England*, London: Macmillan.

Dincecco, Mark (2011), *Political Transformations and Public Finances Europe, 1650–1913*, Cambridge: Cambridge University Press.

Domínguez Ortiz, Antonio (1960), *Política y hacienda de Felipe IV*, Madrid: Editorial de Derecho Financiero.

Drelichman, Mauricio and Voth, Hans-Joachim (2014), *Lending to the Borrower from Hell: Debt, Taxes, and Default in the Age of Philip II*, Princeton, NJ: Princeton University Press.

Falcão, Luis Figueiredo (1607 [1859]), *Livro en que se contem toda a Fazenda e Real Patrimonio dos Reynos de Portugal, India, Ilhas adjacentes* , Lisboa: Imprensa Nacional.

Fritschy, Wantje (2003), "A 'Financial Revolution' Reconsidered: Public Finance in Holland During the Dutch Revolt, 1568–1648", *Economic History Review*, 56, 1, pp. 57–89.

Fritschy, Wantje (2017), *Public Finance of the Dutch Republic in Comparative Perspective. The Viability of an Early Modern Federal State (1570s–1795)*, Leiden: Brill.

Gelderblom, Oscar and Jonker, Joost (2006), *Exploring the market for government bonds in the Dutch Republic (1600–1800)*, Draft: Utrecht University.

Gelderblom, Oscar and Jonker, Joost (2009), "With a View to Hold: The Emergence of Institutional Investors on the Amsterdam Securities Market During the Seventeenth and Eighteenth Centuries", in Atack, Jeremy and Neal, Larry, eds., *The Origins and Development of Financial Markets and Institutions. From the Seventeenth Century to the Present*, Cambridge: Cambridge Univ ersity Press, pp. 71–84.

Henriques, António and Palma, Nuno (2023), "Comparative European Institutions and the Little Divergence, 1385–1800", *Journal of Economic Growth*, 28, 2, pp. 259–294

Hespanha, António Manuel (1994), *As vésperas do Leviathan. Instituições e poder político. Portugal, século XVII,* Lisbon: Almedina.

Li, Ling-Fan (2019), "The Stop of the Exchequer and the Secondary Market for English Sovereign Debt, 1677–1705", *Journal of Economic History, 79*, 1, pp. 176–200.

Magalhães, Joaquim Romero (2012), *Miunças 3, No Portugal Moderno: espaços, tratos e dinheiro*, Coimbra: Imprensa da Universidade de Coimbra.

Miranda, Susana Münch, Rodrigues, Lisbeth and Lopes, Bruno (2024), "The Social Distribution of Public Debt in Portugal, 1529–1680", *e-Journal of Portuguese History*, 22, 1, pp. 29–60.

Neal, Larry (2000), "How It All Began: The Monetary and Financial Architecture of Europe During the First Global Capital Markets, 1648–1815", *Financial History Review*, 7, pp. 117–40.

North, Douglass C. and Weingast, Barry R. (1989), "Constitutions and Commitment: The Evolution of Institutions Governing Public Choice on Seventeenth-Century England", *Journal of Economic* History, 49, 4, pp. 803–32.

Palma, Nuno and Reis, Jaime (2019), "From Convergence to Divergence: Portuguese Economic Growth, 1527–1850", *Journal of Economic History*, 79, 2, pp. 477–506.

Pezzolo, Luciano (2003), "The Venetian Government Debt, 1350–1650", in M. Boone, K. Davids and P. Janssens, eds., *Urban Public Debts, Urban Government and the Market for Annuities in Western Europe (14th-18th Centuries)*, Turnhout: Brepols, pp. 61–74.

Pezzolo, Luciano (2013), "Sovereign Debts, Political Structure, and Institutional Commitments in Italy", in D'Maris Coffman, Adrian Leonard and Larry Neal, eds., *Questioning Credible Commitment: Perspectives on the Rise of Financial Capitalism*, Cambridge: Cambridge University Press, pp. 169–198.

Pimentel, A. F. (2009), "D. Tomás de Almeida (1716–1754)", in Carlos António Moreira de Azevedo, Sandra Costa Saldanha and António Pedro Boto de Oliveira, eds., *Os Patriarcas de Lisboa*, Lisbon: Alêtheia Editores, pp. 7–22.

Quinn, Stephen (2006), *Securitization of Sovereign Debt: Corporations as a Sovereign Debt Restructuring Mechanism in Britain, 1688–1750*, Unpublished Manuscript, Texas Christian University.

Rodrigues, Lisbeth (2019), "Os Padrões de Juro da Misericórdia de Lisboa, 1767–1797", *Ler História*, 74, pp. 137–160.

Rodrigues, Lisbeth (2024), "Institutional Investors in the Portuguese Credit Market (1550–1800): The Case of the Misericórdias", *Revista de Historia Económica/Journal of Iberian and Latin American Economic History*, 42, pp. 1–29

Santos, Catarina Madeira (2006), "Os refluxos do império numa época de crise. A câmara de Lisboa, as Armadas da Índia e as Armadas do Brasil: quatro tempos e uma interrogação (c. 1600–1640)", *Anais de História de Além-Mar*, 7, pp. 81–105.

Stasavage, David (2011), *States of Credit: Size, Power, and the Development of European Polities*, Princeton, NJ: Princeton University Press.

Sussman, Nathan and Yafeh, Yishay (2006), "Institutional Reforms, Financial Development and Sovereign Debt: Britain 1690–1790", *Journal of Economic History*, 66, 4, pp. 906–935.

Toboso Sánchez, Pilar (1987), *La deuda pública castellana durante el Antiguo Régimen (juros) y su liquidación en el siglo* XIX, Madrid: Instituto de Estudios Fiscales.

9 "Es politica segura y obligacion precissa evitar la mayor ruina". Municipal taxation and debt in the Spanish Crown of Aragon (1718–1760)

Íñigo Ena Sanjuán

Introduction

> Having reviewed in the Consejo de Castilla the two petitions – one concerning the granting of permission to the Gobernador and Capitán General and to the Audiencia of Catalonia to authorise *arbitrios* [municipal taxes] to the towns of the Principality of Catalonia, and another, made by the *síndico* of Espluga Calva, to apportion among its inhabitants one eleventh of the fruits of their lands to cover the *censos* [annuities] they owe – the Consejo resolved that the granting of levies, pledging of *propios* [municipal assets], alienations, imposition of annuities, and other similar fiscal measures is so inseparably tied to His Majesty's *regalía* [royal prerogatives] that not even the Consejo itself may grant such faculties without first consulting His Majesty through the customary Friday consultation.
>
> Therefore, it is ordered that the Audiencia shall not admit such faculties or petitions; instead, the towns must submit their requests directly to the Consejo, following the same procedure used in these Kingdoms of Castile.
>
> As for the distribution that the town of Esplugacalva intends to carry out, provided that all residents agree and that it concerns their own production, no license is needed to execute it among those who consent. However, it is to be noted that those who do not consent to the levy cannot be compelled by those who do, since such a measure can only be enforced *inter volentes* [among willing parties]; and in order to bind everyone, including dissenters, a royal faculty must be obtained beforehand.[1]

The royal order promulgated in March 1718 was crystal clear: nobody was entitled to authorise the creation of municipal taxes called "*arbitrios*" except the king. Although the inhabitants of a town consented to apportioning an amount of money to pay municipal debts, nobody could be forced to contribute if the tax had not been approved by the monarch. The royal order was motivated by a consultation submitted by the Real Audiencia of Catalonia to the Consejo de Castilla, the supreme royal council for the affairs of the Crown of Castile and, since the suppression of the Consejo de Aragón in 1711, for the affairs of the Crown of

DOI: 10.4324/9781003653301-10

Aragon. Apart from the little village of Espluga Calva, the Catalan high court had received petitions from towns and villages asking for authorisation to collect new taxes, as municipalities were heavily indebted and could pay neither their creditors nor royal taxes on time. The *oidores* (judges) of the Catalan Audiencia considered that forwarding every petition to the Consejo de Castilla would be slow and would delay the collection of royal taxes, so they suggested that the Capitán General – the highest royal officer in Catalonia – together with the Real Audiencia could authorise the municipal councils to levy taxes. The judges recalled that the viceroy as *alter nos* of the king and the pre-Bourbon Audiencia had such a prerogative. Yet, as the opening quotation shows, the Consejo de Castilla completely deauthorised the Catalan court. Levying *arbitrios* was a *regalía*, an exclusive prerogative of the monarch; not even the Consejo could authorise the creation of municipal taxes without the royal assent.

Although the royal order left no room for doubt, debates around the legitimacy and consequences of municipal taxation and over-indebtedness arose and, unsurprisingly, lasted for more than four decades. Heated controversies involved local parties, the judges of the Reales Audiencias (high courts) of the territories of the Spanish Crown of Aragon, and royal ministers in the court of Madrid. If the order was so clear, why did debates arise? The answer lies in the two sources of legitimacy that underpinned municipal taxation, namely, the monarch's authority and the existence of municipal debt, which had theoretically been authorised by the predecessors of King Felipe V. The debates revolved not only around the town councils' ability to create new *arbitrios*, but also around maintaining existing taxes that may not have been explicitly authorised by the predecessors of Felipe V, but had been earmarked to service debt. Since debt persisted, *arbitrios* and other municipal taxes had to be maintained, too. In short, debates were about the legitimacy and consequences of taxation.

This chapter delves into the discussions about municipal *arbitrios* and annuities in the territories of the Spanish Crown of Aragon during the first half of the eighteenth century. It examines the debates, the arguments, ideas, and motivations of the parties involved, mainly the judges of the Aragonese Reales Audiencias, and the consequences of those debates for the management of the municipal treasuries of the Spanish Crown of Aragon. Discussions revolved around the legitimacy of the taxes and debts created before the arrival of the Bourbons, but also around the persistence of those debts and taxes after the instauration of the French dynasty. Debates were juridical, concerning the legal nature of the *arbitrios* and municipal annuities, but also economic and social, about the consequences of onerous taxation and indebtedness on the economy of the Aragonese regions, and the distribution of the fiscal and financial burden within the Aragonese municipalities. More broadly, the discussions about the legitimacy and consequences of taxation were debates around the Aragonese model, a political, juridical, fiscal, and financial model that emerged in the Middle Ages and persisted almost unaltered until the early eighteenth century, when a series of royal decrees promulgated by the Bourbon king Felipe V challenged its foundations. In short, the chapter examines the effects of the royal policies on redefining municipal taxation.

Since the members of the Consejo de Castilla knew almost nothing about the functioning of municipal taxation in the territories of the former Crown of Aragon, the high courts of the Aragonese territories had to report on this issue several times. This chapter is primarily based on the letters, reports, and verdicts of the judges of the Reales Audiencias of the territories of the Spanish Crown of Aragon. All these documents, together with other reports on municipal debt restructuring in the Aragonese territories, were compiled in a single record, kept at the Spanish National Archives. To my knowledge, this source has never been used for research purposes.[2]

This chapter is structured into five sections. After this introduction, the functioning of the Aragonese town councils from the Late Middle Ages is succinctly described, together with the situation of the municipal councils in the seventeenth and early eighteenth centuries. In the third section, the debates within the Real Audiencia of Catalonia are analysed. Similarly, the fourth section addresses the heated discussions in the Real Audiencia of Aragon, which resulted in an open conflict between the judges and the *fiscal* of the Aragonese high court. Before concluding, the fifth section presents the last phases of the debates, prior to the reform of the municipal treasuries in the 1760s.

Too much debt, too many taxes

The fiscal and financial system of the Aragonese municipal councils took shape in the Late Middle Ages. Permanent taxation at the local level emerged in the fourteenth century as a result of the municipal debt issued using the legal formula of the *censo*, a type of redeemable annuity broadly extended in the Aragonese countries.[3] To regulate taxation and indebtedness, institutional mechanisms had to be devised and implemented. Town councils and permanent deputations of the kingdoms established checks and balances to ensure that debt and taxes were managed properly, thus enhancing credibility.[4] Furthermore, mechanisms to deal with insolvency and over-indebtedness were created. For instance, the municipalities of the Iberian Crown of Aragon (Aragon, Valencia, and Catalonia) adopted a type of agreement called *concordia* to restructure their debts. Similarly, in 1401, the town council of Barcelona inaugurated the first municipal bank in Europe to facilitate economic transactions and relieve municipal finances.[5] This fiscal, financial, and institutional model was partially exported to other Aragonese territories overseas and adapted to local contexts.[6]

From the fourteenth century, the Aragonese cities, towns, and villages experienced boom and bust cycles caused by borrowing and over-indebtedness. When municipal councils found themselves in financial trouble, they normally escaped bankruptcy through the institutional mechanisms mentioned above and by increasing fiscal pressure. As a reward for their donations and for arranging the collection of taxes, the Aragonese monarchs granted the municipalities privileges and charters to manage debt and taxation autonomously, without the intervention of royal officers or authorities external to the town councils. For instance, cities such as Tarragona could freely levy new taxes to pay the annuities that they had issued to fund the military campaigns of the Aragonese monarchy in the Mediterranean.[7]

This model remained mostly unaltered in the following centuries, experiencing slight variations to adapt to changing contexts. Municipal corporations all over the Crown of Aragon enjoyed great independence in managing their own fiscal and financial affairs. Certain institutional mechanisms reinforced this autonomy. For instance, the annuities borrowed by the Crown of Aragon municipalities included a clause of collective and individual responsibility for the debt. This meant that debt was secured against all assets and revenues of the municipality, but also against the entire estates of the individuals that constituted the municipality. In other words, all the *vecinos* or inhabitants of the town, both at the moment of issuing the annuity and in the future, were personally liable for the debt with all their assets. Although this clause increased the security of the debt, as the mortgaged assets and revenues were much larger than just a specific municipal tax, and lowered the interest rate at which annuities were issued, in the long run the clause proved fatal for the town councils and inhabitants.

In the seventeenth century, municipalities had managed to recover from previous financial crises and began issuing annuities again. Borrowing increased suddenly in the 1640s due to the needs of the town councils (purchasing wheat, tackling the effects of devastating plagues), but primarily because of the urgent demands of the monarchy to fund the wars it sustained in Europe.[8] Although the Crown of Aragon had entered a dynastic union with the Crown of Castile and formed the Hispanic monarchy together with other constituents, the Aragonese kingdoms and town councils preserved their own institutional, political, and legal arrangements.[9] Thus, the municipalities continued using the same medieval mechanisms they had used since the fourteenth century: they issued annuities with collective and individual responsibility clauses and created taxes to expand their borrowing capacity and/or to ensure that debt was serviced. As in the Late Middle Ages, they resorted to debt restructuring agreements when they ran into financial trouble.[10]

Over-indebtedness and the subsequent increase in fiscal pressure had a critical impact on the institutional structures and political dynamics of the municipalities of the Crown of Aragon and beyond. While town councils became more oligarchic institutions, the main municipal offices were controlled by an increasingly closed elite whose members were debtholders themselves and oriented municipal taxation towards servicing the debt they owned.[11] This precluded innovation, hindered the arrival of outsiders, discouraged consumption, and had deleterious effects on regional economies, as local production became less competitive.[12] These processes were not exclusive to the Aragonese municipalities, nor even to the towns of the Hispanic monarchy; municipalities all over Western Europe experienced similar problems of indebtedness and taxation.[13] Early modern actors had similar concerns. The correspondence between two ministers of the Bourbon monarchies of Spain and the Two Sicilies reveals that municipal debt and taxation were seen as major social and economic problems in the early modern period. The Neapolitan secretary of state offered an overview of his homeland:

> Throughout Europe, one can now say that the burdens imposed on the municipalities have become intolerable for most of their inhabitants [...]. For over

> two centuries, the Austrians [Habsburgs] have caused greater devastation in this Kingdom [of Naples] than even in the farthest reaches of Sicily. And what renders the ruin complete is having established taxes and then having sold the rights to collect them, so that of all that the oppressed people pay, it seems that barely a third reaches the King, who must maintain the army, the magistrates, the religious institutions, the fortresses, and the court with only that third.

The Spanish Secretary of State informed his Neapolitan counterpart that, in the Spanish monarchy,

> the devastation left by the Austrians is less visible to the public, [but] is at least equal to that of the other country. A civil history of their dynasty would reveal the steps by which they methodically brought about the disappearance of the population, agriculture, manufacturing, commerce, and the wealth that once abounded in countless towns that no longer exist, in others that will recover only with great difficulty, and in many once-famous cities that they reduced to corpses.[14]

The seventeenth century was especially complicated in fiscal, financial, and economic terms. Two factors made the evolution of the municipalities different from previous times. First, the profile of the debtholders changed. While in previous centuries the main municipal creditors were the wealthiest inhabitants of the towns, usually merchants, in the seventeenth century, municipal annuities flowed to ecclesiastical institutions via donations and testaments, to endow chaplaincies and pious works. The change in the profile of creditors in turn brought about a transformation in the way debt was held. Municipal annuities were seen less as an investment and became less mobile capital: after being endowed, they had to ensure the celebration of masses perpetually, so they were not cancelled.[15] Additionally, the Aragonese town councils reached their debt ceiling at different moments in the second half of the seventeenth century. Although this had happened previously, the political context in which municipalities could no longer borrow and experienced solvency problems was different. Traditionally, town councils could refinance debt by issuing annuities at lower interest rates than old *censos*, but from the early eighteenth century, the rollover of debt stopped.

The second main reason for this definitive interruption in borrowing was the Bourbon dynasty's ascension to the Spanish throne after the War of the Spanish Succession (1701–1714) and the subsequent promulgation of the Decretos de Nueva Planta (1707–1716). These were a series of royal orders dictated by Felipe V to punish the Aragonese subjects who had rebelled against him during the succession conflict. Through the decrees, the institutions and laws of the Aragonese territories that remained under Bourbon control (Kingdoms of Aragon, Valencia, and Majorca, and Principality of Catalonia) were abolished either partially or totally, and replaced by laws and institutions inspired by the Castilian model. Since the royal prerogatives were broader in Castile than in Aragon, royal power was reinforced in the Aragonese Crown. Although the importance of the change that the

Nueva Planta represented for the Aragonese territories and for the Spanish monarchy is undeniable, recent historiography has questioned the depth, dimension, and speed of the changes.[16]

In the field of municipal taxation and finances, the Nueva Planta constituted a relevant political and legal change for the town councils, although it was a progressive one. The new Castilian-based town councils (*ayuntamientos*) had more limited capacities than the pre-Bourbon municipal councils. As explained above, municipalities could neither issue annuities nor levy taxes freely. This represented a crucial change both in the source of legitimacy of taxation – from autonomous municipalities granted by former monarchs to the king and only the king – and in the way this legitimacy was expressed – from the will of the inhabitants and council of the town, with the presence of a royal officer, to the explicit authorisation of the monarch. The prohibition was lifted in the late 1710s, but was discussed at length during the following decades until the reforms of the 1750s. It was suggested that the law could have retroactive effects, so the validity of many taxes levied during the medieval and early modern periods, together with the annuities they secured, was called into question. Although some royal ministers suggested defaulting on the municipal annuities to remove the local taxes, the king decided to maintain the existing ones. Yet, the decision to forbid the creation of annuities and taxes, and the new categorisation of the existing municipal taxes as *arbitrios* – an alien concept to the Aragonese tradition – brought to an end the whole fiscal and financial system of the municipalities. This model had worked because debt could be refinanced and serviced by levying new taxes, but the decision to prohibit more debt from being issued and taxes from being created caused it to break down.

In short, the main questions at stake were whether town councils could levy taxes without the explicit consent of the monarch himself, and whether the existing taxes and the annuities they secured had to be considered licit or not, and if they were not, whether they should be annulled. This was tantamount to questioning the autonomy granted by previous rulers to the municipalities to manage their own affairs and, more importantly, the foundations of the Aragonese model that had emerged in the Late Middle Ages.

The initial debates and the conflict in the Catalan Audiencia

As shown above, the debates about the municipalities' ability to levy taxes started in the Principality of Catalonia. Article 32 of the Decreto de Nueva Planta of Catalonia established that the aldermen could not create annuities nor sell municipal properties without "my permission [of the King], or the authorisation of the Court to which we gave permission". All the petitions for levying new taxes had to be sent to the Consejo de Castilla. The apportionment of taxes (*repartimientos*) could only be done *inter volentes*, i.e., among the town's inhabitants who consented to be taxed. Those who refused to pay could not be forced to do so.[17] The order of the monarch generated controversy. The *oidores* of the Reales Audiencias of Catalonia and Majorca raised doubts over the high cost and complexity of forwarding every petition for *arbitrios* to the Consejo de Castilla. The Catalan Audiencia was informed that the prerogatives that the viceroy and the pre-Bourbon Audiencia enjoyed had been extinguished by the Nueva Planta, so everything had to be decided personally by the king.[18]

The judges of the Real Audiencia of Majorca explained that the island's towns and villages had to pay many annuities issued in the previous centuries, and, since they lacked *propios* (assets which belonged to the municipalities and which could therefore be leased by the councils) they had to apportion taxes to service the annuities, which were secured against the entire estates of the towns' inhabitants. The Real Audiencia expressed doubts about the prohibition on giving the town councils permission to create annuities and taxes. They argued that, in case of emergency, Madrid was very far from Majorca, so the process would be very slow. Besides, the refinancing of debt – the cancellation of old annuities by issuing new ones at lower interest rates – was beneficial for the town councils. They also asked the supreme royal council whether the debt service had to be suspended if taxes were not sufficient. The *fiscal* (royal prosecutor) of the Majorcan Audiencia did not agree with the judges. He considered that the island's municipalities – except for the capital, Palma – had to resort to the Consejo de Castilla to request the concession of taxes. According to him, the Audiencia could only authorise the collection of temporary and reduced taxes. He concluded his verdict, saying:

> Lastly, in fulfilment of my duty, I must inform Your Highness [the Consejo de Castilla] that these and many other difficulties that will continue to arise each day stem from the tenacity with which these people cling to their rites and customs, altering for their preservation any interests they may have.[19]

The verdict of the *fiscal* of the Consejo de Castilla was categorical: only the king could authorise the creation of taxes and annuities. There were no such urgent matters that required immediate authorisation.[20]

The king ratified his previous decision, but town councils continued to levy taxes without the consent of the monarch in the following years. In 1729, the Valencian high court submitted a report to the Consejo de Castilla, requesting solutions to the conflicts between municipal creditors on the one hand and town councillors and *vecinos* on the other. The *oidores* of the Real Audiencia of Valencia explained that, after the promulgation of the Decretos de Nueva Planta, many town councils could not service debt, so foreclosures began. Despite the apportionment of taxes, normally without royal permission, creditors had activated the collective and individual responsibility causes of the debt, to seize the private assets of the towns' inhabitants. Some town councils had decided not to collect taxes and to suspend the payment of pensions, causing ruin and conflicts among creditors. The Valencian Audiencia tried to find a middle ground. The *oidores* requested the Consejo de Castilla to authorise them to give permission to the town councils to levy any temporary tax, as well as to promote debt restructuring agreements.[21] As on previous occasions, the Consejo de Castilla left no doubt: if the town councils needed to levy *arbitrios* or other taxes, they had to appeal to the Audiencia, which had to redirect the cases to the Consejo de Castilla so the monarch could decide.[22] The

Consejo's decision did not solve the problem. In the 1730s and 40s, the aldermen of the Valencian cities of Orihuela and Alicante were investigated for collecting non-authorised taxes to compensate for the money they had evaded.[23]

At the same time, a similar debate began in the Real Audiencia of Catalonia. In this case, the discussion went further, fuelled by the conflicts between Catalan- and Castilian-born *oidores*.[24] The dispute about the legitimacy of the annuities and taxes must be contextualised within one of the clashes between the Catalan and the foreign judges. As in Valencia, municipal creditors were foreclosing the assets of private *vecinos* by virtue of the collective and individual responsibility clauses for municipal debt. The Catalan Audiencia received complaints from inhabitants of different towns, protesting against the apportionment of taxes by the town councillors. The dispute revolved around two questions: first, should the municipal annuities, be considered null and void, as they had been issued without royal consent? Should *vecinos* and municipalities be released from the obligation of paying the debt? And second, if municipal annuities were considered legitimate, could the town councillors levy taxes in order to avoid foreclosures? A general report signed by all the *oidores* was sent to the Consejo de Castilla, together with the dissenting vote of the senior *oidor* and another dissenting opinion signed by four judges. In reality, the general report was supported by the Catalan *oidores*, five judges against four dissenting *oidores* and the senior judge, Manuel de Toledo, who all came from the Crown of Castile.[25]

Regarding the first question, the general report explained that, before the Nueva Planta, the authority to issue annuities and levy taxes lay with the towns' general council, not with the councillors. According to the *oidores*, that assembly was the meeting of the town's inhabitants, who could decide freely whether they as a group of private individuals would take on debt and pay taxes to service it. Once made, the decision was binding and could not be overridden. In theory, municipalities could neither issue annuities nor collect taxes to fund them, but by virtue of royal privileges or simply by immemorial custom, they did. After archival research, the *oidores* concluded that the municipal annuities had a general mortgage because the monarchs had promoted that kind of *censos*. They also noted that the royal consent was replaced by the collective and individual responsibility for the debt. The judges pointed out a contradiction: if annuities were null, the Audiencia and the town councils would have made no effort to sign *concordias*, and municipal councillors would have just removed the annuities by not paying them. Moreover, the rescheduling agreements were further proof that the monarchs, even Felipe V himself, had ratified the validity of the annuities. If the mortgage on the municipal assets was declared to be null, the mortgage on the estates of the town inhabitants would remain and would probably be foreclosed by the municipal creditors. The *oidores* concluded that municipal annuities were valid indeed, and that the decision to declare them to be null and void would mean economic ruin for the creditors, mainly ecclesiastical institutions, and judicial chaos produced by an avalanche of lawsuits.

As for the second question, the judges argued that in Catalonia the creation of new taxes should be allowed, as the municipal assets did not suffice to service the debt.

The Real Audiencia had authorised the apportionment of taxes to service annuities created before the Nueva Planta. Overall, the Catalan *oidores* concluded that the municipal annuities should not be declared null and void and that the apportioning of taxes by the town councils to fund debt service had to be authorised.[26]

The dissenting vote of the four Castilian-born judges was surprisingly radical. They thought that municipal annuities – and by extension, the taxes created to pay them – were illegitimate, as most of the Catalan authors agreed that the king had to explicitly authorise the issuance of *censos*. Even the viceroys, who could initially give permission, were no longer allowed to do so once that prerogative had been transferred to the Consejo de Aragón. The invalidation of the municipal annuities would not be negative; on the contrary, it would free many town councils from the burden of the debt. It might be argued that the creditors would be damaged, but since the annuities were secured against the assets of the *vecinos*, the measure would not constitute a default. As for the apportionment of taxes to service the annuities, the *oidores* said that, in Castile, every time the town councillors wanted to levy a new tax, they appealed to the monarch. The royal consent had always been necessary, and, by the early eighteenth century, after the imposition of the new regime and the reaffirmation of the sovereign's prerogatives, the necessity of royal consent was even more evident.[27]

The senior *oidor*, Manuel de Toledo, represented the moderate position that eventually prevailed in the Consejo de Castilla. In his report, he essentially repeated what the king ordered in 1718: the apportionment of taxes was illegal unless the monarch authorised it. Only the collection of taxes *inter volentes* (among people who voluntarily paid them) was legal. In an attempt to ingratiate himself with the monarch and the Consejo de Castilla, the senior judge asserted that the royal approval ensured that the tax revenue was not diverted from the purpose for which it had been allocated. De Toledo acknowledged that, if the general security was invalidated, the towns' inhabitants would have to continue paying the pensions, because the annuities were secured against their entire estates. As for the Castilian law that allowed the town councillors to levy taxes to fund old debts, the senior *oidor* pointed out that it operated only in municipalities that belonged to noble families.[28]

The *fiscal* of the Consejo de Castilla that examined the case adopted Toledo's arguments. He thought that the dissenting vote of the four Castilian *oidores* was well-founded, but invalidating the municipal mortgage on municipal annuities would be a disaster, both in economic and judicial terms. In all cases, the apportionment of taxes had to be authorised by the monarch.[29] The supreme royal council accepted the *fiscal*'s verdict and advised the king to do the same. Felipe V approved it, but the debate would not end yet. The question, which had not been raised so clearly by the Majorcan and Valencian Audiencias, was discussed in all its complexity by the *oidores* of the Real Audiencia of Catalonia. Nobody questioned that, by the eighteenth century, the *regalía* of municipal taxation belonged to the monarch, but had town councils been sovereign entities that could manage their own fiscal and financial affairs? What was the legal status of the municipalities? Why should old annuities be honoured with taxes? Did annuities give legitimacy to the town councillors to levy taxes?

The debates in Aragon

The conflict between the *fiscal* and the *oidores* of the Real Audiencia de Aragón brought all these questions one step further. In 1738, the king repealed all of the *concordias* approved in the Real Audiencia without the intervention of the Consejo de Castilla and the monarch. Felipe V took this measure at the behest of the ecclesiastical estate of the Kingdom of Aragon, which felt aggrieved by the agreements that the Aragonese judges forced them to sign.[30] Following the repeal of the *concordias*, the *fiscal* of the Real Audiencia of Aragon, Pedro Benítez Cantos, sent two letters to the Consejo de Castilla. He argued that debt restructuring agreements were the lesser evil, because the sequestrations demanded by municipal creditors against the private assets of the inhabitants of towns and villages had no legal foundation and had harmful economic consequences. The power to foreclose the assets of a private individual if the town council did not service debt was a "profoundly detrimental abuse to the Kingdom that cannot be found even among the *regalías* of the most absolute of monarchs". The *fiscal* said that the threat of being foreclosed produced depopulation and misery, and cited several Aragonese towns – Ayerbe, Caspe, Alagón, Uncastillo, Sos – whose inhabitants were being foreclosed upon by the Inquisition. As for the collective and individual responsibility clauses, *fiscal* Benítez Campos traced their origins back to the early fourteenth century, to the proxies given to the *síndicos* (syndics) who represented the municipalities in the parliament. Those proxies included a clause by which the decisions made by the *síndicos* would be binding as if the town councillors and all inhabitants of the municipality, assembled in the general council, had made the decision themselves. The clause was improperly extended to the contracts of municipal annuities, according to the *fiscal*.

> Under the freedom granted by the ancient *fueros*, which constituted an almost aristocratic government in this Kingdom, the vassals enjoyed the free use and full ownership of their property. From this, it must be inferred that, although the town council, endowed with authority to enact laws, could be considered the monarch of each town, it could not subject the property of individuals to mortgage without their consent, nor involuntarily enslave their persons [...] with an obligation that would amount to a shackle.[31]

In view of what the *fiscal* argued, the Consejo de Castilla ordered the Real Audiencia de Aragón to report on the issue. The *oidores* sent a short account in which they explained that the town councils enjoyed great prerogatives before the Nueva Planta. After the early eighteenth century, the assemblies and deputies of creditors, mostly clergymen, had used the *concordias* to become "owners, rather than administrators" of the municipal treasuries. The *oidores* had obeyed the decree invalidating the *concordias* and had admitted demands for foreclosure, following the Aragonese *fuero* that the king had re-established in 1711.[32] It is worth remembering that pre-Bourbon laws did not operate when the trial involved royal sovereignty; however, since this was rather a lawsuit between two private parties, the ancient Aragonese laws applied. This meant that the municipalities were not considered part of the royal sovereignty. They were in the royal demesne and the king was the supreme arbiter to whom the municipal corporations appealed, but they were still autonomous. The reforms of the 1760s would transform this situation by creating specific laws for the administration of the municipalities. The application of the *fueros* is not a minor issue, as the municipalities were not judged according to the rules of Castile, as the Decretos de Nueva Planta established, but according to Aragonese law. It is likely that the collective and individual responsibility clauses allowed the judges and the parties to continue applying the pre-Bourbon laws.

While the *oidores* of the Aragonese Audiencia accepted that municipal creditors were entitled to foreclose on assets of private individuals to get their debts repaid, one of them cast a separate vote. Lorenzo Santayana was a judge of the Aragonese court who would write a few years later a reference work about the *corregidor* and, more broadly, about the municipalities in Spain. Santayana was concerned about the governance of the kingdom, especially about the administration of justice, and the improper application of Aragonese civil law.[33] He described the mechanisms of collective and individual responsibility for the debt, and was very critical of it. Santayana questioned first the creation of annuities. He said that town councillors had enjoyed absolute dominion over the municipalities during the pre-Bourbon period. The *oidor* said that municipal annuities had been created for their private benefit rather than for the sake of the common good. The non-redemption of municipal annuities was, for him, the best demonstration that debt had been and still was a private business. Santayana also questioned the council's ability to include the future town inhabitants in the collective and individual responsibility clauses. Finally, he argued that by virtue of the Nueva Planta, the *arbitrios* and *sisas* (excises), called in Aragon *derechos prohibitivos*, had to be repealed. If collateral disappeared, annuities had to be extinguished too. Thus, Santayana thought that the best decision to avoid depopulation and ruin was to default on the annuities. He concluded his report saying:

> The Audiencia well recognises that, should the annulment of the annuities be decreed, even in the case of merely reducing their payments, the entire body of creditors, which is numerous, will protest. However, apart from the fact that this remedy is not truly violent, although it may appear so, as it is dictated by the circumstances of the times, it must also be considered that, even if it is now perceived as highly damaging, in the future it will, for the most part, be acknowledged as a benefit. Moreover, the harm could never be as great as that currently suffered by the people. And in the concurrence of duplicated inconveniences, it is sound policy and a strict obligation to avoid the greater ruin.

Santayana's colleagues did not like his opinion, so the *oidor* had to submit it unofficially, via the secretary of the Consejo de Castilla. In a letter, Santayana said: "I had the misfortune that the report was met with rejection, and that what I understand to be for the greater benefit of this Nation [Aragon] was regarded as an offense".[34] In August 1739, the *fiscal* of the Consejo de Castilla gave his verdict: municipalities and *vecinos* should not be harassed by their creditors. To pay the pensions, the town councillors could either negotiate a *concordia* with the debtholders and/or appeal to the Consejo to request *arbitrios* to pay them.[35]

The Aragonese ecclesiastical estate submitted a memorandum to the king, together with other documents attached: namely, examples of *concordias* that they considered to be harmful and a list of the conditions they tried to impose when it came to signing debt restructuring pacts, such as the composition of the assemblies of creditors and ecclesiastical deputies, the *concordias* signed with the mediation of the Audiencia, or the discounts in the cancellation of annuities. The ecclesiastical debtholders begged the monarch to order the town councils to determine very clearly what their income and expenses were, to prevent abuses. The clergymen preferred to sign rescheduling agreements rather than seizing the *vecinos*' assets, but the Inquisition was willing to foreclose them. In fact, taking advantage of its special jurisdiction, the Holy Office had seized private assets to obtain advantageous conditions in the payment of interest.[36]

Felipe V forwarded the memorandum of the ecclesiastical estate to the Consejo de Castilla. There, the *fiscal* repeated his verdict. If municipalities could not service debt, they had to request *arbitrios* from the Consejo. Furthermore, private inhabitants of the towns should not be harassed by municipal creditors for at least four months. The councillors and the monarch accepted the *fiscal*'s proposal.[37] Yet the conflict in the Real Audiencia de Aragón had only begun. The *fiscal* of the Aragonese court, Benítez Cantos, sent a letter to the Secretary of Grace and Justice, the Marqués de la Compuesta, saying that

> it is evident that the Council has not fully understood the condition in which this kingdom presently finds itself, and thus is unable to adopt, with full knowledge, the resolution that may appear most appropriate.[38]

The *fiscal* accused the municipal creditors of caring only about their money, not about the conservation of the realm. Benítez Cantos explained that, in general, town councillors opted for the *derechos prohibitivos* (duties) which were really harmful to commerce. Furthermore, many municipal assets had been sold without royal permission, including pastures, which had been given to shepherds' guilds ("cofradías de ganaderos", in Aragonese "ligallos") at a very low price. The *fiscal* showed no consideration for the Aragonese legal traditions and suggested correcting these purported abuses by introducing the Castilian laws and procedures. He also suggested creating a single *junta* that would manage the kingdom's local treasuries.[39]

Upon seeing the report, the Consejo de Castilla ordered the Real Audiencia to send a report on the issue. To gain time, the *oidores* sent a report in which they asserted, like their Catalan colleagues one decade earlier, that invalidating the annuities' collective and individual responsibility clauses would cause economic and judicial chaos, and that the municipal taxes collected before the Nueva Planta were legitimate. *Fiscal* Benítez Cantos fiercely attacked the *oidores*, saying that three of them could have personal interests in the issue, as they belonged to the Casa de Ganaderos of Zaragoza, a very powerful corporation of sheep livestock breeding. The *fiscal* also accused the other judges of the Audiencia of trying to avoid addressing the matter. Benítez Cantos finally reported on the ancient *fueros* of the Kingdom of Aragon, "which the fervour of certain legalists [*foristas*] is often prone to portray differently from how they truly were".[40]

Every *oidor* of the Audiencia sent an individual report to the Consejo de Castilla. These responses had to be contextualised within the framework of the invalidation of the *concordias* in 1738 and the debates about reducing the maximum interest rate at which annuities could be created. Most of the Aragonese Audiencia judges thought that municipal annuities were valid and that the solutions to the problems of the kingdom were reducing the maximum interest rate on annuities, continuing the *concordias*, with or without the mediation of the Audiencia, and maintaining municipal taxes.[41]

In his verdict, the *fiscal* of the Consejo de Castilla who examined the case expressed his perplexity. He confessed that he could not decide which arguments were more accurate, so he could not give an opinion about the miserable state of the Kingdom of Aragon, nor about the *arbitrios* and the suppression of the collective and individual responsibility clauses. Regarding the limit in annuity interest, he said that the issue had been repeatedly discussed with the king.[42] No new decision was finally made. The prohibition of levying or apportioning taxes without royal consent remained in force.

Like the Real Audiencia de Cataluña, the high Aragonese court split into two opposing groups; however, on this occasion it was not the birthplace that divided the parties involved. *Fiscal* Benítez Cantos was a radical: he wanted to abolish every vestige of the Aragonese tradition and to replace it with Castilian-imported laws and institutions. Thus, when the *oidores* contradicted his opinion, he opted for attacking them personally, accusing them of being partial and having hidden interests. He even printed a memorandum that generated a great confrontation between him, the Real Audiencia, and the Inquisition.[43] In the debates between the judges and *fiscal* of the Aragonese Audiencia, the economic and social consequences of municipal taxation and debt were as relevant as the legal dimension, which had been broadly discussed since the late 1710s in the cases of Catalonia, Valencia, and Majorca. However, the debates in the Aragonese Real Audiencia show very explicitly how the legitimacy to levy taxes was not the only issue at stake. Like the Castilian-born *oidores* of the Real Audiencia of Catalonia, the *fiscal* of the Aragonese court, Benítez Cantos, thought that the ancient legitimacy of debt to maintain taxes or levy new ones should not prevail over the harmful economic consequences of taxation and over-indebtedness. The king and his ministers could state very clearly what their prerogatives were, but they could not ignore the consequences of abolishing urban taxes or defaulting on municipal debt.

To solve this sort of contradiction, the king generally ratified existing taxes and/or authorised the creation of new ones to ensure debt service. Thus, there was no judicial and economic chaos, the *regalía* of levying and apportioning taxes was not questioned, and debt could be serviced. The situation changed in the 1740s, with the implementation of the so-called *valimiento de arbitrios*. By virtue of this extraordinary fiscal formula, the monarch appropriated 4% and later 54% of the *arbitrios* of every town council in the Spanish monarchy's peninsular territories. This caused a sudden drop in municipal income, so conflicts between town councillors, creditors, and taxpayers arose almost immediately. Furthermore, in 1752 the king ordered the Secretary of the Treasury, the Marqués de la Ensenada, to initiate a revision of all the charters and privileges that entitled town councils to collect taxes. Many *arbitrios* were found to have no legal basis and, therefore, ceased to be collected.[44] Yet problems did not disappear: if taxes were not collected, taxpayers were relieved, but debt could not be serviced, and consequently creditors became angry. The social and political conflicts of the mid-eighteenth century can only be explained within this context of debates regarding the legitimacy, necessity, and consequences of municipal taxation.

Conclusion

In 1753, the Real Audiencia of Aragon reported the complaints of several inhabitants of Barbastro, one of the kingdom's most prominent cities. The aldermen were collecting *arbitrios* without prior authorisation from the king or the Consejo de Castilla. Despite occurring late in the eighteenth century, this case was far from exceptional. Once again, the royal council reiterated the prohibition on levying taxes without explicit royal consent. Nonetheless, the Audiencias of Aragon and Catalonia delayed compliance and again requested the authority to approve temporary taxes in emergencies or to expedite administration. King Fernando VI reaffirmed this prohibition in response to a similar inquiry by the Real Audiencia of Valencia in 1754. Yet, as had occurred under his predecessor, enforcement proved problematic. In Majorca, municipal councils were ordered to report all taxes collected to service the debt, but many suspended both apportionment and collection until the legitimacy of their fiscal instruments was confirmed, leading to a halt in debt servicing and complaints from creditors. As a temporary solution, the Consejo de Castilla authorised a two-year extension of existing taxes, which was renewed in 1756. In Barbastro, despite the *arbitrios* being declared illegal due to their reliance on "ancient *fueros*", they too were extended in 1760 to maintain financial stability.[45]

The prolonged debates over the legitimacy of municipal taxation, sparked by the Decretos de Nueva Planta, persisted until the 1760s, when the reform of municipal treasuries finally began.[46] Until then, the Bourbons' new fiscal policy had little effectiveness. In theory, the king's authorisation to apportion taxes and create and collect *arbitrios* was a *conditio sine qua non* for existing levies to persist and new ones to be created. In practice, however, if every tax without royal authorisation ceased to be collected, municipal debt could not be serviced, and treasuries would go bankrupt. Thus, successive monarchs, royal advisors, officers, and judges had to find a balance between reaffirming the royal sovereignty expressed through the *regalía* of taxation, ensuring debt service, and avoiding the damaging economic consequences of over-taxation. While the native *oidores* of the Aragonese *Reales Audiencias* tended to defend traditional juridical, fiscal, and financial mechanisms and the validity of the existing taxes, the Castilian-born judges and *fiscales* showed a much more radical attitude: if a tax or annuity had not been explicitly authorised by the monarch, it was not valid. The non-Aragonese *oidores* were very critical of the consequences of the autonomy enjoyed by the Crown of Aragon municipalities. Most of them considered the debt's collective and individual responsibility clauses to be abusive, and that the debt should be defaulted on, as the common good and the survival of the town councils had to prevail over the private interest of municipal creditors. More diplomatically than the *fiscal* of the Aragonese Audiencia, the *oidor* Santayana Bustillo argued that "it is sound policy and a strict obligation to prevent greater ruin".[47]

More broadly, the debates represented the terminal phase of a political, juridical, financial, and fiscal model that emerged in the Late Middle Ages and had remained almost unaltered until the early eighteenth century. As in Castile and other European regions, debt and taxation were perceived as major social and economic problems, but fiscal and financial systems were deeply rooted in the political culture of the time. In the Spanish Crown of Aragon, the traditional model came under attack with the Decretos de Nueva Planta in the 1700s and 1710s, but it did not collapse until the mid-eighteenth century, when local conflicts over the management of the municipal treasuries demonstrated the model's inability to satisfy the parties involved. These debates show that the Nueva Planta could not erase centuries of practices and institutions. They also challenge some historiographical views that defend the alleged absolutist character of the Bourbon dynasty. King Felipe V and his ministers had to acknowledge that, although on paper the monarch held the *regalía* of granting taxes and authorising the issuance of municipal annuities, in practice he could not exercise this prerogative without damaging the interests of creditors and causing judicial chaos. In other words, the king's legitimacy was limited by tradition and history.

Notes

1 *Novísima Recopilación*, lib. VII, tít. XVI, ley X. Royal order dictated by King Felipe V, Madrid, 12-III-1718.
2 The reference is Archivo Histórico Nacional (hereafter AHN), Consejos, leg. 22.444. I analysed the reports on debt restructuring in the paper presented at the LVI Settimana di studi organised by the Datini Institute; in Ena Sanjuán, 2026.
3 Placanica, 1982; Fiestas Loza, 1993: 549–614.
4 Sánchez Martínez, Furió, and Sesma Muñoz, 2008: 99–130; Reixach Sala and Verdés Pijuan, 2023: 247–77.
5 Ortí Gost and Verdés Pijuan, 2016: 199–221.
6 Deputations, annuities, and urban taxation were developed similarly in Sicily, and, to a lesser extent, in Sardinia; in Cancila, 2001; Fuertes Broseta, 2023: 85–113.
7 AHCT, municipal minutes, 236, letter 49.
8 This can be clearly observed in the lists of annuities of many town councils in the Crown of Aragon and beyond; see, for instance, the lists of the municipality of Huesca, in AMH, leg. 7, docs. 1058 and 1060 (lists of annuities of 1649 and 1756 respectively).

9 Elliott, 1992: 48–71; Lalinde Abadía, 1993: 155–76. For characterisation of the Crown of Aragon, see Arrieta Alberdi, 2023: 51–102.
10 Peset Reig and Graullera Sanz, 1986: 107–38; Ferrer i Alòs, 2014: 49–90.
11 Stasavage, 2011.
12 Mateos Royo, 2012: 109–32.
13 Andrés Ucendo and Michael Limberger, 2012: 18–33.
14 Archivo General de Simancas (hereafter AGS), Estado, leg. 6099, letters from Tanucci a Grimaldi, Naples, 29-VII-1766, and from Grimaldi to Tanucci, San Ildefonso, 19-VIII-1766.
15 Abadía Irache, 2020: 59–86. An example of this would be Gómez Zorraquino, 2021.
16 Dedieu, 2000: 113–39; Fernández Díaz, 2014; Fox, 2018: 203–31.
17 *Novísima Recopilación*, lib. V, tít. IX, ley I and lib. VII, tít. XVI, ley X.
18 AHN, Consejos, leg. 22.444, nº 11, pieza 3, various letters and verdicts of the Consejo de Castilla and the Real Audiencia of Catalonia, dated in Barcelona and Madrid between III-1717 and III-1718.
19 AHN, Consejos, leg. 22.444, nº 11, pieza 3, various letters and verdicts of the Consejo de Castilla and the Real Audiencia of Catalonia, dated in Barcelona and Madrid between III-1717 and III-1718, letters from the Real Audiencia and the *capitán general* of Majorca to the Consejo de Castilla, and verdict of the *fiscal*, Palma, 2-V and 13-VI-1718.
20 AHN, Consejos, leg. 22.444, nº 11, pieza 3, verdict of the *fiscal* of the Consejo de Castilla, Madrid, 10-VI-1718.
21 AHN, Consejos, leg. 22.444, nº 11, pieza 3, report from the Real Audiencia of Valencia to the Consejo de Castilla, Valencia, 18-X-1729.
22 AHN, Consejos, leg. 22.444, nº 11, pieza 3, resolution of the Consejo de Castilla, Madrid, 18-I-1730.
23 AGS, Secretaría y Superintendencia de Hacienda, leg. 68, report from the Consejo de Castilla to Felipe V, 24-I-1745
24 Molas Ribalta, 1976: 77–87. Although the royal ministers promoted Castilian-born judges to hold offices in the Aragonese Audiencias, they also maintained a minimum of Aragonese-born *oidores* and other judicial officers, to ensure that someone had specific knowledge of the particular civil law which still operated in most of the territories of the Aragonese Crown. The attempts of the conde de Aranda as *presidente* of the Consejo de Castilla to promote the candidates born in the Crown of Aragon for positions in the Aragonese territories in Solé i Cot, 2008: 284–85.
25 Solé i Cot, 2008: 284–85.
26 Archivo de la Corona de Aragón (hereafter ACA), Real Audiencia, registros 143, general report of the Real Audiencia of Catalonia sent to the Consejo de Castilla, Barcelona, 16-X-1729; ff. 197v-214v.
27 ACA, Real Audiencia, registros 143, dissenting vote of the four Castilian *oidores*, Barcelona, 16-X-1729; ff. 226r-232r.
28 ACA, Real Audiencia, registros 143, dissenting vote of senior judge Manuel de Toledo, Barcelona, 16-X-1729; ff. 214v-226r.
29 AHN, Consejos, leg. 22.444, nº 11, pieza 3, verdict of the *fiscal* of the Consejo de Castilla, Madrid, 16-II-1730.
30 Ena Sanjuán, 2026.
31 AHN, Consejos, leg. 22.444, nº 10, pieza 1, two letters from the *fiscal* of the Real Audiencia of Aragon to the Consejo de Castilla, Zaragoza, 16-VI-1738 and 7-IV-1739.
32 The pre-Bourbon laws and institutions of the Kingdom of Aragon were completely abolished in 1707, but Felipe V restored them partially in 1711. The report in AHN,

Consejos, leg. 22.444, nº 10, pieza 1, report from the Real Audiencia of Aragon, Zaragoza, 30-VI-1739.

33 Santayana y Bustillo, 1769. A short biographic profile of Santayana can be found in http://dbe.rah.es/biografias/14692/lorenzo-de-santayana-bustillo.

34 AHN, Consejos, leg. 22.444, nº 10, pieza 1, separate vote of *oidor* Santayana, Zaragoza, 30-VI-1739, and letter from Santayana to Bernardo Santos, secretary of the Cosejo de Castilla, same date.

35 AHN, Consejos, leg. 22.444, nº 10, pieza 1, verdict of the fiscal of the Consejo de Castilla, Madrid, 19-VIII-1739.

36 AHN, Consejos, leg. 22.444, nº 10, pieza 1, from the Aragonese ecclesiastical estate to king Felipe V, VIII-1739. The case of the Inquisition would require a specific study, as it was a clear case of defection from the lobbies of municipal creditors. The Holy Office obtained better conditions in the *concordias* by using their special jurisdiction to free ride. That would lead the *fiscal* of the Aragonese Audiencia Benítez Cantos to question the juridical status of the Inquisition, triggering a heated legal debate with the *oidores* of the Audiencia and the Holy Office. For the *concordias* signed by the Inquisition, see AHN, Inquisición, libro 215. The reply of the Inquisition to the *fiscal*'s accusations can be found in AHN, Inquisición, leg. 3.732, exp. 37.

37 AHN, Consejos, leg. 22.444, nº 10, pieza 1, from Felipe V to cardinal Molina, *gobernador* of the Consejo de Castilla, San Ildefonso, 19-VIII-1739; verdict of the Consejo, Madrid, 23-IX-1739.

38 AHN, Consejos, leg. 22.444, nº 10, pieza 1, from the fiscal Benítez Cantos to the Marqués de la Compuesta, Zaragoza, 9-II-1740.

39 AHN, Consejos, leg. 22.444, nº 10, pieza 1, report from the *fiscal* Benítez Cantos to Felipe V, submitted to the Consejo de Castilla later, Zaragoza, 9-II-1740.

40 AHN, Consejos, leg. 22.444, nº 10, pieza 1, report of the Real Audiencia de Aragón, Zaragoza, 24-V-1740; letter from the *fiscal* Benítez Cantos to the Secretary of the Consejo de Castilla, Zaragoza, 28-VI-1740.

41 AHN, Consejos, leg. 22.444, nº 10, pieza 1, various individual reports from the *oidores* of the Real Audiencia de Aragón to the Consejo de Castilla, Zaragoza, 27 and 28-VI-1740.

42 AHN, Consejos, leg. 22.444, nº 10, pieza 1, verdict of the *fiscal* of the Consejo de Castilla, Madrid, 24-VII-1740. For the issue of the usury limit, see Ena Sanjuán, 2023.

43 AHN, Consejos, leg. 22.444, nº 10, pieza 2; for the conflict with the Holy Office, see AHN, Inquisición, leg. 3.738, expediente 46.

44 García García, 1996: 171–86.

45 AHN, Consejos, leg. 22.444, nº 11, piezas 1 and 2.

46 García García, 1996.

47 AHN, Consejos, leg. 22.444, nº 10, pieza 1, separate vote of *oidor* Santayana, Zaragoza, 30-VI-1739.

Bibliography

Abadía Irache, Alejandro (2020), "Los censos concejiles, la Iglesia Católica y el nuevo gobierno. Las concordias de censualistas", in Jesús Astigarraga and Javier Usoz, eds., *Bajo el velo del bien público: estudios en homenaje a Guillermo Pérez Sarrión*, Zaragoza: Institución Fernando el Católico, pp. 59–86.

Andrés Ucendo, José Ignacio, and Limberger, Michael (2012), "Introduction", in José Ignacio Andrés Ucendo and Michael Limberger, eds., *Taxation and Debt in the Early Modern City*, London: Pickering & Chatto, pp. 18–33.

Arrieta Alberdi, Jon (2023), "La Corona de Aragón como escenario y fuente de disposición de monarquías compuestas", *Pedralbes: Revista d'Història Moderna*, 43, 1, pp. 51–102. https://doi.org/10.1344/pedralbes2023.43-1.3.

Cancila, Rossella (2001), *Fisco, ricchezza, comunità nella Sicilia del Cinquecento*, Roma: Istituto storico italiano per l'età moderna e contemporanea.

Dedieu, Jean-Pierre (2000), "La Nueva Planta en su contexto: Las reformas del aparato del Estado en el reinado de Felipe V", Manuscripts. *Revista d'història moderna*, 18, pp. 113–39.

Elliott, John H (1992), "A Europe of Composite Monarchies", *Past & Present*, 137, pp. 48–71.

Ena Sanjuán, Íñigo (2026), "¿Una medida irrelevante? La reducción de la tasa de censos en la Corona de Aragón (1750): debates previos e impacto en las economías eclesiásticas", *Hispania*, 83, 273, p. e008. https://doi.org/10.3989/hispania.2023.008.

Ena Sanjuán, Íñigo (2026), "From 'util y combeniente, y aun necesario' to 'perjudicialissimas, injustas, y contra todo fundamento legal': redefining municipal debt restructuring in the Spanish Crown of Aragon (1732–1742)", in Ángela Orlandi, ed., *Risk Management, Insolvency, and Bankruptcy in the Pre-Modern World (13th-18th Centuries)*, Firenze: Firenze University Press, pp. 147–165. https://doi.org/10.36253/979-12-215-0963-2.11

Fernández Díaz, Roberto (2014), *Cataluña y el absolutismo borbónico: historia y política*, Barcelona: Crítica/Universitat de Lleida.

Ferrer i Alòs, Llorenç (2014), "Pagar les guerres. Una càrrega fiscal sobre els ajuntaments catalans en els segles XVII i XVIII", in Narcís Figueras Capdevila and Josep Santesmases i Ollé, eds., *Després de les Noves Plantes: canvis i continüitats a les terres de parla catalana: actes del IX Congrés de la CCEPC*, Valls: Cossetània, pp. 49–90.

Fiestas Loza, Alicia (1993), "El censo consignativo, según una fórmula castellana del Antiguo Régimen", *Anuario de historia del derecho español*, 63–64, pp. 549–614.

Fox, Phillip D. (2018), "The Advantage of Legal Diversity for State Formation: Bourbon Reforms and Aragonese Law in Eighteenth-Century Spain", *European History Quarterly*, 48, 2, pp. 203–31. https://doi.org/10.1177/0265691418755601

Fuertes Broseta, Miquel (2023), "Res Publica Sardiniae. Parlamentarismo y Representación Estamental en el Reino de Cerdeña (Siglos XIV-XVIII)", *RiMe. Rivista Dell'lstituto Di Storia Dell'Europa Mediterranea* 12, III, pp. 85–113. https://doi.org/10.7410/1597

García García, Carmen (1996), *La crisis de las haciendas locales: de la reforma administrativa a la reforma fiscal (1743–1845)*, Valladolid: Junta de Castilla y León/ Consejería de Educación y Cultura.

Gómez Zorraquino, José Ignacio (2021), *El control del espacio de culto: el linaje de los Cortés y la iglesia parroquial de San Lorenzo de Huesca (siglos XVI-XVII)*, Huesca: Diputación Provincial.

Lalinde Abadía, Jesús (1993), "La disolución de la Corona de Aragón en la monarquía hispana o católica (sec. XVI a XVIII)", in Carlo Delfin, ed., *La Corona d'Aragona in Italia (secc.XIII-XVIII): XIV Congresso di Storia della Corona d'Aragona 1*, Sassari-Alghero: Regione Autonoma della Sardegna, pp. 155–76.

Mateos Royo, José Antonio (2012), "Public Institutions, Local Politics and Urban Taxation in Seventeenth-Century Aragon", in José Ignacio Andrés Ucendo and Michael Limberger, eds., *Taxation and Debt in the Early Modern City*, London: Pickering & Chatto, pp. 109–32.

Molas Ribalta, Pere (1976), "Las audiencias borbónicas de la Corona de Aragón: aportación a su estudio", *Estudis. Revista de Historia Moderna*, 5, pp. 59–124.

Novísima Recopilación de las Leyes de España, Madrid, 1805.

Ortí Gost, Pere, and Verdés Pijuan, Pere (2016), "The Crisis of Public Finances in the Towns of Late Medieval Catalonia (1350–1500)", in Istituto Internazionale di Storia Economica F. Datini, ed., *Le crisi finanziarie: gestione, implicazioni sociali e conseguenze nell'età preindustriale: selezione di ricerche = The financial crises: their management, their social implications and their consequences in pre-industrial times: selection of essays, Atti delle «Settimane di studi» e altri convegni 47*, Firenze: Firenze University Press, pp. 199–221.

Peset Reig, Mariano, and Graullera Sanz, Vicente (1986), "Els censals i la propietat de la terra al segle XVIII valencià", *Recerques*, 18, pp. 107–38.

Placanica, Augusto (1982), *Moneta, prestiti, usure nel Mezzogiorno moderno*, Napoli: Società Editrice Napoletana.

Reixach Sala, Albert, and Pijuan, Pere Verdés (2023), "Public Debt in Late Medieval Crown of Aragon: A(nother) Financial Revolution?", in Rodrigo Da Costa Domínguez and Amélia Aguiar Andrade, eds., *Portugal in a European Context*, Cham: Springer International Publishing-Palgrave Studies in the History of Finance, pp. 247–77. https://doi.org/10.1007/978-3-031-06227-8_13

Sánchez Martínez, Manuel, Furió, Antoni, and Muñoz, Ángel Sesma (2008), "Old and New Forms of Taxation in the Crown of Aragon (13th-14th Centuries)", in Simonetta Cavaciocchi, ed., *La fiscalità nell'economia Europea secc. XII-XVIII / Fiscal systems in the European economy from the 13th to the 18th centuries. Atti delle «settimane di studi» e altri convegni 39*, Firenze: Firenze University Press, pp. 99–130.

Santayana y Bustillo, Lorenzo (1769), *Gobierno político de los pueblos de España, y el corregidor, alcalde y juez en ellos*, Madrid: Imprenta de la viuda de Eliseo Sánchez, 2ª ed.

Solé i Cot, Sebastiá (2008), *El gobierno del Principado de Cataluña por el Capitán General y la Real Audiencia (el Real Acuerdo) bajo el régimen de Nueva Planta (1716–1808): una aportación al estudio del procedimiento gubernativo a finales del antiguo régimen* , Barcelona: Universitat Pompeu Fabra.

Stasavage, David (2011), *States of Credit: Size, Power, and the Development of European Polities*, Princeton, NJ: Princeton University Press.

10 Economic decline and financial crisis in Flanders and Brabant during the 17th and 18th centuries seen through the eyes of contemporary memoirs

Michael Limberger

Introduction

After the Revolt of the Low Countries, the Southern and Northern provinces went in quite different directions. While the Dutch Republic witnessed its Golden Age and established itself as a new European power with a leading position in global trade and a highly effective system of public finances, the Southern Low Countries remained under Spanish, and later Austrian rule, and underwent economically and financially difficult times.[1] The political circumstances had led to a decentralised financial system with a high degree of autonomy of the territorial estates and the major cities. Moreover, the financial needs of the government were high, partly due to the frequent wars.[2] From the second half of the 17th century onwards, pamphletists, activists, and members of central, regional or local authorities started to write and publish texts in which they gave their own analysis of the country's economic problems and proposed measures to remedy the situation. In this chapter, I analyse some of the principal treatises of the 17th and 18th centuries, such as those by Pieter Cardon, Adrien Foppens, G.A. de Wynants, or J.J. Villain XIIII, and their critiques of the financial system and proposals for improvement. These memoirs were published between 1680 and 1755, in different points of the Low Countries' history. Therefore, also the specific problems mentioned in each of them were different, of course, while on the other hand, some general tendencies and institutional frameworks continued, even though the political regime had changed from a Spanish to a French, then Anglo-Dutch, and finally Austrian government.

From "terres de promission" to economic backwater: the long-term development of the Southern Low Countries

The Low Countries experienced major political and economic changes between their rise in the late Middle Ages and the French Revolution.[3] The principalities constituting the Low Countries were united during the 14th and 15th centuries by the Dukes of Burgundy, who established a prosperous dynastic union. The area was characterised by a high degree of urbanisation and intensive commercial and industrial activity, mainly due to the urban textile industry. The core area of the

DOI: 10.4324/9781003653301-11

Burgundian Low Countries was situated in Flanders, Brabant, and Holland, with Bruges, Ghent, Brussels, Leuven, and Antwerp, and Amsterdam as the major cities. After a period of relative prosperity under Duke Philip the Good, the political situation turned critical under the reign of Charles the Bold, who pursued an aggressive policy of expansion. After the death of Mary of Burgundy, when Maximilian of Habsburg claimed the regency of the realm, the resistance led to civil war. This also had an impact on the economic outlook, with Bruges losing its leading position as an economic and financial centre, giving way to the rise of Antwerp.[4]

During the 16th century, the Low Countries witnessed another economic boom, thanks to international trade via Antwerp and flourishing urban industries. At the same time, Antwerp was an important financial market, together with the Castilian fairs, Lyon and Genoa.[5] The splendour of the Golden Age of the 16th century should not deceive, however; it coincided with Charles V's ambitions in European politics, which brought about almost perpetual warfare and huge financial needs, which required a steady flow of income from taxes, loans, and the princely domain. Dynamic cities like Bruges, Ghent, and Antwerp were formidable centres of capital accumulation, which provided a reliable source of taxation, as well as public credit.[6]

The system of taxation was established in parallel in the different territories during the 13th and 14th centuries. The basis was the classical principle of estate assemblies, with the particular characteristic that the major urban centres became the mouthpiece and representatives of the third estate, and eventually ended up playing the leading role in the assemblies. This was the most notable in Flanders, where the cities of Bruges, Ghent, and Ypres (called the Three Members) were the decisive element of the estates. In neighbouring Brabant, the balance between the estates was more even, partly because of the stronger position of the nobility and the less prominent position of the cities.[7]

The Revolt of the Low Countries, and the Eighty Years' War, lasting from 1568 until 1648, brought about a lasting change in the political and economic outlook of the Low Countries. In 1579, the rebels declared their independence in the Union of Utrecht, and after 1582, the Spanish recovered the southern part, including the city of Antwerp, which was besieged and conquered in 1585. This led to the separation of the Low Countries into the Republic of the United Provinces in the north, and the Southern Low Countries under Spanish government. Besides the immediate consequences of the war, which led to large-scale emigration, the economy of the Southern Low Countries was affected by the new frontier that ran right through the middle of the country, and in particular the loss of the delta of the river Scheldt, which hampered access to the North Sea for the traffic coming from Antwerp. The so-called closure of the Scheldt consisted of a toll barrier and required ships to be unloaded, which significantly increased transport costs and affected the rentability of the port of Antwerp.[8]

The effects of the war led to a major wave of emigration. Between 100,000 and 150,000 people left the Southern Low Countries, especially between 1584 and 1588. Antwerp, Ghent, and Bruges lost almost half of their populations. The emigrants took their capital and know-how with them and contributed to the economic rise of their destinations. They are partly responsible for the start of the Dutch Golden Age.[9] The emigration of Calvinists, but also many Catholics, had consequences for the urban industries of the Southern Low Countries, as well as for trade and finance. Many artisans and merchants left for Germany, England and the Northern provinces, where cities like Amsterdam, Middelburg Leiden or Haarlem offered better opportunities.[10]

After 1590, the Southern provinces saw a degree of economic recovery in the fields of agriculture and urban arts and crafts. The Age of Rubens, or Van Dyck, was called the "Indian Summer" of Antwerp, or the "Age of Silver" of the Southern Low Countries.[11] After the end of the war with the Dutch Republic in 1648, maritime trade with England and Spain was revived, although the wars against France during the second half of the century made it quite risky. However, the control of the Scheldt delta by the Dutch Republic limited the possibilities of trade, which could only take place through the Flemish ports of Ostend, Nieuwpoort, and Dunkirk. The latter was captured, however, by France in 1662. The urban luxury industries, including silk weaving, tapestry and so on, declined during the 17th century.[12]

In the second half of the 17th century, Spain was almost constantly at war with France. The political pressure from France increased especially under Louis XIV, who brought the Low Countries into a series of wars. In 1667, 1672, and 1689, the French invaded the country and occupied a considerable part of its land.[13] The internal politics during this period were enormously unstable. There were seven different governors between 1668 and 1690, but none managed to control the situation.[14]

The economic situation of the Spanish Low Countries therefore significantly deteriorated after the Dutch Revolt. The role of Antwerp had changed from being the leading economic and financial hub of the North Sea area to a more regional centre, with its access to the North Sea severely limited by the frontier and the blockade by the United Provinces. At the same time, the urban industries of the Low Countries suffered from increasing competition and the protectionist politics of neighbouring countries France, the Dutch Republic and England, especially during the last decades of the 17th century.[15]

Import and export tariffs: "*the origin of the ruin and poverty of the Spanish Low Countries*"

It is in this context that we have to understand the title of the treatise "the origin of the ruin and poverty of the Spanish Low Countries", attributed to the Antwerp merchant Pieter Cardon.[16] Cardon's treatise is generally considered to be the classical example of mercantilist ideas in the Southern Low Countries in the late 17th century. Cardon was quite active with different initiatives to improve the trade situation in the Southern Low Countries. In 1682, he presented a project to build a canal between Ostend and the cities of Ghent and Antwerp, which was one of the main issues of the economic conferences convened by the Treasurer General of the Southern Low Countries, the Count of Bergeyck, in Brussels in 1699, to find solutions for the country's economic difficulties.[17] This mercantilist treatise is presented in the form of a dialogue between a Brabant nobleman and a Flemish merchant, who meet in a stagecoach. The background of the text is a critique of the reduction in import and export tariffs of the Spanish Low Countries in 1680, which he describes as a major economic disaster. The background of this highly debated tariff goes back to the war with the United Provinces when it was introduced as an exceptional permit to trade between the northern and southern provinces during wartime. This trade seems to have been economically necessary for the provision of the country; the tariffs provided a practical solution and, at the time, a valuable source of income for the state treasury.[18] With the end of the hostilities in 1648, the measure became obsolete and was abolished temporarily. However, already by 1654, the existing tariffs of England, France, and the Dutch Republic, as well as the financial necessities of the treasury required the government to re-introduce them.[19]

The tariffs were heavily contested by the Estates of Brabant, and in particular by the Antwerp merchants, who saw the tariffs as a major threat to their economic recovery and an infraction of the age-old privileges of the Duchy of Brabant, which said that there should not be any toll barriers within the territories of the Low Countries. The resistance against the tariffs went on for decades, leading to temporary exemptions, the re-introduction of tariffs, and even periods of tax refusal by the Antwerp guild masters, before eventually being reinstated with a reduced tariff, which was therefore also called the List of Antwerp.[20]

According to Cardon, cheap imports destroy domestic production. Therefore, imports of goods that can be produced at home should not be allowed. This is not the case for raw materials for local industry which should be exempt. The imports of cheap goods are the real reason for the ruin and poverty of the Low Countries. "There is no money", he says,

> the country is thrown into deep poverty, because of the lack of money, and nobody has work, and there are no industries to earn a living. All imports of goods result in an outflow of money. Therefore, all imported goods that can be produced in our country should be charged with sufficiently high tariffs or banned totally.[21]

Instead of becoming more expensive, as a result of tariffs, products would become cheaper because of higher production. Moreover, more money would circulate within the country, without flowing out to foreign producers. Raw materials could be imported from Spain and its overseas territories, which were receiving various products from the Low Countries and, therefore, did not cause a drain on the local economy.[22] The ideas defended by Cardon are very much in line with the economic mainstream of his time, that is, mercantilist or cameralist ideas of protecting the domestic export industry by means of import and export tariffs, thus promoting economic development and welfare.[23] For example, Philip Wilhelm von Hörnigk's classical treatise "Österreich über Alles" (Austria above all), first published in 1684, also focused on the protection of local industries against imports of luxury goods from England or the Netherlands, the use of local raw materials and, in case of necessity, imports from friendly nations like Spain.[24]

"Capricious and ignorant": The secret correspondence of Adrien Foppens

Cardon was not the only contemporary author advocating for strong import and export tariffs in response to French and British mercantilist policies. Another activist, who is often associated with Cardon is the Brussels gazetteer Adrien Foppens.[25] Foppens was the publisher of the only journal in Brussels at that time, titled *Rélations véritables*. As a gazetteer, he had correspondents in the major European cities, including some influential members of the nobility and government circles. It is in these secret correspondences that Foppens reported on the political situation in the Low Countries. In short, fragmentary notes, he wrote openly about the disastrous state of the Spanish troops, which took to plundering, pillaging or begging, about the destroyed and abandoned countryside, the oppressive tax burden, and the constant military pressure from France. The correspondence was confiscated when Foppens was arrested in 1685 on suspicion of instigating public unrest and a revolt in Brussel and the notes were kept as proof in the case file.

Among other issues, Foppens also takes a position on the issue of the import and export tariffs. Upon the publication of the new, reduced tariff in 1680, Foppens declares that "this tariff could not be more harmful for the people of these provinces, nor for the finances of the king, and at this moment it had just seen the light, we will see without any doubt 200 requests to his Highness, from the concerned."[26] "The errors that have been made are irreparable and now they made a list of tariffs like nobody has ever seen before, so capricious and ignorant."[27] "The deputies of the Estates of Flanders have an endless number of complaints about Antwerp, because it is them who have to be blamed, as well as some individuals, who are factors or commissioners of foreigners, who have distributed money among the communities, and incited them to push the court to act as they did."[28] "The tariff is made by the intervention of some mutineers of Antwerp, corrupted by factions of foreigners, in order to ruin the trade of his Majesty's subjects."[29] In these passages, Foppens points out the particular political climate of Antwerp, a city based on an ideology of trade, in the tradition of the 16th-century idea of an Antwerp Golden Age, which contrasted with the general tendency towards industrial protectionism.[30]

Foppens' protectionist ideas seem to have been in line with the opinion of the central government. In the instructions for Governor Iñigo Melchor de Velasco in 1668, the latter was supposed to

> "take care of the reestablishment of trade, in order to avoid the entry of foreign commodities and manufactures, which exhaust the subsistence of our subjects, especially for voluntary and superfluous expenses, serving only for ostentation and to imitate the habits of foreign peoples and nations, for which you would best publish edicts, prohibitions, and pragmatic sanctions for the greater profit of our subjects which you find convenient.[31]

The argument of the Antwerp town council had been quite the opposite. In a memoir from 1655, titled *Politieke consideratiën*, they declared that trade was a country's source of welfare. Therefore, the authorities had to make efforts to restore and conserve profitable trade by keeping tariffs on trade as low as possible, because "the merchants will always send their goods at the lowest possible cost, in order to obtain profit." If this was not the case, trade would leave the Low Countries, all capital and employment would disappear, cities would shrink, and the ports would not receive any ships. As a result, consumption would decline, and with it, the source of taxation and the finances of the King of Spain. As a result of the latter's insolvency, he would be unable to take out loans and would ultimately depend on Amsterdam and London.[32] In 1669, after the withdrawal of the exemption for Antwerp citizens, the Antwerp pensionaries, the leading urban officials next to the mayor, declared that the silks and woollens imported to be finished and re-exported, were taxed twice, once upon entering the country and again when re-exported, which prevented them from offering a competitive price like the merchants of France, England, and Holland. As such, they preferred to leave their profession rather than sell at a loss, and hundreds of families left the country to settle abroad where silks and other crafts were made that used to exist only in the Low Countries.[33]

The conflict about the course of economic policy and the role of tariffs was finally debated in 1699, during a series of conferences in the Brussels town hall, initiated by the Treasurer General of the Low Countries, Jan van Brouchoven, Count of Bergeyck. For these conferences, representatives of the major cities of the Southern Low Countries gathered as experts in the field of commerce and industry.[34] They resulted in an edict in which a more consistent protectionist policy was declared. However, the resistance of neighbouring countries and internal disputes about the policies to be chosen led to the edict's immediate withdrawal.[35] The political situation at that moment of full competition between Atlantic powers, and in the midst of the Nine-years' War and the War of the Spanish Succession, did not allow for drastic protectionist measures.[36]

Very difficult, long, and almost inexcusable negotiations: Charles d'Hovyne's "Briefve memoire" about State Institutions and Taxation

The issue of the "licenten" was not just one of priorities of economic policy; it was also about privileges and political power. The Estates of Brabant, following the concerns of the Antwerp merchant class, insisted that the collection of these tariffs was against their privileges, considering that the medieval constitution of Brabant, the so-called Blijde Inkomst (Solemn Entry) stated that no tolls were to be collected within the territory of the Duchy of Brabant.[37] Of course, this privilege was granted in the fourteenth century, long before the separation of the Low Countries into two states.[38] Charles d'Hovyne, chief-president of the Privy Council between 1653 and 1671, authored a political memoir dating from the period between 1656 and 1671, which clearly reflects the point of view of the central government in Brussels:

> and according to this treaty (the treaty of Munster of 1648), the levy of tariffs may be and must be continued on one side and the other, to which all the other provinces of obedience are conforming, except the one of Brabant, which insists stubbornly and with much insolence that this levy is against their privileges.[39]

During several decades, the Estates of Brabant used their constitutional rights to resist the imposition of import and export tariffs by writing petitions, through direct negotiations with the governor in Brussels, by sending an envoy to Madrid to present the issue to the King personally, and finally by means of a fiscal boycott. The system of taxation required the consent of the Estates to any proposed tax. In Brabant, the clergy and the nobility, representing the first two estates, generally consented without major objections. The representatives of the principal cities, Brussels, Louvain, and Antwerp, however had to respond to the City Council, where the merchants and craft guilds often put up heavy resistance. Hence, between 1668 and 1680, the Antwerp representatives of the citizens and the guilds refused to consent to the subsidies proposed to the Estates of Brabant, resulting in a boycott of the proposal since unanimity was required.[40]

d'Hovyne is frustrated about the political autonomy of the Estates of Brabant,

> because more than any other province, they have the inclination to disrespect the royal authorities. And, as they cannot do so directly, they do so by linking conditions to their acceptation of taxes and subsidies, about questions of justice and police, with protestations that they will not consent to the subsidies or taxes, if their conditions are not satisfied. Therefore, the government is continually embarrassed and the prince reduced to a necessity of being either frustrated about his taxes or to accept their conditions, which curtails the authority of the sovereign and the conducting of justice and police.[41]

The negotiations with the estates were, therefore, "very difficult, very long and almost inexcusable", the author goes on to say. It may take two or three years until an agreement can be obtained about a subsidy.

> One is their claim to unanimity. Although from the king's side they insist that the decision has to be taken by majority, they always include the condition that they would only consent if all the other estates also agree. Furthermore, once the subsidy is accepted, they discuss the kind of taxation to apply to find the required amount, to the extent that they do not accept the interference of the royal authority by means of justice, which extends the process to infinity.

In the Estates of Flanders, the other big province of the Low Countries, the negotiations were "without any comparison, quicker and easier than those with Brabant".[42]

The political system provided one way to avoid a blockade of the process of taxation, which was called conformation or *vervankenisse*. This compromise could be applied when one city, or even one fraction in a city refused to consent to a proposal of taxation. In that case, the rest of the estates, or fractions, could overrule the vote, without requiring the opposing fraction to contribute. In the "briefve memoire", the author suggests extending the principle of conformation from one to two fractions. This would make it easier to obtain a favourable vote despite the refusal of one, or even two fractions. This would be an important secret to making the decision of taxes easier, at least "if the practice were as easy as the theory".

> Another abuse and bad principle among the Brabant Estates is the fact that their deputies are permanent for life, whereas other provinces change from time to time, generally every three years, which leads the said deputies to attribute to themselves a sovereign authority, and they do everything without any control and censorship, to such an extent that they render their accounts among each other, without any intervention of any official of the crown, although they used to present their accounts to the Chamber of Accounts. They hardly accept any justice, neither from the Brabant Council, nor the Privy Council, to such an extent that it is a state organism that is totally deregulated and full of confusion, abuses and errors that are being committed among the permanent deputies.[43]

Also in the correspondence of Adrien Foppens, the issue of taxation and the role of the Estates of Brabant is mentioned. He directly accuses the Estates of malpractice and embezzlement "There is great dissatisfaction about the Estates of Brabant that they have not done their duty to collect the money of the imposts on beer and wine in the countryside.[44] And they recognise more than ever the corruption."[45]

> The estates collect more than was actually agreed upon as a subsidy, as if it had been agreed a second time, which is against the privileges, because you cannot collect any taxes without the agreement of the people. Farmers had to sell their cow or horse, just when the peace has started, and the owners were not capable to relieve them. The people paid taxes like under the former governments, but the troops were never so badly paid.[46]

At another moment, he pointed out that "most of inhabitants are ruined and a large part of the land is not cultivated since several years."[47] "Because it is the practice to raise the double and more, and this is the origin of the ruin of the villages and the countryside."[48]

The population's frustration over taxation also affected Governor Alexander Farnese, Prince of Parma. In 1681, Foppens mentions, "It will be difficult to obtain the consent of the third estate and the cities of Brussels, Antwerp and Leuven, because there is quite some resentment against the Prince of Parma." When he passes in his chariot of triumph in the streets, the humble people scream in Flemish: "Here are our subsidies, and our 20th pennies well employed, while leaving the soldiers without money and the cause of the thefts they commit unpunished in the city and in the countryside and the excesses they commit here in our streets!" "If ever there was a disarmed authority it is here, where the communities were assembled in the city hall, about the small impost, which they refuse, if their demands are not satisfied."

> Because the country is so exhausted of money and the people so poor, that no more subsidies can be raised, at this moment, and the deputies of the estates of all provinces have so liberally accepted to the marquis de Grana, because they raise more than they give in form of subsidy.[49]

Hence, the blame for the fiscal pressure, and especially the practice of raising more taxes than agreed in the negotiations with the government, is put on the Estates, particularly those of the Duchy of Brabant. The complaints against the Estates of Brabant and the issue of taxation were quite broad in the last decades of the 17th century. While d'Hovyne, the author of the *brievfe mmoire* mainly sees the difficulties in the negotiations and the long procedure to obtain consent for a proposed subsidy, Foppens points more directly at the corruption and malpractice of the Estates, which collected more taxes than negotiated with the government, keeping the rest for themselves.

Goswin Arnold de Wynants, 1730: the four branches of incomes of the sovereign

In later memoirs, dating from the first decades of the 18th century, we obtain more precise information about the fiscal dimensions of the tensions between the government and the provincial estates. Meanwhile, the country had undergone major political and institutional changes. The War of the Spanish Succession had actually led to a total regime change, from Spanish to Austrian authority. However, at the provincial and local level, a high degree of institutional continuity can be observed. On the economic level, the country took quite a while to recover from the war, and also suffered from the consequences of the Barrier Treaties imposed by Great Britain and the Dutch Republic to create a military buffer-zone against a potential French invasion.[50] A very detailed analysis of the government's organisation in the Austrian Low Countries is to be found in the "Mémoires de tout ce qui concerne le governement des Pay-Bas" by the vicomte Goswin Arnold de Wynants, a councillor at the Council of Brabant in the 1690s, and later at the Supreme Council of the Low Countries at Vienna.[51] His opinions are generally characterised as being centralistic and loyal to the Prince. At the same time, he was a strong defender of the Brabantine constitutionalist tradition, in particular the requirement of the Estates' consent for taxation. The sovereign and his subjects are bound together by a mutual relation which forms the constitutional basis of the state.[52] In his memoir, dating from 1730, just two years before his death, he also gives a systematic overview of the types of income of the King in the Low Countries, including the domain of the sovereign, aides, subsidies, and subventions granted by the Estates of the Provinces, entry and exit rights, and finally, occasional income.

The domains formed since ancient times the patrimony of the princes to sustain their house and the other expenses of their sovereignty. They are inalienable without the consent of the Estates of the province where they are situated. The cruel wars to which the country was exposed in the Low Countries during the reign of Philip II required the sovereigns to seek money by alienating many parts of their domain, with the consent of the provincial estates, partly by sale, partly by engagement, that is, temporarily.[53]

In 1726, an attempt was made to rent out the domain incomes altogether, in a so-called admodiation, in the hope of a higher income than if by direct administration. This led to major complications, however, as the consortium that had made the highest offer disputed the conditions, and then refused to pay and were finally forced by means of confiscation to pay its rent and was arrested.[54] During the process, many councils and political offices were not paid for a period of two years. Wynants finally proposed a plan to recover part of the engaged offices, including the creation of different classes of incomes, and a list of rents to be cancelled, which would eventually help to discharge the domain. And, considering the fact that the rents were being paid with huge delays, the rent holders would be pleased to receive their capital without claiming the arrears, just to get relief from the constant delays.

The second type of income, taxes and subsidies, went entirely to cover military expenses, but they were far from sufficient, so that the government had to find ways to compensate for them. Although a general tax, or "*bede*", of 50,000 guilders was collected in Brabant, it cannot be counted among the income of the royal treasury, which meant that his majesty did not receive a penny, as the needs of the State required the sovereigns to sell such a high amount of rents on the tax income, with the consent of the Estates of Brabant, that the rent service absorbed the entire tax income and more. Therefore, there was nihil on this point, even though the subjects of Brabant paid for it. If the inhabitants were only to contribute to the taxes and subsidies, they would not complain, Wynants adds, but rent charges varied depending on how well or poorly the finances had been managed in the past. It is certain that in certain places, the rents are higher than what they pay in taxes, impositions and subsidies.[55]

For Wynants, it is the County of Flanders that poses the most serious problem. He declares, that

> among all the provinces none is in such disorder as the one of Flanders, because of the bad (méchante) behaviour of the members, the castellanies, and low administrations which compose them, so that we don't know where to put hands on to find a remedy. The subsidies, once they are granted, are collected through loans, the cities take another loan for their share, the castellanies a third for theirs, and the smaller towns and villages a fourth. Thus, at least 25% interest for one subsidy, on top of which the costs of the loan have to be added, which are quite considerable, as well as the costs of collection and accounting. This province, being stronger and bigger than Brabant, contributes more apparently, but if you consider the reduction they have, as mentioned before, the latter ultimately contributes more to the treasury than the former. In Brabant, everyone has to put their hand in their pocket to pay the charges of the moment. The Estates do not take out any loans on interest in order to pay the subsidy, and they do not allow

> that those of the countryside nor the cities, big or small, do so. That means that the existing rent charges do not increase through those of the current year.
>
> The magistrates of the cities with a vote (in the Estates) are easily convinced to consent to high taxes in order to keep their employment or to be re-elected without caring too much about the increasing tax charge and, like the governors general, they think only of the term of their office of three or six years. It is often the members of the clergy who cause difficulties, and those of the Franc of Bruges, the former because they cannot be put in any magistrate position, and the others because their charge is for life.[56]

Here, the author points out the marquis de Prié, minister plenipotentiary and governor ad interim between 1716 and 1724, who managed to negotiate extremely high tax quota with the Estates of Flanders. The loans are so frequent and the interest so high that the public pays almost as much as a double subsidy. As a result, the province had reached a point that its letters of exchange and obligations were protested, the traders and holders attacked them and exhausted them everywhere, its bankruptcy was almost certain as well as the ruin of the greatest part of its creditors, and its debt rose to more than 1,300,000 fl. That is the result of this kind of negotiations, which destroys the tree down to its roots, instead of being content to profit from it by collecting the fruit of each year. De Prié tried to reach the same result in Brabant, by presenting the example of Flanders to the Estates, but the bishop of Antwerp, the head of the clergy in the Estates, answered that we have to live and to let live, and not try to eat in one year what one needs to subsist during the following years.[57]

Wynants adds a general reflection concerning taxes: everybody agrees on the close relationship between the Prince and his subjects. The Prince has to love them and treat them as a father and protect them as a sovereign master. The subjects, on the other hand, are obliged to assist him in conscience and honour with their goods and their life to maintain and sustain his State, so that he can defend them against all outside enemies and govern them from within, with the decency due to his representatives and with the necessary expense for the internal government. These two goals cannot be achieved without the required funds during times of war, more than in times of peace. In any case, it is absolutely indispensable to take into consideration the capability of the subjects. If one is not careful and overtaxes the population to the point of exhausting their resources or threatening their subsistence, the system will collapse. When resources are consumed before they can regenerate – like eating grain before it has grown – the means of subsistence are depleted, leading to a general breakdown that harms both the people and the Prince alike. It seems necessary, therefore, that the ministers have clear knowledge of the country's economic situation, year by year…that is, the harvests, the profits which one can obtain, the state of domestic and foreign trade, the industries, the workers they employ, the cattle, the families which depend on them. These considerations make it possible to engage the subjects to increase their subsidies and their contributions, in order to show their zeal to fulfil their obligation to employ their goods for both the maintenance of the Prince's State and for their own preservation.

Finally, Wynants also touches upon the issue of tariffs. This type of public charge has been introduced by royal authority in all the kingdoms, states and provinces, not just in Europe, but also in the other three parts of the world. This right, depending on the times and circumstances, can be extremely favourable for commerce, industries and the balance of trade, but when badly managed it causes damage that cannot be repaired, or at least not without great difficulty. It is a very sharp razor, but governed by inept, it cuts the living flesh and the wounds are very difficult to heal. Each sovereign has the authority to establish tariffs for entry, exit and transit, at least if his authority is not limited or tied by peace treaties or commercial agreements, or other such arrangements. Wynants' ideas about the general welfare and role of the State are very much in line with the Cameralist teachings, which predominated in large parts of Continental Europe during the 17th and 18th century – a system of thought that aimed at economic growth and development, full employment, price stability, free markets, equal distribution of income, welfare systems, and market integration, in order to "largely remedy the economic evils which afflicted the states".[58]

Reducing interest rates: J. J. Vilain XIIII: Réflexions sur l'état présent des finances de Flandre (1755)

In de Wynants' memoir, the County of Flanders, and particularly the Estates of the latter principality, are the most critical element of the Southern Low Countries. The dominant position of Ghent and Bruges, led to a political system in which the two cities decided on the basis of their own interest, yet involving the taxpayers of the whole principality in their policies. Especially the rural districts were not included in the major decisions. In 1753 and 1754, the problems within the estates led to a crisis which required a fundamental reform, that is, giving full representation to the rural districts, and stricter control of provincial finances by the central government. The financial reforms included a reduction of expenses, lower interest rates, debt amortisation, and fiscal reforms.[59]

A key figure in these reforms was Jean Jacques Vilain XIIII, first alderman of Ghent, and president of the Estates of Flanders at the time, a highly influential, but also controversial figure.[60] In 1755, he published a memoir in which he reflects on the financial problems of Flanders, and proposes some solutions.[61] His criticism is mainly directed at the administration of the previous 30 years which, according to the author, left enormous disorder in the province' finances, with taxes multiplied, limitless debt, and its credit considerably impacted, if not totally ruined.[62] Despite years of peace between 1712 and 1743, public debt increased. This is the result of a principle whereby the secrets of an administration are not supposed to be known, even by those most concerned, not even the sovereign. It is perhaps in the interest of some that the affairs of the State would be opaque, because it allows them to harvest in times of difficulty, but the people as a whole are interested in the economy and lower taxes. The basis of credit is lender confidence in the surety of repayment. These sureties are the state incomes. So, if the tax incomes are sufficient to pay for the annuities of the rents, in order to pay off a considerable part of the debt every year, and if there are some resources left for a new need, in that case one may say that the credit is intact and merits the public's confidence. Therefore, it is indispensable for the reestablishment of the public credit to give exact information about all details of the public administration.[63]

One issue that receives particular attention is the burden of public debt. Villain XIIII considers it a great vice to neglect the cancellation of the public debt, which is "like a worm who ends up destroying the woodwork." Some people think, he argues, that it is a good thing if the State is indebted to itself. This would multiply wealth and increase the circulation of the system. Yet on the contrary, this idea leads only to disadvantages, because

> the taxes levied and perpetuated for the payment of interest are harmful for agriculture and industry, making the labour more expensive. The real income of the State is transferred from those who work and have activity and industry, to idle people, by giving the means to work to those who do not, and the difficulties to those who do work.

"The rentiers, rich people, who become richer through the interest paid by the poor: a member which grows monstrously on the account of the subsistence of others, who become dry and paralytic." Therefore, the public debt in Flanders is twice destructive for agriculture, commerce, and industry, first because they turn taxes into perpetual charges of the artisan and labourer. Second, if the interests of the State are higher than what is employed on land, agriculture will be abandoned, money flows out of commerce, ultimately leading to the fall of industry, the sources of tax income and, in turn, the income itself.[64]

The advantage of low interests comes down to an increase in cultivated land, incomes, productions, commerce and fabrics, liberation from debt, lower taxes and charges, for the benefit of the poor as well as the wider population.[65] He therefore proposes a plan to cancel the existing annuities and replace them with bonds at reduced interest. To reduce the public debt, which amounted to several million guilders, he proposed an amortisation scheme, which would take 30 years. The State officials would make a list of those eligible and offer them to choose between cancelling their rents, or a reduction in the interest rate to 4% (penny 25). The benefits of this transaction would go into an amortisation fund, which would be used to for further debt reduction. The reduction of interest rates was a general concern for state authorities. In fact, government and town authorities frequently tried to apply reductions by replacing existing bonds for others with lower interest rates. While it was, of course, advantageous to reduce interest rates for existing loans, the existing agreements had to be respected in order not to lose the credibility of the lenders.[66]

As for taxes, Vilain XIIII acknowledged the necessity of taxes for the State, but instead of head taxes he concentrated on the optimised use of the existing taxes of consumption. As long as the necessities of the State are ensured, the fewer taxes collected, the better. Nevertheless, it is obvious that a minimum level of taxation is necessary for providing the means for the State. The tax rates should be transparent and clear in order to convince the public of their legitimacy.

General reflections

The authors of the memoirs analysed in this chapter all address the economic and financial problems of their time and present them as the result of mismanagement and abuses by individuals, or as failures of the financial system, and they propose solutions based on alternative forms of financial organisation and political reforms. The opinions about the role of import and export tariffs were quite polarised in the last decades of the 17th century. Pieter Cardon was very clear in attributing the country's ruin to the low tariffs issued in 1680, as this led to mass imports of cheap goods from foreign countries, such as England and France. He is seconded by the central government which, in the instructions for Governor Melchor de Velasco in 1668, speaks of superfluous expenses, ostentation, and the imitation of foreign nations. These arguments fit very well into the general protectionist politics of mercantilism and cameralism of the time.[67]

The Antwerp city council, on the other hand, backed by the Estates of Brabant, insisted on the negative impact of tariffs on trade. They were not only against the fundamental constitutional rights of the Brabant citizens, but they would also ruin trade and force merchants and artisans to leave the country. The Antwerp merchants argued that high trade tariffs would ruin trade and force merchants and artisans to leave the country, causing a decline in consumption and tax incomes. As a final result, public loans would have to be taken out in London or Amsterdam. The resistance of Antwerp was related to their particular historical dependence on foreign trade, which resulted in an ideology of free trade. The Brussels gazetteer Adrien Foppens sees a conspiracy in these arguments, led by foreign merchants with the goal of ruining the trade of the Low Countries. The political circumstances at the end of the 17th century, and the politics of the Barrier Treaties, imposed as a measure to protect British and Dutch interests after the War of the Spanish Succession, prevented the Austrian Low Countries from undertaking a proper customs policy in the first decades of the 18th century. It would take until the middle of the 18th century for such a policy to be put into practice.

The debate about import and export tariffs was also linked to another debate, which is the question of political privileges and constitutional rights. The Estates of Brabant interpreted the imposition of the licenten as an infraction upon their political privileges and, therefore, they resisted the tariffs in their negotiations on taxation during several decades, between 1654 and 1680. One of the fractions represented in the Estates, the citizens and craft guilds of Antwerp, took their protest to the limit by refusing to agree to the prolongation of the yearly taxation, and thus de facto boycotted tax collection. This practice of resistance of the Brabant Estates and the high degree of autonomy is sharply criticised by the author of the "briefve memoire", as it is diametrically opposed to the absolutistic logic of princely power. The author complains about the lack of respect and submission of the Estates and the resulting frustration of the central authorities about their own lack of power. This high degree of autonomy seems to have been particularly strong in Brabant. In Flanders, de Wynants claims that the Estates could be manipulated fairly well by offering them the option of staying in office for a long period or being re-elected. According to him, they did not care very much about the long-term consequences of their decisions, but only thought of the short-term interests of their office. Only those representatives who were nominated for life or who did not have any magistrate positions could not be manipulated so easily.

Another problem most authors agree upon is the high degree of financial autonomy and lack of transparency of the provincial estates of Flanders and Brabant. The central authorities had only limited control of the collection of taxes and of the accounts of the Estates. So, they either agreed to higher taxes than they actually could deliver, or they managed to collect more taxes than negotiated with the government, and kept a considerable part for themselves, without any possibility of control by the central authorities. The high degree of autonomy and lack of control of the provincial and municipal finances was a major concern of the central governments of both the Spanish and the Austrian Empire. Throughout the 18th century, the Austrian government tried to gain greater control of the different financial and administrative practices of their territories by introducing administrative reforms and financial surveys. Also, Vilain XIIII speaks about a lack of transparency, in this case about public debt. He even sees this lack of transparency as a principle of a corrupt system, which serves a group of privileged rentiers, and deprives the working population of their means of subsistence. A high public debt at high interest rates is bad for the economy, agriculture, and trade, making labour more expensive. Income is transferred from those who work to idle people, that is rentiers, rich people.

The memoirs of de Wynants and Vilain XIIII have the common objective of proposing a general plan of taxation on the one hand, and the reduction of the public debt on the other. Both authors agree that taxes are necessary for the functioning of the state. But it is necessary to assess very clearly the population's capacity to contribute, so not to over-tax them, which would lead to a general breakdown. In good cameralist fashion, De Wynants pleads, therefore, for a careful survey of the country's economic situation, including agriculture, trade, industry, employment, and consumption, to achieve a good assessment of fiscal potential. Vilain XIIII also aims at such a detailed survey of the economy and a clear, transparent form of taxation.

This aim for increasing centralisation and transparency was one of the principles of the economic and financial policy of the Austrian government of the Low Countries in the 18th century. In the field of financial policy, the government made a major effort to perform a complete survey of the public finances of the country and the regional and local authorities. The government created so called *jointes*, or *juntas*, to create a general survey of the public finances, with the ultimate aim of coming to a more unified and transparent organisation of public finances.

Notes

1 For the Dutch Republic, a classical study is de Vries and van der Woude, 1997. For public finance, Fritschy, 2017; for the Spanish Low Countries, see Janssens, 2006; *Oostenrijks België, 1713–1794: de Zuidelijke Nederlanden onder de Oostenrijkse Habsburgers*, 1987.

2 Janssens, 2012: 67–92. For the 18th century, Coppens, 1992.

3 "Terres de promission" is a reference to the period of Duke Philipp the Good by the fifteenth-century chronicler Philippe de Commynes. See van Uytven, 1961: 281–317.

4 Blockmans, 2010.

5 Braudel, 1979: 17–24.
6 Tracy, 1985.
7 For Flanders, see Blockmans, 1978. For Brabant, Damen, 2018; Limberger, 2023: 103–129.
8 Thijs, 1986: 165–273.
9 Israel, 2006b: 25–28; Gelderblom, 2000.
10 Van der Wee, 2006: 16–21.
11 Israel, 2006b: 28. See also Brulez, 1967: 75–99; and Baetens, 1976.
12 Van Damme, 2003: 6–40.
13 Israel, 2006a: 43–47.
14 The marquis of Castel Rodrigo (1664–1668), Iñigo de Velasco (1668–1675), the count of Monterey (1675), the duke of Villa Hermosa (1675–1677), Alexander Farnese (1678–1682) the marquis of Grana (1682–1685), marquis of Gastañaga (1685–1691): Lefèvre, 1954: 91–122.
15 Morsa, 2006: 100–134; Everaert, 1979: 185–202.
16 *'Den oorspronck van de ruïne en armoede der Spaensche Nederlanden', Liege, 1686 and 1699,* reprinted in Beutels, 1991.
17 Galesloot, 1870: 10; d'Hoker, 1970: 167–214. See also De Schryver, 1965.
18 Kernkamp, 1931.
19 Voeten, 1957; Dhondt, 2023: 763–64.
20 Van Damme, 2003; Limberger, 2014: 95–108.
21 Cardon, 1991: 40–42.
22 Beutels, 1991: 64. See also Galesloot, 1870: 1–154.
23 Rössner, 2016: 3–24.
24 von Hörnigk (1983), cited in Seitschek, 2019: 103–130. See also the English edition by Robinson, 2018.
25 Galesloot, 1877: 369–472.
26 Galesloot, 1877: 408–409, 29 January 1681.
27 Galesloot, 1877: 410, 5 February 1681.
28 Galesloot, 1877: 410, 9 February 1681.
29 Galesloot, 1877: 415, 2 March 1681.
30 Van Damme, 2003. See also Lindemann, 2014.
31 BSA, Audience 1225bis, fol. 53–65. Also, Van Damme, 2003, points at the moral debate about foreign fashion trends.
32 Cited in Van Damme, 2003: 28–29.
33 Antwerp City Archives, Minutes of pensionary Valkenisse, 21 memoire of pensionaries 1669.
34 Beutels, 1991 and De Schryver, 1965: 85.
35 d'Hoker, 1970; De Schryver, 1965.
36 Findlay and O'Rourke, 2007: 247–251.
37 "Note sur les droits d'entrée et sortie", cited in Van Damme, 2003: 33.
38 Vrancken, 2018.
39 "Et selon le dit traité la levée des licentes peut et doit etre continué d'une part et d'autre à quoi toutes les autres provinces de l'obeissance sont accomodées sauf celle de Brabant, qui soutient opiniatrement et avec beaucoup d 'insolence cette levée etre contraire à ses privileges". Charles d'Hovyne, *'Briefve memoire de la forme des ressorts du gouvernement politique des provinces des Pays Bas soub l'obeissance de sa majesté'. s.d. (between 1656 and 1671)*: ARAB, Aud. 1225bis. fo. 104. The date of the document can be established on the basis of the reference to Esteban de Gamarra as a resident in the Hague (1654–1671), and to the revolts taking place in Antwerp in 1655–1656. See also: Brants, 1909, 1. A modified version was published under title *Gouvernement*

politique du Pays-Bas soubs l'obéissance de sa Majesté Catholique, in Leiden, by Habraham Gogat (s.d.).

40 Van Damme, 2003; Limberger, 2014.
41 D'Hovyne, *Briefve memoire.*
42 D'Hovyne, *Briefve memoire.*
43 D'Hovyne, *Briefve memoire.*
44 Galesloot, 1870: 423–424, 28 May 1681. Imposts were indirect taxes on basic goods of consumption, including beer, wine, bread and meat, which were collected in the rural districts throughout the Low Countries since the 1540's. As a consequence of the sale of annuities by the provincial estates, the collection of these taxes came under the control of the Estates. See Tracy, 1985; Maddens, 1979: 342–363.
45 Galesloot, 1877: 424.
46 Galesloot, 1877: 390, 25 September 1680.
47 Galesloot, 1877: 422, 7 May 1681.
48 Galesloot, 1877: 461, 6 September 1682.
49 Galesloot, 1877: 462, 23 September 1682.
50 Van Gelder, 2016.
51 Wynants, 1721. See also Van de Perre, 1995: 185–187.
52 Dhondt, 2023: 749–755.
53 Van Cauwenberghe, 1982: 61; Baelde, 1963: 14–33.
54 Coppens, 1992: 64.
55 Wynants, 1721: 138.
56 Wynants, 1721: 140–141.
57 Wynants, 1721: 142.
58 Rössner, 2018: 29–40; Seppel, 2017: 5.
59 Lenders, 1956. See also, Coppens, 1993: 174–176.
60 Lenders, 1986: 159–177.
61 Vilain XIIII, 1755.
62 Vilain XIIII, 1755: 193–195.
63 Vilain XIIII, 1755: 9–11.
64 Vilain XIIII, 1755: 137–144. This problem was also observed Spain as early as in 1600 by Martín Gonçález de Cellorigo in his *Memorial de la politica necessaria, y vtil restauracion à la republica de España, y estados de ella, y del desempeño universal de estos reynos*, see, Lanza García, 2023: 10.
65 Vilain XIIII, 1755: 145.
66 De Vijlder and Limberger, 2014: 301–326. For the Habsburg Monarchy, see Seitschek, 2019: 115.
67 Findlay and O'Rourke, 2007: 227–310.

Bibliography

Archival Sources

Antwerp City Archives (ACA), Minutes of pensionary Valkenisse, 21 memoire of pensionaries 1669.

Bussels State Archives (BSA), Audience 1225bis, (Charles d'Hovyne) *'Briefve memoire de la forme des ressorts du gouvernement politique des provinces des Pays Bas soub l'obeissance de sa majesté'.* s.d. (between 1656 and 1671).

Wynants, Goswin-Arnold, de, *Mémoires contenant des notions générales de tout ce qui concerne le gouvernement des Pays-Bas. Etat général de tous les revenus et de toutes les charges des Pays-Bas autrichiens*, manuscript, 1721.

Printed Sources

Cardon, Pieter (1991), Den oorspronck van de ruïne en armoede der Spaensche Nederlanden, 1686–1699, in Robert Beutels, ed., *Over het mercantilisme in de Spaanse Nederlanden*, Tielt, Lanoo Publishers.

Galesloot, Louis V. (1877), "Mémoires secrets d'Adrien Foppens sur le gouvernement et les affaires des Pays-Bas pendant les années 1680–1682", in *Compte-rendu des séances de la commission royale d'histoire. Deuxième Série*, 4, pp. 369–472.

Vilain XIIII, Jean Jacques Philippe (1755), *Réflexions sur les finances de la Flandre, et nommement à l'égard de ses Taxes, Revenues & ses Dettes sur la nature & Administration des Premieres, sur l'Origine, Progrès, Consequences & Necessités de diminuer les dernieres*, Ghent: de Goesin.

von Hörnigk, Philipp Wilhelm (1983), *Österreich über alles, wann es nur will (1708). Eingeleitet und kommentiert von Horst Knapp*, Wien: Klassiker der österreichischen Nationalökonomie. English edition by Philipp Robinson Rössner and Philipp Wilhelm von Hörnigk, *Austria Supreme (if It so Wishes) (1684). A Strategy for European Economic Supremacy*, London: Anthem, 2018.

Literature

Baelde, M. (1963), "Financiële politiek en domaniale evolutie in de Nederlanden onder Karel V en Filips II", *Tijdschrift voor Geschiedenis*, 76, pp. 14–33.

Baetens, Roland (1976), *De nazomer van Antwerpens welvaart. De diaspora en het handelshuis De Groote tijdens de eerste helft der 17e eeuw*, Brussel: Gemeentekrediet van België, 2 vols.

Beutels, Robert (1991), *Over het mercantilisme in de Spaanse Nederlanden: economisch-historische duiding van een merkwaardig nederlandstalig mercantilistisch traktaat van Pieter Cardon: 'De oorsprong van de ruïne en armoede der Spaanse Nederlanden', 1686–1699*, Tielt: Lanoo Publishers.

Blockmans, Wim (1978), *De Volksvertegenwoordiging in Vlaanderen in de overgang van Middeleeuwen naar Nieuwe Tijden (1384-1506)*, Brussels: Koninklijke academie voor wetenschappen, letteren en schone kunsten van België.

Blockmans, Wim (2010), *Metropolen Aan De Noordzee: De Geschiedenis Van Nederland 1100–1560*, Amsterdam: Bakker.

Brants, Victor (1909), "Le mémoire politique sur le gouvernement des Pays-Bas de Ch. d'Hovyne, chef-président du conseil privé (1653–1671)", *Annales de la Fédération archéologique et historique de Belgique*, 21, 1, pp. 49–66.

Braudel, Fernand (1979), *Le temps du monde, Civilisation matérielle, économie et capitalisme, XVe - XVIIIe siècle*, III, Paris: Flammarion.

Brulez, Wilfried (1967), "Anvers de 1585 à 1650", *Vierteljahrsschriften für Sozial- und Wirtschaftsgeschichte*, 53, pp. 75–99.

Coppens, Herman (1992), *De financiën van de centrale regering van de Zuidelijke Nederlanden aan het einde van het Spaanse en onder Oostenrijks bewind (ca. 1680-1788)*, Brussels: Koninklijke academie voor wetenschappen, letteren en schone kunsten van België.

Coppens, Herman (1993), *Het institutioneel kader van de centrale overheidsfinanciën in de Spaanse en Oostenrijkse Nederlanden tijdens het late Ancien Régime (c.1680–1788)*, Brussels: Algemeen Rijksarchief en Rijksarchief in de Provinciën.

d'Hoker, Marc (1970), "De economische conferenties te Brussel in 1699. Bijdrage tot de geschiedenis van de economische politiek in de Zuidelijke Nederlanden". *Bijdragen en Mededelingen betreffende de Geschiedenis der Nederlanden*, 85, pp. 167–214.

Damen, Mario (2018), "The Nobility in the Estates of the Late Medieval Duchy of Brabant", in Mario Damen, Jelle Haemers and Alastair J. Mann, eds., *Political Representation: Communities, Ideas and Institutions in Europe (c. 1200 - c. 1690)*, Leiden: Brill, pp. 161–181.

De Schryver, Reginald (1965), *Jan Van Brouchoven, graaf van Bergeyck 1644–1725: een halve eeuw staatkunde in de Spaanse Nederlanden en in Europa*, Brussels: Koninklijke Vlaamse academie voor wetenschappen, letteren en schone kunsten van België.

De Vijlder, Nicolas and Michael Limberger (2014), "Public or Private Interests? The Investment Behaviour of Public Officials in Antwerp During the Early Modern Period", *Financial History Review*, 21, 3, pp. 301–326.

De Vries, Jan and Ad van der Woude (1997), *The First Modern Economy: Success, Failure, and Perseverance of the Dutch Economy, 1500–1815*, Cambridge: Cambridge University Press.

Dhondt, Frederik (2023), "Constitutional Identity in the 18th Century Austrian Low Countries: Count Goswin de Wynants's Viennese Mémoires (1730)", in Peter Hilpold and Christoph Perathoner, eds., *Europäisches Minderheitenrecht. Festschrift Gilbert Gornig* I, Vienna: Facultas, pp. 749–769.

Everaert, John (1979), "Handel in de Zuidelijke Nederlanden 1650–1795", in D.P. Blok, ed., *Algemene Geschiedenis der Nederlanden*, Bussum: Unieboek, pp. 185–202.

Findlay, Ronald and Kevin H. O'Rourke (2007), *Power and Plenty: Trade, War, and the World Economy in the Second Millennium*, Princeton, NJ: Princeton University Press.

Fritschy, Wantje (2017), *Public Finance of the Dutch Republic in Comparative Perspective. The Viability of an Early Modern Federal State (1570s–1795)*, Leiden: Brill.

Galesloot, Louis (1870), "Troubles de Bruxelles de 1698 et 1699. L'avocat Vander Meulen et les doyens des métiers traduits devant le conseil de Brabant", *Annales de l'academie d'archéologie de Belgique*, XXVI, 2e série, VI, pp. 1–154.

Gelderblom, Oscar (2000), *Zuid-Nederlandse kooplieden en de opkomst van de Amsterdamse stapelmarkt (1578–1630)*, Hilversumm: Verloren.

Israel, Jonathan (2006a), "De Franse opmars en de anti-Franse coalitie in de late 17de eeuw, 1668–1702", in *De Spaanse Nederlanden en het prinsbisdom Luik. Deel 1: Politiek*, Ghent: Snoeck, pp. 43–47.

Israel, Jonathan, (2006b), "Oorlog en vrede. Het lot van de Spaanse Nederlanden, Reïntegratie in het Spaanse imperiaal bestel, 1584–1598", in *De Spaanse Nederlanden en het prinsbisdom Luik. Deel 1: Politiek*, Ghent: Snoeck, pp. 25–28.

Janssens, Paul, ed. (2006), *België in de 17de eeuw. De Spaanse Nederlanden en het prinsbisdom Luik (1585–1715)*, Ghent: Dexia Bank-Snoeck, 2 vols.

Janssens, Paul (2012), "Taxation in the Habsburg Low Countries and Belgium, 1579–1914", in Bartolomé Yun-Casalilla and Patrick K. O'Brien, eds., *The Rise of Fiscal States: A Global History 1500–1914*, Cambridge: Cambridge University Press, pp. 67–92.

Kernkamp, Johannes Hermann (1931), *De Handel op den Vijand*, Utrecht: Kemink en zoon.

Lanza García, Ramón (2023), "A modo de introducción", in Ramón Lanza García, ed., *Los dineros de la Corona. Finanzas y cambio fiscal en la monarchía hispánica (siglos XVI-XVII)*, Granada: Comares, pp. 1–20.

Lefèvre, J. (1954), "Het slotbedrijf van het Spaanse régime in de Zuidelijke Nederlanden (1648–1700)", in J.A. Van Houtte, et al, eds., *Algemene Geschiedenis der Nederlanden, VII, Op gescheiden wegen, (1648-1748)* , Utrecht: De Haan, pp. 91–122.

Lenders, Piet S. J. (1956), *De politieke crisis in Vlaanderen omstreeks het midden der achttiende eeuw. Bijdrage tot de geschiedenis der Aufklärung in België*, Brussels: Paleis der Academiën.

Lenders, Piet S. J. (1986), "De Gentse voorschepen J. J. P. Vilain XIIII (1755–1777). Enkele trekken van zijn persoonlijkheid", *Handelingen der Maatschappij voor Geschiedenis en Oudheidkunde te Gent*, 40, 1, pp. 159–177.

Limberger, Michael (2023), "El establecimiento de una deuda provincial por los Estados de Brabante en el siglo XVI y sus consecuencias fiscales", in Ramón Lanza García, ed., *Los dineros de la corona. Finanzas y cambio fiscal en la Monarquía Hispánica (siglos XVI-XVII)*, Granada: Comares, pp. 103–129.

Limberger, Michael (2014), "Trade and war in the North Sea: Antwerp's struggle concerning trade tariffs during and after the Dutch revolt", in Angela Schottenhammer, ed., *Tribute, trade and smuggling. Tributo, comercio y contrabando: commercial, scientific and human interaction in the middle period and early modern world. Interacciones comerciales, científicas y humanas en el mundo de la Edad media y moderna* , Wiesbaden: Harrassowitz, pp. 95–108.

Lindemann, Mary (2014), *The Merchant Republics: Amsterdam, Antwerp, and Hamburg, 1648–1790*, Cambridge: Cambridge University Press.

Maddens, Niklaas (1979), "De invoering van de "nieuwe middelen" in het graafschap Vlaanderen tijdens de regering van Keizer Karel V", *Belgisch Tijdschrift voor Filologie en geschiedenis/ Revue Belge de Philologie et d'Histoire*, 57, 2, pp. 342–363.

Morsa, Denis (2006), "Een ongelukseeuw?", in *België in de 17de eeuw. De Spaanse Nederlanden en het prinsbisdom Luik. Deel 1: Politiek*, Ghent: Snoeck, pp. 100–134.

Oostenrijks België, 1713–1794: de Zuidelijke Nederlanden onder de Oostenrijkse Habsburgers (1987), Brussels: Gemeentekrediet van België.

Rössner, Philipp R. (2016), "New Inroads into Well-Known Territory? On the Virtues of Re-discovering Pre-classical Political Economy", in Philipp R. Rössner, ed., *Economic Growth and the Origins of Modern Political Economy. Economic reasons of state, 1500–2000*, London: Routledge, pp. 3–24.

Rössner, Philipp R. (2018), "Cameralism-Baroque-o-nomics. Cameralist Economic Theory", in Philipp Wilhelm von Hörnigk, ed., *Austria Supreme (if it so wishes) 1684. A Strategy for European Economic Supemacy*, edited with an introduction by Philipp Robinson Rössner, London: Anthem Press, pp. 29–40.

Seitschek, Franz-Stefan (2019), "Tradition als Innovation. Finanzverwaltung in der Habsburgermonarchie um 1700", in Harald Heppner, and Sabine Jesner, eds., *The 18th Century as Period of Innovation, Yearbook of the Society for 18th Century Studies on South Eastern Europe*, 2, pp. 103–130.

Seppel, Marten (2017), "Introduction: Cameralism in Practice", in Marten Seppel and Keith Tribe, eds., *Cameralism in Practice: State Administration and Economy in Early Modern Europe*, Woodbridge: Boydell & Brewer, pp. 1–16, 5.

Thijs, Alfons (1986), "The River Scheldt Closed for Two Centuries", in Fernand Suykens, e.a., eds., *Antwerp. A Port for all Seasons*, Deurne: MIM N.V., pp. 165–273.

Tracy, James D. (1985), *A Financial Revolution in the Habsburg Netherlands. Renten and Renteniers in the County of Holland, 1515–1565*, Berkley: University of California Press.

Van Cauwenberghe, Eddy (1982), *Het vorstelijk domein en de overheidsfinanciën in de Nederlanden (15de en 16de eeuw). Een quantitative analyse van Vlaamse en Brabantse domeinrekeningen*, Brussels: Gemeentekrediet van België.

Van Damme, Ilja (2003), "Het vertrek van Mercurius. Historiografische en hypothetische verkenningen van het economisch wedervaren van Antwerpen in de tweede helft van de zeventiende eeuw", *NEHA Jaarboek*, pp. 6–40.

Van de Perre, Stijn (1995), "Goswin-Arnold de Wynants en zijn Traité des charges publiques", in Paul Janssens, ed., *Fiscaal recht geboekstaafd. Geschiedenis van Het Belastingrecht van Perkament Tot Databank*, Brussels: Fiscale Hogeschool-HUB, pp. 185–187.

Van der Wee, Herman (2006), "De Nederlanden op de drempel van de 17de eeuw: de erfenis van het verleden", in *België in de 17de eeuw. De Spaanse Nederlanden en het prinsbisdom Luik. Deel 1: Politiek*, Ghent: Snoeck, pp. 16–21.

Van Gelder, Klaas (2016), *Regime Change at a Distance: Austria and the Southern Netherlands Following the War of the Spanish Succession (1716–1725)*, Leuven: Peters Publishers.

Van Uytven, Raymond (1961), "La Flandre et le Brabant, « terres de promission » sous les ducs de Bourgogne?", *Revue du Nord*, 43, 172, pp. 281–317.

Voeten, Petrus (1957), "Antwerpens verzet tegen de licenten tussen 1648 en 1670", *Bijdragen tot de geschiedenis*, 40, pp. 72–73.

Vrancken, Valerie (2018), *De Blijde Inkomsten van de Brabantse hertogen. Macht, opstand en privileges in de vijftiende eeuw*, Brussels: ASP.

Index

Note: Page references in *italics* refer to figures and **bold** refers to tables, and with "n" refer to endnotes.

For Product Safety Concerns and Information please contact our EU representative GPSR@taylorandfrancis.com
Taylor & Francis Verlag GmbH, Kaufingerstraße 24, 80331 München, Germany

www.ingramcontent.com/pod-product-compliance
Lightning Source LLC
LaVergne TN
LVHW010650300926
849161LV00005B/1082
* 9 7 8 1 0 4 1 1 0 0 8 2 9 *